MW00352066

Mastering PyTorch

Build powerful neural network architectures using
advanced PyTorch 1.x features

Ashish Ranjan Jha

BIRMINGHAM—MUMBAI

Mastering PyTorch

Group Product Manager: Kunal Parikh

Publishing Product Manager: Devika Battike

Senior Editor: Roshan Kumar

Content Development Editor: Tazeen Shaikh

Technical Editor: Sonam Pandey

Copy Editor: Safis Editing

Project Coordinator: Aishwarya Mohan

Proofreader: Safis Editing

Indexer: Priyanka Dhadke

Production Designer: Nilesh Mohite

First published: February 2021
Production reference: 2090221

Published by Packt Publishing Ltd.
Livery Place
35 Livery Street
Birmingham
B3 2PB, UK.

ISBN 978-1-78961-438-1

www.packt.com

To my mother and best-friend - Rani Jha, my father and idol - Bibhuti Bhushan Jha,
for their sacrifices and constant support and for being the driving forces of my life and career.
Without their love, none of this would matter. To my sisters, Sushmita, Nivedita, and Shalini,
for teaching me what and what not to do in life.

Packt.com

Subscribe to our online digital library for full access to over 7,000 books and videos, as well as industry leading tools to help you plan your personal development and advance your career. For more information, please visit our website.

Why subscribe?

- Spend less time learning and more time coding with practical eBooks and videos from over 4,000 industry professionals

- Improve your learning with Skill Plans built especially for you

- Get a free eBook or video every month

- Fully searchable for easy access to vital information

- Copy and paste, print, and bookmark content

Did you know that Packt offers eBook versions of every book published, with PDF and ePub files available? You can upgrade to the eBook version at packt.com and, as a print book customer, you are entitled to a discount on the eBook copy. Get in touch with us at customercare@packtpub.com for more details.

At www.packt.com, you can also read a collection of free technical articles, sign up for a range of free newsletters, and receive exclusive discounts and offers on Packt books and eBooks.

Foreword

I am happy to know that Ashish, who was my student on the artificial neural networks course 8 years ago at IIT Roorkee, has now authored this hands-on book that covers a range of deep learning topics in reasonable depth.

Learning by coding is something every deep learning enthusiast wants to undertake, but tends to leave half way through. The effort needed to go through documentation and extract useful information to run deep learning projects is cumbersome. I have seen far too many students become frustrated during the process. There are tons of resources available for any beginner to become an expert. However, it is easy for any beginner to lose sight of the learning task while trying to strike a balance between concept-oriented courses and the coding-savvy approach of many academic programs.

PyTorch is uniquely placed as being pythonic and very flexible. It is appealing both to beginners who have just started coding machine learning models and to experts who like to meddle in the finer parameters of model designing and training. PyTorch is one library I am happy to recommend to any enthusiast, regardless of their level of expertise.

The best way to learn machine learning and deep learning models is by practicing coding in PyTorch. This book navigates the world of deep learning through PyTorch in a very engaging way. It starts from the basic building blocks of deep learning. The visual appeal of learning the data pipeline is one of its strong points. The PyTorch modules used for model building and training are introduced in the simplest of ways. Any student will appreciate the hands-on approach of this book. Every concept is explained through codes, and every step of the code is well documented. It should not be assumed that this book is just for beginners. Instead, any beginner can become an expert by following this book.

Starting from basic model building, such as the popular VGG16 or ResNet, to advanced topics, such as AutoML and distributed learning, all these aspects are covered here. The book further encompasses concepts such as AI explainability, deep reinforcement learning, and GANs. The exercises in this book range from building an image captioning model to music generation and neural style transfer models, as well as building PyTorch model servers in production systems. This helps you to prepare for any niche deep learning ventures.

I recommend this book to anyone who wants to master PyTorch for deploying deep learning models with the latest libraries.

Dr. Gopinath Pillai
Head Of Department, Electrical Engineering, IIT Roorkee

Contributors

About the author

Ashish Ranjan Jha received his bachelor's degree in electrical engineering from IIT Roorkee (India), his master's degree in computer science from EPFL (Switzerland), and an MBA degree from the Quantic School of Business (Washington). He received distinctions in all of his degrees. He has worked for a variety of tech companies, including Oracle and Sony, and tech start-ups, such as Revolut, as a machine learning engineer.

Aside from his years of work experience, Ashish is a freelance ML consultant, an author, and a blogger (datashines). He has worked on products/projects ranging from using sensor data for predicting vehicle types to detecting fraud in insurance claims. In his spare time, Ashish works on open source ML projects and is active on StackOverflow and kaggle (arj7192).

About the reviewer

Javier Abascal Carrasco has a master's degree in telecommunication engineering from the University of Seville (Spain). He also studied abroad at TU Dresden (Germany) and Thomas College (ME, USA), where he obtained his MBA. Since his career started, Javier has been passionate about the world of data and analytics. He has had the chance to work with and help all manner of companies, ranging from small start-ups to big corporations, including the consulting firm EY and Facebook. In addition, for the last 3 years, he has been a part-time lecturer on the data science space. He truly believes that PyTorch is bringing a new, fresh style to programming and work involving deep learning, generating a friendly competitor landscape in relation to TensorFlow.

Packt is searching for authors like you

If you're interested in becoming an author for Packt, please visit `authors.packtpub.com` and apply today. We have worked with thousands of developers and tech professionals, just like you, to help them share their insight with the global tech community. You can make a general application, apply for a specific hot topic that we are recruiting an author for, or submit your own idea.

Table of Contents

Section 2: Working with Advanced Neural Network Architectures

3
Deep CNN Architectures

4
Deep Recurrent Model Architectures

5
Hybrid Advanced Models

Section 3: Generative Models and Deep Reinforcement Learning

6
Music and Text Generation with PyTorch

Section 4: PyTorch in Production Systems

10
Operationalizing PyTorch Models into Production

11
Distributed Training

12
PyTorch and AutoML

13
PyTorch and Explainable AI

14
Rapid Prototyping with PyTorch

Other Books You May Enjoy

Index

Preface

Deep learning (**DL**) is driving the AI revolution, and PyTorch is making it easier than ever for people to build DL applications. This book will help you discover expert techniques to get the most out of your data and build complex neural network models.

The book starts with a quick overview of PyTorch and explores **convolutional neural network** (**CNN**) architectures for image classification. You will explore **recurrent neural network** (**RNN**) architectures as well as Transformers and use them for sentiment analysis. As you advance, you'll apply DL across different domains, such as music, text, and image generation, using generative models. After that, you'll delve into the world of **generative adversarial networks** (**GANs**), build and train your own deep reinforcement learning models in PyTorch, and interpret DL models. You will not only learn how to build models but also deploy PyTorch models into production using expert tips and techniques. Finally, you will master the skill of training large models efficiently in a distributed fashion, search neural architectures effectively with AutoML, and rapidly prototype models using PyTorch and fast.ai.

By the end of this PyTorch book, you'll be well equipped to perform complex DL tasks using PyTorch to build smart **artificial intelligence** models.

Who this book is for

This book is for data scientists, machine learning researchers, and DL practitioners looking to implement advanced DL paradigms using PyTorch 1.x. Working knowledge of DL with Python programming is required.

What this book covers

Chapter 1, Overview of Deep Learning Using PyTorch, includes brief notes on various DL terms and concepts that are will help you to understand later parts of the book. This chapter also gives you a quick overview of PyTorch as a language and the tools that will be used throughout this book to build DL models. Finally, we will train a neural network model using PyTorch.

Chapter 2, Combining CNNs and LSTMs, walks us through an example where we will build a neural network model with a CNN and **long short-term memory (LSTM)** that generates text/captions as output when given images as input using PyTorch.

Chapter 3, Deep CNN Architectures, gives a rundown of the most advanced deep CNN model architectures in recent years. We use PyTorch to create many of these models and train them for different tasks.

Chapter 4, Deep Recurrent Model Architectures, goes through the recent advancements in recurrent neural architectures, specifically RNNs, LSTMs, and **gated recurrent units (GRUs)**. Upon completion of this chapter, you will be able to create your own complex recurrent architectures in PyTorch.

Chapter 5, Hybrid Advanced Models, discusses some advanced, unique hybrid neural architectures, such as Transformers, which have revolutionized the world of natural language processing. This chapter also discusses RandWireNNs, taking a peek into the world of neural architecture search using PyTorch.

Chapter 6, Music and Text Generation with PyTorch, demonstrates the use of PyTorch to create DL models that can compose music and write text with practically nothing being provided to them at runtime.

Chapter 7, Neural Style Transfer, discusses a special type of generative neural network model that can mix multiple input images and generate artistic-looking arbitrary images.

Chapter 8, Deep Convolutional GANs, explains GANs and sees you train one on a specific task using PyTorch.

Chapter 9, Deep Reinforcement Learning, explores how PyTorch can be used to train agents in a deep reinforcement learning task, such as a video game.

Chapter 10, Operationalizing PyTorch Models into Production, runs through the process of deploying a DL model written in PyTorch into a real production system using Flask and Docker as well as TorchServe. Then, we'll learn how to export PyTorch models using TorchScript and ONNX. We'll also learn how to ship PyTorch code as a C++ application. Finally, we will also learn how to use PyTorch on some of the popular cloud computing platforms.

Chapter 11, Distributed Training, explores how to efficiently train large models with limited resources through distributed training practices in PyTorch.

Chapter 12, PyTorch and AutoML, walks us through setting up machine learning experiments effectively using AutoML with PyTorch.

Chapter 13, PyTorch and Explainable AI, focuses on making machine learning models interpretable to a layman using tools such as Captum combined with PyTorch.

Chapter 14, Rapid Prototyping with PyTorch, discusses various tools and libraries such as fast.ai and PyTorch Lightning that make the process of model training in PyTorch several times faster.

To get the most out of this book

Hands-on Python experience as well as basic knowledge of PyTorch is expected. Because most exercises in this book are in the form of notebooks, experience of working with Jupyter notebooks is expected. Some of the exercises in some of the chapters might require a GPU for faster model training, and therefore having an NVIDIA GPU is a plus. Finally, having registered accounts with cloud computing platforms such as AWS, Google Cloud, and Microsoft Azure will be helpful to navigate parts of *Chapter 10, Operationalizing PyTorch Models into Production*, and *Chapter 11, Distributed Training*, where you will distribute training over several virtual machines.

Software/hardware covered in the book	OS requirements
Jupyter Notebook	Windows, macOS X, or Linux (any)
Preferably an NVIDIA GPU, but this is not mandatory	Windows, macOS X, or Linux (any)
Python and PyTorch	Windows, macOS X, or Linux (any)
AWS, Google Cloud, and Azure accounts	Windows, macOS X, or Linux (any)

If you are using the digital version of this book, we advise you to type the code yourself or access the code via the GitHub repository (link available in the next section). Doing so will help you avoid any potential errors related to the copying and pasting of code.

Download the example code files

You can download the example code files for this book from GitHub at `https://github.com/PacktPublishing/Mastering-PyTorch`. In case there's an update to the code, it will be updated on the existing GitHub repository.

We also have other code bundles from our rich catalog of books and videos available at `https://github.com/PacktPublishing/`. Check them out!

Download the color images

We also provide a PDF file that has color images of the screenshots/diagrams used in this book. You can download it here: `https://static.packt-cdn.com/downloads/9781789614381_ColorImages.pdf`.

Conventions used

There are a number of text conventions used throughout this book.

`Code in text`: Indicates code words in text, database table names, folder names, filenames, file extensions, pathnames, dummy URLs, user input, and Twitter handles. Here is an example: "And because `batch_size` is now coupled with `world_size`, we provide it as an input argument for an easier training interface."

A block of code is set as follows:

```
# define the optimization schedule for both G and D
opt_gen = torch.optim.Adam(gen.parameters(), lr=lrate)
opt_disc = torch.optim.Adam(disc.parameters(), lr=lrate)
```

When we wish to draw your attention to a particular part of a code block, the relevant lines or items are set in bold:

```
def main():
    parser.add_argument('--num-gpu-processes', default=1,
type=int)
    args.world_size = args.num_gpu_processes * args.num_
machines
    mp.spawn(train, nprocs=args.num_gpu_processes,
args=(args,))
```

Any command-line input or output is written as follows:

```
jupyter==1.0.0
torch==1.4.0
torchvision==0.5.0
matplotlib==3.1.2
pytorch-lightning==1.0.5
fastai==2.1.8
```

Bold: Indicates a new term, an important word, or words that you see onscreen. For example, words in menus or dialog boxes appear in the text like this. Here is an example: "First, the random noise input vector of size **64** is reshaped and projected into **128** feature maps of size **16x16** each."

> **Tips or important notes**
> Appear like this.

Get in touch

Feedback from our readers is always welcome.

General feedback: If you have questions about any aspect of this book, mention the book title in the subject of your message and email us at customercare@packtpub.com.

Errata: Although we have taken every care to ensure the accuracy of our content, mistakes do happen. If you have found a mistake in this book, we would be grateful if you would report this to us. Please visit www.packtpub.com/support/errata, selecting your book, clicking on the Errata Submission Form link, and entering the details.

Piracy: If you come across any illegal copies of our works in any form on the Internet, we would be grateful if you would provide us with the location address or website name. Please contact us at copyright@packt.com with a link to the material.

If you are interested in becoming an author: If there is a topic that you have expertise in and you are interested in either writing or contributing to a book, please visit authors.packtpub.com.

Reviews

Please leave a review. Once you have read and used this book, why not leave a review on the site that you purchased it from? Potential readers can then see and use your unbiased opinion to make purchase decisions, we at Packt can understand what you think about our products, and our authors can see your feedback on their book. Thank you!

For more information about Packt, please visit packt.com.

Section 1: PyTorch Overview

This section includes a refresher on deep learning concepts, as well as PyTorch essentials. Upon completing this section, you will be able to identify how to train your own PyTorch models, as well as how to build a neural network model that generates text/captions as output when given images as input using PyTorch.

This section comprises the following chapters:

- *Chapter 1, Overview of Deep Learning Using PyTorch*
- *Chapter 2, Combining CNNs and LSTMs*

1
Overview of Deep Learning using PyTorch

Deep learning is a class of machine learning methods that has revolutionized the way computers/machines are used to perform cognitive tasks in real life. Based on the mathematical concept of deep neural networks, deep learning uses large amounts of data to learn non-trivial relationships between inputs and outputs in the form of complex nonlinear functions. Some of the inputs and outputs, as demonstrated in *Figure 1.1*, could be the following:

- *Input*: An image of a text; *output*: Text
- *Input*: Text; *output*: A natural voice speaking the text
- *Input*: A natural voice speaking the text; *output*: Transcribed text

And so on. Here is a figure to support the preceding explanation:

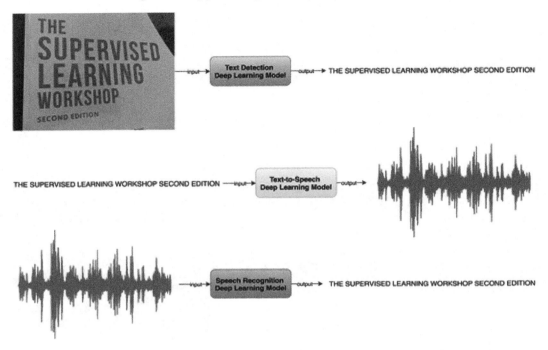

Figure 1.1 – Deep learning model examples

Deep neural networks involve a lot of mathematical computations, linear algebraic equations, complex nonlinear functions, and various optimization algorithms. In order to build and train a deep neural network from scratch using a programming language such as Python, it would require us to write all the necessary equations, functions, and optimization schedules. Furthermore, the code would need to be written such that large amounts of data can be loaded efficiently, and training can be performed in a reasonable amount of time. This amounts to implementing several lower-level details each time we build a deep learning application.

Deep learning libraries such as **Theano** and **TensorFlow**, among various others, have been developed over the years to abstract these details out. **PyTorch** is one such Python-based deep learning library that can be used to build deep learning models.

TensorFlow was introduced as an open source deep learning Python (and C++) library by Google in late 2015, which revolutionized the field of applied deep learning. Facebook, in 2016, responded with its own open source deep learning library and called it **Torch**. Torch was initially used with a scripting language called **Lua**, and soon enough, the Python equivalent emerged called **PyTorch**. Around the same time, Microsoft released its own library – **CNTK**. Amidst the hot competition, PyTorch has been growing fast to become one of the most used deep learning libraries.

This book is meant to be a hands-on resource on some of the most advanced deep learning problems, how they are solved using complex deep learning architectures, and how PyTorch can be effectively used to build, train, and evaluate these complex models. While the book keeps PyTorch at the center, it also includes comprehensive coverage of some of the most recent and advanced deep learning models. The book is intended for data scientists, machine learning engineers, or researchers who have a working knowledge of Python and who, preferably, have used PyTorch before.

Due to the hands-on nature of this book, it is highly recommended to try the examples in each chapter by yourself on your computer to become proficient in writing PyTorch code. We begin with this introductory chapter and subsequently explore various deep learning problems and model architectures that will expose the various functionalities PyTorch has to offer.

This chapter will review some of the concepts behind deep learning and will provide a brief overview of the PyTorch library. We conclude this chapter with a hands-on exercise where we train a deep learning model using PyTorch.

The following topics will be covered in this chapter:

- A refresher on deep learning
- Exploring the PyTorch library
- Training a neural network using PyTorch

Technical requirements

We will be using Jupyter notebooks for all of our exercises. And the following is the list of Python libraries that shall be installed for this chapter using `pip`. For example, run `pip install torch==1.4.0` on the command line:

```
jupyter==1.0.0
torch==1.4.0
torchvision==0.5.0
matplotlib==3.1.2
```

All code files relevant to this chapter are available at `https://github.com/PacktPublishing/Mastering-PyTorch/tree/master/Chapter01`.

A refresher on deep learning

Neural networks are a sub-type of machine learning methods that are inspired by the structure and function of the human brain. In neural networks, each computational unit, analogically called a neuron, is connected to other neurons in a layered fashion. When the number of such layers is more than two, the neural network thus formed is called a **deep neural network**. Such models are generally called **deep learning models**.

Deep learning models have proven superior to other classical machine learning models because of their ability to learn highly complex relationships between input data and the output (ground truth). In recent times, deep learning has gained a lot of attention and rightly so, primarily because of the following two reasons:

- The availability of powerful computing machines, especially in the cloud
- The availability of huge amounts of data

Owing to Moore's law, which states that the processing power of computers will double every 2 years, we are now living in a time when deep learning models with several hundreds of layers can be trained within a realistic and reasonably short amount of time. At the same time, with the exponential increase in the use of digital devices everywhere, our digital footprint has exploded, resulting in gigantic amounts of data being generated across the world every moment.

Hence, it has been possible to train deep learning models for some of the most difficult cognitive tasks that were either intractable earlier or had sub-optimal solutions through other machine learning techniques.

Deep learning, or neural networks in general, has another advantage over the classical machine learning models. Usually, in a classical machine learning-based approach, **feature engineering** plays a crucial role in the overall performance of a trained model. However, a deep learning model does away with the need to manually craft features. With large amounts of data, deep learning models can perform very well without requiring hand-engineered features and can outperform the traditional machine learning models. The following graph indicates how deep learning models can leverage large amounts of data better than the classical machine models:

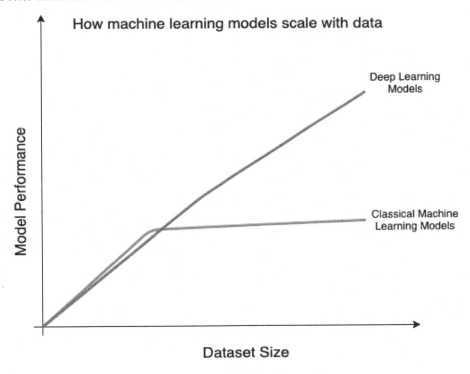

Figure 1.2 – Model performance versus dataset size

As can be seen in the graph, deep learning performance isn't necessarily distinguished up to a certain dataset size. However, as the data size starts to further increase, deep neural networks begin outperforming the non-deep learning models.

A deep learning model can be built based on various types of neural network architectures that have been developed over the years. A prime distinguishing factor between the different architectures is the type and combination of layers that are used in the neural network. Some of the well-known layers are the following:

- **Fully-connected** or **linear**: In a fully connected layer, as shown in the following diagram, all neurons preceding this layer are connected to all neurons succeeding this layer:

Fully Connected Layer

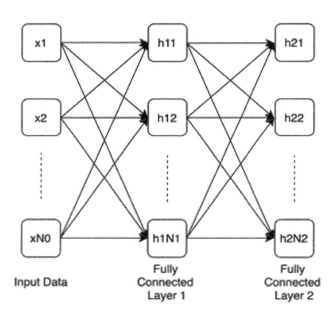

Figure 1.3 – Fully connected layer

This example shows two consecutive fully connected layers with **N1** and **N2** number of neurons, respectively. Fully connected layers are a fundamental unit of many – in fact, most – deep learning classifiers.

- **Convolutional**: The following diagram shows a convolutional layer, where a convolutional kernel (or filter) is convolved over the input:

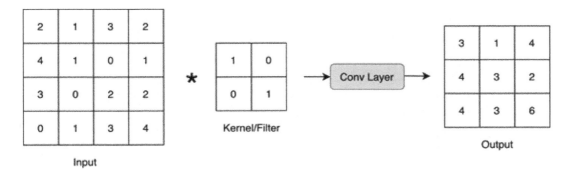

Figure 1.4 – Convolutional layer

Convolutional layers are a fundamental unit of **convolutional neural networks** (**CNNs**), which are the most effective models for solving computer vision problems.

- **Recurrent**: The following diagram shows a recurrent layer. While it looks similar to a fully connected layer, the key difference is the recurrent connection (marked with bold curved arrows):

Recurrent layer

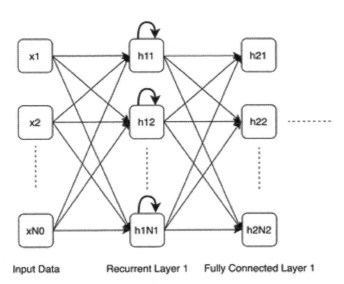

Figure 1.5 – Recurrent layer

Recurrent layers have an advantage over fully connected layers in that they exhibit memorizing capabilities, which comes in handy working with sequential data where one needs to remember past inputs along with the present inputs.

- **DeConv** (the reverse of a convolutional layer): Quite the opposite of a convolutional layer, a **deconvolutional layer** works as shown in the following diagram:

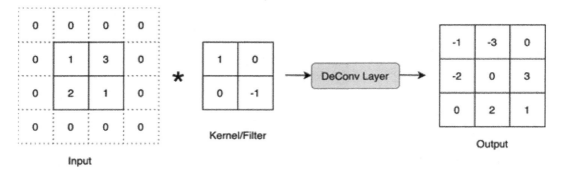

Figure 1.6 – Deconvolutional layer

This layer expands the input data spatially and hence is crucial in models that aim to generate or reconstruct images, for example.

- **Pooling**: The following diagram shows the max-pooling layer, which is perhaps the most widely used kind of pooling layer:

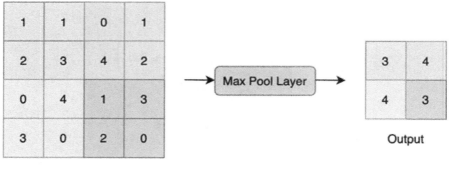

Figure 1.7 – Pooling layer

This is a max-pooling layer that pools the highest number each from 2x2 sized subsections of the input. Other forms of pooling are **min-pooling** and **mean-pooling**.

- **Dropout**: The following diagram shows how dropout layers work. Essentially, in a dropout layer, some neurons are temporarily switched off (marked with **X** in the diagram), that is, they are disconnected from the network:

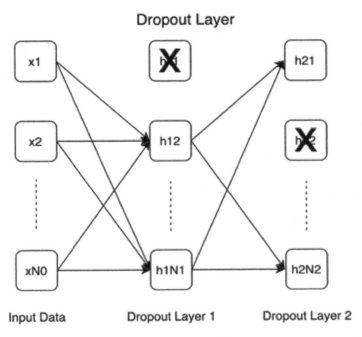

Figure 1.8 – Dropout layer

Dropout helps in model regularization as it forces the model to function well in sporadic absences of certain neurons, which forces the model to learn generalizable patterns instead of memorizing the entire training dataset.

A number of well-known architectures based on the previously mentioned layers are shown in the following diagram:.

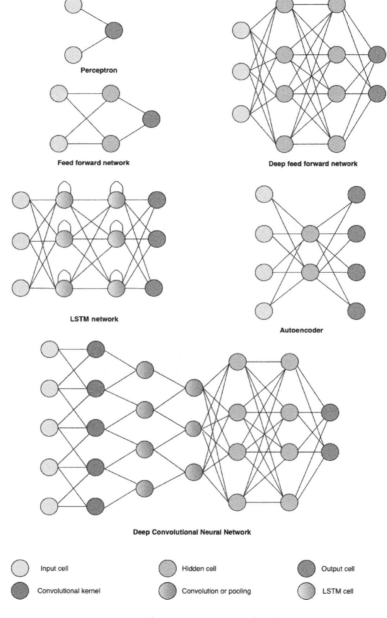

Figure 1.9 – Different neural network architectures

A more exhaustive set of neural network architectures can be found here: https://www.asimovinstitute.org/neural-network-zoo/.

Besides the types of layers and how they are connected in a network, other factors such as **activation functions** and the **optimization schedule** also define the model.

Activation functions

Activation functions are crucial to neural networks as they add the non-linearity without which, no matter how many layers we add, the entire neural network would be reduced to a simple linear model. The different types of activation functions listed here are basically different nonlinear mathematical functions.

Some of the popular activation functions are as follows:

- **Sigmoid**: A sigmoid (or logistic) function is expressed as follows:

$$y = f(x) = \frac{1}{1 + e^{-x}}$$

The function is shown in graph form as follows:

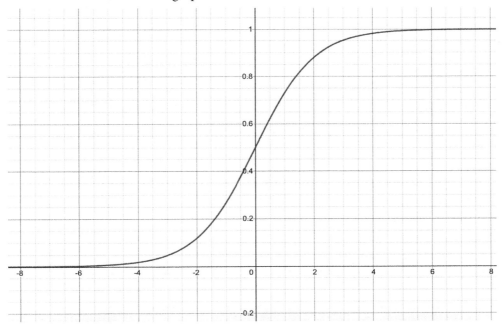

Figure 1.10 – Sigmoid function

As can be seen from the graph, the sigmoid function takes in a numerical value x as input and outputs a value y in the range (0, 1).

- **TanH**: TanH is expressed as follows:

$$y = f(x) = \frac{e^x - e^{-x}}{e^x + e^{-x}}$$

The function is shown in graph form as follows:

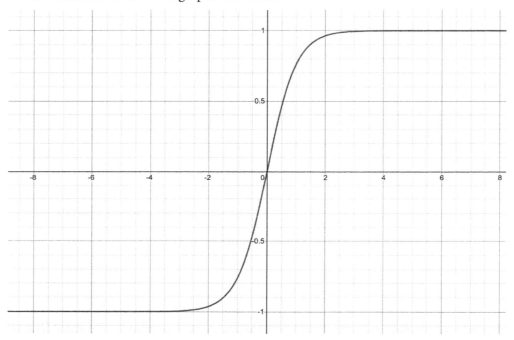

Figure 1.11 – TanH function

Contrary to sigmoid, the output y varies from -1 to 1 in the case of the TanH activation function. Hence, this activation is useful in cases where we need both positive as well as negative outputs.

- **Rectified linear units (ReLUs)**: ReLUs are more recent than the previous two and are simply expressed as follows:

$$y = f(x) = max(0, x)$$

The function is shown in graph form as follows:

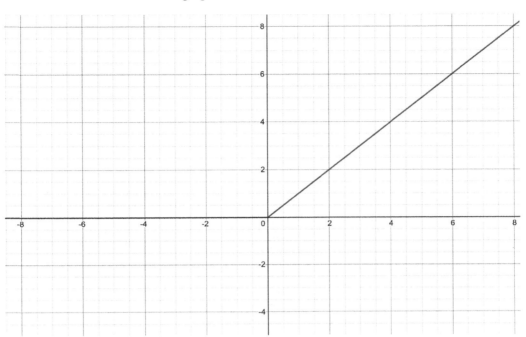

Figure 1.12 – ReLU function

A distinct feature of ReLU in comparison with the sigmoid and TanH activation functions is that the output keeps growing with the input whenever the input is greater than 0. This prevents the gradient of this function from diminishing to 0 as in the case of the previous two activation functions. Although, whenever the input is negative, both the output and the gradient will be 0.

- **Leaky ReLU**: ReLUs entirely suppress any incoming negative input by outputting 0. We may, however, want to also process negative inputs for some cases. Leaky ReLUs offer the option of processing negative inputs by outputting a fraction k of the incoming negative input. This fraction k is a parameter of this activation function, which can be mathematically expressed as follows:

$$y = f(x) = max(kx, x)$$

The following graph shows the input-output relationship for leaky ReLU:

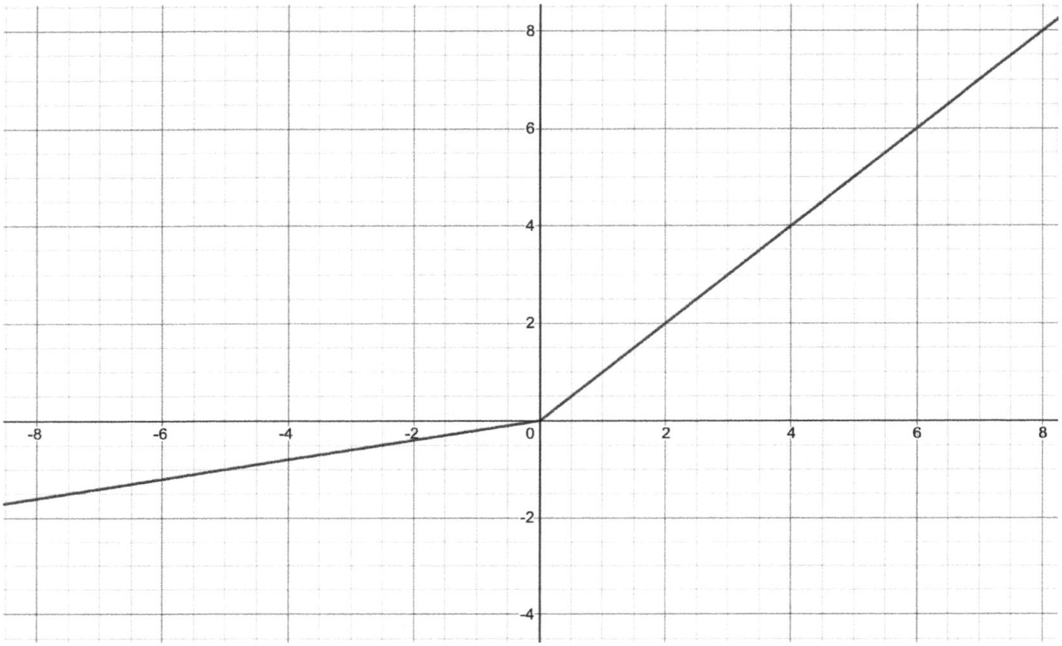

Figure 1.13 – Leaky ReLU function

Activation functions are an actively evolving area of research within deep learning. It will not be possible to list all of the activation functions here but I encourage you to check out the recent developments in this domain. Many activation functions are simply nuanced modifications of the ones mentioned in this section.

Optimization schedule

So far, we have spoken of how a neural network structure is built. In order to train a neural network, we need to adopt an **optimization schedule**. Like any other parameter-based machine learning model, a deep learning model is trained by tuning its parameters. The parameters are tuned through the process of **backpropagation**, wherein the final or output layer of the neural network yields a loss. This loss is calculated with the help of a loss function that takes in the neural network's final layer's outputs and the corresponding ground truth target values. This loss is then backpropagated to the previous layers using *gradient descent* and the *chain rule of differentiation*.

The parameters or weights at each layer are accordingly modified in order to minimize the loss. The extent of modification is determined by a coefficient, which varies from 0 to 1, also known as the **learning rate**. This whole procedure of updating the weights of a neural network, which we call the **optimization schedule**, has a significant impact on how well a model is trained. Therefore, a lot of research has been done in this area and is still ongoing. The following are a few popular optimization schedules:

- **Stochastic Gradient Descent (SGD)**: It updates the model parameters in the following fashion:

$$\beta = \beta - \alpha * \frac{\delta L(X, y, \beta)}{\delta \beta}$$

β is the parameter of the model and X and y are the input training data and the corresponding labels respectively. L is the loss function and α is the learning rate. SGD performs this update for every training example pair (X, y). A variant of this – mini-batch gradient descent – performs updates for every k examples, where k is the batch size. Gradients are calculated altogether for the whole mini-batch. Another variant, batch gradient descent, performs parameter updates by calculating the gradient across the entire dataset.

- **Adagrad**: In the previous optimization schedule, we used a single learning rate for all the parameters of the model. However, different parameters might need to be updated at different paces, especially in cases of sparse data, where some parameters are more actively involved in feature extraction than others. Adagrad introduces the idea of per-parameter updates, as shown here:

$$\beta_i^{t+1} = \beta_i^t - \frac{\alpha}{\sqrt{SSG_i^t + \epsilon}} * \frac{\delta L(X, y, \beta)}{\delta \beta_i^t}$$

Here, we use the subscript i to denote the ith parameter and the superscript t is used to denote the time step t of the gradient descent iterations. SSG_i^t is the *sum of squared gradients* for the ith parameter starting from time step 0 to time step t. ϵ is used to denote a small value added to SSG to avoid division by zero. Dividing the global learning rate α by the square root of SSG ensures that the learning rate for frequently changing parameters lowers faster than the learning rate for rarely updated parameters.

- **Adadelta**: In Adagrad, the denominator of the learning rate is a term that keeps on rising in value due to added squared terms in every time step. This causes the learning rates to decay to vanishingly small values. To tackle this problem, Adadelta introduces the idea of computing the sum of squared gradients only up to previous time steps. In fact, we can express it as a running decaying average of the past gradients:

$$SSG_i^t = \gamma * SSG_i^{t-1} + (1 - \gamma) * (\frac{\delta L(X, y, \beta)}{\delta \beta_i^t})^2$$

γ here is the decaying factor we wish to choose for the previous sum of squared gradients. With this formulation, we ensure that the sum of squared gradients does not accumulate to a large value, thanks to the decaying average. Once SSG_i^t is defined, we can use the *Adagrad equation* to define the update step for Adadelta.

However, if we look closely at the *Adagrad equation*, the root mean squared gradient is not a dimensionless quantity and hence should ideally not be used as a coefficient for the learning rate. To resolve this, we define another running average, this time for the squared parameter updates. Let's first define the parameter update:

$$\Delta \beta_i^t = \beta_i^{t+1} - \beta_i^t = - \frac{\alpha}{\sqrt{SSG_i^t + \epsilon}} * \frac{\delta L(X, y, \beta)}{\delta \beta_i^t}$$

And then, similar to the *running decaying average of the past gradients* equation (the first equation under *Adadelta*), we can define the square sum of parameter updates as follows:

$$SSPU_i^t = \gamma * SSPU_i^{t-1} + (1 - \gamma) * (\Delta \beta_i^t)^2$$

Here, *SSPU* is the sum of squared parameter updates. Once we have this, we can adjust for the dimensionality problem in the *Adagrad equation* with the final Adadelta equation:

$$\beta_i^{t+1} = \beta_i^t - \frac{\sqrt{SSPU_i^t + \epsilon}}{\sqrt{SSG_i^t + \epsilon}} * \frac{\delta L(X, y, \beta)}{\delta \beta_i^t}$$

Noticeably, the final Adadelta equation doesn't require any learning rate. One can still however provide a learning rate as a multiplier. Hence, the only mandatory hyperparameter for this optimization schedule is the decaying factors..

- **RMSprop**: We have implicitly discussed the internal workings of RMSprop while discussing Adadelta as both are pretty similar. The only difference is that RMSProp does not adjust for the dimensionality problem and hence the update equation stays the same as the equation presented in the *Adagrad* section, wherein the SSG_i^t is obtained from the first equation in the *Adadelta* section. This essentially means that we do need to specify both a base learning rate as well as a decaying factor in the case of RMSProp.

- **Adaptive Moment Estimation (Adam)**: This is another optimization schedule that calculates customized learning rates for each parameter. Just like Adadelta and RMSprop, Adam also uses the decaying average of the previous squared gradients as demonstrated in the first equation in the *Adadelta* section. However, it also uses the decaying average of previous gradient values:

$$SG_i^t = \gamma' * SG_i^{t-1} + (1 - \gamma') * \frac{\delta L(X, y, \beta)}{\delta \beta_i^t}$$

SG and SSG are mathematically equivalent to estimating the first and second moments of the gradient respectively, hence the name of this method – **adaptive moment estimation**. Usually, γ and γ' are close to 1 and in that case, the initial values for both SG and SSG might be pushed towards zero. To counteract that, these two quantities are reformulated with the help of bias correction:

$$SG_i^t = \frac{SG_i^t}{1 - \gamma'} \qquad \text{and} \qquad SSG_i^t = \frac{SSG_i^t}{1 - \gamma}$$

Once they are defined, the parameter update is expressed as follows:

$$\beta_i^{t+1} = \beta_i^t - \frac{\alpha}{\sqrt{SSG_i^t + \epsilon}} * SG_i^t$$

Basically, the gradient on the extreme right-hand side of the equation is replaced by the decaying average of the gradient. Noticeably, Adam optimization involves three hyperparameters – the base learning rate, and the two decaying rates for the gradients and squared gradients. Adam is one of the most successful, if not the most successful, optimization schedule in recent times for training complex deep learning models.

So, which optimizer shall we use? It depends. If we are dealing with sparse data, then the adaptive optimizers (numbers 2 to 5) will be advantageous because of the per-parameter learning rate updates. As mentioned earlier, with sparse data, different parameters might be worked at different paces and hence a customized per-parameter learning rate mechanism can greatly help the model in reaching optimal solutions. SGD might also find a decent solution but will take much longer in terms of training time. Among the adaptive ones, Adagrad has the disadvantage of vanishing learning rates due to a monotonically increasing learning rate denominator.

RMSProp, Adadelta, and Adam are quite close in terms of their performance on various deep learning tasks. RMSprop is largely similar to Adadelta, except for the use of the base learning rate in RMSprop versus the use of the decaying average of previous parameter updates in Adadelta. Adam is slightly different in that it also includes the first-moment calculation of gradients and accounts for bias correction. Overall, Adam could be the optimizer to go with, all else being equal. We will use some of these optimization schedules in the exercises in this book. Feel free to switch them with another one to observe changes in the following:

- Model training time and trajectory (convergence)
- Final model performance

In the coming chapters, we will use many of these architectures, layers, activation functions, and optimization schedules in solving different kinds of machine learning problems with the help of PyTorch. In the example included in this chapter, we will create a convolutional neural network that contains convolutional, linear, max-pooling, and dropout layers. **Log-Softmax** is used for the final layer and ReLU is used as the activation function for all the other layers. And the model is trained using an Adadelta optimizer with a fixed learning rate of 0 . 5.

Exploring the PyTorch library

PyTorch is a machine learning library for Python based on the Torch library. PyTorch is extensively used as a deep learning tool both for research as well as building industrial applications. It is primarily developed by Facebook's machine learning research labs. PyTorch is competition for the other well-known deep learning library – TensorFlow, which is developed by Google. The initial difference between these two was that PyTorch was based on **eager execution** whereas TensorFlow was built on **graph-based deferred execution**. Although, TensorFlow now also provides an eager execution mode.

Eager execution is basically an imperative programming mode where mathematical operations are computed immediately. A deferred execution mode would have all the operations stored in a computational graph without immediate calculations and then the entire graph would be evaluated later. Eager execution is considered advantageous for reasons such as intuitive flow, easy debugging, and less scaffolding code.

PyTorch is more than just a deep learning library. With its NumPy-like syntax/interface, it provides tensor computation capabilities with strong acceleration using GPUs. But what is a tensor? Tensors are computational units, very similar to NumPy arrays, except that they can also be used on GPUs to accelerate computing.

With accelerated computing and the facility to create dynamic computational graphs, PyTorch provides a complete deep learning framework. Besides all that, it is truly Pythonic in nature, which enables PyTorch users to exploit all the features Python provides, including the extensive Python data science ecosystem.

In this section, we will take a look at some of the useful PyTorch modules that extend various functionalities helpful in loading data, building models, and specifying the optimization schedule during the training of a model. We will also expand on what a tensor is and how it is implemented with all of its attributes in PyTorch.

PyTorch modules

The PyTorch library, besides offering the computational functions as NumPy does, also offers a set of modules that enable developers to quickly design, train, and test deep learning models. The following are some of the most useful modules.

torch.nn

When building a neural network architecture, the fundamental aspects that the network is built on are the number of layers, the number of neurons in each layer, and which of those are learnable, and so on. The PyTorch nn module enables users to quickly instantiate neural network architectures by defining some of these high-level aspects as opposed to having to specify all the details manually. The following is a one-layer neural network initialization without using the nn module:

```
import math
# we assume a 256-dimensional input and a 4-dimensional output
for this 1-layer neural network
# hence, we initialize a 256x4 dimensional matrix filled with
random values
weights = torch.randn(256, 4) / math.sqrt(256)
```

```
# we then ensure that the parameters of this neural network
ar trainable, that is, the numbers in the 256x4 matrix can be
tuned with the help of backpropagation of gradients
```
```
weights.requires_grad_()
```
```
# finally we also add the bias weights for the 4-dimensional
output, and make these trainable too
```
```
bias = torch.zeros(4, requires_grad=True)
```

We can instead use nn.Linear(256, 4) to represent the same thing.

Within the torch.nn module, there is a submodule called torch.nn.functional. This submodule consists of all the functions within the torch.nn module whereas all the other submodules are classes. These functions are **loss functions**, **activating functions**, and also **neural functions** that can be used to create neural networks in a functional manner (that is, when each subsequent layer is expressed as a function of the previous layer) such as *pooling*, *convolutional*, and *linear* functions. An example of a loss function using the torch.nn.functional module could be the following:

```
import torch.nn.functional as F
loss_func = F.cross_entropy
loss = loss_func(model(X), y)
```

Here, X is the input, y is the target output, and model is the neural network model.

torch.optim

As we train a neural network, we back-propagate errors to tune the weights or parameters of the network – the process that we call **optimization**. The optim module includes all the tools and functionalities related to running various types of optimization schedules while training a deep learning model. Let's say we define an optimizer during a training session using the torch.optim modules, as shown in the following snippet:

```
opt = optim.SGD(model.parameters(), lr=lr)
```

Then, we don't need to manually write the optimization step as shown here:

```
with torch.no_grad():
    # applying the parameter updates using stochastic gradient
descent
    for param in model.parameters(): param -= param.grad * lr
    model.zero_grad()
```

We can simply write this instead:

```
opt.step()
opt.zero_grad()
```

Next, we will look at the `utis.data` module.

torch.utils.data

Under the `utis.data` module, torch provides its own dataset and `DatasetLoader` classes, which are extremely handy due to their abstract and flexible implementations. Basically, these classes provide intuitive and useful ways of iterating and performing other such operations on tensors. Using these, we can ensure high performance due to optimized tensor computations and also have fail-safe data I/O. For example, let's say we use `torch.utils.data.DataLoader` as follows:

```
from torch.utils.data import (TensorDataset, DataLoader)
train_dataset = TensorDataset(x_train, y_train)
train_dataloader = DataLoader(train_dataset, batch_size=bs)
```

Then, we don't need to iterate through batches of data manually, like this:

```
for i in range((n-1)//bs + 1):
    x_batch = x_train[start_i:end_i]
    y_batch = y_train[start_i:end_i]
    pred = model(x_batch)
```

We can simply write this instead:

```
for x_batch,y_batch in train_dataloader:
    pred = model(x_batch)
```

Let's now look at tensor modules.

Tensor modules

As mentioned earlier, tensors are conceptually similar to NumPy arrays. A tensor is an n-dimensional array on which we can operate mathematical functions, accelerate computations via GPUs, and tensors can also be used to keep track of a computational graph and gradients, which prove vital for deep learning. To run a tensor on a GPU, all we need is to cast the tensor into a certain data type.

Here is how we can instantiate a tensor in PyTorch:

```
points = torch.tensor([1.0, 4.0, 2.0, 1.0, 3.0, 5.0])
```

To fetch the first entry, simply write the following:

```
float(points[0])
```

We can also check the shape of the tensor using this:

```
points.shape
```

In PyTorch, tensors are implemented as views over a one-dimensional array of numerical data stored in contiguous chunks of memory. These arrays are called storage instances. Every PyTorch tensor has a storage attribute that can be called to output the underlying storage instance for a tensor as shown in the following example:

```
points = torch.tensor([[1.0, 4.0], [2.0, 1.0], [3.0, 5.0]])
points.storage()
```

This should output the following:

```
points = torch.tensor([[1.0, 4.0], [2.0, 1.0], [3.0, 5.0]])
points.storage()
 1.0
 4.0
 2.0
 1.0
 3.0
 5.0
[torch.FloatStorage of size 6]
```

Figure 1.14 – PyTorch tensor storage

When we say a tensor is a view on the storage instance, the tensor uses the following information to implement the view:

- Size
- Storage
- Offset
- Stride

Let's look into this with the help of our previous example:

```
points = torch.tensor([[1.0, 4.0], [2.0, 1.0], [3.0, 5.0]])
```

Let's investigate what these different pieces of information mean:

```
points.size()
```

This should output the following:

```
points.size()

torch.Size([3, 2])
```

Figure 1.15 – PyTorch tensor size

As we can see, `size` is similar to the `shape` attribute in NumPy, which tells us the number of elements across each dimension. The multiplication of these numbers equals the length of the underlying storage instance (6 in this case).

As we have already examined what the `storage` attribute means, let's look at `offset`:

```
points.storage_offset()
```

This should output the following:

```
points.storage_offset()

0
```

Figure 1.16 – PyTorch tensor storage offset 1

The offset here represents the index of the first element of the tensor in the `storage` array. Because the output is `0`, it means that the first element of the tensor is the first element in the `storage` array.

Let's check this:

```
points[1].storage_offset()
```

This should output the following:

```
points[1].storage_offset()

2
```

Figure 1.17 – PyTorch tensor storage offset 2

Because `points[1]` is `[2.0, 1.0]` and the `storage` array is `[1.0, 4.0, 2.0, 1.0, 3.0, 5.0]`, we can see that the first element of the tensor `[2.0, 1.0]`, that is, `.2.0` is at index 2 of the `storage` array.

Finally, we'll look at the `stride` attribute:

```
points.stride()
```

```
points.stride()
```

```
(2, 1)
```

Figure 1.18 – PyTorch tensor stride

As we can see, `stride` contains, for each dimension, the number of elements to be skipped in order to access the next element of the tensor. So, in this case, along the first dimension, in order to access the element after the first one, that is, `1.0` we need to skip 2 elements (that is, `1.0` and `4.0`) to access the next element, that is, `2.0`. Similarly, along the second dimension, we need to skip 1 element to access the element after `1.0`, that is, `4.0`. Thus, using all these attributes, tensors can be derived from a contiguous one-dimensional storage array.

The data contained within tensors is of numeric type. Specifically, PyTorch offers the following data types to be contained within tensors:

- `torch.float32` or `torch.float`—32-bit floating-point
- `torch.float64` or `torch.double`—64-bit, double-precision floating-point
- `torch.float16` or `torch.half`—16-bit, half-precision floating-point
- `torch.int8`—Signed 8-bit integers
- `torch.uint8`—Unsigned 8-bit integers
- `torch.int16` or `torch.short`—Signed 16-bit integers
- `torch.int32` or `torch.int`—Signed 32-bit integers
- `torch.int64` or `torch.long`—Signed 64-bit integers

An example of how we specify a certain data type to be used for a tensor is as follows:

```
points = torch.tensor([[1.0, 2.0], [3.0, 4.0]], dtype=torch.
float32)
```

Besides the data type, tensors in PyTorch also need a device specification where they will be stored. A device can be specified as instantiation:

```
points = torch.tensor([[1.0, 2.0], [3.0, 4.0]], dtype=torch.
float32, device='cpu')
```

Or we can also create a copy of a tensor in the desired device:

```
points_2 = points.to(device='cuda')
```

As seen in the two examples, we can either allocate a tensor to a CPU (using `device='cpu'`), which happens by default if we do not specify a device, or we can allocate the tensor to a GPU (using `device='cuda'`).

> **Note**
> PyTorch currently supports only GPUs that support CUDA.

When a tensor is placed on a GPU, the computations speed up and because the tensor APIs are largely uniform across CPU and GPU placed tensors in PyTorch, it is quite convenient to move the same tensor across devices, perform computations, and move it back.

If there are multiple devices of the same type, say more than one GPU, we can precisely locate the device we want to place the tensor in using the device index, such as the following:

```
points_3 = points.to(device='cuda:0')
```

You can read more about PyTorch-CUDA here: `https://pytorch.org/docs/stable/notes/cuda.html`. And you can read more generally about CUDA here: `https://developer.nvidia.com/about-cuda`.

Now that we have explored the PyTorch library and understood the PyTorch and Tensor modules, let's learn how to train a neural network using PyTorch.

Training a neural network using PyTorch

For this exercise, we will be using the famous MNIST dataset (available at http://yann.lecun.com/exdb/mnist/), which is a sequence of images of handwritten postcode digits, zero through nine, with corresponding labels. The MNIST dataset consists of 60,000 training samples and 10,000 test samples, where each sample is a grayscale image with 28 x 28 pixels. PyTorch also provides the MNIST dataset under its Dataset module.

In this exercise, we will use PyTorch to train a deep learning multi-class classifier on this dataset and test how the trained model performs on the test samples:

1. For this exercise, we will need to import a few dependencies. Execute the following import statements:

```
import torch
import torch.nn as nn
import torch.nn.functional as F
import torch.optim as optim
from torch.utils.data import DataLoader
from torchvision import datasets, transforms
import matplotlib.pyplot as plt
```

2. Next, we define the model architecture as shown in the following diagram:

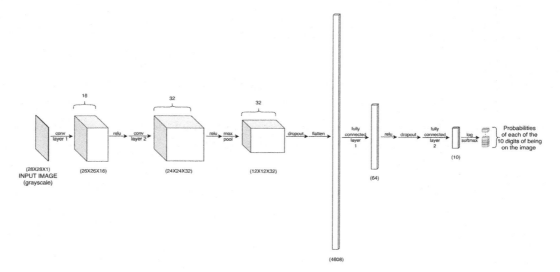

Figure 1.19 – Neural network architecture

The model consists of convolutional layers, dropout layers, as well as linear/fully connected layers, all available through the `torch.nn` module:

```python
class ConvNet(nn.Module):
    def __init__(self):
        super(ConvNet, self).__init__()
        self.cn1 = nn.Conv2d(1, 16, 3, 1)
        self.cn2 = nn.Conv2d(16, 32, 3, 1)
        self.dp1 = nn.Dropout2d(0.10)
        self.dp2 = nn.Dropout2d(0.25)
        self.fc1 = nn.Linear(4608, 64) # 4608 is
basically 12 X 12 X 32
        self.fc2 = nn.Linear(64, 10)
    def forward(self, x):
        x = self.cn1(x)
        x = F.relu(x)
        x = self.cn2(x)
        x = F.relu(x)
        x = F.max_pool2d(x, 2)
        x = self.dp1(x)
        x = torch.flatten(x, 1)
        x = self.fc1(x)
        x = F.relu(x)
        x = self.dp2(x)
        x = self.fc2(x)
        op = F.log_softmax(x, dim=1)
        return op
```

The `__init__` function defines the core architecture of the model, that is, all the layers with the number of neurons at each layer. And the `forward` function, as the name suggests, does a forward pass in the network. Hence it includes all the activation functions at each layer as well as any pooling or dropout used after any layer. This function shall return the final layer output, which we call the prediction of the model, which has the same dimensions as the target output (the ground truth).

Notice that the first convolutional layer has a 1-channel input, a 16-channel output, a kernel size of 3, and a stride of 1. The 1-channel input is essentially for the grayscale images that will be fed to the model. We decided on a kernel size of 3x3 for various reasons. Firstly, kernel sizes are usually odd numbers so that the input image pixels are symmetrically distributed around a central pixel. 1x1 would be too small because then the kernel operating on a given pixel would not have any information about the neighboring pixels. 3 comes next, but why not go further to 5, 7, or, say, even 27?

Well, at the extreme high end, a 27x27 kernel convolving over a 28x28 image would give us very coarse-grained features. However, the most important visual features in the image are fairly local and hence it makes sense to use a small kernel that looks at a few neighboring pixels at a time, for visual patterns. 3x3 is one of the most common kernel sizes used in CNNs for solving computer vision problems.

Note that we have two consecutive convolutional layers, both with 3x3 kernels. This, in terms of spatial coverage, is equivalent to using one convolutional layer with a 5x5 kernel. However, using multiple layers with a smaller kernel size is almost always preferred because it results in deeper networks, hence more complex learned features as well as fewer parameters due to smaller kernels.

The number of channels in the output of a convolutional layer is usually higher than or equal to the input number of channels. Our first convolutional layer takes in one channel data and outputs 16 channels. This basically means that the layer is trying to detect 16 different kinds of information from the input image. Each of these channels is called a **feature map** and each of them has a dedicated kernel extracting features for them.

We escalate the number of channels from 16 to 32 in the second convolutional layer, in an attempt to extract more kinds of features from the image. This increment in the number of channels (or image depth) is common practice in CNNs. We will read more on this under *width-based CNNs* in *Chapter 3, Deep CNN Architectures*.

Finally, the stride of 1 makes sense, as our kernel size is just 3. Keeping a larger stride value – say, 10 – would result in the kernel skipping many pixels in the image and we don't want to do that. If, however, our kernel size was 100, we might have considered 10 as a reasonable stride value. The larger the stride, the lower the number of convolution operations but the smaller the overall field of view for the kernel.

3. We then define the training routine, that is, the actual backpropagation step. As can be seen, the `torch.optim` module greatly helps in keeping this code succinct:

```python
def train(model, device, train_dataloader, optim, epoch):
    model.train()
    for b_i, (X, y) in enumerate(train_dataloader):
        X, y = X.to(device), y.to(device)
        optim.zero_grad()
        pred_prob = model(X)
        loss = F.nll_loss(pred_prob, y) # nll is the
negative likelihood loss
        loss.backward()
        optim.step()
        if b_i % 10 == 0:
            print('epoch: {} [{}/{} ({:.0f}%)]\t training
loss: {:.6f}'.format(
                epoch, b_i * len(X), len(train_
                    dataloader.dataset),
                100. * b_i / len(train_dataloader), loss.
                    item()))
```

This iterates through the dataset in batches, makes a copy of the dataset on the given device, makes a forward pass with the retrieved data on the neural network model, computes the loss between the model prediction and the ground truth, uses the given optimizer to tune model weights, and prints training logs every 10 batches. The entire procedure done once qualifies as 1 epoch, that is, when the entire dataset has been read once.

4. Similar to the preceding training routine, we write a test routine that can be used to evaluate the model performance on the test set:

```python
def test(model, device, test_dataloader):
    model.eval()
    loss = 0
    success = 0
    with torch.no_grad():
        for X, y in test_dataloader:
            X, y = X.to(device), y.to(device)
            pred_prob = model(X)
            loss += F.nll_loss(pred_prob, y,
reduction='sum').item()  # loss summed across the batch
            pred = pred_prob.argmax(dim=1,
                keepdim=True)  # us argmax to get the most
                likely prediction
            success += pred.eq(y.view_as(pred)).sum().
item()
    loss /= len(test_dataloader.dataset)
    print('\nTest dataset: Overall Loss: {:.4f}, Overall
Accuracy: {}/{} ({:.0f}%)\n'.format(
        loss, success, len(test_dataloader.dataset),
        100. * success / len(test_dataloader.dataset)))
```

Most of this function is similar to the preceding `train` function. The only difference is that the loss computed from the model predictions and the ground truth is not used to tune the model weights using an optimizer. Instead, the loss is used to compute the overall test error across the entire test batch.

5. Next, we come to another critical component of this exercise, which is loading the dataset. Thanks to PyTorch's `DataLoader` module, we can set up the dataset loading mechanism in a few lines of code:

```python
# The mean and standard deviation values are calculated
as the mean of all pixel values of all images in the
training dataset
train_dataloader = torch.utils.data.DataLoader(
    datasets.MNIST('../data', train=True, download=True,
                transform=transforms.Compose([
                    transforms.ToTensor(),
```

```
                            transforms.Normalize((0.1302,),
    (0.3069,))])), # train_X.mean()/256. and train_X.
    std()/256.
        batch_size=32, shuffle=True)


test_dataloader = torch.utils.data.DataLoader(
    datasets.MNIST('../data', train=False,
                transform=transforms.Compose([
                    transforms.ToTensor(),
                    transforms.Normalize((0.1302,),
    (0.3069,))
                ])),
        batch_size=500, shuffle=False)
```

As you can see, we set batch_size to 32, which is a fairly common choice. Usually, there is a trade-off in deciding the batch size. A very small batch size can lead to slow training due to frequent gradient calculations and can lead to extremely noisy gradients. Very large batch sizes can, on the other hand, also slow down training due to a long waiting time to calculate gradients. It is mostly not worth waiting long before a single gradient update. It is rather advisable to make frequent, less precise gradients as it will eventually lead the model to a better set of learned parameters.

For both the training and test dataset, we specify the local storage location we want to save the dataset to, and the batch size, which determines the number of data instances that constitute one pass of a training and test run. We also specify that we want to randomly shuffle training data instances to ensure a uniform distribution of data samples across batches. Finally, we also normalize the dataset to a normal distribution with a specified mean and standard deviation.

6. We defined the training routine earlier. Now is the time to actually define which optimizer and device we will use to run the model training. And we will finally get the following:

```
torch.manual_seed(0)
device = torch.device("cpu")

model = ConvNet()
optimizer = optim.Adadelta(model.parameters(), lr=0.5)
```

We define the device for this exercise as cpu. We also set a seed to avoid unknown randomness and ensure repeatability. We will use AdaDelta as the optimizer for this exercise with a learning rate of 0.5. While discussing optimization schedules earlier in the chapter, we mentioned that Adadelta could be a good choice if we are dealing with sparse data. And this is a case of sparse data, because not all pixels in the image are informative. Having said that, I encourage you to try out other optimizers such as Adam on this same problem to see how it affects the training process and model performance.

7. And then we start the actual process of training the model for *k* number of epochs, and we also keep testing the model at the end of each training epoch:

```
for epoch in range(1, 3):
    train(model, device, train_dataloader, optimizer,
epoch)
    test(model, device, test_dataloader)
```

For demonstration purposes, we will run the training for only two epochs. The output will be as follows:

```
epoch: 1 [0/60000 (0%)]  training loss: 2.306125
epoch: 1 [320/60000 (1%)]        training loss: 1.623073
epoch: 1 [640/60000 (1%)]        training loss: 0.998695
epoch: 1 [960/60000 (2%)]        training loss: 0.953389
epoch: 1 [1280/60000 (2%)]       training loss: 1.054391
epoch: 1 [1600/60000 (3%)]       training loss: 0.393427
epoch: 1 [1920/60000 (3%)]       training loss: 0.235708
epoch: 1 [2240/60000 (4%)]       training loss: 0.284237
epoch: 1 [2560/60000 (4%)]       training loss: 0.203838
epoch: 1 [2880/60000 (5%)]       training loss: 0.292076
epoch: 1 [3200/60000 (5%)]       training loss: 0.541438
epoch: 1 [3520/60000 (6%)]       training loss: 0.411091
epoch: 1 [3840/60000 (6%)]       training loss: 0.323946
epoch: 1 [4160/60000 (7%)]       training loss: 0.296546



epoch: 2 [56000/60000 (93%)]     training loss: 0.072877
epoch: 2 [56320/60000 (94%)]     training loss: 0.112689
epoch: 2 [56640/60000 (94%)]     training loss: 0.003503
epoch: 2 [56960/60000 (95%)]     training loss: 0.002715
epoch: 2 [57280/60000 (95%)]     training loss: 0.089225
epoch: 2 [57600/60000 (96%)]     training loss: 0.184287
epoch: 2 [57920/60000 (97%)]     training loss: 0.044174
epoch: 2 [58240/60000 (97%)]     training loss: 0.097794
epoch: 2 [58560/60000 (98%)]     training loss: 0.018629
epoch: 2 [58880/60000 (98%)]     training loss: 0.062386
epoch: 2 [59200/60000 (99%)]     training loss: 0.031968
epoch: 2 [59520/60000 (99%)]     training loss: 0.009200
epoch: 2 [59840/60000 (100%)]    training loss: 0.021790

Test dataset: Overall Loss: 0.0489, Overall Accuracy: 9850/10000 (98%)
```

Figure 1.20 – Training logs

8. Now that we have trained a model, with a reasonable test set performance, we can also manually check whether the model inference on a sample image is correct:

```
test_samples = enumerate(test_dataloader)
b_i, (sample_data, sample_targets) = next(test_samples)

plt.imshow(sample_data[0][0], cmap='gray',
interpolation='none')
```

The output will be as follows:

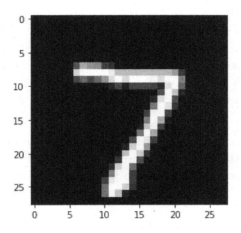

Figure 1.21 – Sample handwritten image

And now we run the model inference for this image and compare it with the ground truth:

```
print(f"Model prediction is : {model(sample_data).data.
max(1)[1][0]}")
print(f"Ground truth is : {sample_targets[0]}")
```

Note that, for predictions, we first calculate the class with maximum probability using the max function on **axis=1**. The max function outputs two lists – a list of probabilities of classes for every sample in sample_data and a list of class labels for each sample. Hence, we choose the second list using index [1]. We further select the first class label by using index [0] to look at only the first sample under sample_data. The output will be as follows:

```
Model prediction is : 7
Ground truth is : 7
```

Figure 1.22 – PyTorch model prediction

This appears to be the correct prediction. The forward pass of the neural network done using `model()` produces probabilities. Hence, we use the `max` function to output the class with the maximum probability.

> **Note**
> The code pattern for this exercise is derived from the official PyTorch examples repository, which can be found here: `https://github.com/pytorch/examples/tree/master/mnist`.

Summary

In this chapter, we refreshed deep learning concepts such as layers, activation functions, and optimization schedules and how they contribute towards building varied deep learning architectures. We explored the PyTorch deep learning library, including some of the important modules, such as `torch.nn`, `torch.optim`, and `torch.data`, as well as tensor modules.

We then ran a hands-on exercise on training a deep learning model from scratch. We built a CNN for our exercise using PyTorch modules. We also wrote relevant PyTorch code to load the dataset, train and evaluate the model, and finally, make predictions from the trained model.

In the next chapter, we will explore a slightly more complex model architecture that involves multiple sub-models and use this type of hybrid model to tackle the real-world task of describing an image using natural text. Using PyTorch, we will implement such a system and generate captions for unseen images.

2
Combining CNNs and LSTMs

Convolutional Neural Networks (CNNs) are a type of deep learning model known to solve machine learning problems related to images and video, such as image classification, object detection, segmentation, and more. This is because CNNs use a special type of layer called **convolutional layers**, which have shared learnable parameters. The weight or parameter sharing works because the patterns to be learned in an image (such as edges or contours) are assumed to be independent of the location of the pixels in the image. Just as CNNs are applied to images, **Long Short-Term Memory (LSTM)** networks – which are a type of **Recurrent Neural Network (RNN)** – prove to be extremely effective at solving machine learning problems related to **sequential data**. An example of sequential data could be text. For example, in a sentence, each word is dependent on the previous word(s). LSTM models are meant to model such sequential dependencies.

These two different types of networks – CNNs and LSTMs – can be cascaded to form a hybrid model that takes in images or video and outputs text. One well-known application of such a hybrid model is image captioning, where the model takes in an image and outputs a plausible textual description of the image. Since 2010, machine learning has been used to perform the task of image captioning (`https://dl.acm.org/doi/10.5555/1858681.1858808`).

However, neural networks were first successfully used for this task in around 2014/2015 (https://www.cv-foundation.org/openaccess/content_cvpr_2015/html/Vinyals_Show_and_Tell_2015_CVPR_paper.html). Ever since, image captioning has been actively researched. With significant improvements each year, this deep learning application might help the visually impaired better visualize the world.

This chapter first discusses the architecture of such a hybrid model, along with the related implementational details in PyTorch, and at the end of the chapter, we will build an image captioning system from scratch using PyTorch. This chapter covers the following topics:

- Building a neural network with CNNs and LSTMs
- Building an image caption generator using PyTorch

Technical requirements

We will be using Jupyter notebooks for all of our exercises. The following is the list of Python libraries that should be installed for this chapter using pip. For example, run pip install torch==1.4.0 on the command line, and so on:

```
jupyter==1.0.0
torch==1.4.0
torchvision==0.5.0
nltk==3.4.5
Pillow==6.2.2
pycocotools==2.0.0
```

All the code files relevant to this chapter are available at https://github.com/PacktPublishing/Mastering-PyTorch/tree/master/Chapter02.

Building a neural network with CNNs and LSTMs

A CNN-LSTM network architecture consists of a convolutional layer(s) for extracting features from the input data (image), followed by an LSTM layer(s) to perform sequential predictions. This kind of model is both spatially and temporally deep. The convolutional part of the model is often used as an **encoder** that takes in an input image and outputs high-dimensional features or embeddings.

In practice, the CNN used for these hybrid networks is often pre-trained on, say, an image classification task. The last hidden layer of the pre-trained CNN model is then used as an input to the LSTM component, which is used as a **decoder** to generate text.

When we are dealing with textual data, we need to transform the words and other symbols (punctuation, identifiers, and more) – together referred to as **tokens** – into numbers. We do so by representing each token in the text with a unique corresponding number. In the following sub-section, we will demonstrate an example of text encoding.

Text encoding demo

Let's assume we're building a machine learning model with textual data; say, for example, that our text is as follows:

```
<start> PyTorch is a deep learning library. <end>
```

Then, we would map each of these words/tokens to numbers, as follows:

```
<start> : 0
PyTorch : 1
is : 2
a : 3
deep : 4
learning : 5
library : 6
. : 7
<end> : 8
```

Once we have the mapping, we can represent this sentence numerically as a list of numbers:

```
<start> PyTorch is a deep learning library. <end> -> [0, 1, 2,
3, 4, 5, 6, 7, 8]
```

Also, for example, `<start> PyTorch is deep. <end>` would be encoded as `-> [0, 1, 2, 4, 7, 8]` and so on. This mapping, in general, is referred to as **vocabulary**, and building a vocabulary is a crucial part of most text-related machine learning problems.

The LSTM model, which acts as the decoder, takes in a CNN embedding as input at $t=0$. Then, each LSTM cell makes a token prediction at each time-step, which is fed as the input to the next LSTM cell. The overall architecture thus generated can be visualized as shown in the following diagram:

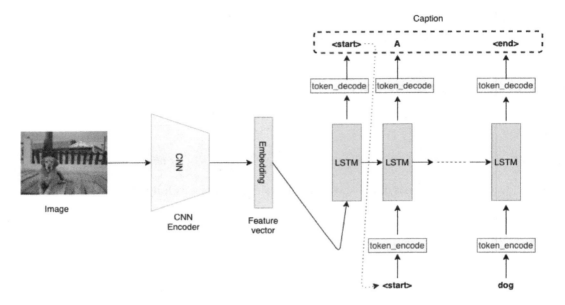

Figure 2.1 – Example CNN-LSTM architecture

The demonstrated architecture is suitable for the image captioning task. If instead of just having a single image we had a sequence of images (say, in a video) as the input to the CNN layer, then we would include the CNN embedding as the LSTM cell input at each time-step, not just at $t=0$. This kind of architecture would be useful for applications such as activity recognition or video description.

In the next section, we will implement an image captioning system in PyTorch that includes building a hybrid model architecture as well as data loading, preprocessing, model training, and model evaluation pipelines.

Building an image caption generator using PyTorch

For this exercise, we will be using the **Common Objects in Context (COCO)** dataset (available at http://cocodataset.org/#overview), which is a large-scale object detection, segmentation, and captioning dataset.

This dataset consists of over 200,000 labeled images with five captions for each image. The COCO dataset emerged in 2014 and has helped significantly in the advancement of object recognition-related computer vision tasks. It stands as one of the most commonly used datasets for benchmarking tasks such as object detection, object segmentation, instance segmentation, and image captioning.

In this exercise, we will use PyTorch to train a CNN-LSTM model on this dataset and use the trained model to generate captions for unseen samples. Before we do that, though, there are a few pre-requisites that we need to carry out.

> **Note**
>
> We will be referring to only the important snippets of code for illustration purposes. The full exercise code can be found at `https://github.com/PacktPublishing/Mastering-PyTorch/blob/master/Chapter02/image_captioning_pytorch.ipynb`

Downloading the image captioning datasets

Before we begin building the image captioning system, we need to download the required datasets. If you do not have the datasets downloaded, then run the following script with the help of Jupyter Notebook. This should help with downloading the datasets locally.

> **Note**
>
> We are using a slightly older version of the dataset as it is slightly smaller in size, enabling us to get the results faster.

The training and validation datasets are 13 GB and 6 GB in size, respectively. Downloading and extracting the dataset files, as well as cleaning and processing them, might take a while. A good idea is to execute these steps as follows and let them finish overnight:

```
# download images and annotations to the data directory
!wget http://msvocds.blob.core.windows.net/annotations-1-0-3/captions_train-val2014.zip -P ./data_dir/
!wget http://images.cocodataset.org/zips/train2014.zip -P ./data_dir/
!wget http://images.cocodataset.org/zips/val2014.zip -P ./data_dir/
# extract zipped images and annotations and remove the zip files
```

```
!unzip ./data_dir/captions_train-val2014.zip -d ./data_dir/
!rm ./data_dir/captions_train-val2014.zip
!unzip ./data_dir/train2014.zip -d ./data_dir/
!rm ./data_dir/train2014.zip
!unzip ./data_dir/val2014.zip -d ./data_dir/
!rm ./data_dir/val2014.zip
```

You should see the following output:

```
--2020-05-19 06:45:20--  http://msvocds.blob.core.windows.net/annotations-1-0-3/captions_train-val2014.zip
Resolving msvocds.blob.core.windows.net (msvocds.blob.core.windows.net)... 52.176.224.96
Connecting to msvocds.blob.core.windows.net (msvocds.blob.core.windows.net)|52.176.224.96|:80... connected.
HTTP request sent, awaiting response... 200 OK
Length: 19673183 (19M) [application/octet-stream Charset=UTF-8]
Saving to: './data/captions_train-val2014.zip'

captions_train-val2 100%[===================>]  18.76M   220KB/s    in 6m 46s

2020-05-19 06:52:07 (47.4 KB/s) - './data/captions_train-val2014.zip' saved [19673183/19673183]

--2020-05-19 06:52:07--  http://images.cocodataset.org/zips/train2014.zip
Resolving images.cocodataset.org (images.cocodataset.org)... 52.216.143.4
Connecting to images.cocodataset.org (images.cocodataset.org)|52.216.143.4|:80... connected.
HTTP request sent, awaiting response... 200 OK
Length: 13510573713 (13G) [application/zip]
Saving to: './data/train2014.zip'

train2014.zip         63%[===========>          ]   8.03G  --.-KB/s    in 4h 54m
                                      .
                                      .
                                      .

extracting: ./data/val2014/COCO_val2014_000000014526.jpg
extracting: ./data/val2014/COCO_val2014_000000154892.jpg
extracting: ./data/val2014/COCO_val2014_000000535313.jpg
extracting: ./data/val2014/COCO_val2014_000000008483.jpg
extracting: ./data/val2014/COCO_val2014_000000259087.jpg
extracting: ./data/val2014/COCO_val2014_000000030667.jpg
extracting: ./data/val2014/COCO_val2014_000000132288.jpg
extracting: ./data/val2014/COCO_val2014_000000155617.jpg
extracting: ./data/val2014/COCO_val2014_000000049682.jpg
extracting: ./data/val2014/COCO_val2014_000000382438.jpg
extracting: ./data/val2014/COCO_val2014_000000488693.jpg
extracting: ./data/val2014/COCO_val2014_000000324492.jpg
extracting: ./data/val2014/COCO_val2014_000000543836.jpg
extracting: ./data/val2014/COCO_val2014_000000551804.jpg
extracting: ./data/val2014/COCO_val2014_000000045516.jpg
extracting: ./data/val2014/COCO_val2014_000000347233.jpg
extracting: ./data/val2014/COCO_val2014_000000154202.jpg
extracting: ./data/val2014/COCO_val2014_000000038210.jpg
extracting: ./data/val2014/COCO_val2014_000000113113.jpg
extracting: ./data/val2014/COCO_val2014_000000441814.jpg
```

Figure 2.2 – Data download and extraction

This step basically creates a data folder (`./data_dir`), downloads the zipped images and annotation files, and extracts them inside the data folder.

Preprocessing caption (text) data

The downloaded image captioning datasets consist of both text (captions) and images. In this section, we will preprocess the text data to make it usable for our CNN-LSTM model. The exercise is laid out as a sequence of steps. The first three steps are focused on processing the text data:

1. For this exercise, we will need to import a few dependencies. Some of the crucial modules we will import for this chapter are as follows:

    ```
    import nltk
    from pycocotools.coco import COCO
    import torch.utils.data as data
    import torchvision.models as models
    import torchvision.transforms as transforms
    from torch.nn.utils.rnn import pack_padded_sequence
    ```

    `nltk` is the natural language toolkit, which will be helpful in building our vocabulary, while `pycocotools` is a helper tool to work with the COCO dataset. The various Torch modules we have imported here have already been discussed in the previous chapter, except the last one – that is, `pack_padded_sequence`. This function will be useful to transform sentences with variable lengths (number of words) into fixed-length sentences by applying padding.

    Besides importing the `nltk` library, we will also need to download its `punkt` tokenizer model, as follows:

    ```
    nltk.download('punkt')
    ```

    This will enable us to tokenize given text into constituent words.

2. Next, we build the vocabulary – that is, a dictionary that can convert actual textual tokens (such as words) into numeric tokens. This step is essential for any text-related tasks. The approximate code here gives an idea of what is being done at this step:

    ```
    def build_vocabulary(json, threshold):
        """Build a vocab wrapper."""
        coco = COCO(json)
        counter = Counter()
    ```

```
ids = coco.anns.keys()
for i, id in enumerate(ids):
    caption = str(coco.anns[id]['caption'])
    tokens = nltk.tokenize.word_tokenize(caption.
lower())
    counter.update(tokens)
    if (i+1) % 1000 == 0:
        print("[{}/{}] Tokenized the
captions.".format(i+1, len(ids)))
```

First, inside the vocabulary builder function, JSON text annotations are loaded, and individual words in the annotation/caption are tokenized or converted into numbers and stored in a counter.

Then, inside the vocabulary builder function, tokens with fewer than a certain number of occurrences are discarded, and the remaining tokens are added to a vocabulary object beside some wildcard tokens – start (of the sentence), end, unknown_word, and padding tokens, as follows:

```
# If word freq < 'thres', then word is discarded.
tokens = [token for token, cnt in counter.items() if
cnt >= threshold]
# Create vocab wrapper + add special tokens.
vocab = Vocab()
vocab.add_token('<pad>')
vocab.add_token('<start>')
vocab.add_token('<end>')
vocab.add_token('<unk>')
# Add words to vocab.
for i, token in enumerate(tokens):
    vocab.add_token(token)
return vocab
```

Finally, the vocabulary builder function, called a vocabulary object, is created and saved locally for further reuse, as shown in the following code:

```
vocab = build_vocabulary(json='data_dir/annotations/
captions_train2014.json', threshold=4)
vocab_path = './data_dir/vocabulary.pkl'
with open(vocab_path, 'wb') as f:
    pickle.dump(vocab, f)
```

```
print("Total vocabulary size: {}".format(len(vocab)))
print("Saved the vocabulary wrapper to '{}'".
format(vocab_path))
```

The output for this is as follows:

```
loading annotations into memory...
Done (t=0.79s)
creating index...
index created!
[1000/414113] Tokenized the captions.
[2000/414113] Tokenized the captions.
[3000/414113] Tokenized the captions.
[4000/414113] Tokenized the captions.
[5000/414113] Tokenized the captions.
[6000/414113] Tokenized the captions.
[7000/414113] Tokenized the captions.
[8000/414113] Tokenized the captions.
[9000/414113] Tokenized the captions.
[10000/414113] Tokenized the captions.




[407000/414113] Tokenized the captions.
[408000/414113] Tokenized the captions.
[409000/414113] Tokenized the captions.
[410000/414113] Tokenized the captions.
[411000/414113] Tokenized the captions.
[412000/414113] Tokenized the captions.

[413000/414113] Tokenized the captions.
[414000/414113] Tokenized the captions.
Total vocabulary size: 9956
Saved the vocabulary wrapper to './data_dir/vocab.pkl'
```

Figure 2.3 – Vocabulary creation

In this step, we define a vocabulary object, vocab, where we add the tokens, which will eventually provide us with the mapping between the textual tokens and numeric tokens. The vocabulary object is also saved locally to save us from having to re-run the vocabulary builder for re-training the model later.

The build_vocabulary function reads the annotations from the annotations file downloaded in step 1 via the pycocotools helper library. After reading all the annotations, it loops over the text tokens and adds every newly discovered text token to the mapping.

Once we have built the vocabulary, we can deal with the textual data by transforming it into numbers at runtime.

Preprocessing image data

After downloading the data and building the vocabulary for the text captions, we need to perform some preprocessing for the image data.

Because the images in the dataset can come in various sizes or shapes, we need to reshape all the images to a fixed shape so that they can be inputted to the first layer of our CNN model, as follows:

```python
def reshape_images(image_path, output_path, shape):
    images = os.listdir(image_path)
    num_im = len(images)
    for i, im in enumerate(images):
        with open(os.path.join(image_path, im), 'r+b') as f:
            with Image.open(f) as image:
                image = reshape_image(image, shape)
                image.save(os.path.join(output_path, im),
image.format)
        if (i+1) % 100 == 0:
            print ("[{}/{}] Resized the images and saved into
'{}'.".format(i+1, num_im, output_path))
reshape_images(image_path, output_path, image_shape)
```

The output for this will be as follows:

```
[100/82783] Resized the images and saved into './data_dir/resized_images/'.
[200/82783] Resized the images and saved into './data_dir/resized_images/'.
[300/82783] Resized the images and saved into './data_dir/resized_images/'.
[400/82783] Resized the images and saved into './data_dir/resized_images/'.
[500/82783] Resized the images and saved into './data_dir/resized_images/'.
[600/82783] Resized the images and saved into './data_dir/resized_images/'.
[700/82783] Resized the images and saved into './data_dir/resized_images/'.
[800/82783] Resized the images and saved into './data_dir/resized_images/'.
[900/82783] Resized the images and saved into './data_dir/resized_images/'.
[1000/82783] Resized the images and saved into './data_dir/resized_images/'.


[82000/82783] Resized the images and saved into './data_dir/resized_images/'.
[82100/82783] Resized the images and saved into './data_dir/resized_images/'.
[82200/82783] Resized the images and saved into './data_dir/resized_images/'.
[82300/82783] Resized the images and saved into './data_dir/resized_images/'.
[82400/82783] Resized the images and saved into './data_dir/resized_images/'.
[82500/82783] Resized the images and saved into './data_dir/resized_images/'.
[82600/82783] Resized the images and saved into './data_dir/resized_images/'.
[82700/82783] Resized the images and saved into './data_dir/resized_images/'.
```

Figure 2.4 – Image preprocessing (reshaping)

We have reshaped all the images to 256 X 256 pixels, which makes them compatible with our CNN model architecture.

Defining the image captioning data loader

We have already downloaded and preprocessed the image captioning data. Now it is time to cast this data as a PyTorch dataset object. This dataset object can subsequently be used to define a PyTorch data loader object, which we will use in our training loop to fetch batches of data as follows:

1. Now, we will implement our own custom `Dataset` module and a custom data loader:

```
class CustomCocoDataset(data.Dataset):
    """COCO Dataset compatible with torch.utils.data.
DataLoader."""
    def __init__(self, data_path, coco_json_path,
vocabulary, transform=None):
        """Set path for images, texts and vocab wrapper.

        Args:
            data_path: image directory.
            coco_json_path: coco annotation file path.
            vocabulary: vocabulary wrapper.
            transform: image transformer.
        """
        ...
    def __getitem__(self, idx):
        """Returns one data sample (X, y)."""
        ...
        return image, ground_truth
    def __len__(self):
        return len(self.indices)
```

First, in order to define our custom PyTorch `Dataset` object, we have defined our own __init__, __get_item__, and __len__ methods for instantiation, fetching items, and returning the size of the dataset, respectively.

2. Next, we define `collate_function`, which returns mini batches of data in the form of X, y, as follows:

```
def collate_function(data_batch):
    """Creates mini-batches of data
    We build custom collate function rather than using
standard collate function,
    because padding is not supported in the standard
version.
    Args:
        data: list of (image, caption)tuples.
            - image: tensor of shape (3, 256, 256).
            - caption: tensor of shape (:); variable
length.
    Returns:
        images: tensor of size (batch_size, 3, 256, 256).
        targets: tensor of size (batch_size, padded_
length).
        lengths: list.
    """

    ...
    return imgs, tgts, cap_lens
```

Usually, we would not need to write our own `collate` function, but we do so to deal with variable-length sentences so that when the length of a sentence (say, k) is less than the fixed length, n, then we need to pad the n-k tokens with padding tokens using the `pack_padded_sequence` function.

3. Finally, we will implement the `get_loader` function, which returns a custom data loader for the COCO dataset in the following code:

```
def get_loader(data_path, coco_json_path, vocabulary,
transform, batch_size, shuffle, num_workers):
    # COCO dataset
    coco_dataset = CustomCocoDataset(data_path=data_path,
                        coco_json_path=coco_json_path,
                        vocabulary=vocabulary,
                        transform=transform)
    custom_data_loader = torch.utils.data.
DataLoader(dataset=coco_dataset, batch_size=batch_size,
```

```
        shuffle=shuffle, num_workers=num_workers, collate_
        fn=collate_function)
            return custom_data_loader
```

During the training loop, this function will be extremely useful in fetching mini batches of data.

This completes the work needed to set up the data pipeline for model training. We will now work toward the actual model itself.

Defining the CNN-LSTM model

In this section, we will define the model architecture, which involves a CNN as well as an LSTM component.

Now that we have set up our data pipeline, we will define the model architecture as per the description in *Figure 2.1*, as follows:

```
class CNNModel(nn.Module):
    def __init__(self, embedding_size):
        """Load pretrained ResNet-152 & replace last fully
connected layer."""
        super(CNNModel, self).__init__()
        resnet = models.resnet152(pretrained=True)
        module_list = list(resnet.children())[:-1]        #
delete last fully connected layer.
        self.resnet_module = nn.Sequential(*module_list)
        self.linear_layer = nn.Linear(resnet.fc.in_features,
embedding_size)
        self.batch_norm = nn.BatchNorm1d(embedding_size,
momentum=0.01)

    def forward(self, input_images):
        """Extract feats from images."""
        with torch.no_grad():
            resnet_features = self.resnet_module(input_images)
        resnet_features = resnet_features.reshape(resnet_
features.size(0), -1)
        final_features = self.batch_norm(self.linear_
layer(resnet_features))
        return final_features
```

We have defined two sub-models – that is, a CNN model and an RNN model. For the CNN part, we use a pre-trained CNN model available under the PyTorch models repository: the ResNet 152 architecture. While we will learn more about ResNet in detail in the next chapter, this deep CNN model with 152 layers is pre-trained on the ImageNet dataset (http://www.image-net.org/). The ImageNet dataset contains over 1.4 million RGB images labeled over 1,000 classes. These 1,000 classes belong to categories such as plants, animals, food, sports, and more.

We remove the last layer of this pre-trained ResNet model and replace it with a fully connected layer followed by a batch normalization layer. Why are we able to replace the fully connected layer? Well, the neural network can be seen as a sequence of weight matrices starting from the weight matrix between the input layer and the first hidden layer straight up to the weight matrix between the penultimate layer and the output layer. A pre-trained model can then be seen as a sequence of nicely tuned weight matrices.

By replacing the final layer, we are essentially replacing the final weight matrix ($K x 1000$-dimensional, assuming K number of neurons in the penultimate layer) with a new randomly initialized weight matrix ($K x 256$-dimensional, where 256 is the new output size).

The batch normalization layer normalizes the fully connected layer outputs with a mean of 0 and a standard deviation of 1 across the entire batch. This is similar to the standard input data normalization that we perform using torch.transforms. Performing batch normalization helps limit the extent to which the hidden layer output values fluctuate. It also generally helps with faster learning. We can use higher learning rates because of a more uniform (0 mean, 1 standard deviation) optimization hyperplane.

Since this is the final layer of the CNN sub-model, batch normalization helps insulate the LSTM sub-model against any data shifts that the CNN might introduce. If we do not use batch-norm, then in the worst-case scenario, the CNN final layer could output values with, say, mean > 0.5 and standard deviation = 1 during training. But during inference, if for a certain image the CNN outputs values with mean < 0.5 and standard deviation = 1, then the LSTM sub-model would struggle to operate on this unforeseen data distribution.

Coming back to the fully connected layer, we introduce our own layer because we do not need the 1,000 class probabilities of the ResNet model. Instead, we want to use this model to generate an embedding vector for each image. This embedding can be thought of as a one-dimensional, numerically encoded version of a given input image. This embedding is then fed to the LSTM model.

We will explore LSTMs in detail in *Chapter 4*, *Deep Recurrent Model Architectures*. But, as we have seen in *Figure 2.1*, the LSTM layer takes in the embedding vectors as input and outputs a sequence of words that should ideally describe the image from which the embedding was generated:

```
class LSTMModel(nn.Module):
    def __init__(self, embedding_size, hidden_layer_size,
vocabulary_size, num_layers, max_seq_len=20):
        . . .
        self.lstm_layer = nn.LSTM(embedding_size, hidden_layer_
size, num_layers, batch_first=True)
        self.linear_layer = nn.Linear(hidden_layer_size,
vocabulary_size)
        . . .

    def forward(self, input_features, capts, lens):
        . . .
        hidden_variables, _ = self.lstm_layer(lstm_input)
        model_outputs = self.linear_layer(hidden_variables[0])
        return model_outputs
```

The LSTM model consists of an LSTM layer followed by a fully connected linear layer. The LSTM layer is a recurrent layer, which can be imagined as LSTM cells unfolded along the time dimension, forming a temporal sequence of LSTM cells. For our use case, these cells will output word prediction probabilities at each time-step and the word with the highest probability is appended to the output sentence.

The LSTM cell at each time-step also generates an internal cell state, which is passed on as input to the LSTM cell of the next time-step. The process continues until an LSTM cell outputs an <end> token/word. The <end> token is appended to the output sentence. The completed sentence is our predicted caption for the image.

Note that we also specify the maximum allowed sequence length as 20 under the max_seq_len variable. This will essentially mean that any sentence shorter than 20 words will have empty word tokens padded at the end and sentences longer than 20 words will be curtailed to just the first 20 words.

Why do we do it and why 20? If we truly want our LSTM to handle sentences of any length, we might want to set this variable to an extremely large value, say, 9,999 words. However, (a) not many image captions come with that many words, and (b), more importantly, if there were ever such extra-long outlier sentences, the LSTM would struggle with learning temporal patterns across such a huge number of time-steps.

We know that LSTMs are better than RNNs at dealing with longer sequences; however, it is difficult to retain memory across such sequence lengths. We choose 20 as a reasonable number given the usual image caption lengths and the maximum length of captions we would like our model to generate.

Both the LSTM layer and the linear layer objects in the previous code are derived from nn.module and we define the __init__ and forward methods to construct the model and run a forward pass through the model, respectively. For the LSTM model, we additionally implement a sample method, as shown in the following code, which will be useful for generating captions for a given image:

```python
def sample(self, input_features, lstm_states=None):
    """Generate caps for feats with greedy search."""
    sampled_indices = []
    ...
    for i in range(self.max_seq_len):
        ...
        sampled_indices.append(predicted_outputs)
        ...
    sampled_indices = torch.stack(sampled_indices, 1)
    return sampled_indices
```

The sample method makes use of greedy search to generate sentences; that is, it chooses the sequence with the highest overall probability.

This brings us to the end of the image captioning model definition step. We are now all set to train this model.

Training the CNN-LSTM model

As we have already defined the model architecture in the previous section, we will now train the CNN-LSTM model. Let's examine the details of this step one by one:

1. First, we define the device. If there is a GPU available, use it for training; otherwise, use the CPU:

    ```
    # Device configuration
    device = torch.device('cuda' if torch.cuda.is_available()
    else 'cpu')
    ```

    Although we have already reshaped all the images to a fixed shape, (256, 256), that is not enough. We still need to normalize the data. Normalization is important because different data dimensions might have different distributions, which might skew the overall optimization space and lead to inefficient gradient descent (think of an ellipse versus a circle).

2. We will use PyTorch's transform module to normalize the input image pixel values:

    ```
    # Image pre-processing, normalization for pretrained
    resnet
    transform = transforms.Compose([
        transforms.RandomCrop(224),
        transforms.RandomHorizontalFlip(),
        transforms.ToTensor(),
        transforms.Normalize((0.485, 0.456, 0.406),
                             (0.229, 0.224, 0.225))])
    ```

    Furthermore, we augment the available dataset. This helps not only in generating larger volumes of training data but also in making the model robust against potential variations in input data. Using PyTorch's transform module, we perform two data augmentation techniques here:

    i) Random cropping, resulting in the reduction of the image size from (256, 256) to (224, 224).

    ii) Horizontal flipping of the images.

3. Next, we load the vocabulary that we built in the *Preprocessing caption (text) data* section. We also initialize the data loader using the `get_loader` function defined in the *Defining the image captioning data loader* section:

```
# Load vocab wrapper
with open('data_dir/vocabulary.pkl', 'rb') as f:
    vocabulary = pickle.load(f)


# Instantiate data loader
custom_data_loader = get_loader('data_dir/resized_
images', 'data_dir/annotations/captions_train2014.json',
vocabulary,
                                transform, 128,
                                shuffle=True, num_workers=2)
```

4. Next, we come to the main section of this step, where we instantiate the CNN and LSTM models in the form of encoder and decoder models. Furthermore, we also define the loss function – **cross entropy loss** – and the optimization schedule – the **Adam optimizer** – as follows:

```
# Build models
encoder_model = CNNModel(256).to(device)
decoder_model = LSTMModel(256, 512, len(vocabulary),
1).to(device)



# Loss & optimizer
loss_criterion = nn.CrossEntropyLoss()
parameters = list(decoder_model.parameters()) +
list(encoder_model.linear_layer.parameters()) +
list(encoder_model.batch_norm.parameters())
optimizer = torch.optim.Adam(parameters, lr=0.001)
```

As discussed in *Chapter 1, Overview of Deep Learning Using PyTorch*, Adam is possibly the best choice for an optimization schedule when dealing with sparse data. Here, we are dealing with both images and text – perfect examples of sparse data because not all pixels contain useful information and numericized/vectorized text is a sparse matrix in itself.

5. Finally, we run the training loop (for five epochs) where we use the data loader to fetch a mini batch of the COCO dataset, run a forward pass with the mini batch through the encoder and decoder networks, and finally, tune the parameters of the CNN-LSTM model using backpropagation (backpropagation through time, for the LSTM network):

```
for epoch in range(5):
    for i, (imgs, caps, lens) in enumerate(custom_data_
loader):
        tgts = pack_padded_sequence(caps, lens, batch_
first=True)[0]
        # Forward pass, backward propagation
        feats = encoder_model(imgs)
        outputs = decoder_model(feats, caps, lens)
        loss = loss_criterion(outputs, tgts)
        decoder_model.zero_grad()
        encoder_model.zero_grad()
        loss.backward()
        optimizer.step()
```

Every 1,000 iterations into the training loop, we save a model checkpoint. For demonstration purposes, we have run the training for just two epochs, as follows:

```
        # Log training steps
        if i % 10 == 0:
            print('Epoch [{}/{}], Step [{}/{}], Loss:
{:.4f}, Perplexity: {:5.4f}'
                  .format(epoch, 5, i, total_num_steps,
loss.item(), np.exp(loss.item())))
        # Save model checkpoints
        if (i+1) % 1000 == 0:
            torch.save(decoder_model.state_dict(),
os.path.join(
                'models_dir/', 'decoder-{}-{}.ckpt'.
format(epoch+1, i+1)))
            torch.save(encoder_model.state_dict(),
os.path.join(
                'models_dir/', 'encoder-{}-{}.ckpt'.
format(epoch+1, i+1)))
```

The output will be as follows:

```
loading annotations into memory...
Done (t=0.95s)
creating index...
index created!
```

```
Downloading: "https://download.pytorch.org/models/resnet152-b121ed2d.pth" to /Users/ashish.jha/.cache/torch/checkpoin
ts/resnet152-b121ed2d.pth
```

```
100%                                230M/230M [21:30:44<00:00, 3.12kB/s]
```

```
Epoch [0/5], Step [0/3236], Loss: 9.2069, Perplexity: 9965.6803
Epoch [0/5], Step [10/3236], Loss: 5.8838, Perplexity: 359.1789
Epoch [0/5], Step [20/3236], Loss: 5.1500, Perplexity: 172.4289
Epoch [0/5], Step [30/3236], Loss: 4.9295, Perplexity: 138.3147
Epoch [0/5], Step [40/3236], Loss: 4.5292, Perplexity: 92.6851
Epoch [0/5], Step [50/3236], Loss: 4.3870, Perplexity: 80.3971
Epoch [0/5], Step [60/3236], Loss: 4.2046, Perplexity: 66.9942
Epoch [0/5], Step [70/3236], Loss: 4.0149, Perplexity: 55.4195
Epoch [0/5], Step [80/3236], Loss: 3.9087, Perplexity: 49.8341
Epoch [0/5], Step [90/3236], Loss: 3.8128, Perplexity: 45.2768
Epoch [0/5], Step [100/3236], Loss: 3.7193, Perplexity: 41.2363
Epoch [0/5], Step [110/3236], Loss: 3.8261, Perplexity: 45.8836
Epoch [0/5], Step [120/3236], Loss: 3.6833, Perplexity: 39.7769
Epoch [0/5], Step [130/3236], Loss: 3.4806, Perplexity: 32.4807
Epoch [0/5], Step [140/3236], Loss: 3.6516, Perplexity: 38.5349
Epoch [0/5], Step [150/3236], Loss: 3.6148, Perplexity: 37.1424
Epoch [0/5], Step [160/3236], Loss: 3.6043, Perplexity: 36.7555
Epoch [0/5], Step [170/3236], Loss: 3.4089, Perplexity: 30.2317
Epoch [0/5], Step [180/3236], Loss: 3.5103, Perplexity: 33.4576
Epoch [0/5], Step [190/3236], Loss: 3.4509, Perplexity: 31.5299
Epoch [0/5], Step [200/3236], Loss: 3.3716, Perplexity: 29.1259
                                    |
                                    |
                                    |
                                    |
                                    |
Epoch [1/5], Step [3100/3236], Loss: 1.9792, Perplexity: 7.2366
Epoch [1/5], Step [3110/3236], Loss: 2.0225, Perplexity: 7.5575
Epoch [1/5], Step [3120/3236], Loss: 1.9827, Perplexity: 7.2626
Epoch [1/5], Step [3130/3236], Loss: 2.1007, Perplexity: 8.1719
Epoch [1/5], Step [3140/3236], Loss: 2.0461, Perplexity: 7.7378
Epoch [1/5], Step [3150/3236], Loss: 2.1792, Perplexity: 8.8390
Epoch [1/5], Step [3160/3236], Loss: 2.0305, Perplexity: 7.6180

Epoch [1/5], Step [3170/3236], Loss: 2.0086, Perplexity: 7.4526
Epoch [1/5], Step [3180/3236], Loss: 2.0680, Perplexity: 7.9090
Epoch [1/5], Step [3190/3236], Loss: 2.1530, Perplexity: 8.6106
Epoch [1/5], Step [3200/3236], Loss: 1.9798, Perplexity: 7.2412
Epoch [1/5], Step [3210/3236], Loss: 2.0868, Perplexity: 8.0591
Epoch [1/5], Step [3220/3236], Loss: 2.0150, Perplexity: 7.5010
Epoch [1/5], Step [3230/3236], Loss: 2.0978, Perplexity: 8.1480
```

Figure 2.5 – Model training loop

Generating image captions using the trained model

We have trained an image captioning model in the previous section. In this section, we will use the trained model to generate captions for images previously unseen by the model:

1. We have stored a sample image, `sample.jpg`, to run inference on. Just as we did during training, we define the device to the GPU if available; otherwise, we define it to the CPU. Then, we define a function to load the image and reshape it to `(224, 224)` pixels. Finally, we define the transformation module to normalize the image pixels, as follows:

```
image_file_path = 'sample.jpg'
# Device config
device = torch.device('cuda' if torch.cuda.is_available()
else 'cpu')
def load_image(image_file_path, transform=None):
    img = Image.open(image_file_path).convert('RGB')
    img = img.resize([224, 224], Image.LANCZOS)
    if transform is not None:
        img = transform(img).unsqueeze(0)
    return img
# Image pre-processing
transform = transforms.Compose([
    transforms.ToTensor(),
    transforms.Normalize((0.485, 0.456, 0.406),
                         (0.229, 0.224, 0.225))])
```

2. Next, we load the vocabulary and instantiate the encoder and decoder models:

```
# Load vocab wrapper
with open('data_dir/vocabulary.pkl', 'rb') as f:
    vocabulary = pickle.load(f)
# Build models
encoder_model = CNNModel(256).eval()  # eval mode
(batchnorm uses moving mean/variance)
decoder_model = LSTMModel(256, 512, len(vocabulary), 1)
encoder_model = encoder_model.to(device)
decoder_model = decoder_model.to(device)
```

3. Once we have the model scaffold ready, we will use the latest saved checkpoint from the two epochs of training to set the model parameters:

```
# Load trained model params
encoder_model.load_state_dict(torch.load('models_dir/
encoder-2-3000.ckpt'))
decoder_model.load_state_dict(torch.load('models_dir/
decoder-2-3000.ckpt'))
```

After this point, the model is ready to use for inference.

4. Next comes the main part of this step, where we actually load the image and run inference on it – that is, first we use the encoder model to generate embeddings from the image, and then we feed this embedding to the decoder network to generate sequences, as follows:

```
# Prepare image
img = load_image(image_file_path, transform)
img_tensor = img.to(device)
# Generate caption text from image
feat = encoder_model(img_tensor)
sampled_indices = decoder_model.sample(feat)
sampled_indices = sampled_indices[0].cpu().
numpy()           # (1, max_seq_length) -> (max_seq_
length)
```

5. At this stage, the caption predictions are still in the form of numeric tokens. We need to convert the numeric tokens into actual text using the vocabulary by applying the mapping between textual and numeric tokens in reverse:

```
# Convert numeric tokens to text tokens
predicted_caption = []
for token_index in sampled_indices:
    word = vocabulary.i2w[token_index]
    predicted_caption.append(word)
    if word == '<end>':
        break
predicted_sentence = ' '.join(predicted_caption)
```

6. Once we have transformed our output into text, we can visualize both the image
    as well as the generated caption:

```
# Print image & generated caption text
print (predicted_sentence)
img = Image.open(image_file_path)
plt.imshow(np.asarray(img))
```

The output will be as follows:

```
<start> a dog is standing on a sidewalk near a building . <end>
```

Figure 2.6 – Model inference on a sample image

It seems that although the model is not absolutely perfect, within two epochs, it is already
trained well enough to generate sensible captions.

Summary

This chapter discussed the concept of combining a CNN model and an LSTM model
in an encoder-decoder framework, jointly training them, and using the combined model
to generate captions for an image. We first described what the model architecture for such
a system would look like and how minor changes to the architecture could lead to solving
different applications, such as *activity recognition* and *video description*. We also explored
what building a vocabulary for a text dataset means in practice.

In the second and final part of this chapter, we actually implemented an image captioning system using PyTorch. We downloaded datasets, wrote our own custom PyTorch dataset loader, built a vocabulary based on the caption text dataset, and applied transformations to images, such as reshaping, normalizing, random cropping, and horizontal flipping. We then defined the CNN-LSTM model architecture, along with the loss function and optimization schedule, and finally, we ran the training loop. Once the model was trained, we generated captions on a sample image and the model seemed to be working reasonably well.

We have used CNNs both in this and the previous chapter's exercises.

In the next chapter, we will take a deeper look at the gamut of different CNN architectures developed over the years, how each of them is uniquely useful, and how they can be easily implemented using PyTorch.

Section 2: Working with Advanced Neural Network Architectures

In this section, we'll use PyTorch to showcase some of the most advanced neural network architectures at the time of writing, as well as demonstrate their applications in real-life problems. Upon completing this section, you will be up to date with the most cutting-edge technologies in the world of convolutional, recurrent, and hybrid deep learning models and will be able to apply these models to advanced machine learning tasks.

This section comprises the following chapters:

- *Chapter 3, Deep CNN Architectures*
- *Chapter 4, Deep Recurrent Model Architectures*
- *Chapter 5, Hybrid Advanced Models*

3
Deep CNN Architectures

In this chapter, we will first briefly review the evolution of CNNs (in terms of architectures), and then we will study the different CNN architectures in detail. We will implement these CNN architectures using PyTorch and in doing so, we aim to exhaustively explore the tools (modules and built-in functions) that PyTorch has to offer in the context of building **Deep CNNs**. Building strong CNN expertise in PyTorch will enable us to solve a number of deep learning problems involving CNNs. This will also help us in building more complex deep learning models or applications of which CNNs are a part.

This chapter will cover the following topics:

- Why are CNNs so powerful?
- Evolution of CNN architectures
- Developing LeNet from scratch
- Fine-tuning the AlexNet model
- Running a pre-trained VGG model
- Exploring GoogLeNet and Inception v3
- Discussing ResNet and DenseNet architectures
- Understanding EfficientNets and the future of CNN architectures

Technical requirements

We will be using Jupyter Notebooks for all of our exercises. The following is the list of Python libraries that should be installed for this chapter using `pip`. For example, use `run pip install torch==1.4.0` on the command line, and so on:

```
jupyter==1.0.0
torch==1.4.0
torchvision==0.5.0
nltk==3.4.5
Pillow==6.2.2
pycocotools==2.0.0
```

All the code files relevant to this chapter are available at `https://github.com/PacktPublishing/Mastering-PyTorch/tree/master/Chapter03`.

Why are CNNs so powerful?

CNNs are among the most powerful machine learning models at solving challenging problems such as image classification, object detection, object segmentation, video processing, natural language processing, and speech recognition. Their success is attributed to various factors, such as the following:

- **Weight sharing**: This makes CNNs parameter-efficient, that is, different features are extracted using the same set of weights or parameters. **Features** are the high-level representations of input data that the model generates with its parameters.

- **Automatic feature extraction**: Multiple feature extraction stages help a CNN to automatically learn feature representations in a dataset.

- **Hierarchical learning**: The multi-layered CNN structure helps CNNs to learn low-, mid-, and high-level features.

- The ability to explore both **spatial and temporal** correlations in the data, such as in video processing tasks.

Besides these pre-existing fundamental characteristics, CNNs have advanced over the years with the help of improvements in the following areas:

- The use of better **activation** and **loss functions**, such as using **ReLU** to overcome the **vanishing gradient problem**. What is the vanishing gradient problem? Well, we know backpropagation in neural networks works on the basis of the *chain rule of differentiation*.

According to the chain rule, the gradient of the loss function with respect to the input layer parameters can be written as a product of gradients at each layer. If these gradients are all less than 1 – and worse still, tending toward 0 – then the product of these gradients will be a vanishingly small value. The vanishing gradient problem can cause serious troubles in the optimization process by preventing the network parameters from changing their values, which is equivalent to stunted learning.

- **Parameter optimization**, such as using an optimizer based on **Adaptive Momentum (Adam)** instead of simple **Stochastic Gradient Descent**.

- **Regularization**: Applying dropouts and batch normalization besides L2 regularization.

But some of the most significant drivers of development in CNNs over the years have been the various *architectural innovations*:

- **Spatial exploration-based CNNs**: The idea behind **spatial exploration** is using different kernel sizes in order to explore different levels of visual features in input data. The following diagram shows a sample architecture for a spatial exploration-based CNN model:

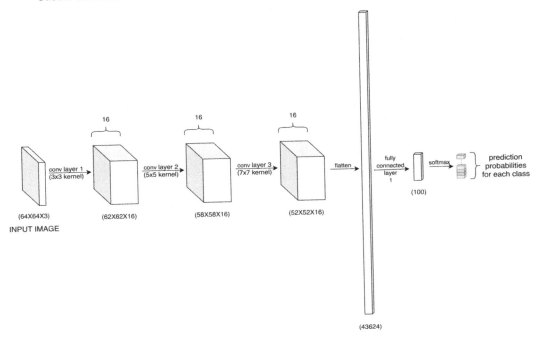

Figure 3.1 – Spatial exploration-based CNN

- **Depth-based CNNs**: The **depth** here refers to the depth of the neural network, that is, the number of layers. So, the idea here is to create a CNN model with multiple convolutional layers in order to extract highly complex visual features. The following diagram shows an example of such a model architecture:

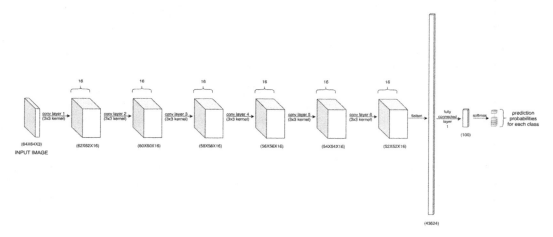

Figure 3.2 – Depth-based CNN

- **Width-based CNNs**: **Width** refers to the number of channels or feature maps in the data or features extracted from the data. So, width-based CNNs are all about increasing the number of feature maps as we go from the input to the output layers, as demonstrated in the following diagram:

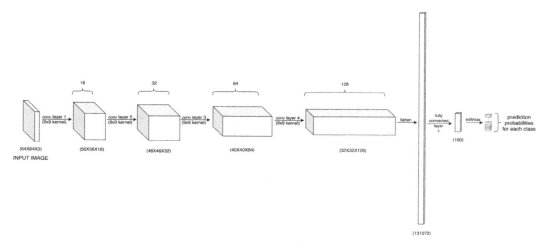

Figure 3.3 – Width-based CNN

- **Multi-path-based CNNs**: So far, the preceding three types of architectures have monotonicity in connections between layers, that is, direct connections exist only between consecutive layers. **Multi-path CNNs** brought the idea of making shortcut connections or skip connections between non-consecutive layers. The following diagram shows an example of a multi-path CNN model architecture:

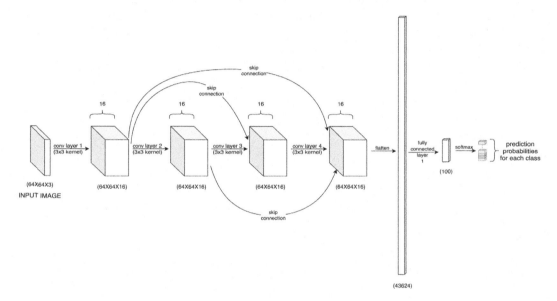

Figure 3.4 – Multi-path CNN

A key advantage of multi-path architectures is a better flow of information across several layers, thanks to the skip connections. This, in turn, also lets the gradient flow back to the input layers without too much dissipation.

Having looked at the different architectural setups found in CNN models, we will now look at how CNNs have evolved over the years ever since they were first used.

Evolution of CNN architectures

CNNs have been in existence since 1989, when the first multilayered CNN, called **ConvNet**, was developed by Yann LeCun. This model could perform visual cognition tasks such as identifying handwritten digits. In 1998, LeCun developed an improved ConvNet model called **LeNet**. Due to its high accuracy in optical recognition tasks, LeNet was adopted for industrial use soon after its invention. Ever since, CNNs have been one of the most successful machine learning models, both in industry as well as academia. The following diagram shows a brief timeline of architectural developments in the lifetime of CNNs, starting from 1989 all the way to 2020:

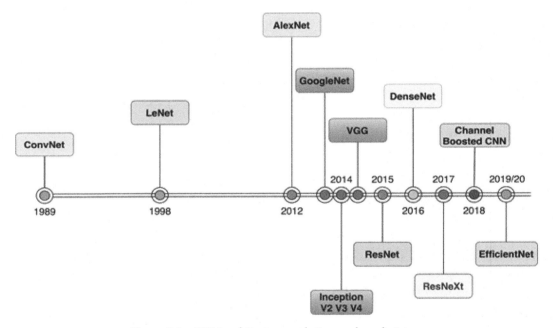

Figure 3.5 – CNN architecture evolution – a broad picture

As we can see, there is a significant gap between the years 1998 and 2012. This was primarily because there wasn't a dataset big and suitable enough to demonstrate the capabilities of CNNs, especially deep CNNs. And on the existing small datasets of the time, such as MNIST, classical machine learning models such as SVMs were starting to beat CNN performance. During those years, a few CNN developments took place.

The ReLU activation function was designed in order to deal with the gradient explosion and decay problem during backpropagation. Non-random initialization of network parameter values proved to be crucial. **Max-pooling** was invented as an effective method for subsampling. GPUs were getting popular for training neural networks, especially CNNs at scale. Finally, and most importantly, a large-scale dedicated dataset of annotated images called **ImageNet** (`http://www.image-net.org/`) was created by a research group at Stanford. This dataset is still one of the primary benchmarking datasets for CNN models to date.

With all of these developments compounding over the years, in 2012, a different architectural design brought about a massive improvement in CNN performance on the `ImageNet` dataset. This network was called **AlexNet** (named after the creator, Alex Krizhevsky). AlexNet, along with having various novel aspects such as random cropping and pre-training, established the trend of uniform and modular convolutional layer design. The uniform and modular layer structure was taken forward by repeatedly stacking such modules (of convolutional layers), resulting in very deep CNNs also known as **VGGs**.

Another approach of branching the blocks/modules of convolutional layers and stacking these branched blocks on top of each other proved extremely effective for tailored visual tasks. This network was called **GoogLeNet** (as it was developed at Google) or **Inception v1** (inception being the term for those branched blocks). Several variants of the **VGG** and **Inception** networks followed, such as **VGG16**, **VGG19**, **Inception v2**, **Inception v3**, and so on.

The next phase of development began with **skip connections**. To tackle the problem of gradient decay while training CNNs, non-consecutive layers were connected via skip connections lest information dissipated between them due to small gradients. A popular type of network that emerged with this trick, among other novel characteristics such as batch normalization, was **ResNet**.

A logical extension of ResNet was **DenseNet**, where layers were densely connected to each other, that is, each layer gets the input from all the previous layers' output feature maps. Furthermore, hybrid architectures were then developed by mixing successful architectures from the past such as **Inception-ResNet** and **ResNeXt**, where the parallel branches within a block were increased in number.

Lately, the **channel boosting** technique has proven useful in improving CNN performance. The idea here is to learn novel features and exploit pre-learned features through transfer learning. Most recently, automatically designing new blocks and finding optimal CNN architectures has been a growing trend in CNN research. Examples of such CNNs are **MnasNets** and **EfficientNets**. The approach behind these models is to perform a neural architecture search to deduce an optimal CNN architecture with a uniform model scaling approach.

In the next section, we will go back to one of the earliest CNN models and take a closer look at the various CNN architectures developed since. We will build these architectures using PyTorch, training some of the models on real-world datasets. We will also explore PyTorch's pre-trained CNN models repository, popularly known as **model-zoo**. We will learn how to fine-tune these pre-trained models as well as running predictions on them.

Developing LeNet from scratch

LeNet, originally known as **LeNet-5**, is one of the earliest CNN models, developed in 1998. The number *5* in LeNet-5 represents the *total number of layers* in this model, that is, two convolutional and three fully connected layers. With roughly 60,000 total parameters, this model gave state-of-the-art performance on image recognition tasks for handwritten digit images in the year 1998. As expected from a CNN model, LeNet demonstrated rotation, position, and scale invariance as well as robustness against distortion in images. Contrary to the classical machine learning models of the time, such as SVMs, which treated each pixel of the image separately, LeNet exploited the correlation among neighboring pixels.

Note that although LeNet was developed for handwritten digit recognition, it can certainly be extended for other image classification tasks, as we shall see in our next exercise. The following diagram shows the architecture of a LeNet model:

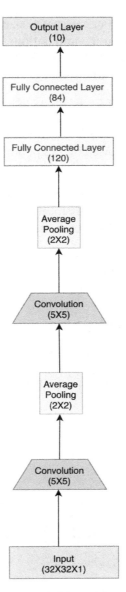

Figure 3.6 – LeNet architecture

As mentioned earlier, there are two convolutional layers followed by three fully connected layers (including the output layer). This approach of stacking convolutional layers followed by fully connected layers later became a trend in CNN research and is still applied to the latest CNN models. Besides these layers, there are pooling layers in between. These are basically subsampling layers that reduce the spatial size of image representation, thereby reducing the number of parameters and computations. The pooling layer used in LeNet was an average pooling layer that had trainable weights. Soon after, **max pooling** emerged as the most commonly used pooling function in CNNs.

The numbers in brackets in each layer in the figure demonstrate the dimensions (for input, output, and fully connected layers) or window size (for convolutional and pooling layers). The expected input for a grayscale image is 32x32 pixels in size. This image is then operated on by 5x5 convolutional kernels, followed by 2x2 pooling, and so on. The output layer size is 10, representing the 10 classes.

In this section, we will use PyTorch to build LeNet from scratch and train and evaluate it on a dataset of images for the task of image classification. We will see how easy and intuitive it is to build the network architecture in PyTorch using the outline from *Figure 3.6*.

Furthermore, we will demonstrate how effective LeNet is, even on a dataset different from the ones it was originally developed on (that is, MNIST) and how PyTorch makes it easy to train and test the model in a few lines of code.

Using PyTorch to build LeNet

Observe the following steps to build the model:

1. For this exercise, we will need to import a few dependencies. Execute the following `import` statements:

    ```python
    import numpy as np
    import matplotlib.pyplot as plt
    import torch
    import torchvision
    import torch.nn as nn
    import torch.nn.functional as F
    import torchvision.transforms as transforms
    torch.manual_seed(55)
    ```

    Here, we are importing all the `torch` modules necessary for the exercise. We also import `numpy` and `matplotlib` to display images during the exercise. Besides imports, we also set the random seed to ensure the reproducibility of this exercise.

2.   Next, we will define the model architecture based on the outline given in *Figure 3.6*:

```python
class LeNet(nn.Module):
    def __init__(self):
        super(LeNet, self).__init__()
        # 3 input image channel, 6 output feature maps
and 5x5 conv kernel
        self.cn1 = nn.Conv2d(3, 6, 5)
        # 6 input image channel, 16 output feature maps
and 5x5 conv kernel
        self.cn2 = nn.Conv2d(6, 16, 5)
        # fully connected layers of size 120, 84 and 10
        self.fc1 = nn.Linear(16 * 5 * 5, 120)  # 5*5 is
the spatial dimension at this layer
        self.fc2 = nn.Linear(120, 84)
        self.fc3 = nn.Linear(84, 10)
    def forward(self, x):
        # Convolution with 5x5 kernel
        x = F.relu(self.cn1(x))
        # Max pooling over a (2, 2) window
        x = F.max_pool2d(x, (2, 2))
        # Convolution with 5x5 kernel
        x = F.relu(self.cn2(x))
        # Max pooling over a (2, 2) window
        x = F.max_pool2d(x, (2, 2))
        # Flatten spatial and depth dimensions into a
single vector
        x = x.view(-1, self.flattened_features(x))
        # Fully connected operations
        x = F.relu(self.fc1(x))
        x = F.relu(self.fc2(x))
        x = self.fc3(x)
        return x
    def flattened_features(self, x):
        # all except the first (batch) dimension
        size = x.size()[1:]
        num_feats = 1
```

```
        for s in size:
            num_feats *= s
        return num_feats
lenet = LeNet()
print(lenet)
```

In the last two lines, we instantiate the model and print the network architecture. The output will be as follows:

```
LeNet(
  (cn1): Conv2d(3, 6, kernel_size=(5, 5), stride=(1, 1))
  (cn2): Conv2d(6, 16, kernel_size=(5, 5), stride=(1, 1))
  (fc1): Linear(in_features=400, out_features=120, bias=True)
  (fc2): Linear(in_features=120, out_features=84, bias=True)
  (fc3): Linear(in_features=84, out_features=10, bias=True)
)
```

Figure 3.7 – LeNet PyTorch model object

There are the usual __init__ and forward methods for architecture definition and running a forward pass, respectively. The additional flattened_features method is meant to calculate the total number of features in an image representation layer (usually an output of a convolutional layer or pooling layer). This method helps to flatten the spatial representation of features into a single vector of numbers, which is then used as input to fully connected layers.

Besides the details of the architecture mentioned earlier, ReLU is used throughout the network as the activation function. Also, contrary to the original LeNet network, which takes in single-channel images, the current model is modified to accept RGB images, that is, three channels as input. This is done in order to adapt to the dataset that is used for this exercise.

3. We then define the training routine, that is, the actual backpropagation step:

```
def train(net, trainloader, optim, epoch):
    # initialize loss
    loss_total = 0.0
    for i, data in enumerate(trainloader, 0):
        # get the inputs; data is a list of [inputs,
labels]
        # ip refers to the input images, and ground_truth
refers to the output classes the images belong to
        ip, ground_truth = data
        # zero the parameter gradients
        optim.zero_grad()
```

```
        # forward-pass + backward-pass + optimization
-step
        op = net(ip)
        loss = nn.CrossEntropyLoss()(op, ground_truth)
        loss.backward()
        optim.step()
        # update loss
        loss_total += loss.item()
         # print loss statistics
        if (i+1) % 1000 == 0:      # print at the interval
of 1000 mini-batches
            print('[Epoch number : %d, Mini-batches: %5d]
loss: %.3f' % (epoch + 1, i + 1, loss_total / 200))
            loss_total = 0.0
```

For each epoch, this function iterates through the entire training dataset, runs a forward pass through the network and, using backpropagation, updates the parameters of the model based on the specified optimizer. After iterating through every 1,000 mini-batches of the training dataset, this method also logs the calculated loss.

4. Similar to the training routine, we will define the test routine that we will use to evaluate model performance:

```
def test(net, testloader):
    success = 0
    counter = 0
    with torch.no_grad():
        for data in testloader:
            im, ground_truth = data
            op = net(im)
            _, pred = torch.max(op.data, 1)
            counter += ground_truth.size(0)
            success += (pred == ground_truth).sum().item()
    print('LeNet accuracy on 10000 images from test
dataset: %d %%' % (100 * success / counter))
```

This function runs a forward pass through the model for each test-set image, calculates the correct number of predictions, and prints the percentage of correct predictions on the test set.

5. Before we get on to training the model, we need to load the dataset. For this exercise, we will be using the CIFAR-10 dataset.

> **Dataset citation**
>
> *Learning Multiple Layers of Features from Tiny Images*, Alex Krizhevsky, 2009

This dataset consists of 60,000 32x32 RGB images labeled across 10 classes, with 6,000 images per class. The 60,000 images are split into 50,000 training images and 10,000 test images. More details can be found here: https://www. cs.toronto.edu/~kriz/cifar.html. Torch supports the CIFAR dataset under the torchvision.datasets module. We will be using the module to directly load the data and instantiate train and test dataloaders as demonstrated in the following code:

```python
# The mean and std are kept as 0.5 for normalizing pixel
values as the pixel values are originally in the range 0
to 1
train_transform = transforms.Compose([transforms.
RandomHorizontalFlip(),
transforms.RandomCrop(32, 4),
transforms.ToTensor(),
transforms.Normalize((0.5, 0.5, 0.5), (0.5, 0.5, 0.5))])
trainset = torchvision.datasets.CIFAR10(root='./data',
train=True, download=True, transform=train_transform)
trainloader = torch.utils.data.DataLoader(trainset,
batch_size=8, shuffle=True, num_workers=1)
test_transform = transforms.Compose([transforms.
ToTensor(), transforms.Normalize((0.5, 0.5, 0.5), (0.5,
0.5, 0.5))])
testset = torchvision.datasets.CIFAR10(root='./data',
train=False, download=True, transform=test_transform)
testloader = torch.utils.data.DataLoader(testset, batch_
size=10000, shuffle=False, num_workers=2)
# ordering is important
classes = ('plane', 'car', 'bird', 'cat', 'deer', 'dog',
'frog', 'horse', 'ship', 'truck')
```

> **Note**
>
> In the previous chapter, we manually downloaded the dataset and wrote a custom dataset class and a `dataloader` function. We will not need to write those here, thanks to the `torchvision.datasets` module.

Because we set the `download` flag to `True`, the dataset will be downloaded locally. Then, we shall see the following dialog box:

```
Downloading https://www.cs.toronto.edu/~kriz/cifar-10-python.tar.gz to ./data/cifar-10-python.tar.gz

          170500096/? [02:40<00:00, 934685.86it/s]

Extracting ./data/cifar-10-python.tar.gz to ./data
Files already downloaded and verified
```

Figure 3.8 – CIFAR-10 dataset download

The transformations used for training and testing datasets are different because we apply some data augmentation to the training dataset, such as flipping and cropping, which are not applicable to the test dataset. Also, after defining `trainloader` and `testloader`, we declare the 10 classes in this dataset with a pre-defined ordering.

6. After loading the datasets, let's investigate how the data looks:

```python
# define a function that displays an image
def imageshow(image):
    # un-normalize the image
    image = image/2 + 0.5
    npimage = image.numpy()
    plt.imshow(np.transpose(npimage, (1, 2, 0)))
    plt.show()
# sample images from training set
dataiter = iter(trainloader)
images, labels = dataiter.next()
# display images in a grid
num_images = 4
imageshow(torchvision.utils.make_grid(images[:num_images]))
# print labels
print('    '+'  ||  '.join(classes[labels[j]] for j in range(num_images)))
```

The preceding code shows us four sample images with their respective labels from the training dataset. The output will be as follows:

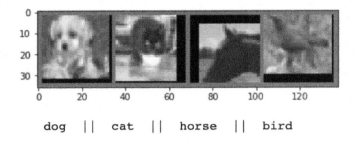

Figure 3.9 – CIFAR-10 dataset samples

The preceding output shows us four color images, which are 32x32 pixels in size. These four images belong to four different labels, as displayed in the text following the images.

We will now train the LeNet model.

Training LeNet

Now we are ready to train the model. Let's do so with the help of the following steps:

1. We will define optimizer and start the training loop as shown here:

```
# define optimizer
optim = torch.optim.Adam(lenet.parameters(), lr=0.001)
# training loop over the dataset multiple times
for epoch in range(50):
    train(lenet, trainloader, optim, epoch)
    print()
    test(lenet, testloader)
    print()
print('Finished Training')
```

The output will be as follows:

```
[Epoch number : 1, Mini-batches:  1000] loss: 9.901
[Epoch number : 1, Mini-batches:  2000] loss: 8.828
[Epoch number : 1, Mini-batches:  3000] loss: 8.350
[Epoch number : 1, Mini-batches:  4000] loss: 8.125
[Epoch number : 1, Mini-batches:  5000] loss: 7.935
[Epoch number : 1, Mini-batches:  6000] loss: 7.619

LeNet accuracy on 10000 images from test dataset: 48 %

            ⋮

[Epoch number : 50, Mini-batches:  1000] loss: 5.027
[Epoch number : 50, Mini-batches:  2000] loss: 5.143
[Epoch number : 50, Mini-batches:  3000] loss: 5.079
[Epoch number : 50, Mini-batches:  4000] loss: 5.159
[Epoch number : 50, Mini-batches:  5000] loss: 5.065
[Epoch number : 50, Mini-batches:  6000] loss: 4.977

LeNet accuracy on 10000 images from test dataset: 67 %

Finished Training
```

Figure 3.10 – Training LeNet

2. Once the training is finished, we can save the model file locally:

```
model_path = './cifar_model.pth'
torch.save(lenet.state_dict(), model_path)
```

Having trained the LeNet model, we will now test its performance on the test dataset in the next section.

Testing LeNet

The following steps need to be observed to test the LeNet model:

1. Let's make predictions by loading the saved model and running it on the test dataset:

```
# load test dataset images
d_iter = iter(testloader)
im, ground_truth = d_iter.next()
# print images and ground truth
imageshow(torchvision.utils.make_grid(im[:4]))
print('Label:      ', ' '.join('%5s' % classes[ground_
truth[j]] for j in range(4)))
# load model
lenet_cached = LeNet()
```

```
lenet_cached.load_state_dict(torch.load(model_path))
# model inference
op = lenet_cached(im)
# print predictions
_, pred = torch.max(op, 1)
print('Prediction: ', ' '.join('%5s' % classes[pred[j]]
for j in range(4)))
```

The output will be as follows:

```
Label:          cat  ship  ship plane
Prediction:     cat  ship  ship plane
```

Figure 3.11 – LeNet predictions

Evidently, all four predictions are correct.

2. Finally, we will check the overall accuracy of this model on the test dataset as well as per class accuracy:

```
success = 0
counter = 0
with torch.no_grad():
    for data in testloader:
        im, ground_truth = data
        op = lenet_cached(im)
        _, pred = torch.max(op.data, 1)
        counter += ground_truth.size(0)
        success += (pred == ground_truth).sum().item()
print('Model accuracy on 10000 images from test dataset:
%d %%' % (
    100 * success / counter))
```

The output will be as follows:

```
Model accuracy on 10000 images from test dataset: 67 %
```

Figure 3.12 – LeNet overall accuracy

3. For per class accuracy, the code is as follows:

```
class_sucess = list(0. for i in range(10))
class_counter = list(0. for i in range(10))
with torch.no_grad():
    for data in testloader:
        im, ground_truth = data
        op = lenet_cached(im)
        _, pred = torch.max(op, 1)
        c = (pred == ground_truth).squeeze()
        for i in range(10000):
            ground_truth_curr = ground_truth[i]
            class_sucess[ground_truth_curr] += c[i].item()
            class_counter[ground_truth_curr] += 1
for i in range(10):
    print('Model accuracy for class %5s : %2d %%' % (
        classes[i], 100 * class_sucess[i] / class_
counter[i]))
```

The output will be as follows:

```
Model accuracy for class plane : 68 %
Model accuracy for class   car : 87 %
Model accuracy for class  bird : 57 %
Model accuracy for class   cat : 56 %
Model accuracy for class  deer : 59 %
Model accuracy for class   dog : 39 %
Model accuracy for class  frog : 83 %
Model accuracy for class horse : 62 %
Model accuracy for class  ship : 82 %
Model accuracy for class truck : 75 %
```

Figure 3.13 – LeNet per class accuracy

Some classes have better performance than others. Overall, the model is far from perfect (that is, 100% accuracy) but much better than a model making random predictions, which would have an accuracy of 10% (due to the 10 classes).

Having built a LeNet model from scratch and evaluated its performance using PyTorch, we will now move on to a successor of LeNet – **AlexNet**. For LeNet, we built the model from scratch, trained, and tested it. For AlexNet, we will use a pre-trained model, fine-tune it on a smaller dataset, and test it.

Fine-tuning the AlexNet model

In this section, we will first take a quick look at the AlexNet architecture and how to build one by using PyTorch. Then we will explore PyTorch's pre-trained CNN models repository, and finally, use a pre-trained AlexNet model for fine-tuning on an image classification task, as well as making predictions.

AlexNet is a successor of LeNet with incremental changes in the architecture, such as 8 layers (5 convolutional and 3 fully connected) instead of 5, and 60 million model parameters instead of 60,000, as well as using `MaxPool` instead of `AvgPool`. Moreover, AlexNet was trained and tested on a much bigger dataset – ImageNet, which is over 100 GB in size, as opposed to the MNIST dataset (on which LeNet was trained), which amounts to a few MBs. AlexNet truly revolutionized CNNs as it emerged as a significantly more powerful class of models on image-related tasks than the other classical machine learning models, such as SVMs. *Figure 3.14* shows the AlexNet architecture:

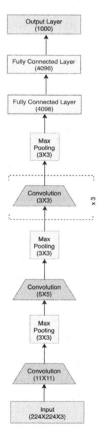

Figure 3.14 – AlexNet architecture

As we can see, the architecture follows the common theme from LeNet of having convolutional layers stacked sequentially, followed by a series of fully connected layers toward the output end. PyTorch makes it easy to translate such a model architecture into actual code. This can be seen in the following PyTorch code equivalent of the architecture:

```python
class AlexNet(nn.Module):
    def __init__(self, number_of_classes):
        super(AlexNet, self).__init__()
        self.feats = nn.Sequential(
            nn.Conv2d(in_channels=3, out_channels=64, kernel_size=11, stride=4, padding=5),
            nn.ReLU(),
            nn.MaxPool2d(kernel_size=2, stride=2),
            nn.Conv2d(in_channels=64, out_channels=192, kernel_size=5, padding=2),
            nn.ReLU(),
            nn.MaxPool2d(kernel_size=2, stride=2),
            nn.Conv2d(in_channels=192, out_channels=384, kernel_size=3, padding=1),
            nn.ReLU(),
            nn.Conv2d(in_channels=384, out_channels=256, kernel_size=3, padding=1),
            nn.ReLU(),
            nn.Conv2d(in_channels=256, out_channels=256, kernel_size=3, padding=1),
            nn.ReLU(),
            nn.MaxPool2d(kernel_size=2, stride=2),
        )
        self.clf = nn.Linear(in_features=256, out_features=number_of_classes)
    def forward(self, inp):
        op = self.feats(inp)
        op = op.view(op.size(0), -1)
        op = self.clf(op)
        return op
```

The code is quite self-explanatory, wherein the __init__ function contains the initialization of the whole layered structure, consisting of convolutional, pooling, and fully connected layers, along with ReLU activations. The `forward` function simply runs a data point *x* through this initialized network. Please note that the second line of the `forward` method already performs the flattening operation so that we need not define that function separately as we did for LeNet.

But besides the option of initializing the model architecture and training it ourselves, PyTorch, with its `torchvision` package, provides a `models` sub-package, which contains definitions of CNN models meant for solving different tasks, such as image classification, semantic segmentation, object detection, and so on. Following is a list of available models for the task of image classification (source: `https://pytorch.org/docs/stable/torchvision/models.html`):

- AlexNet
- VGG
- ResNet
- SqueezeNet
- DenseNet
- Inception v3
- GoogLeNet
- ShuffleNet v2
- MobileNet v2
- ResNeXt
- Wide ResNet
- MNASNet

In the next section, we will use a pre-trained AlexNet model as an example and demonstrate how to fine-tune it using PyTorch in the form of an exercise.

Using PyTorch to fine-tune AlexNet

In the following exercise, we will load a pre-trained AlexNet model and fine-tune it on an image classification dataset different from ImageNet (on which it was originally trained). Finally, we will test the fine-tuned model's performance to see if it could transfer-learn from the new dataset. Some parts of the code in the exercise are trimmed for readability but you can find the full code here: `https://github.com/PacktPublishing/Mastering-PyTorch/blob/master/Chapter03/transfer_learning_alexnet.ipynb`.

For this exercise, we will need to import a few dependencies. Execute the following `import` statements:

```
import os
import time
import copy
import numpy as np
import matplotlib.pyplot as plt
import torch
import torchvision
import torch.nn as nn
import torch.optim as optim
from torch.optim import lr_scheduler
from torchvision import datasets, models, transforms
torch.manual_seed(0)
```

Next, we will download and transform the dataset. For this fine-tuning exercise, we will use a small image dataset of bees and ants. There are 240 training images and 150 validation images divided equally between the two classes (bees and ants).

We download the dataset from `https://www.kaggle.com/ajayrana/hymenoptera-data` and store it in the current working directory. More information about the dataset can be found at `https://hymenoptera.elsiklab.missouri.edu/`.

Dataset citation

Elsik CG, Tayal A, Diesh CM, Unni DR, Emery ML, Nguyen HN, Hagen DE. Hymenoptera Genome Database: integrating genome annotations in HymenopteraMine. Nucleic Acids Research 2016 Jan 4;44(D1):D793-800. doi: 10.1093/nar/gkv1208. Epub 2015 Nov 17. PubMed PMID: 26578564.

In order to download the dataset, you will need to log into Kaggle. If you do not already have a Kaggle account, you will need to register:

```
ddir = 'hymenoptera_data'
# Data normalization and augmentation transformations for train
dataset
# Only normalization transformation for validation dataset
# The mean and std for normalization are calculated as the mean
of all pixel values for all images in the training set per each
image channel - R, G and B
data_transformers = {
    'train': transforms.Compose([transforms.
RandomResizedCrop(224), transforms.RandomHorizontalFlip(),
                                transforms.ToTensor(),
                                transforms.
Normalize([0.490, 0.449, 0.411], [0.231, 0.221, 0.230])]),
    'val': transforms.Compose([transforms.Resize(256),
transforms.CenterCrop(224), transforms.ToTensor(), transforms.
Normalize([0.490, 0.449, 0.411], [0.231, 0.221, 0.230])])}
img_data = {k: datasets.ImageFolder(os.path.join(ddir, k),
data_transformers[k]) for k in ['train', 'val']}
dloaders = {k: torch.utils.data.DataLoader(img_data[k], batch_
size=8, shuffle=True, num_workers=0)
            for k in ['train', 'val']}
dset_sizes = {x: len(img_data[x]) for x in ['train', 'val']}
classes = img_data['train'].classes
dvc = torch.device("cuda:0" if torch.cuda.is_available() else
"cpu")
```

Now that we have completed the pre-requisites, let's begin:

1. Let's visualize some sample training dataset images:

```
def imageshow(img, text=None):
    img = img.numpy().transpose((1, 2, 0))
    avg = np.array([0.490, 0.449, 0.411])
    stddev = np.array([0.231, 0.221, 0.230])
    img = stddev * img + avg
```

```
        img = np.clip(img, 0, 1)
        plt.imshow(img)
        if text is not None:
            plt.title(text)
# Generate one train dataset batch
imgs, cls = next(iter(dloaders['train']))
# Generate a grid from batch
grid = torchvision.utils.make_grid(imgs)
imageshow(grid, text=[classes[c] for c in cls])
```

The output will be as follows:

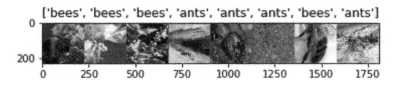

Figure 3.15 – Bees versus ants dataset

2. We now define the fine-tuning routine, which is essentially a training routine performed on a pre-trained model:

```
def finetune_model(pretrained_model, loss_func, optim,
epochs=10):
    ...
    for e in range(epochs):
        for dset in ['train', 'val']:
            if dset == 'train':
                pretrained_model.train()  # set model to
train mode (i.e. trainbale weights)
            else:
                pretrained_model.eval()   # set model to
validation mode
            # iterate over the (training/validation)
data.
            for imgs, tgts in dloaders[dset]:
                ...
                optim.zero_grad()
                with torch.set_grad_enabled(dset ==
'train'):
```

```
                ops = pretrained_model(imgs)
                _, preds = torch.max(ops, 1)
                loss_curr = loss_func(ops, tgts)
                # backward pass only if in training
mode
                if dset == 'train':
                    loss_curr.backward()
                    optim.step()
            loss += loss_curr.item() * imgs.size(0)
                successes += torch.sum(preds == tgts.
data)
            loss_epoch = loss / dset_sizes[dset]
            accuracy_epoch = successes.double() / dset_
sizes[dset]
            if dset == 'val' and accuracy_epoch >
accuracy:
                accuracy = accuracy_epoch
                model_weights = copy.deepcopy(pretrained_
model.state_dict())
    # load the best model version (weights)
    pretrained_model.load_state_dict(model_weights)
    return pretrained_model
```

In this function, we require the pre-trained model (that is, the architecture as well as weights) as input along with the loss function, optimizer, and number of epochs. Basically, instead of starting from a random initialization of weights, we start with the pre-trained weights of AlexNet. The other parts of this function are pretty similar to our previous exercises.

3. Before starting to fine-tune (train) the model, we will define a function to visualize the model predictions:

```
def visualize_predictions(pretrained_model, max_num_
imgs=4):
    was_model_training = pretrained_model.training
    pretrained_model.eval()
    imgs_counter = 0
    fig = plt.figure()
    with torch.no_grad():
```

```
        for i, (imgs, tgts) in enumerate(dloaders['val']):
            imgs = imgs.to(dvc)
            tgts = tgts.to(dvc)
            ops = pretrained_model(imgs)
            _, preds = torch.max(ops, 1)
            for j in range(imgs.size()[0]):
                imgs_counter += 1
                ax = plt.subplot(max_num_imgs//2, 2,
imgs_counter)
                ax.axis('off')
                ax.set_title(f'Prediction: {class_
names[preds[j]]}, Ground Truth: {class_names[tgts[j]]}')
                imshow(inputs.cpu().data[j])
                if imgs_counter == max_num_imgs:
    pretrained_model.train(mode=was_training)
                    return
        model.train(mode=was_training)
```

4. Finally, we get to the interesting part. Let's use PyTorch's `torchvision.models` sub-package to load the pre-trained AlexNet model:

```
model_finetune = models.alexnet(pretrained=True)
```

This model object has the following two main components:

i) `features`: The feature extraction component, which contains all the convolutional and pooling layers

ii) `classifier`: The classifier block, which contains all the fully connected layers leading to the output layer

5. We can visualize these components as shown here:

```
print(model_finetune.features)
```

This should output the following:

```
Sequential(
  (0): Conv2d(3, 64, kernel_size=(11, 11), stride=(4, 4), padding=(2, 2))
  (1): ReLU(inplace=True)
  (2): MaxPool2d(kernel_size=3, stride=2, padding=0, dilation=1, ceil_mode=False)
  (3): Conv2d(64, 192, kernel_size=(5, 5), stride=(1, 1), padding=(2, 2))
  (4): ReLU(inplace=True)
  (5): MaxPool2d(kernel_size=3, stride=2, padding=0, dilation=1, ceil_mode=False)
  (6): Conv2d(192, 384, kernel_size=(3, 3), stride=(1, 1), padding=(1, 1))
  (7): ReLU(inplace=True)
  (8): Conv2d(384, 256, kernel_size=(3, 3), stride=(1, 1), padding=(1, 1))
  (9): ReLU(inplace=True)
  (10): Conv2d(256, 256, kernel_size=(3, 3), stride=(1, 1), padding=(1, 1))
  (11): ReLU(inplace=True)
  (12): MaxPool2d(kernel_size=3, stride=2, padding=0, dilation=1, ceil_mode=False)
)
```

Figure 3.16 – AlexNet feature extractor

6. Now, we will run the `classifier` feature as follows:

```
print(model_finetune.classifier)
```

This should output the following:

```
Sequential(
  (0): Dropout(p=0.5, inplace=False)
  (1): Linear(in_features=9216, out_features=4096, bias=True)
  (2): ReLU(inplace=True)
  (3): Dropout(p=0.5, inplace=False)
  (4): Linear(in_features=4096, out_features=4096, bias=True)
  (5): ReLU(inplace=True)
  (6): Linear(in_features=4096, out_features=1000, bias=True)
)
```

Figure 3.17 – AlexNet classifier

7. As you may have noticed, the pre-trained model has the output layer of size `1000`, but we only have 2 classes in our fine-tuning dataset. So, we shall alter that, as shown here:

```
# change the last layer from 1000 classes to 2 classes
model_finetune.classifier[6] = nn.Linear(4096,
len(classes))
```

8. And now, we are all set to define the optimizer and loss function, and thereafter run the training routine as follows:

```
loss_func = nn.CrossEntropyLoss()
optim_finetune = optim.SGD(model_finetune.parameters(),
lr=0.0001)
# train (fine-tune) and validate the model
model_finetune = finetune_model(model_finetune, loss_
func, optim_finetune, epochs=10)
```

The output will be as follows:

```
Epoch number 0/9
====================
train loss in this epoch: 0.7761217306871884, accuracy in this epoch: 0.4959016393442623
val loss in this epoch: 0.6042805251732372, accuracy in this epoch: 0.6666666666666666

Epoch number 1/9
====================
train loss in this epoch: 0.5759895355975042, accuracy in this epoch: 0.6639344262295082
val loss in this epoch: 0.4689261562684003, accuracy in this epoch: 0.7908496732026143

Epoch number 2/9
====================
train loss in this epoch: 0.5033335646644967, accuracy in this epoch: 0.75
val loss in this epoch: 0.3966531710687026, accuracy in this epoch: 0.8431372549019608

                                    I
                                    I
                                    I
                                    I

Epoch number 8/9
====================
train loss in this epoch: 0.3300624494669867, accuracy in this epoch: 0.860655737704918
val loss in this epoch: 0.27101927756764044, accuracy in this epoch: 0.934640522875817

Epoch number 9/9
====================
train loss in this epoch: 0.3026028309689193, accuracy in this epoch: 0.8729508196721312
val loss in this epoch: 0.2609025729710565, accuracy in this epoch: 0.9215686274509803

Training finished in 4.0mins 30.213629007339478secs
Best validation set accuracy: 0.934640522875817
```

Figure 3.18 – AlexNet fine-tuning loop

9. Let's visualize some of the model predictions to see whether the model has indeed learned the relevant features from this small dataset:

```
visualize_predictions(model_finetune)
```

This should output the following:

Figure 3.19 – AlexNet predictions

Clearly, the pretrained AlexNet model has been able to transfer-learn on this rather tiny image classification dataset. This both demonstrates the power of transfer learning as well as the speed and ease with which we can fine-tune well known models using PyTorch.

In the next section, we will discuss an even deeper and more complex successor of AlexNet – the VGG network. We have demonstrated the model definition, dataset loading, model training (or fine-tuning), and evaluation steps in detail for LeNet and AlexNet. In subsequent sections, we will focus mostly on model architecture definition, as the PyTorch code for other aspects (such as data loading and evaluation) will be similar.

Running a pre-trained VGG model

We have already discussed LeNet and AlexNet, two of the foundational CNN architectures. As we progress in the chapter, we will explore increasingly complex CNN models. Although, the key principles in building these model architectures will be the same. We will see a modular model-building approach in putting together convolutional layers, pooling layers, and fully connected layers into blocks/modules and then stacking these blocks sequentially or in a branched manner. In this section, we look at the successor to AlexNet – VGGNet.

The name VGG is derived from the **Visual Geometry Group of Oxford University**, where this model was invented. Compared to the 8 layers and 60 million parameters of AlexNet, VGG consists of 13 layers (10 convolutional layers and 3 fully connected layers) and 138 million parameters. VGG basically stacks more layers onto the AlexNet architecture with smaller size convolution kernels (2x2 or 3x3). Hence, VGG's novelty lies in the unprecedented level of depth that it brings with its architecture. *Figure 3.20* shows the VGG architecture:

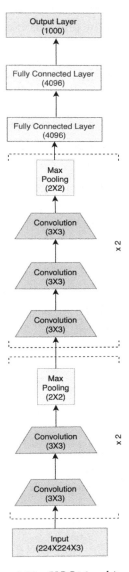

Figure 3.20 – VGG16 architecture

The preceding VGG architecture is called **VGG13**, because of the 13 layers. Other variants are VGG16 and VGG19, consisting of 16 and 19 layers, respectively. There is another set of variants – **VGG13_bn**, **VGG16_bn**, and **VGG19_bn**, where **bn** suggests that these models also consist of **batch-normalization layers**.

PyTorch's `torchvision.model` sub-package provides the pre-trained `VGG` model (with all of the six variants discussed earlier) trained on the ImageNet dataset. In the following exercise, we will use the pre-trained `VGG13` model to make predictions on a small dataset of bees and ants (used in the previous exercise). We will focus on the key pieces of code here, as most other parts of our code will overlap with that of the previous exercises. We can always refer to our notebooks to explore the full code: `https://github.com/PacktPublishing/Mastering-PyTorch/blob/master/Chapter03/vgg13_pretrained_run_inference.ipynb`:

1. First, we need to import dependencies, including `torchvision.models`.

2. Download the data and set up the ants and bees dataset and dataloader, along with the transformations.

3. In order to make predictions on these images, we will need the 1,000 labels of the ImageNet dataset, which can be found here: `https://gist.github.com/yrevar/942d3a0ac09ec9e5eb3a`.

4. Once downloaded, we need to create a mapping between the class indices 0 to 999 and the corresponding class labels, as shown here:

```
import ast
with open('./imagenet1000_clsidx_to_labels.txt') as f:
    classes_data = f.read()
classes_dict = ast.literal_eval(classes_data)
print({k: classes_dict[k] for k in list(classes_dict)
[:5]})
```

This should output the first five class mappings, as shown in the following screenshot:

```
{0: 'tench, Tinca tinca', 1: 'goldfish, Carassius auratus', 2: 'great white shark, white shark, man-eater, man-eating
shark, Carcharodon carcharias', 3: 'tiger shark, Galeocerdo cuvieri', 4: 'hammerhead, hammerhead shark'}
```

Figure 3.21 – ImageNet class mappings

5. Define the model prediction visualization function that takes in the pre-trained model object and the number of images to run predictions on. This function should output the images with predictions.

6. Load the pretrained VGG13 model:

```
model_finetune = models.vgg13(pretrained=True)
```

This should output the following:

```
Downloading: "https://download.pytorch.org/models/vgg13-c768596a.pth" to /Users/ashish.jha/.cache/torch/checkpoints/v
gg13-c768596a.pth
100%  ████████████████████████  508M/508M [21:36<00:00, 411kB/s]
```

Figure 3.22 – Loading the VGG13 model

The 508 MB VGG13 model is downloaded in this step.

7. Finally, we run predictions on our ants and bees dataset using this pre-trained model:

```
visualize_predictions(model_finetune)
```

This should output the following:

Figure 3.23 – VGG13 predictions

The VGG13 model trained on an entirely different dataset seems to predict all the test samples correctly in the ants and bees dataset. Basically, the model grabs the two most similar animals from the dataset out of the 1,000 classes and finds them in the images. By doing this exercise, we see that the model is still able to extract relevant visual features out of the images and the exercise demonstrates the utility of PyTorch's out-of-the-box inference feature.

In the next section, we are going to study a different type of CNN architecture – one that involves modules that have multiple parallel convolutional layers. The modules are called **Inception modules** and the resulting network is called the **Inception network**. We will explore the various parts of this network and the reasoning behind its success. We will also build the inception modules and the Inception network architecture using PyTorch.

Exploring GoogLeNet and Inception v3

As we have discovered the progression of CNN models from LeNet to VGG so far, we have observed the sequential stacking of more convolutional and fully connected layers. This resulted in deep networks with a lot of parameters to train. *GoogLeNet* emerged as a radically different type of CNN architecture that is composed of a module of parallel convolutional layers called the inception module. Because of this, GoogLeNet is also called **Inception v1** (v1 marked the first version as more versions came along later). Some of the drastically new elements introduced in GoogLeNet were the following:

- The **inception module** – a module of several parallel convolutional layers
- Using **1x1 convolutions** to reduce the number of model parameters
- **Global average pooling** instead of a fully connected layer – reduces overfitting
- Using **auxiliary classifiers** for training – for regularization and gradient stability

GoogLeNet has 22 layers, which is more than the number of layers of any VGG model variant. Yet, due to some of the optimization tricks used, the number of parameters in GoogLeNet is 5 million, which is far less than the 138 million parameters of VGG. Let's expand on some of the key features of this model.

Inception modules

Perhaps the single most important contribution of this model was the development of a convolutional module with several convolutional layers running in parallel, which are finally concatenated to produce a single output vector. These parallel convolutional layers operate with different kernel sizes ranging from 1x1 to 3x3 to 5x5. The idea is to extract all levels of visual information from the image. Besides these convolutions, a 3x3 max-pooling layer adds another level of feature extraction. *Figure 3.24* shows the inception block diagram along with the overall GoogLeNet architecture:

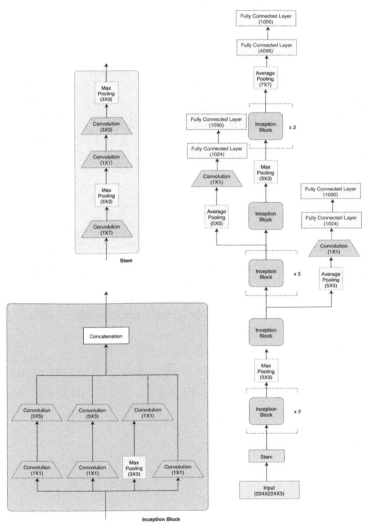

Figure 3.24 – GoogLeNet architecture

By using this architecture diagram, we can build the inception module in PyTorch as shown here:

```python
class InceptionModule(nn.Module):
    def __init__(self, input_planes, n_channels1x1, n_
channels3x3red, n_channels3x3, n_channels5x5red, n_channels5x5,
pooling_planes):
        super(InceptionModule, self).__init__()
        # 1x1 convolution branch
        self.block1 = nn.Sequential(
            nn.Conv2d(input_planes, n_channels1x1, kernel_
size=1),nn.BatchNorm2d(n_channels1x1),nn.ReLU(True),)
        # 1x1 convolution -> 3x3 convolution branch
        self.block2 = nn.Sequential(
            nn.Conv2d(input_planes, n_channels3x3red, kernel_
size=1),nn.BatchNorm2d(n_channels3x3red),
            nn.ReLU(True),nn.Conv2d(n_channels3x3red, n_
channels3x3, kernel_size=3, padding=1),nn.BatchNorm2d(n_
channels3x3),nn.ReLU(True),)
        # 1x1 conv -> 5x5 conv branch
        self.block3 = nn.Sequential(
            nn.Conv2d(input_planes, n_channels5x5red, kernel_
size=1),nn.BatchNorm2d(n_channels5x5red),nn.ReLU(True),
            nn.Conv2d(n_channels5x5red, n_channels5x5, kernel_
size=3, padding=1),nn.BatchNorm2d(n_channels5x5),nn.ReLU(True),
            nn.Conv2d(n_channels5x5, n_channels5x5, kernel_
size=3, padding=1),nn.BatchNorm2d(n_channels5x5),
            nn.ReLU(True),)
        # 3x3 pool -> 1x1 conv branch
        self.block4 = nn.Sequential(
            nn.MaxPool2d(3, stride=1, padding=1),
```

```
            nn.Conv2d(input_planes, pooling_planes, kernel_
size=1),
            nn.BatchNorm2d(pooling_planes),
            nn.ReLU(True),)
    def forward(self, ip):
        op1 = self.block1(ip)
        op2 = self.block2(ip)
        op3 = self.block3(ip)
        op4 = self.block4(ip)
        return torch.cat([op1,op2,op3,op4], 1)
```

Next, we will look at another important feature of GoogLeNet – 1x1 convolutions.

1x1 convolutions

In addition to the parallel convolutional layers in an inception module, each parallel layer has a preceding **1x1 convolutional layer**. The reason behind using these 1x1 convolutional layers is *dimensionality reduction*. 1x1 convolutions do not change the width and height of the image representation but can alter the depth of an image representation. This trick is used to reduce the depth of the input visual features before performing the 1x1, 3x3, and 5x5 convolutions parallelly. Reducing the number of parameters not only helps build a lighter model but also combats overfitting.

Global average pooling

If we look at the overall GoogLeNet architecture in *Figure 3.24*, the penultimate output layer of the model is preceded by a 7x7 average pooling layer. This layer again helps in reducing the number of parameters of the model, thereby reducing overfitting. Without this layer, the model would have millions of additional parameters due to the dense connections of a fully connected layer.

Auxiliary classifiers

Figure 3.24 also shows two extra or auxiliary output branches in the model. These auxiliary classifiers are supposed to tackle the vanishing gradient problem by adding to the gradients' magnitude during backpropagation, especially for the layers towards the input end. Because these models have a large number of layers, vanishing gradients can become a bottleneck. Hence, using auxiliary classifiers has proven useful for this 22-layer deep model. Additionally, the auxiliary branches also help in regularization. Please note that these auxiliary branches are switched off/discarded while making predictions.

Once we have the inception module defined using PyTorch, we can easily instantiate the entire Inception v1 model as follows:

```python
class GoogLeNet(nn.Module):
    def __init__(self):
        super(GoogLeNet, self).__init__()
        self.stem = nn.Sequential(
            nn.Conv2d(3, 192, kernel_size=3, padding=1),
            nn.BatchNorm2d(192),
            nn.ReLU(True),)
        self.im1 = InceptionModule(192,   64,   96, 128, 16,  32,
32)
        self.im2 = InceptionModule(256, 128, 128, 192, 32,  96,
64)
        self.max_pool = nn.MaxPool2d(3, stride=2, padding=1)
        self.im3 = InceptionModule(480, 192,   96, 208,
16,  48,   64)
        self.im4 = InceptionModule(512, 160, 112, 224,
24,  64,   64)
        self.im5 = InceptionModule(512, 128, 128, 256,
24,  64,   64)
        self.im6 = InceptionModule(512, 112, 144, 288,
32,  64,   64)
        self.im7 = InceptionModule(528, 256, 160, 320, 32, 128,
128)
        self.im8 = InceptionModule(832, 256, 160, 320, 32, 128,
128)
        self.im9 = InceptionModule(832, 384, 192, 384, 48, 128,
128)
```

```
        self.average_pool = nn.AvgPool2d(7, stride=1)
        self.fc = nn.Linear(4096, 1000)
    def forward(self, ip):
        op = self.stem(ip)
        out = self.im1(op)
        out = self.im2(op)
        op = self.maxpool(op)
        op = self.a4(op)
        op = self.b4(op)
        op = self.c4(op)
        op = self.d4(op)
        op = self.e4(op)
        op = self.max_pool(op)
        op = self.a5(op)
        op = self.b5(op)
        op = self.avgerage_pool(op)
        op = op.view(op.size(0), -1)
        op = self.fc(op)
        return op
```

Besides instantiating our own model, we can always load a pre-trained GoogLeNet with just two lines of code:

```
import torchvision.models as models
model = models.googlenet(pretrained=True)
```

Finally, as mentioned earlier, a number of versions of the Inception model were developed later. One of the eminent ones was Inception v3, which we will briefly discuss next.

Inception v3

This successor of Inception v1 has a total of 24 million parameters as compared to 5 million in v1. Besides the addition of several more layers, this model introduced different kinds of inception modules, which are stacked sequentially. *Figure 3.25* shows the different inception modules and the full model architecture:

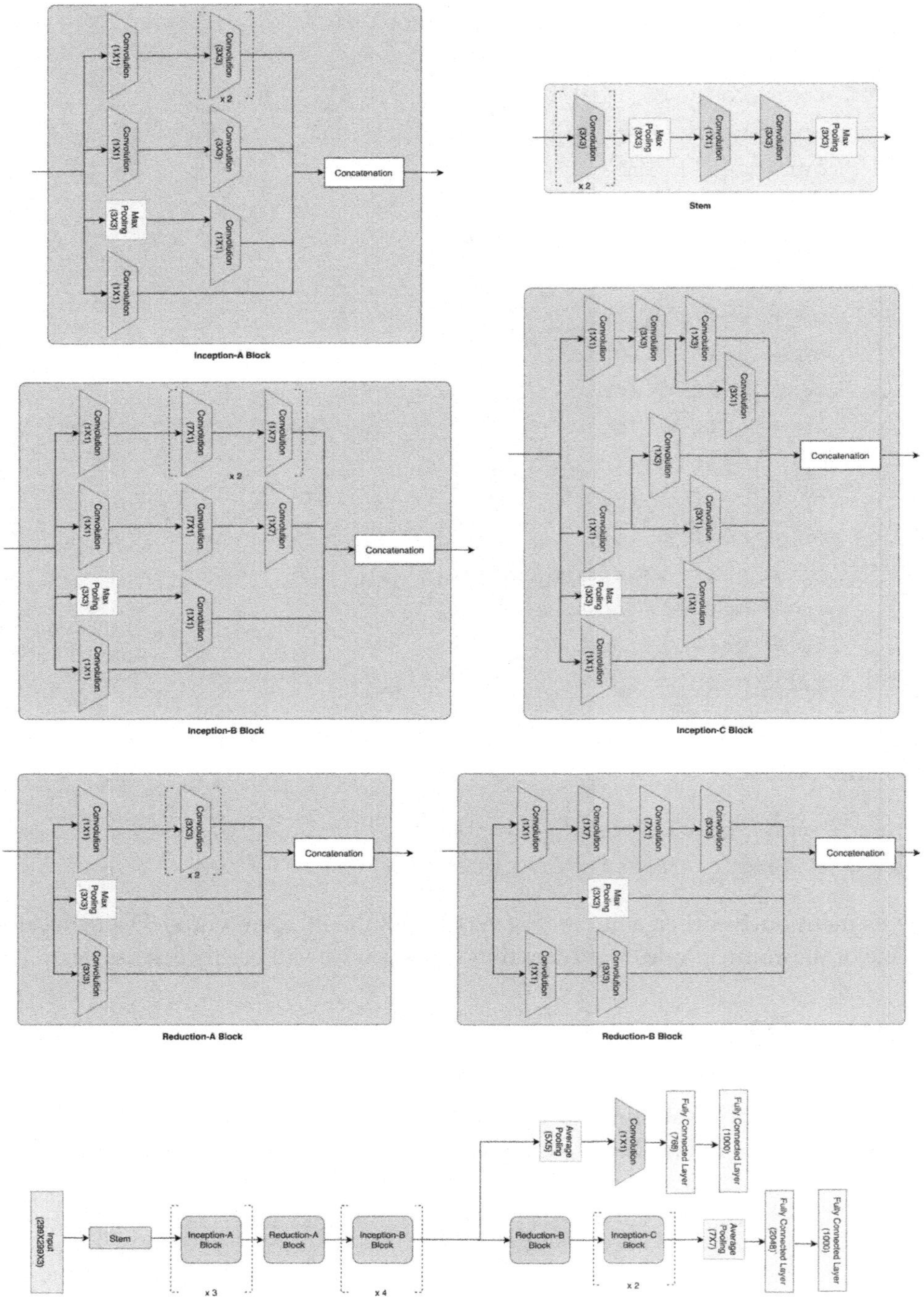

Fig 3.25 – Inception v3 architecture

It can be seen from the architecture that this model is an architectural extension of the Inception v1 model. Once again, besides building the model manually, we can use the pre-trained model from PyTorch's repository as follows:

```
import torchvision.models as models
model = models.inception_v3(pretrained=True)
```

In the next section, we will go through the classes of CNN models that have effectively combatted the vanishing gradient problem in very deep CNNs – **ResNet** and **DenseNet**. We will learn about the novel techniques of skip connections and dense connections and use PyTorch to code the fundamental modules behind these advanced architectures.

Discussing ResNet and DenseNet architectures

In the previous section, we explored the Inception models, which had a reduced number of model parameters as the number of layers increased, thanks to the 1x1 convolutions and global average pooling. Furthermore, auxiliary classifiers were used to combat the vanishing gradient problem.

ResNet introduced the concept of **skip connections**. This simple yet effective trick overcomes the problem of both parameter overflow and vanishing gradients. The idea, as shown in the following diagram, is quite simple. The input is first passed through a non-linear transformation (convolutions followed by non-linear activations) and then the output of this transformation (referred to as the residual) is added to the original input. Each block of such computation is called a **residual block**, hence the name of the model – **residual network** or **ResNet**.

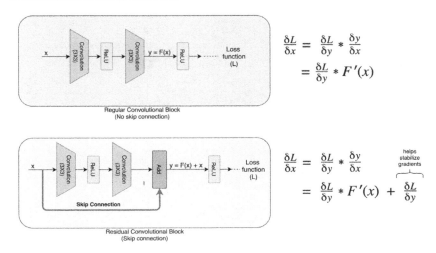

Figure 3.26 – Skip connections

Using these skip (or shortcut) connections, the number of parameters is limited to 26 million parameters for a total of 50 layers (ResNet-50). Due to the limited number of parameters, ResNet has been able to generalize well without overfitting even when the number of layers is increased to 152 (ResNet-152). The following diagram shows the ResNet-50 architecture:

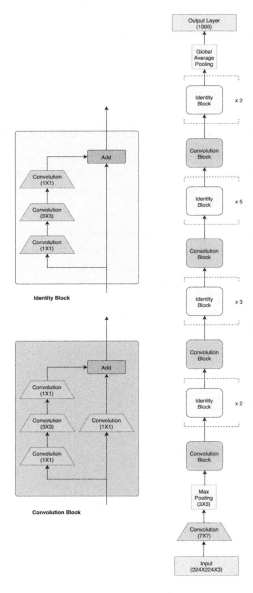

Figure 3.27 – ResNet architecture

There are two kinds of residual blocks – **convolutional** and **identity**, both having skip connections. For the convolutional block, there is an added 1x1 convolutional layer, which further helps to reduce dimensionality. A residual block for ResNet can be implemented in PyTorch as shown here:

```python
class BasicBlock(nn.Module):
    multiplier=1
    def __init__(self, input_num_planes, num_planes, strd=1):
        super(BasicBlock, self).__init__()
        self.conv_layer1 = nn.Conv2d(in_channels=input_num_planes, out_channels=num_planes, kernel_size=3, stride=stride, padding=1, bias=False)
        self.batch_norm1 = nn.BatchNorm2d(num_planes)
        self.conv_layer2 = nn.Conv2d(in_channels=num_planes, out_channels=num_planes, kernel_size=3, stride=1, padding=1, bias=False)
        self.batch_norm2 = nn.BatchNorm2d(num_planes)
        self.res_connnection = nn.Sequential()
        if strd > 1 or input_num_planes != self.multiplier*num_planes:
            self.res_connnection = nn.Sequential(
                nn.Conv2d(in_channels=input_num_planes, out_channels=self.multiplier*num_planes, kernel_size=1, stride=strd, bias=False),
                nn.BatchNorm2d(self.multiplier*num_planes))
    def forward(self, inp):
        op = F.relu(self.batch_norm1(self.conv_layer1(inp)))
        op = self.batch_norm2(self.conv_layer2(op))
        op += self.res_connnection(inp)
        op = F.relu(op)
        return op
```

To get started quickly with ResNet, we can always use the pre-trained ResNet model from PyTorch's repository:

```
import torchvision.models as models
model = models.resnet50(pretrained=True)
```

ResNet uses the identity function (by directly connecting input to output) to preserve the gradient during backpropagation (as the gradient will be 1). Yet, for extremely deep networks, this principle might not be sufficient to preserve strong gradients from the output layer back to the input layer.

The CNN model we will discuss next is designed to ensure a strong gradient flow, as well as a further reduction in the number of required parameters.

DenseNet

The skip connections of ResNet connected the input of a residual block directly to its output. However, the inter-residual-blocks connection is still sequential, that is, residual block number 3 has a direct connection with block 2 but no direct connection with block 1.

DenseNet, or dense networks, introduced the idea of connecting every convolutional layer with every other layer within what is called a **dense block**. And every dense block is connected to every other dense block in the overall DenseNet. A dense block is simply a module of two 3x3 densely connected convolutional layers.

These dense connections ensure that every layer is receiving information from all of the preceding layers of the network. This ensures that there is a strong gradient flow from the last layer down to the very first layer. Counterintuitively, the number of parameters of such a network setting will also be low. As every layer is receiving the feature maps from all the previous layers, the required number of channels (depth) can be fewer. In the earlier models, the increasing depth represented the accumulation of information from earlier layers, but we don't need that anymore, thanks to the dense connections everywhere in the network.

One key difference between ResNet and DenseNet is also that, in ResNet, the input was added to the output using skip connections. But in the case of DenseNet, the preceding layers' outputs are concatenated with the current layer's output. And the concatenation happens in the depth dimension.

This might raise a question about the exploding size of outputs as we proceed further in the network. To combat this compounding effect, a special type of block called the **transition block** is devised for this network. Composed of a 1x1 convolutional layer followed by a 2x2 pooling layer, this block standardizes or resets the size of the depth dimension so that the output of this block can then be fed to the subsequent dense block(s). The following diagram shows the DenseNet architecture:

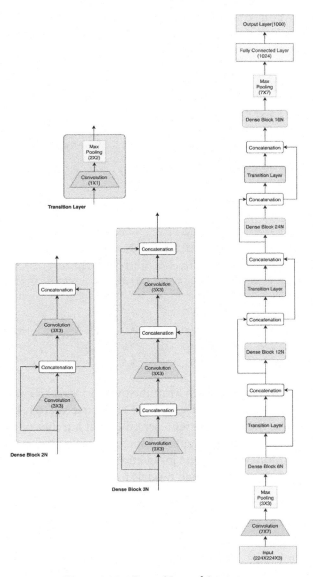

Figure 3.28 – DenseNet architecture

As mentioned earlier, there are two types of blocks involved – the **dense block** and the **transition block**. These blocks can be written as classes in PyTorch in a few lines of code, as shown here:

```python
class DenseBlock(nn.Module):
    def __init__(self, input_num_planes, rate_inc):
        super(DenseBlock, self).__init__()
        self.batch_norm1 = nn.BatchNorm2d(input_num_planes)
        self.conv_layer1 = nn.Conv2d(in_channels=input_num_
planes, out_channels=4*rate_inc, kernel_size=1, bias=False)
        self.batch_norm2 = nn.BatchNorm2d(4*rate_inc)
        self.conv_layer2 = nn.Conv2d(in_channels=4*rate_inc,
out_channels=rate_inc, kernel_size=3, padding=1, bias=False)
    def forward(self, inp):
        op = self.conv_layer1(F.relu(self.batch_norm1(inp)))
        op = self.conv_layer2(F.relu(self.batch_norm2(op)))
        op = torch.cat([op,inp], 1)
        return op
class TransBlock(nn.Module):
    def __init__(self, input_num_planes, output_num_planes):
        super(TransBlock, self).__init__()
        self.batch_norm = nn.BatchNorm2d(input_num_planes)
        self.conv_layer = nn.Conv2d(in_channels=input_num_
planes, out_channels=output_num_planes, kernel_size=1,
bias=False)
    def forward(self, inp):
        op = self.conv_layer(F.relu(self.batch_norm(inp)))
        op = F.avg_pool2d(op, 2)
        return op
```

These blocks are then stacked densely to form the overall DenseNet architecture. DenseNet, like ResNet, comes in variants such as **DenseNet121**, **DenseNet161**, **DenseNet169**, and **DenseNet201**, where the numbers represent the total number of layers. Such large numbers of layers are obtained by the repeated stacking of the dense and transition blocks plus a fixed 7x7 convolutional layer at the input end and a fixed fully connected layer at the output end. PyTorch provides pre-trained models for all of these variants:

```python
import torchvision.models as models
densenet121 = models.densenet121(pretrained=True)
densenet161 = models.densenet161(pretrained=True)
densenet169 = models.densenet169(pretrained=True)
densenet201 = models.densenet201(pretrained=True)
```

DenseNet outperforms all the models discussed so far on the ImageNet dataset. Various hybrid models have been developed by mixing and matching the ideas presented in the previous sections. The Inception-ResNet and ResNeXt models are examples of such hybrid networks. The following diagram shows the ResNeXt architecture:

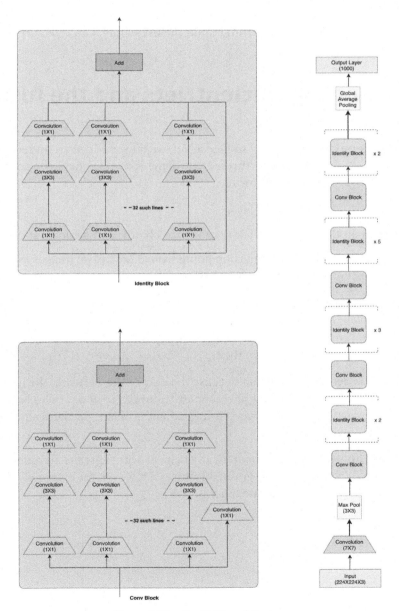

Figure 3.29 – ResNeXt architecture

As you can see, it looks like a wider variant of a *ResNet + Inception* hybrid because there is a large number of parallel convolutional branches in the residual blocks – and the idea of parallelism is derived from the inception network.

In the next and last section of this chapter, we are going to look at the current best performing CNN architectures – EfficientNets. We will also discuss the future of CNN architectural development while touching upon the use of CNN architectures for tasks beyond image classification.

Understanding EfficientNets and the future of CNN architectures

So far in our exploration from LeNet to DenseNet, we have noticed an underlying theme in the advancement of CNN architectures. That theme is the expansion or scaling of the CNN model through one of the following:

- An increase in the number of layers
- An increase in the number of feature maps or channels in a convolutional layer
- An increase in the spatial dimension going from 32x32 pixel images in LeNet to 224x224 pixel images in AlexNet and so on

These three different aspects on which scaling can be performed are identified as *depth*, *width*, and *resolution*, respectively. Instead of manually scaling these attributes, which often leads to suboptimal results, **EfficientNets** use neural architecture search to calculate the optimal scaling factors for each of them.

Scaling up depth is deemed important because the deeper the network, the more complex the model, and hence it can learn highly complex features. However, there is a trade-off because, with increasing depth, the vanishing gradient problem escalates along with the general problem of overfitting.

Similarly, scaling up width should theoretically help, as with a greater number of channels, the network should learn more fine-grained features. However, for extremely wide models, the accuracy tends to saturate quickly.

Finally, higher resolution images, in theory, should work better as they have more fine-grained information. Empirically, however, the increase in resolution does not yield a linearly equivalent increase in the model performance. All of this is to say that there are trade-offs to be made while deciding the scaling factors and hence, neural architecture search helps in finding the optimal scaling factors.

EfficientNet proposes finding the architecture that has the right balance between depth, width, and resolution, and all three of these aspects are scaled together using a global scaling factor. The EfficientNet architecture is built in two steps. First, a basic architecture (called the **base network**) is devised by fixing the scaling factor to 1. At this stage, the relative importance of depth, width, and resolution is decided for the given task and dataset. The base network obtained is pretty similar to a well-known CNN architecture – **MnasNet**, short for **Mobile Neural Architecture Search Network**. PyTorch offers the pre-trained MnasNet model, which can be loaded as shown here:

```
import torchvision.models as models
model = models.mnasnet1_0()
```

Once the base network is obtained in the first step, the optimal global scaling factor is then computed with the aim of maximizing the accuracy of the model and minimizing the number of computations (or flops). The base network is called **EfficientNet B0** and the subsequent networks derived for different optimal scaling factors are called **EfficientNet B1-B7**.

As we go forward, efficient scaling of CNN architecture is going to be a prominent direction of research along with the development of more sophisticated modules inspired by the inception, residual, and dense modules. Another aspect of CNN architecture development is minimizing the model size while retaining performance. **MobileNets** (https://pytorch.org/hub/pytorch_vision_mobilenet_v2/) are a prime example and there is a lot of ongoing research on this front.

Besides the top-down approach of looking at architectural modifications of a pre-existing model, there will be continued efforts adopting the bottom-up view of fundamentally rethinking the units of CNNs such as the convolutional kernels, pooling mechanism, more effective ways of flattening, and so on. One concrete example of this could be **CapsuleNet** (https://en.wikipedia.org/wiki/Capsule_neural_network), which revamped the convolutional units to cater to the third dimension (depth) in images.

CNNs are a huge topic of study in themselves. In this chapter, we have touched upon the architectural development of CNNs, mostly in the context of image classification. However, these same architectures are used across a wide variety of applications. One well-known example is the use of ResNets for object detection and segmentation in the form of **RCNNs** (`https://en.wikipedia.org/wiki/Region_Based_Convolutional_Neural_Networks`). Some of the improved variants of RCNNs are **Faster R-CNN**, **Mask-RCNN**, and **Keypoint-RCNN**. PyTorch provides pre-trained models for all three variants:

```
faster_rcnn = models.detection.fasterrcnn_resnet50_fpn()
mask_rcnn = models.detection.maskrcnn_resnet50_fpn()
keypoint_rcnn = models.detection.keypointrcnn_resnet50_fpn()
```

PyTorch also provides pre-trained models for ResNets that are applied to video-related tasks such as video classification. Two such ResNet-based models used for video classification are **ResNet3D** and **ResNet Mixed Convolution**:

```
resnet_3d = models.video.r3d_18()
resnet_mixed_conv = models.video.mc3_18()
```

While we do not extensively cover these different applications and corresponding CNN models in this chapter, we encourage you to read more on them. PyTorch's website can be a good starting point: `https://pytorch.org/docs/stable/torchvision/models.html#object-detection-instance-segmentation-and-person-keypoint-detection`.

Summary

This chapter has been all about CNN architectures. First, we briefly discussed the history and evolution of CNNs. We then explored in detail one of the earliest CNN models – LeNet. Using PyTorch, we built the model from scratch and trained and tested it on an image classification dataset. We then explored LeNet's successor – AlexNet. Instead of building it from scratch, we used PyTorch's pre-trained model repository to load a pre-trained AlexNet model. We then fine-tuned the loaded model on a different dataset and evaluated its performance.

Next, we looked at the VGG model, which is a deeper and a more advanced successor to AlexNet. We loaded a pre-trained VGG model using PyTorch and used it to make predictions on a different image classification dataset. We then successively discussed the GoogLeNet and Inception v3 models that are composed of several inception modules. Using PyTorch, we wrote the implementation of an inception module and the whole network. Moving on, we discussed ResNet and DenseNet. For each of these architectures, we implemented their building blocks, that is, residual blocks and dense blocks, using PyTorch. We also briefly looked at an advanced hybrid CNN architecture – ResNeXt.

Finally, we concluded the chapter with an overview of the current state-of-the-art CNN model – EfficientNet. We discussed the idea behind it and the related pre-trained models available under PyTorch, such as MnasNet. We also provided plausible future directions for CNN architectural developments, along with briefly mentioning other CNN architectures specific to object detection and video classification, such as RCNNs and ResNet3D respectively.

Although this chapter does not cover every possible topic under the concept of CNN architectures, it still provides an elaborate understanding of the progression of CNNs from LeNet to EfficientNet and beyond. Moreover, this chapter highlights the effective use and application of PyTorch for the various CNN architectures that we have discussed.

In the next chapter, we will explore a similar journey but for another important type of neural network – recurrent neural networks. We will discuss the various recurrent net architectures and use PyTorch to effectively implement, train, and test them.

4
Deep Recurrent Model Architectures

Neural networks are powerful machine learning tools that are used to help us learn complex patterns between the inputs (X) and outputs (y) of a dataset. In the previous chapter, we discussed convolutional neural networks, which learn a one-to-one mapping between X and y; that is, each input, X, is independent of the other inputs and each output, y, is independent of the other outputs of the dataset.

In this chapter, we will discuss a class of neural networks that can model sequences where X (or y) is not just a single independent data point, but a temporal sequence of data points [X1, X2, .. Xt] (or [y1, y2, .. yt]). Note that X2 (which is the data point at time step 2) is dependent on X1, X3 is dependent on X2 and X1, and so on.

Such networks are classified as **recurrent neural networks** (**RNNs**). These networks are capable of modeling the temporal aspect of data by including additional weights in the model that create cycles in the network. This helps maintain a state, as shown in the following diagram:

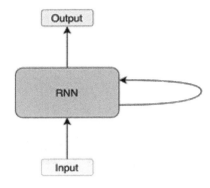

Figure 4.1 – RNN

The concept of cycles explains the term *recurrence*, and this recurrence helps establish the concept of memory in these networks. Essentially, such networks facilitate the use of intermediate outputs at *time step t* as inputs for *time step t+1*, while maintaining a hidden internal state. These connections across time steps are called **recurrent connections**.

This chapter will focus on the various recurrent neural network architectures that have been developed over the years, such as different types of RNNs, **long short-term memory** (**LSTM**), and **gated recurrent units** (**GRUs**). We will use PyTorch to implement some of these architectures and train and test recurrent models on real-world sequential modeling tasks. Besides model training and testing, we will also learn how to efficiently use PyTorch to load and preprocess sequential data. By the end of this chapter, you will be ready to solve machine learning problems with sequential datasets using (RNNs) in PyTorch.

This chapter covers the following topics:

- Exploring the evolution of recurrent networks
- Training RNNs for sentiment analysis
- Building a bidirectional LSTM
- Discussing GRUs and attention-based models

Technical requirements

We will be using Jupyter notebooks for all our exercises. The following is a list of Python libraries that must be installed for this chapter using `pip`; for example, run `pip install torch==1.4.0` on the command line:

```
jupyter==1.0.0
torch==1.4.0
tqdm==4.43.0
matplotlib==3.1.2
torchtext==0.5.0
```

All the code files that are relevant to this chapter are available at `https://github.com/PacktPublishing/Mastering-PyTorch/blob/master/Chapter04`.

Exploring the evolution of recurrent networks

Recurrent networks have been around since the 80s. In this section, we will explore the evolution of the recurrent network architecture since its inception. We will discuss and reason about the developments that were made to the architecture by going through the key milestones in the evolution of (RNNs). Before jumping right into the timelines, we'll quickly review the different types of RNNs and how they relate to a general feed-forward neural network.

Types of recurrent neural networks

While most supervised machine learning models model one-to-one relationships, (RNNs) can model the following types of input-output relationships:

- **Many-to-many (instantaneous)**
  Example: Named-entity-recognition: Given a sentence/text, tag the words with named entity categories such as names, organizations, locations, and so on.

- **Many-to-many (encoder-decoder)**
  Example: Machine translation (say, from English text to German text): Takes in a sentence/piece of text in a natural language, encodes it into a consolidated fixed size representation, and decodes that representation to produce an equivalent sentence/piece of text in another language.

- **Many-to-one**
  Example: Sentiment analysis: Given a sentence/piece of text, classify it as positive, negative, neutral, and so on.

- **One-to-many**

  Example: Image captioning: Given an image, produce a sentence/piece of text describing it.

- **One-to-one** (although not very useful)

  Example: Image classifications (by processing image pixels sequentially).

The following diagram shows these RNN types in contrast to the regular NN:

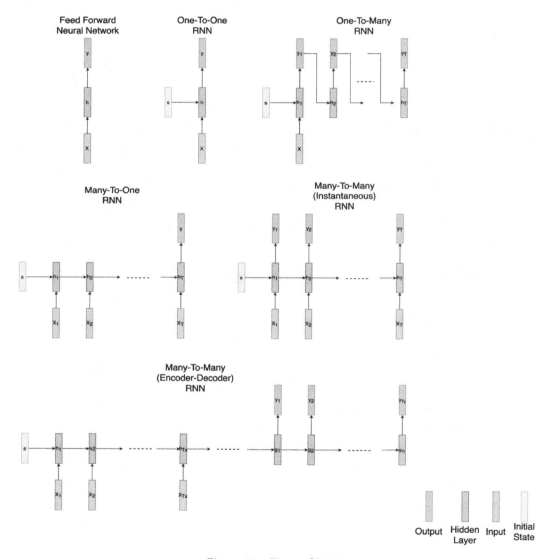

Figure 4.2 – Types of RNNs

> **Note**
>
> We provided an example of a one-to-many recurrent neural network in the image captioning exercise in *Chapter 2, Combining CNNs and LSTMs*.

As we can see, recurrent neural architectures have recurrent connections that do not exist in regular NNs. These recurrent connections are unfolded along the time dimension in the preceding diagram. The following diagram shows the structure of an RNN in both **time-folded** and **time-unfolded** forms:

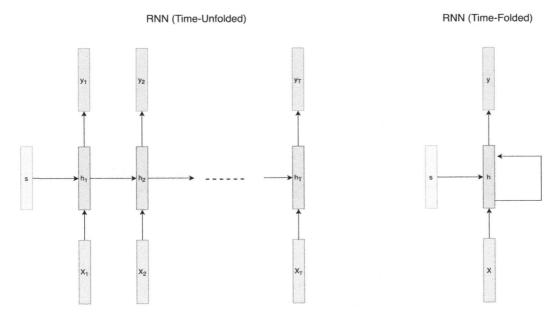

Figure 4.3 – Temporal unfolding of an RNN

In the following sections, we will be using the time-unfolded version to demonstrate RNN architectures. In the preceding diagrams, we have marked the RNN layer in red as the hidden layer of the neural network. Although the network might seem to just have one hidden layer, once this hidden layer is unrolled along the time dimension, we can see that the network actually has T hidden layers. Here, T is the total number of time steps in the sequential data.

One of the powerful features of RNNs is that they can deal with sequential data of varying sequence lengths (T). One way of dealing with this variability in length is by padding shorter sequences and truncating longer sequences, as we will see in the exercises provided later in this chapter.

Next, we will delve into the history and evolution of recurrent architectures, starting with basic RNNs.

RNNs

The idea behind RNNs became evident with the emergence of the Hopfield network in 1982, which is a special type of RNN that tries to emulate the workings of the human memory. RNNs later came into their own existence based on the works of David Rumelhart, among others, in 1986. These RNNs were able to process sequences with an underlying concept of memory. From here, a series of improvements were made to its architecture, as shown in the following diagram:

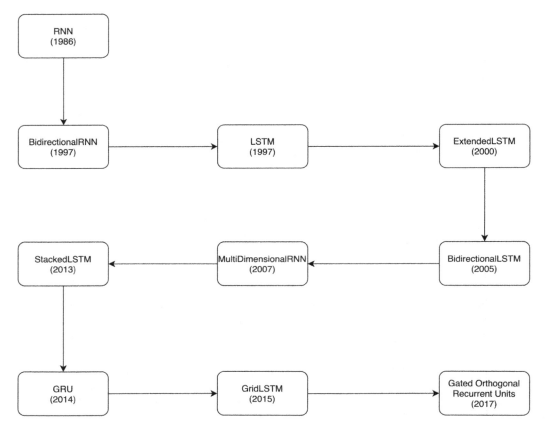

Figure 4.4 – RNN architecture evolution – a broad picture

The preceding diagram does not cover the entire history of the architecture evolution of RNNs, but it does cover the important checkpoints. Next, we will discuss the successors of RNNs chronologically, starting with bidirectional RNNs.

Bidirectional RNNs

Although RNNs performed well on sequential data, it was later realized that some sequence-related tasks, such as language translation, can be done more efficiently by looking at both past and future information. For example, *I see you* in English would be translated to *Je te vois* in French. Here, *te* means *you* and *vois* means *see*. Hence, in order to correctly translate English into French, we need all three words in English before writing the second and third words in French.

To overcome this limitation, **bidirectional RNNs** were invented in 1997. These are pretty similar to conventional RNNs except that bidirectional RNNs have two RNNs working internally: one running the sequence from start to end, and another running the sequence backward from end to start, as shown in the following diagram:

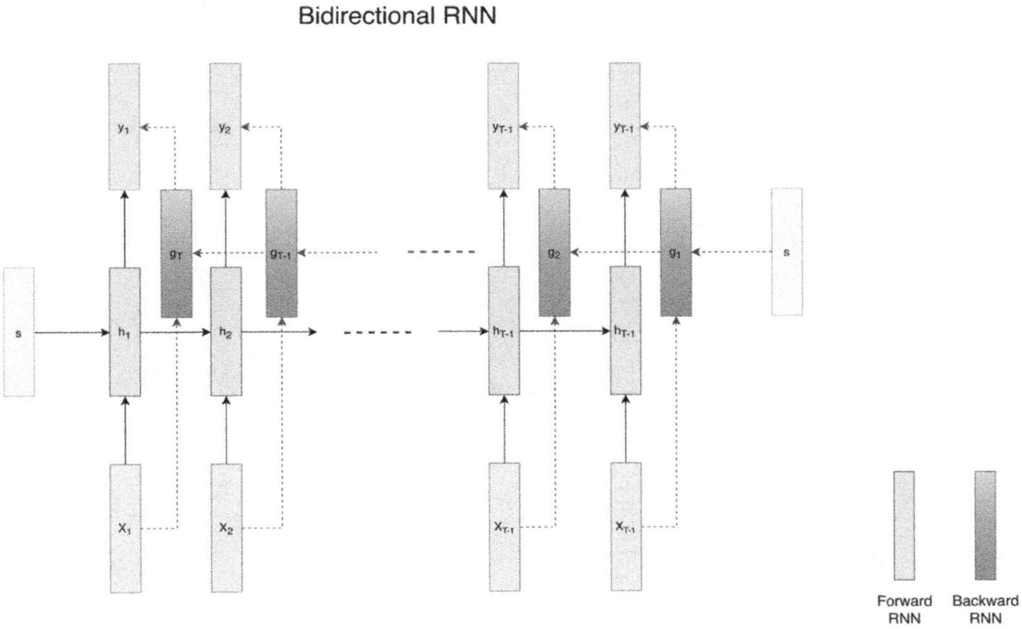

Figure 4.5 – Bidirectional RNNs

Next, we will learn about LSTMs.

LSTMs

While RNNs were able to deal with sequential data and remember information, they suffered from the problem of exploding and vanishing gradients. This happened because of the extremely deep networks that resulted from unfolding the recurrent networks in the time dimension.

In 1997, a different approach was devised. The RNN cell was replaced with a more sophisticated memory cell – the **long short-term memory (LSTM)** cell. The RNN cell usually has a **sigmoid** or a **tanh** activation function. These functions are chosen because of their ability to control the output between the values of 0 (no information flow) to 1 (complete information flow), or -1 to 1 in the case of tanh.

Tanh is additionally advantageous for providing a 0 mean output value and larger gradients in general – both of which contribute to faster learning (convergence). These activation functions are applied to the concatenation of the current time step's input and the previous time step's hidden state, as shown in the following diagram:

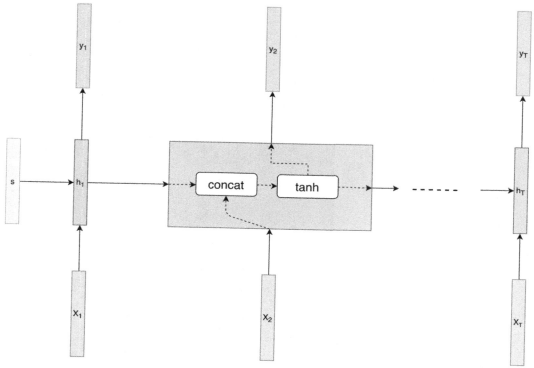

Figure 4.6 – RNN cell

During **backpropagation**, the gradient either keeps diminishing across several of these RNN cells or keeps growing, due to the multiplication of gradient terms across time-unfolded RNN cells. So, while RNNs can remember the sequential information across short sequences, they tend to struggle with long sequences due to the larger number of multiplications. LSTMs resolve this issue by controlling their input and output using gates.

An LSTM layer essentially consists of various time-unfolded LSTM cells. Information passes from one cell to another in the form of cell states. These cell states are controlled or manipulated using multiplications and additions using the mechanism of gates. These gates, as shown in the following diagram, control the flow of information to the next cell while preserving or forgetting the information that's coming in from the previous cell:

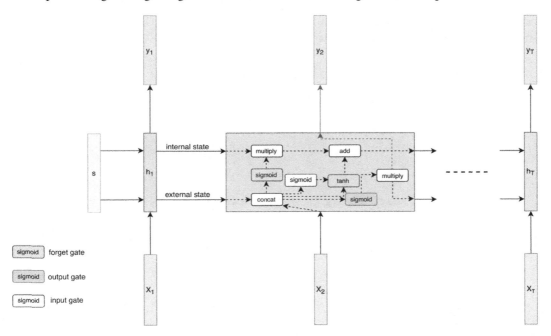

Figure 4.7 – LSTM network

LSTMs revolutionized recurrent networks as they can efficiently deal with much longer sequences. Next, we discuss more advanced variants of LSTMs.

Extended and bidirectional LSTMs

Originally, in 1997, LSTMs were invented with just the input and output gates. Soon after, in 2000, an extended LSTM was developed with forget gates, which is mostly used nowadays. A few years later, bidirectional LSTMs were developed in 2005, which are similar in concept to bidirectional RNNs.

Multi-dimensional RNNs

In 2007, **multi-dimensional RNNs (MDRNNs)** were invented. Here, a single recurrent connection between RNN cells is replaced by as many connections as there are dimensions in the data. This was useful in video processing, for example, where the data is a sequence of images that is inherently two-dimensional.

Stacked LSTMs

Although single-layer LSTM networks did seem to overcome the problem of vanishing and exploding gradients, stacking more LSTM layers proved more helpful in learning highly complex patterns across various sequential processing tasks, such as speech recognition. These powerful models were called **stacked LSTMs**. The following diagram shows a stacked LSTM model with two LSTM layers:

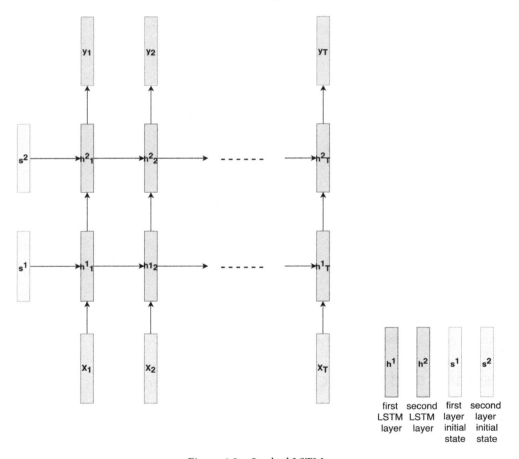

Figure 4.8 – Stacked LSTMs

LSTM cells are, by their very nature, stacked in the time dimension of an LSTM layer. Stacking several such layers in the space dimension provides them with the additional depth in space they need. The downside of these models is that they are significantly slower to train due to the extra depth and extra recurrent connections they have. Furthermore, the additional LSTM layers need to be unrolled (in the time dimension) at every training iteration. Hence, training stacked recurrent models in general is not parallelizable.

GRUs

The LSTM cell has two states – internal and external – as well as three different gates – **input gate**, **forget gate**, and **output gate**. A similar type of cell, named **gated recurrent unit** (**GRU**), was invented in 2014 with the goal of learning long-term dependencies while effectively dealing with the exploding and vanishing gradients problem. GRUs have just one state and only two gates – a **reset gate** (a combination of the input and forget gates) and an **update gate**. The following diagram shows a GRU network:

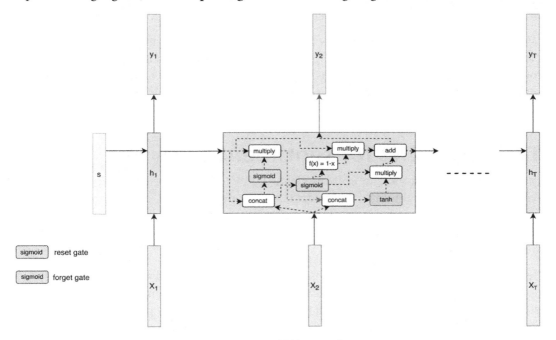

Figure 4.9 – GRU network

Next up is the grid LSTM.

Grid LSTMs

A year later, in 2015, the **grid LSTM** model was developed as a successor to the MDLSTM model, as the LSTM equivalent of multi-dimensional RNNs. LSTM cells are arranged into a multi-dimensional grid in a grid LSTM model. These cells are connected along the spatiotemporal dimensions of the data, as well as between the network layers.

Gated orthogonal recurrent units

In 2017, **gated orthogonal recurrent units** were devised, which brought together the ideas of GRUs and **unitary RNNs**. Unitary RNNs are based on the idea of using **unitary matrices** (which are **orthogonal matrices**) as the **hidden-state loop matrices** of RNNs to deal with the problem of exploding and vanishing gradients. This works because deviating gradients are attributed to deviating the **eigenvalues** of the **hidden-to-hidden** weight matrices from one. Due to this, these matrices have been replaced with orthogonal matrices to solve the gradients problem. You can read more about unitary RNNs in the original paper: `https://arxiv.org/pdf/1511.06464.pdf`.

We briefly covered the evolution of recurrent neural architectures in this section. Next, we will dive deep into RNNs by performing an exercise with a simple RNN model architecture based on a text classification task. We will also explore how PyTorch plays an important role in processing sequential data, as well as building and evaluating recurrent models.

Training RNNs for sentiment analysis

In this section, we will train an RNN model using PyTorch for a text classification task – sentiment analysis. In this task, the model takes in a piece of text – a sequence of words – as input and outputs either 1 (meaning positive sentiment) or 0 (negative sentiment). For this binary classification task involving sequential data, we will use a **unidirectional single-layer RNN**.

Before training the model, we will manually process the textual data and convert it into a usable numeric form. Upon training the model, we will test it on some sample texts. We will demonstrate the use of various PyTorch functionalities to efficiently perform this task. The code for this exercise can be found at `https://github.com/PacktPublishing/Mastering-PyTorch/blob/master/Chapter04/rnn.ipynb`.

Loading and preprocessing the text dataset

For this exercise, we will need to import a few dependencies:

1. First, execute the following `import` statements:

```
import os
import time
import numpy as np
from tqdm import tqdm
from string import punctuation
from collections import Counter
import matplotlib.pyplot as plt

import torch
import torch.nn as nn
import torch.optim as optim
from torch.utils.data import DataLoader, TensorDataset
device = torch.device('cuda' if torch.cuda.is_available()
else 'cpu')
torch.manual_seed(123)
```

Besides importing the regular `torch` dependencies, we have also imported `punctuation` and `Counter` for text processing. We have also imported `matplotlib` to display images, `numpy` for array operations, and `tqdm` for visualizing progress bars. Besides imports, we have also set the random seed to ensure reproducibility of this exercise, as shown in the last line of the code snippet.

2. Next, we will read the data from the text files. For this exercise, we will be using the IMDb sentiment analysis dataset, which can be found here: `https://ai.stanford.edu/~amaas/data/sentiment/`. This IMDb dataset consists of several movie reviews as texts and corresponding sentiment labels (positive or negative). First, we will download the dataset and run the following lines of code in order to read and store the list of texts and corresponding sentiment labels:

```
# read sentiments and reviews data from the text files
review_list = []
label_list = []
for label in ['pos', 'neg']:
    for fname in tqdm(os.listdir(f'./aclImdb/train/
{label}/')):
        if 'txt' not in fname:
            continue
```

```
            with open(os.path.join(f'./aclImdb/train/
{label}/', fname), encoding="utf8") as f:
                review_list += [f.read()]
                label_list += [label]
    print ('Number of reviews :', len(review_list))
```

This should output the following:

```
100%|████████████| 12500/12500 [00:03<00:00, 3393.39it/s]
100%|████████████| 12500/12500 [00:03<00:00, 3707.12it/s]

Number of reviews : 25000
```

Figure 4.10 – IMDb dataset loading

As we can see, there are a total of 25,000 movie reviews, with 12,500 positive and 12,500 negative.

> **Dataset Citation**
>
> Andrew L. Maas, Raymond E. Daly, Peter T. Pham, Dan Huang, Andrew Y. Ng, and Christopher Potts. (2011). *Learning Word Vectors for Sentiment Analysis.* The 49th Annual Meeting of the Association for Computational Linguistics (ACL 2011).

3. Following the data loading step, we will now start processing the text data, as follows:

```
# pre-processing review text
review_list = [review.lower() for review in review_list]
review_list = [''.join([letter for letter in review if
letter not in punctuation]) for review in tqdm(review_
list)]
# accumulate all review texts together
reviews_blob = ' '.join(review_list)
# generate list of all words of all reviews
review_words = reviews_blob.split()
# get the word counts
count_words = Counter(review_words)
# sort words as per counts (decreasing order)
total_review_words = len(review_words)
sorted_review_words = count_words.most_common(total_
review_words)
print(sorted_review_words[:10])
```

This should output the following:

```
[('the', 334691), ('and', 162228), ('a', 161940), ('of', 145326), ('to',
135042), ('is', 106855), ('in', 93028), ('it', 77099), ('i', 75719), ('th
is', 75190)]
```

Figure 4.11 – Word counts

As you can see, first, we lower-cased the entire text corpus and subsequently removed all punctuation marks from the review texts. Then, we accumulated all the words in all the reviews together to get word counts and sorted them in decreasing order of counts, to see the most popular words. Note that the most popular words are all **non-nouns** such as determiners, pronouns, and more, as shown in the preceding screenshot.

Ideally, these non-nouns, also referred to as **stop words**, would be removed from the corpus as they do not carry a lot of meaning. However, we will skip those advanced text processing steps to keep things simple.

4.   We will continue with data processing by converting these individual words into numbers or tokens. This is a crucial step because machine learning models only understand numbers, not words:

```
# create word to integer (token) dictionary in order to
encode text as numbers
vocab_to_token = {word:idx+1 for idx, (word, count) in
enumerate(sorted_review_words)}
print(list(vocab_to_token.items())[:10])
```

This should output the following:

```
[('the', 1), ('and', 2), ('a', 3), ('of', 4), ('to', 5), ('is', 6),
('in', 7), ('it', 8), ('i', 9), ('this', 10)]
```

Figure 4.12 – Word token generation

Starting with the most popular word, numbers are assigned to words 1 onward.

5.   We obtained the word-to-integer mapping in the previous step, which is also known as the vocabulary of our dataset. In this step, we will use the vocabulary to translate movie reviews in our dataset into a list of numbers:

```
reviews_tokenized = []
for review in review_list:
    word_to_token = [vocab_to_token[word] for word in
review.split()]
```

```
reviews_tokenized.append(word_to_token)
print(review_list[0])
print()
print (reviews_tokenized[0])
```

This should output something like the following:

```
for a movie that gets no respect there sure are a lot of memorable quotes listed for this gem
imagine a movie where joe piscopo is actually funny maureen stapleton is a scene stealer the
moroni character is an absolute scream watch for alan the skipper hale jr as a police sgt

[15, 3, 17, 11, 201, 56, 1165, 47, 242, 23, 3, 168, 4, 891, 4325, 3513, 15, 10, 1514, 822, 3,
17, 112, 884, 14623, 6, 155, 161, 7307, 15816, 6, 3, 134, 20049, 1, 32064, 108, 6, 33, 1492,
1943, 103, 15, 1550, 1, 18993, 9055, 1809, 14, 3, 549, 6906]
```

Figure 4.13 – Numericalized text

6.   We shall also encode the sentiment targets – pos and neg – into numbers 1 and 0, respectively:

```
# encode sentiments as 0 or 1
encoded_label_list = [1 if label =='pos' else 0 for label
in label_list]
reviews_len = [len(review) for review in reviews_
tokenized]
reviews_tokenized = [reviews_tokenized[i] for i, l in
enumerate(reviews_len) if l>0 ]
encoded_label_list = np.array([encoded_label_list[i]
for i, l in enumerate(reviews_len) if l> 0 ],
dtype='float32')
```

7.   Before we train the model, we need a final data-processing step. Different reviews can be of different lengths. However, we will define our simple RNN model for a fixed sequence length. Hence, we need to normalize different length reviews so that they're all same length.

For this, we will define a sequence length L (512, in this case), and then pad sequences that are smaller than L in length and truncate sequences that are longer than L:

```
def pad_sequence(reviews_tokenized, sequence_length):
    ''' returns the tokenized review sequences padded
with 0's or truncated to the sequence_length.
    '''
    padded_reviews = np.zeros((len(reviews_tokenized),
sequence_length), dtype = int)
```

```
        for idx, review in enumerate(reviews_tokenized):
            review_len = len(review)
            if review_len <= sequence_length:
                zeroes = list(np.zeros(sequence_length-
    review_len))
                new_sequence = zeroes+review
            elif review_len > sequence_length:
                new_sequence = review[0:sequence_length]
            padded_reviews[idx,:] = np.array(new_sequence)
        return padded_reviews
sequence_length = 512
padded_reviews = pad_sequence(reviews_tokenized=reviews_
tokenized, sequence_length=sequence_length)
plt.hist(reviews_len);
```

The output will be as follows:

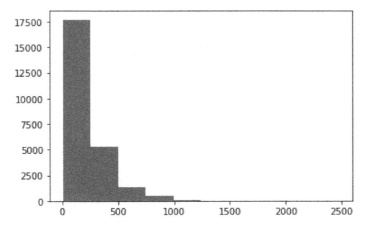

Figure 4.14 – Histogram of review lengths

As we can see, the reviews are mostly below 500, so we have chosen 512 (a power of 2) as the sequence length for our model and modified the sequences that are not exactly 512 words long accordingly.

8. Finally, we can train the model. To do this, we must split our dataset into training and validation sets with a 75:25 ratio:

```
train_val_split = 0.75
train_X = padded_reviews[:int(train_val_split*len(padded_
reviews))]
```

```
train_y = encoded_label_list[:int(train_val_
split*len(padded_reviews))]
validation_X = padded_reviews[int(train_val_
split*len(padded_reviews)):]
validation_y = encoded_label_list[int(train_val_
split*len(padded_reviews)):]
```

9. At this stage, we can start using PyTorch to generate the `dataset` and `dataloader` objects from the processed data:

```
# generate torch datasets
train_dataset = TensorDataset(torch.from_numpy(train_X).
to(device), torch.from_numpy(train_y).to(device))
validation_dataset = TensorDataset(torch.from_
numpy(validation_X).to(device), torch.from_
numpy(validation_y).to(device))
batch_size = 32
# torch dataloaders (shuffle data)
train_dataloader = DataLoader(train_dataset, batch_
size=batch_size, shuffle=True)
validation_dataloader = DataLoader(validation_dataset,
batch_size=batch_size, shuffle=True)
```

10. To get a feeling of what the data looks like before we feed it to the model, let's visualize a batch of 32 reviews and the corresponding sentiment labels:

```
# get a batch of train data
train_data_iter = iter(train_dataloader)
X_example, y_example = train_data_iter.next()
print('Example Input size: ', X_example.size()) # batch_
size, seq_length
print('Example Input:\n', X_example)
print()
print('Example Output size: ', y_example.size()) # batch_
size
print('Example Output:\n', y_example)
```

The output will be as follows:

```
Example Input size:  torch.Size([32, 512])
Example Input:
  tensor([[    0,      0,      0,  ...,     1,    875,    520],
          [    0,      0,      0,  ...,   482,    800,   1794],
          [    0,      0,      0,  ...,     3,   1285,  70251],
          ...,
          [    0,      0,      0,  ...,     4,      1,   1374],
          [    0,      0,      0,  ...,     2,   8268,  17117],
          [    0,      0,      0,  ...,  6429,    271,    116]])

Example Output size:  torch.Size([32])
Example Output:
  tensor([1., 0., 1., 0., 0., 1., 0., 1., 1., 0., 1., 1., 0., 0., 0., 1., 1., 1.,
          1., 1., 1., 0., 1., 1., 1., 1., 1., 1., 0., 1., 1., 1.])
```

Figure 4.15 – Sample data point

Having loaded and processed the textual dataset into sequences of numerical tokens, next, we will create the RNN model object in PyTorch and train the RNN model.

Instantiating and training the model

Now that we have prepared our datasets, we can instantiate our unidirectional single-layer RNN model. Firstly, PyTorch makes it incredibly compact through its **nn.RNN** module to instantiate the RNN layer. All it takes in is the input/embedding dimension, the hidden-to-hidden state dimension, and the number of layers. Let's get started:

1. Let's define our own wrapper RNN class. This instantiates the whole RNN model, which is composed of the embedding layer, followed by the RNN layer, and finally followed by a fully connected layer, as follows:

```python
class RNN(nn.Module):
    def __init__(self, input_dimension, embedding_
dimension, hidden_dimension, output_dimension):
        super().__init__()
        self.embedding_layer = nn.Embedding(input_
dimension, embedding_dimension)
        self.rnn_layer = nn.RNN(embedding_dimension,
hidden_dimension, num_layers=1)
        self.fc_layer = nn.Linear(hidden_dimension,
output_dimension)
    def forward(self, sequence):
```

```
        # sequence shape = (sequence_length, batch_size)
        embedding = self.embedding_layer(sequence)
        # embedding shape = [sequence_length, batch_size,
embedding_dimension]
        output, hidden_state = self.rnn_layer(embedding)
        # output shape = [sequence_length, batch_size,
hidden_dimension]
        # hidden_state shape = [1, batch_size, hidden_
dimension]
        final_output = self.fc_layer(hidden_state[-
1,:,:].squeeze(0))
        return final_output
```

The embedding layer's functionality is provided under the nn.Embedding module, which stores word embeddings (in the form of a lookup table) and retrieves them using indices. In this exercise, we set the embeddings dimension to 100. This implies that if we have a total of 1,000 words in our vocabulary, then the embeddings lookup table will be 1000x100 in size.

For example, the word *it*, which is tokenized as number *8* in our vocabulary, will be stored as a vector of size 100 at the 8th row in this lookup table. You can initialize the embeddings lookup table with pre-trained embeddings for better performance, but we will be training it from scratch in this exercise.

2. In the following code, we are instantiating the RNN model:

```
input_dimension = len(vocab_to_token)+1 # +1 to account
for padding
embedding_dimension = 100
hidden_dimension = 32
output_dimension = 1
rnn_model = RNN(input_dimension, embedding_dimension,
hidden_dimension, output_dimension)
optim = optim.Adam(rnn_model.parameters())
loss_func = nn.BCEWithLogitsLoss()
rnn_model = rnn_model.to(device)
loss_func = loss_func.to(device)
```

We use the nn.BCEWithLogitsLoss module to compute losses. This PyTorch module provides a numerically stable computation of a **Sigmoid** function, followed by a **binary cross-entropy** function, which is exactly what we want as a loss function for our binary classification problem. The hidden dimension of 32 simply means that each RNN cell (hidden) state will be a vector of size 32.

3. We will also define an accuracy metric to measure the performance of our trained model on the validation set. We will be using simple 0-1 accuracy for this exercise:

```python
def accuracy_metric(predictions, ground_truth):
    """
    Returns 0-1 accuracy for the given set of predictions
and ground truth
    """
    # round predictions to either 0 or 1
    rounded_predictions = torch.round(torch.
sigmoid(predictions))
    success = (rounded_predictions == ground_truth).
float() #convert into float for division
    accuracy = success.sum() / len(success)
    return accuracy
```

4. Once we've completed the model instantiation and metrics definition, we can define the training and validation routines. The code for the training routine is as follows:

```python
def train(model, dataloader, optim, loss_func):
    loss = 0
    accuracy = 0
    model.train()
    for sequence, sentiment in dataloader:
        optim.zero_grad()
        preds = model(sequence.T).squeeze()
        loss_curr = loss_func(preds, sentiment)
        accuracy_curr = accuracy_metric(preds, sentiment)
        loss_curr.backward()
        optim.step()
        loss += loss_curr.item()
        accuracy += accuracy_curr.item()
    return loss/len(dataloader), accuracy/len(dataloader)
```

The code for the validation routine is as follows:

```python
def validate(model, dataloader, loss_func):
    loss = 0
    accuracy = 0
    model.eval()
    with torch.no_grad():
        for sequence, sentiment in dataloader:
            preds = model(sequence.T).squeeze()
            loss_curr = loss_func(preds, sentiment)
            accuracy_curr = accuracy_metric(preds,
sentiment)
            loss += loss_curr.item()
            accuracy += accuracy_curr.item()
    return loss/len(dataloader), accuracy/len(dataloader)
```

5. Finally, we are now ready to train the model:

```python
num_epochs = 10
best_validation_loss = float('inf')
for ep in range(num_epochs):
    time_start = time.time()
    training_loss, train_accuracy = train(rnn_model,
train_dataloader, optim, loss_func)
    validation_loss, validation_accuracy = validate(rnn_
model, validation_dataloader, loss_func)
    time_end = time.time()
    time_delta = time_end - time_start
    if validation_loss < best_validation_loss:
        best_validation_loss = validation_loss
        torch.save(rnn_model.state_dict(), 'rnn_model.
pt')
    print(f'epoch number: {ep+1} | time elapsed: {time_
delta}s')
    print(f'training loss: {training_loss:.3f} | training
accuracy: {train_accuracy*100:.2f}%')
    print(f'\tvalidation loss: {validation_loss:.3f}
| validation accuracy: {validation_accuracy*100:.2f}%')
```

The output will be as follows:

```
epoch number: 1 | time elapsed: 136.13723397254944s
training loss: 0.627 | training accuracy: 66.23%
validation loss: 1.048 |  validation accuracy: 19.65%

epoch number: 2 | time elapsed: 150.36637210845947s
training loss: 0.533 | training accuracy: 73.80%
validation loss: 0.858 |  validation accuracy: 54.43%

epoch number: 3 | time elapsed: 186.54570603370667s
training loss: 0.438 | training accuracy: 80.39%
validation loss: 0.551 |  validation accuracy: 78.56%

                         ⋮

epoch number: 8 | time elapsed: 199.3309519290924s
training loss: 0.198 | training accuracy: 92.92%
validation loss: 0.971 |  validation accuracy: 66.19%

epoch number: 9 | time elapsed: 185.76586294174194s
training loss: 0.315 | training accuracy: 87.93%
validation loss: 0.950 |  validation accuracy: 62.34%

epoch number: 10 | time elapsed: 188.916706085205508s
training loss: 0.193 | training accuracy: 93.08%
validation loss: 1.042 |  validation accuracy: 62.71%
```

Figure 4.16 – RNN model training logs

The model seems to have learned especially well on the training set through overfitting. The model has 512 layers in the time dimension, which explains why this powerful model can learn the training set quite well. The performance of the validation set starts from a low value but then rises and fluctuates.

6. Let's quickly define a helper function to make real-time inference on the trained model:

```
def sentiment_inference(model, sentence):
    model.eval()
    # text transformations
    sentence = sentence.lower()
    sentence = ''.join([c for c in sentence if c not in
punctuation])
    tokenized = [vocab_to_token.get(token, 0) for token
in sentence.split()]
```

```
        tokenized = np.pad(tokenized, (512-len(tokenized),
   0), 'constant')
        # model inference
        model_input = torch.LongTensor(tokenized).to(device)
        model_input = model_input.unsqueeze(1)
        pred = torch.sigmoid(model(model_input))
        return pred.item()
```

7. As the last step of this exercise, we will test the performance of this model on some manually entered review texts:

```
print(sentiment_inference(rnn_model, "This film is
horrible"))
print(sentiment_inference(rnn_model, "Director tried too
hard but this film is bad"))
print(sentiment_inference(rnn_model, "Decent movie,
although could be shorter"))
print(sentiment_inference(rnn_model, "This film will be
houseful for weeks"))
print(sentiment_inference(rnn_model, "I loved the movie,
every part of it"))
```

The output will be as follows:

```
0.05216024070978165
0.17682921886444092
0.7510029077529907
0.9689022898674011
0.9829260110855103
```

Figure 4.17 – RNN inference output

Here, we can see that the model indeed picks up on the notion of positive and negative. Also, it seems to be able to deal with sequences of variable lengths, even if they are all much shorter than 512 words.

In this exercise, we have trained a rather simple RNN model that has limitations not only on the model architecture aspect, but also on the data processing side. In the next exercise, we will use a more evolved recurrent architecture – a bidirectional LSTM model – to tackle the same task. We will use some regularization methods to overcome the problem of overfitting that we observed in this exercise. Moreover, we will use PyTorch's torchtext module to handle the data loading and processing pipelines more efficiently and concisely.

Building a bidirectional LSTM

So far, we have trained and tested a simple RNN model on the sentiment analysis task, which is a binary classification task based on textual data. In this section, we will try to improve our performance on the same task by using a more advanced recurrent architecture – LSTMs.

LSTMs, as we know, are more capable of handling longer sequences due to their memory cell gates, which help retain important information from several time steps before and forget irrelevant information even if it was recent. With the exploding and vanishing gradients problem in check, LSTMs should be able to perform well when processing long movie reviews.

Moreover, we will be using a bidirectional model as it broadens the context window at any time step for the model to make a more informed decision about the sentiment of the movie review. The RNN model we looked at in the previous exercise overfitted the dataset during training, so to tackle that, we will be using dropouts as a regularization mechanism in our LSTM model.

Loading and preprocessing text dataset

In this exercise, we will demonstrate the power of PyTorch's `torchtext` module. In the previous exercise, we roughly dedicated half of the exercise to loading and processing the text dataset. Using `torchtext`, we will do the same in less than 10 lines of code.

Instead of manually downloading the dataset, we will use the pre-existing IMDb dataset under `torchtext.datasets` to load it. We will also use `torchtext.data` to tokenize words and generate vocabulary. Finally, we will use the `nn.LSTM` module to directly pad sequences instead of manually padding them. The code for this exercise can be found at `https://github.com/PacktPublishing/Mastering-PyTorch/blob/master/Chapter04/lstm.ipynb`. Let's get started:

1. For this exercise, we will need to import a few dependencies. First, we will execute the same `import` statements as we did for the previous exercise. However, we will also need to import the following:

    ```
    import random
    from torchtext import (data, datasets)
    ```

2. Next, we will use the datasets submodule from the `torchtext` module to directly download the IMDb sentiment analysis dataset. We will separate the review texts and the sentiment labels into two separate fields and split the dataset into training, validation, and test sets:

```
TEXT_FIELD = data.Field(tokenize = data.get_
tokenizer("basic_english"), include_lengths = True)
LABEL_FIELD = data.LabelField(dtype = torch.float)
train_dataset, test_dataset = datasets.IMDB.splits(TEXT_
FIELD, LABEL_FIELD)
train_dataset, valid_dataset = train_dataset.
split(random_state = random.seed(123))
```

3. Next, we will use the `build_vocab` method of `torchtext.data.Field` and `torchtext.data.LabelField` to build the vocabulary for the movie reviews text dataset and the sentiment labels, respectively:

```
MAX_VOCABULARY_SIZE = 25000
TEXT_FIELD.build_vocab(train_dataset,
                 max_size = MAX_VOCABULARY_SIZE)
LABEL_FIELD.build_vocab(train_dataset)
```

As we can see, it takes just three lines of code to build the vocabulary using the predefined functions.

4. Before we get into the model-related details, we will also create dataset iterators for the training, validation, and test sets.

Now that we've loaded and processed the dataset and derived the dataset iterators, let's create the LSTM model object and train the LSTM model.

Instantiating and training the LSTM model

In this section, we will instantiate the LSTM model object. We will then define the optimizer, the loss function, and the model training performance metrics. Finally, we will run the model training loop using the defined model training and model validation routines. Let's get started:

1. First, we must instantiate the bidirectional LSTM model with dropout. While most of the model instantiation looks the same as in the previous exercise, the following line of code is the key difference:

```
self.lstm_layer = nn.LSTM(embedding_dimension,
                          hidden_dimension,
```

```
                             num_layers=1,
                             bidirectional=True,
                             dropout=dropout)
```

2. We have added two special types of tokens – unknown_token (for words that do not exist in our vocabulary) and padding_token (for tokens that are just added for padding the sequence) – to our vocabulary. Hence, we will need to set the embeddings to all zeros for these two tokens:

```
UNK_INDEX = TEXT_FIELD.vocab.stoi[TEXT_FIELD.unk_token]

lstm_model.embedding_layer.weight.data[UNK_INDEX] =
torch.zeros(EMBEDDING_DIMENSION)

lstm_model.embedding_layer.weight.data[PAD_INDEX] =
torch.zeros(EMBEDDING_DIMENSION)
```

3. Next, we will define the optimizer (*Adam*) and the loss function (*Sigmoid* followed by *binary cross-entropy*). We will also define an accuracy metric calculation function, as we did in the previous exercise.

4. We will then define the training and validation routines.

5. Finally, we will run the training loop with 10 epochs. This should output the following:

```
epoch number: 1 | time elapsed: 1212.3228149414062s
training loss: 0.686 | training accuracy: 54.57%
validation loss: 0.666 |  validation accuracy: 60.02%

epoch number: 2 | time elapsed: 1138.5317480564117s
training loss: 0.650 | training accuracy: 61.54%
validation loss: 0.607 |  validation accuracy: 68.02%

epoch number: 3 | time elapsed: 1141.8038160800934s
training loss: 0.579 | training accuracy: 69.60%
validation loss: 0.654 |  validation accuracy: 67.09%

                           ⋮

epoch number: 8 | time elapsed: 1066.7158658504486s
training loss: 0.383 | training accuracy: 83.04%
validation loss: 0.653 |  validation accuracy: 74.60%

epoch number: 9 | time elapsed: 1046.7357511520386s
training loss: 0.389 | training accuracy: 83.21%
validation loss: 0.586 |  validation accuracy: 75.98%

epoch number: 10 | time elapsed: 1029.34814786911s
training loss: 0.351 | training accuracy: 84.87%
validation loss: 0.549 |  validation accuracy: 77.66%
```

Figure 4.18 – LSTM model training logs

As we can see, the model is learning well as the epochs progress. Also, dropout seems to control overfitting as both the training and validation set accuracies are increasing at a similar pace. However, compared to RNNs, LSTMs are slower to train. As we can see, the epoch time for LSTMs is roughly 9 to 10 times that of RNNs. This is also because we are using a bidirectional network in this exercise.

6.   The previous step also saves the best performing model. In this step, we will load the best performing model and evaluate it on the test set:

```
lstm_model.load_state_dict(torch.load('lstm_model.pt'))
test_loss, test_accuracy = validate(lstm_model, test_
data_iterator, loss_func)
print(f'test loss: {test_loss:.3f} | test accuracy:
{test_accuracy*100:.2f}%')
```

This should output the following:

```
test loss: 0.585 | test accuracy: 76.19%
```

Figure 4.19 – LSTM test set accuracy

7.   Finally, we will define a sentiment inference function, as we did in the previous exercise, and run some manually entered movie reviews against the trained model:

```
print(sentiment_inference(rnn_model, "This film is
horrible"))
print(sentiment_inference(rnn_model, "Director tried too
hard but this film is bad"))
print(sentiment_inference(rnn_model, "Decent movie,
although could be shorter"))
print(sentiment_inference(rnn_model, "This film will be
houseful for weeks"))
print(sentiment_inference(rnn_model, "I loved the movie,
every part of it"))
```

This should output the following:

```
0.06318538635969162
0.015872443094849586
0.37745001912117004
0.8425034284591675
0.9304025769233704
```

Figure 4.20 – LSTM model inference output

Clearly, the LSTM model has outperformed the RNN models in terms of performance on the validation set. Dropout helped to prevent overfitting, and the bidirectional LSTM architecture seems to have learned the sequential patterns in the movie review text sentences.

The previous two exercises have both been about a many-to-one type sequence task, where the input is a sequence and output is a binary label. These two exercises, together with the one-to-many exercise in *Chapter 2, Combining CNNs and LSTMs*, should have provided you with enough context to get hands-on with different recurrent architectures using PyTorch.

In the next and final section, we will briefly discuss GRUs and how to use them in PyTorch. Then, we will introduce the concept of attention and how it is used in recurrent architectures.

Discussing GRUs and attention-based models

In the final section of this chapter, we will briefly look at GRUs, how they are similar yet different from LSTMs, and how to initialize a GRU model using PyTorch. We will also look at attention-based (RNNs). We will conclude this section by describing how attention-only (no recurrence or convolutions)-based models outperform the recurrent family of neural models when it comes to sequence modeling tasks.

GRUs and PyTorch

As we discussed in the *Exploring the evolution of recurrent networks* section, GRUs are a type of memory cell with two gates – a reset gate and an update gate, as well as one hidden state vector. In terms of configuration, GRUs are simpler than LSTMs and yet equally effective in dealing with the exploding and vanishing gradients problem. Tons of research has been done to compare the performance of LSTMs and GRUs. While both perform better than the simple RNNs on various sequence-related tasks, one is slightly better than the other on some tasks and vice versa.

GRUs train faster than LSTMs and on many tasks such as language modeling, GRUs can perform as well as LSTMs with much less training data. However, theoretically, LSTMs are supposed to retain information from longer sequences than GRUs. PyTorch provides the nn.GRU module to instantiate a GRU layer in one line of code. The following code creates a deep GRU network with two bidirectional GRU layers, each with 80% recurrent dropout:

```
self.gru_layer = nn.GRU(input_size, hidden_size, num_layers=2,
dropout=0.8, bidirectional=True)
```

As we can see, it takes one line of code to get started with a PyTorch GRU model. I encourage you to plug the `gru` layer instead of the `lstm` layer or `rnn` layer into the previous exercises and see how it impacts the model training time, as well as model performance.

Attention-based models

The models we have discussed in this chapter have been pathbreaking in solving problems related to sequential data. However, in 2017, a novel attention-only-based approach was invented that subsequently took the shine off these recurrent networks. The concept of attention is derived from the idea of how we, as humans, pay different levels of attention to different parts of a sequence (say, text) at different times.

For example, if we were to complete the statement *Martha sings beautifully, I am hooked to ___ voice.*, we would pay more attention to the word *Martha* to guess that the missing word might be *her*. On the other hand, if we were to complete the statement *Martha sings beautifully, I am hooked to her ____.*, then we would pay more attention to the word *sings* to guess that the missing word is either *voice*, *songs*, *singing*, and so on.

In all our recurrent architectures, a mechanism for focusing on specific parts of the sequence in order to predict the output at the current time step does not exist. Instead, the recurrent models can only get a summary of the past sequence in the form of a condensed hidden state vector.

Attention-based recurrent networks were the first ones to exploit the concept of attention around the years 2014-2015. In these models, an additional attention layer was added on top of the usual recurrent layer. This attention layer learned attention weights for each of the preceding words in the sequence.

A context vector was computed as an attention-weighted average of all the preceding words' hidden state vectors. This context vector was fed to the output layer, in addition to the regular hidden state vector at any time step, t. The following diagram shows the architecture of an attention-based (RNNs):

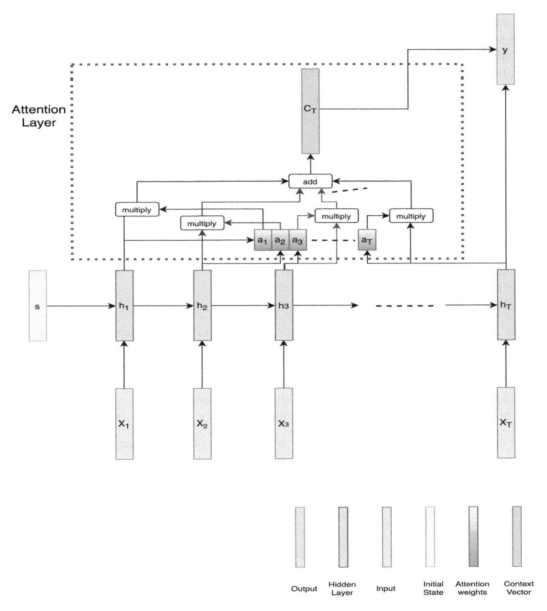

Figure 4.21 – Attention-based RNN

In this architecture, a global context vector is being calculated at each time step. Variants of this architecture were then devised using a local context vector – not paying attention to all the preceding words but only k previous words. Attention-based RNNs outperformed the state-of-the-art recurrent models on tasks such as machine translation.

A couple of years later, in 2017, it was realized that attention was all we needed for dealing with sequential data to outperform the various recurrent models we've discussed so far. Not only did this lead to achieving better accuracy on tasks, but more importantly, it significantly reduced the model training (and inference) time.

Recurrent networks need to be unrolled in time, which makes them non-parallelizable. However, a new model called the **transformer** model, which we will discuss in the next chapter, has no recurrent (and convolutional) layers, making it both parallelizable and lightweight (in terms of computation flops).

Summary

In this chapter, we have extensively explored recurrent neural architectures. First, we learned about various RNN types: one-to-many, many-to-many, and so on. We then delved into the history and evolution of RNN architectures. From here, we looked at simple RNNs, LSTMs, and GRUs to bidirectional, multi-dimensional, and stacked models. We also inspected what each of these individual architectures looked like and what was novel about them.

Next, we performed two hands-on exercises on a many-to-one sequence classification task based on sentiment analysis. Using PyTorch, we trained a unidirectional RNN model, followed by a bidirectional LSTM model with dropout on the IMDb movie reviews dataset. In the first exercise, we manually loaded and processed the data. In the second exercise, using PyTorch's `torchtext` module, we demonstrated how to load the dataset and process the text data, including vocabulary generation, efficiently and concisely.

In the final section of this chapter, we discussed GRUs, how to use them in PyTorch, and compared them to LSTMs. Finally, we explored the attention mechanism in recurrent models and discussed the architecture of an attention-based RNN model. We concluded by discussing attention-only-based models – known as transformers – that are devoid of recurrent layers and have outperformed recurrent models both in terms of (training) speed and accuracy.

In the next chapter, we will elaborate on transformers and other such model architectures, which are neither purely recurrent nor convolutional yet have achieved state-of-the art results.

5
Hybrid Advanced Models

In the previous two chapters, we learned extensively about the various convolutional and recurrent network architectures available, along with their implementations in PyTorch. In this chapter, we will take a look at some other deep learning model architectures that have proven to be successful on various machine learning tasks and are neither purely convolutional nor recurrent in nature. We will continue from where we left off in both *Chapter 3, Deep CNN Architectures*, and *Chapter 4, Deep Recurrent Model Architectures*.

First, we will explore transformers, which, as we learnt toward the end of *Chapter 4, Deep Recurrent Model Architectures*, have outperformed recurrent architectures on various sequential tasks. Then, we will pick up from the **EfficientNets** discussion at the end of *Chapter 3, Deep CNN Architectures*, and explore the idea of generating randomly wired neural networks, also known as **RandWireNNs**.

With this chapter, we aim to conclude our discussion of different kinds of neural network architectures in this book. After completing this chapter, you will have a detailed understanding of transformers and how to apply these powerful models to sequential tasks using PyTorch. Furthermore, by building your own RandWireNN model, you will have hands-on experience of performing a neural architecture search in PyTorch. This chapter is broken down into the following topics:

- Building a transformer model for language modeling
- Developing a RandWireNN model from scratch

Technical requirements

We will be using Jupyter notebooks for all our exercises. The following is a list of Python libraries that must be installed for this chapter using `pip`. Here, you must run `pip install torch==1.4.0` on the command line and then use the following commands:

```
jupyter==1.0.0
torch==1.4.0
tqdm==4.43.0
matplotlib==3.1.2
torchtext==0.5.0
torchvision==0.5.0
torchviz==0.0.1
networkx==2.4
```

All the code files that are relevant to this chapter are available at `https://github.com/PacktPublishing/Mastering-PyTorch/tree/master/Chapter05`.

Building a transformer model for language modeling

In this section, we will explore what transformers are and build one using PyTorch for the task of language modeling. We will also learn how to use some of its successors, such as **BERT** and **GPT**, via PyTorch's pretrained model repository. Before we start building a transformer model, let's quickly recap what language modeling is.

Reviewing language modeling

Language modeling is the task of figuring out the probability of the occurrence of a word or a sequence of words that should follow a given sequence of words. For example, if we are given *French is a beautiful* _____ as our sequence of words, what is the probability that the next word will be *language* or *word*, and so on? These probabilities are computed by modeling the language using various probabilistic and statistical techniques. The idea is to observe a text corpus and learn the grammar by learning which words occur together and which words never occur together. This way, a language model establishes probabilistic rules around the occurrence of different words or sequences, given various different sequences.

Recurrent models have been a popular way of learning a language model. However, as with many sequence-related tasks, transformers have outperformed recurrent networks on this task as well. We will implement a transformer-based language model for the English language by training it on the Wikipedia text corpus.

Now, let's start training a transformer for language modeling. During this exercise, we will demonstrate only the most important parts of the code. The full code can be accessed at https://github.com/PacktPublishing/Mastering-PyTorch/blob/master/Chapter05/transformer.ipynb.

We will delve deeper into the various components of the transformer architecture in-between the exercise.

For this exercise, we will need to import a few dependencies. One of the important import statements is listed here:

```
from torch.nn import TransformerEncoder,
TransformerEncoderLayer
```

Besides importing the regular torch dependencies, we must import some modules specific to the transformer model; these are provided directly under the torch library. We'll also import torchtext in order to download a text dataset directly from the available datasets under torchtext.datasets.

In the next section, we will define the transformer model architecture and look at the details of the model's components.

Understanding the transformer model architecture

This is perhaps the most important step of this exercise. Here, we define the architecture of the transformer model.

First, let's briefly discuss the model architecture and then look at the PyTorch code for defining the model. The following diagram shows the model architecture:

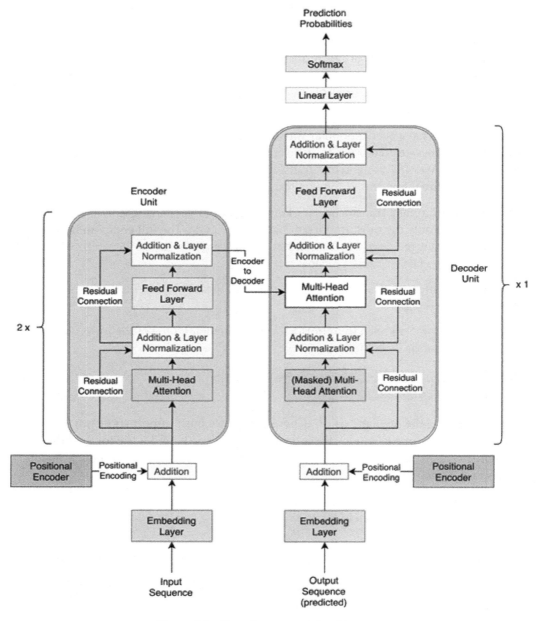

Figure 5.1 – Transformer model architecture

The first thing to notice is that this is essentially an encoder-decoder based architecture, with the **Encoder Unit** on the left (in purple) and the **Decoder Unit** (in orange) on the right. The encoder and decoder units can be tiled multiple times for even deeper architectures. In our example, we have two cascaded encoder units and a single decoder unit. This encoder-decoder setup essentially means that the encoder takes a sequence as input and generates as many embeddings as there are words in the input sequence (that is, one embedding per word). These embeddings are then fed to the decoder, along with the predictions made thus far by the model.

Let's walk through the various layers in this model:

- **Embedding Layer**: This layer is simply meant to perform the traditional task of converting each input word of the sequence into a vector of numbers; that is, an embedding. As always, here, we use the `torch.nn.Embedding` module to code this layer.

- **Positional Encoder**: Note that transformers do not have any recurrent layers in their architecture, yet they outperform recurrent networks on sequential tasks. How? Using a neat trick known as *positional encoding*, the model is provided the sense of sequentiality or sequential-order in the data. Basically, vectors that follow a particular sequential pattern are added to the input word embeddings.

  These vectors are generated in a way that enables the model to understand that the second word comes after the first word and so on. The vectors are generated using the `sinusoidal` and `cosinusoidal` functions to represent a systematic periodicity and distance between subsequent words, respectively. The implementation of this layer for our exercise is as follows:

```
class PosEnc(nn.Module):
    def __init__(self, d_m, dropout=0.2, size_
limit=5000):
        # d_m is same as the dimension of the embeddings
        pos = torch.arange(0, size_limit, dtype=torch.
float).unsqueeze(1)
        divider = torch.exp(torch.arange(0, d_m,
2).float() * (-math.log(10000.0) / d_m))
        # divider is the list of radians, multiplied by
position indices of words, and fed to the sinusoidal and
cosinusoidal function.
        p_enc[:, 0::2] = torch.sin(pos * divider)
        p_enc[:, 1::2] = torch.cos(pos * divider)
    def forward(self, x):
```

```
        return self.dropout(x + self.p_enc[:x.size(0),
 :])
```

As you can see, the `sinusoidal` and `cosinusoidal` functions are used alternatively to give the sequential pattern. There are many ways to implement positional encoding though. Without a positional encoding layer, the model will be clueless about the order of the words.

- **Multi-Head Attention**: Before we look at the multi-head attention layer, let's first understand what a **self-attention layer** is. We covered the concept of attention in *Chapter 4, Deep Recurrent Model Architectures*, with respect to recurrent networks. Here, as the name suggests, the attention mechanism is applied to self; that is, each word of the sequence. Each word embedding of the sequence goes through the self-attention layer and produces an individual output that is exactly the same length as the word embedding. The following diagram describes the process of this in detail:

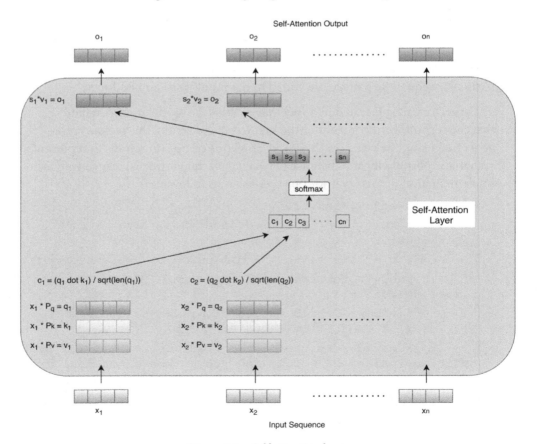

Figure 5.2 – Self-attention layer

As we can see, for each word, three vectors are generated through three learnable parameter matrices (**Pq**, **Pk**, and **Pv**). The three vectors are query, key, and value vectors. The query and key vectors are dot-multiplied to produce a number for each word. These numbers are normalized by dividing the square root of the key vector length for each word. The resultant numbers for all words are then Softmaxed at the same time to produce probabilities that are finally multiplied by the respective value vectors for each word. This results in one output vector for each word of the sequence, with the lengths of the output vector and the input word embedding being the same.

A multi-head attention layer is an extension of the self-attention layer where multiple self-attention modules compute outputs for each word. These individual outputs are concatenated and matrix-multiplied with yet another parameter matrix (**Pm**) to generate the final output vector, whose length is equal to the input embedding vector's. The following diagram shows the multi-head attention layer, along with two self-attention units that we will be using in this exercise:

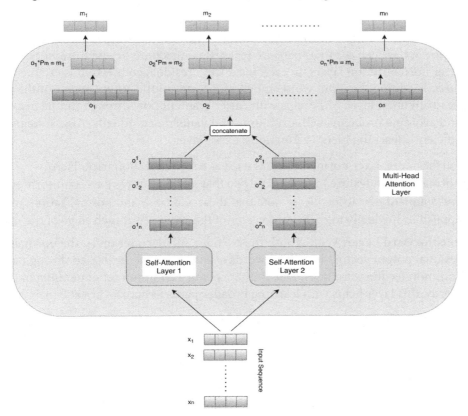

Figure 5.3 – Multi-head attention layer with two self-attention units

Having multiple self-attention heads helps different heads focus on different aspects of the sequence word, similar to how different feature maps learn different patterns in a convolutional neural network. Due to this, the multi-head attention layer performs better than an individual self-attention layer and will be used in our exercise.

Also, note that the masked multi-head attention layer in the decoder unit works in exactly the same way as a multi-head attention layer, except for the added masking; that is, given time step *t* of processing the sequence, all words from *t+1* to *n* (length of the sequence) are masked/hidden.

During training, the decoder is provided with two types of inputs. On one hand, it receives query and key vectors from the final encoder as inputs to its (unmasked) multi-head attention layer, where these query and key vectors are matrix transformations of the final encoder output. On the other hand, the decoder receives its own predictions from previous time steps as sequential input to its masked multi-head attention layer.

- **Addition and Layer Normalization**: We discussed the concept of a residual connection in *Chapter 3, Deep CNN Architectures*, while discussing ResNets. In *Figure 5.1*, we can see that there are residual connections across the addition and layer normalization layers. In each instance, a residual connection is established by directly adding the input word embedding vector to the output vector of the multi-head attention layer. This helps with easier gradient flow throughout the network and avoiding problems with exploding and vanishing gradients. Also, it helps with efficiently learning identity functions across layers.

  Furthermore, layer normalization is used as a normalization trick. Here, we normalize each feature independently so that all the features have a uniform mean and standard deviation. Please note that these additions and normalizations are applied individually to each word vector of the sequence at each stage of the network.

- **Feedforward Layer**: Within both the encoder and decoder units, the normalized residual output vectors for all the words of the sequence are passed through a common feedforward layer. Due to there being a common set of parameters across words, this layer helps with learning broader patterns across the sequence.

- **Linear and Softmax Layer**: So far, each layer is outputting a sequence of vectors, one per word. For our task of language modeling, we need a single final output. The linear layer transforms the sequence of vectors into a single vector whose size is equal to the length of our word vocabulary. The **Softmax** layer converts this output into a vector of probabilities summing to 1. These probabilities are the probabilities that the respective words (in the vocabulary) occur as the next words in the sequence.

Now that we have elaborated on the various elements of a transformer model, let's look at the PyTorch code for instantiating the model.

Defining a transformer model in PyTorch

Using the architecture details described in the previous section, we will now write the necessary PyTorch code for defining a transformer model, as follows:

```
class Transformer(nn.Module):
    def __init__(self, num_token, num_inputs, num_heads, num_
hidden, num_layers, dropout=0.3):
        self.position_enc = PosEnc(num_inputs, dropout)
        layers_enc = TransformerEncoderLayer(num_inputs, num_
heads, num_hidden, dropout)
        self.enc_transformer = TransformerEncoder(layers_enc,
num_layers)
        self.enc = nn.Embedding(num_token, num_inputs)
        self.num_inputs = num_inputs
        self.dec = nn.Linear(num_inputs, num_token)
```

As we can see, in the __init__ method of the class, thanks to PyTorch's TransformerEncoder and TransformerEncoderLayer functions, we do not need to implement these ourselves. For our language modeling task, we just need a single output for the input sequence of words. Due to this, the decoder is just a linear layer that transforms the sequence of vectors from an encoder into a single output vector. A position encoder is also initialized using the definition that we discussed earlier.

In the forward method, the input is positionally encoded and then passed through the encoder, followed by the decoder:

```
    def forward(self, source):
        source = self.enc(source) * math.sqrt(self.num_inputs)
        source = self.position_enc(source)
        op = self.enc_transformer(source, self.mask_source)
        op = self.dec(op)
        return op
```

Now that we have defined the transformer model architecture, we shall load the text corpus to train it on.

Loading and processing the dataset

In this section, we will discuss the steps related to loading a text dataset for our task and making it usable for the model training routine. Let's get started:

1. For this exercise, we will be using texts from Wikipedia, all of which are available as the `WikiText-2` dataset.

   > **Dataset Citation**
   > `https://blog.einstein.ai/the-wikitext-long-term-dependency-language-modeling-dataset/`.

   We'll use the functionality of `torchtext` to download the dataset (available under `torchtext` datasets), tokenize its vocabulary, and split the dataset into training, validation, and test sets:

   ```
   TEXT = torchtext.data.Field(tokenize=get_
   tokenizer("basic_english"), lower=True, eos_
   token='<eos>', init_token='<sos>')
   training_text, validation_text, testing_text = torchtext.
   datasets.WikiText2.splits(TEXT)
   TEXT.build_vocab(training_text)
   device = torch.device("cuda" if torch.cuda.is_available()
   else "cpu")
   ```

2. We'll also define the batch sizes for training and evaluation and declare a batch generation function, as shown here:

   ```
   def gen_batches(text_dataset, batch_size):
       text_dataset = TEXT.numericalize([text_dataset.
   examples[0].text])
       # distribute dataset across batches evenly
       text_dataset = text_dataset.view(batch_size, -1).t().
   contiguous()
       return text_dataset.to(device)
   training_batch_size = 32
   training_data = gen_batches(training_text, training_
   batch_size)
   ```

3. Next, we must define the maximum sequence length and write a function that will generate input sequences and output targets for each batch, accordingly:

```
max_seq_len = 64
def return_batch(src, k):
    sequence_length = min(max_seq_len, len(src) - 1 - k)
    sequence_data = src[k:k+sequence_length]
    sequence_label = src[k+1:k+1+sequence_length].view(-1)
    return sequence_data, sequence_label
```

Having defined the model and prepared the training data, we will now train the transformer model.

Training the transformer model

In this section, we will define the necessary hyperparameters for model training, define the model training and evaluation routines, and finally execute the training loop. Let's get started:

1. In this step, we define all the model hyperparameters and instantiate our transformer model. The following code is self-explanatory:

```
num_tokens = len(TEXT.vocab.stoi) # vocabulary size
embedding_size = 256 # dimension of embedding layer
num_hidden_params = 256 # transformer encoder's hidden
(feed forward) layer dimension
num_layers = 2 # num of transformer encoder layers within
transformer encoder
num_heads = 2 # num of heads in (multi head) attention
models
dropout = 0.25 # value (fraction) of dropout
loss_func = nn.CrossEntropyLoss()
lrate = 4.0 # learning rate
transformer_model = Transformer(num_tokens, embedding_
size, num_heads, num_hidden_params, num_layers, dropout).
to(device)
```

2. Before starting the model training and evaluation loop, we need to define the training and evaluation routines:

```
def train_model():
    num_tokens = len(TEXT.vocab.stoi)
    for b, i in enumerate(range(0, training_data.size(0)
- 1, max_seq_len)):
        train_data_batch, train_label_batch = return_
batch(training_data, i)
        optim_module.zero_grad()
        op = transformer_model(train_data_batch)
        loss_curr = loss_func(op.view(-1, num_tokens),
train_label_batch)
        loss_curr.backward()
torch.nn.utils.clip_grad_norm_(transformer_model.
parameters(), 0.6)
        optim_module.step()
        loss_total += loss_curr.item()
def eval_model(eval_model_obj, eval_data_source):
    ...
```

3. Finally, we must run the model training loop. For demonstration purposes, we are training the model for 5 epochs, but you are encouraged to run it for longer in order to get better performance:

```
min_validation_loss = float("inf")
eps = 5
best_model_so_far = None
for ep in range(1, eps + 1):
    ep_time_start = time.time()
    train_model()
    validation_loss = eval_model(transformer_model,
validation_data)
    if validation_loss < min_validation_loss:
        min_validation_loss = validation_loss
        best_model_so_far = transformer_model
```

This should result in the following output:

```
epoch 1, 100/1018 batches, training loss 8.50, training perplexity 4901.66
epoch 1, 200/1018 batches, training loss 7.16, training perplexity 1286.24
epoch 1, 300/1018 batches, training loss 6.76, training perplexity 865.43
epoch 1, 400/1018 batches, training loss 6.55, training perplexity 702.21
epoch 1, 500/1018 batches, training loss 6.45, training perplexity 631.90
epoch 1, 600/1018 batches, training loss 6.31, training perplexity 548.01
epoch 1, 700/1018 batches, training loss 6.25, training perplexity 516.28
epoch 1, 800/1018 batches, training loss 6.11, training perplexity 450.42
epoch 1, 900/1018 batches, training loss 6.09, training perplexity 441.72
epoch 1, 1000/1018 batches, training loss 6.08, training perplexity 436.78

epoch 1, validation loss 5.82, validation perplexity 336.19

epoch 2, 100/1018 batches, training loss 5.98, training perplexity 394.64
epoch 2, 200/1018 batches, training loss 5.90, training perplexity 364.08
                                  ⋮



epoch 5, 700/1018 batches, training loss 5.22, training perplexity 185.69
epoch 5, 800/1018 batches, training loss 5.07, training perplexity 158.79
epoch 5, 900/1018 batches, training loss 5.13, training perplexity 169.36
epoch 5, 1000/1018 batches, training loss 5.19, training perplexity 179.63

epoch 5, validation loss 5.23, validation perplexity 186.53
```

Figure 5.4 – Transformer training logs

Besides the cross-entropy loss, the perplexity is also reported. **Perplexity** is a popularly used metric in natural language processing to indicate how well a **probability distribution** (a language model, in our case) fits or predicts a sample. The lower the perplexity, the better the model is at predicting the sample. Mathematically, perplexity is just the exponential of the cross-entropy loss. Intuitively, this metric is used to indicate how perplexed or confused the model is while making predictions.

4. Once the model has been trained, we can conclude this exercise by evaluating the model's performance on the test set:

```
testing_loss = eval_model(best_model_so_far, testing_
data)
print(f"testing loss {testing_loss:.2f}, testing
perplexity {math.exp(testing_loss):.2f}")
```

This should result in the following output:

```
testing loss 5.14, testing perplexity 171.47
```

Figure 5.5 – Transformer evaluation results

In this exercise, we built a transformer model using PyTorch for the task of language modeling. We explored the transformer architecture in detail and how it is implemented in PyTorch. We used the `WikiText-2` dataset and `torchtext` functionalities to load and process the dataset. We then trained the transformer model for 5 epochs and evaluated it on a separate test set. This shall provide us with all the information we need to get started on working with transformers.

Besides the original transformer model, which was devised in 2017, a number of successors have since been developed over the years, especially around the field of language modeling, such as the following:

- **Bidirectional Encoder Representations from Transformers (BERT)**, 2018
- **Generative Pretrained Transformer (GPT)**, 2018
- **GPT-2**, 2019
- **Conditional Transformer Language Model (CTRL)**, 2019
- **Transformer-XL**, 2019
- **Distilled BERT (DistilBERT)**, 2019
- **Robustly optimized BERT pretraining Approach (RoBERTa)**, 2019
- **GPT-3**, 2020

While we will not cover these models in detail in this chapter, you can nonetheless get started with using these models with PyTorch thanks to the `transformers` library, developed by HuggingFace (`https://github.com/huggingface/transformers`). It provides pre-trained transformer family models for various tasks, such as language modeling, text classification, translation, question-answering, and so on.

Besides the models themselves, it also provides tokenizers for the respective models. For example, if we wanted to use a pre-trained BERT model for language modeling, we would need to write the following code once we have installed the `transformers` library:

```
import torch
from transformers import BertForMaskedLM, BertTokenizer
bert_model = BertForMaskedLM.from_pretrained('bert-base-
uncased')
```

```
token_gen = BertTokenizer.from_pretrained('bert-base-uncased')
ip_sequence = token_gen("I love PyTorch !", return_
tensors="pt")["input_ids"]
op = bert_model(ip_sequence, labels=ip_sequence)
total_loss, raw_preds = op[:2]
```

As we can see, it takes just a couple of lines to get started with a BERT-based language model. This demonstrates the power of the PyTorch ecosystem. You are encouraged to explore this with more complex variants, such as *Distilled BERT* or *RoBERTa*, using the transformers library. For more details, please refer to their GitHub page, which was mentioned previously.

This concludes our exploration of transformers. We did this by both building one from scratch as well as by reusing pre-trained models. The invention of transformers in the natural language processing space has been paralleled with the ImageNet moment in the field of computer vision, so this is going to be an active area of research. PyTorch will have a crucial role to play in the research and deployment of these types of models.

In the next and final section of this chapter, we will resume the neural architecture search discussions we provided at the end of *Chapter 3, Deep CNN Architectures*, where we briefly discussed the idea of generating optimal network architectures. We will explore a type of model where we do not decide what the model architecture will look like, and instead run a network generator that will find an optimal architecture for the given task. The resultant network is called a **randomly wired neural network** (**RandWireNN**) and we will develop one from scratch using PyTorch.

Developing a RandWireNN model from scratch

We discussed EfficientNets in *Chapter 3, Deep CNN Architectures*, where we explored the idea of finding the best model architecture instead of specifying it manually. RandWireNNs, or randomly wired neural networks, as the name suggests, are built on a similar concept. In this section, we will study and build our own RandWireNN model using PyTorch.

Understanding RandWireNNs

First, a random graph generation algorithm is used to generate a random graph with a predefined number of nodes. This graph is converted into a neural network by a few definitions being imposed on it, such as the following:

- **Directed**: The graph is restricted to be a directed graph, and the direction of edge is considered to be the direction of data flow in the equivalent neural network.

- **Aggregation**: Multiple incoming edges to a node (or neuron) are aggregated by weighted sum, where the weights are learnable.

- **Transformation**: Inside each node of this graph, a standard operation is applied: ReLU followed by 3x3 separable convolution (that is, a regular 3x3 convolution followed by a 1x1 pointwise convolution), followed by batch normalization. This operation is also referred to as a **ReLU-Conv-BN triplet**.

- **Distribution**: Lastly, multiple outgoing edges from each neuron carry a copy of the aforementioned triplet operation.

One final piece in the puzzle is to add a single input node (source) and a single output node (sink) to this graph in order to fully transform the random graph into a neural network. Once the graph is realized as a neural network, it can be trained for various machine learning tasks.

In the **ReLU-Conv-BN triplet unit**, the output number of channels/features are the same as the input number of channels/features for repeatability reasons. However, depending on the type of task at hand, you can stage several of these graphs with an increasing number of channels downstream (and decreasing spatial size of the data/images). Finally, these staged graphs can be connected to each other by connecting the sink of one to the source of the other in a sequential manner.

Next, in the form of an exercise, we will build a RandWireNN model from scratch using PyTorch.

Developing RandWireNNs using PyTorch

We will now develop a RandWireNN model for an image classification task. This will be performed on the CIFAR-10 dataset. We will start from an empty model, generate a random graph, transform it into a neural network, train it for the given task on the given dataset, evaluate the trained model, and finally explore the resulting model that was generated. In this exercise, we will only show the important parts of the code for demonstration purposes. In order to access the full code, visit `https://github.com/PacktPublishing/Mastering-PyTorch/blob/master/Chapter05/rand_wire_nn.ipynb`.

Defining a training routine and loading data

In the first sub-section of this exercise, we will define the training function that will be called by our model training loop and define our dataset loader, which will provide us with batches of data for training. Let's get started:

1. First, we need to import some libraries. Some of the new libraries that will be used in this exercise are as follows:

    ```
    from torchviz import make_dot
    import networkx as nx
    ```

2. Next, we must define the training routine, which takes in a trained model that can produce prediction probabilities given an RGB input image:

    ```
    def train(model, train_dataloader, optim, loss_func,
    epoch_num, lrate):
        for training_data, training_label in train_
    dataloader:
            pred_raw = model(training_data)
            curr_loss = loss_func(pred_raw, training_label)
            training_loss += curr_loss.data
        return training_loss / data_size, training_accuracy /
    data_size
    ```

3. Next, we define the dataset loader. We will use the `CIFAR-10` dataset for this image classification task, which is a well-known database of 60,000 32x32 RGB images labeled across 10 different classes containing 6,000 images per class. We will use the `torchvision.datasets` module to directly load the data from the torch dataset repository.

    > **Dataset Citation**
    >
    > *Learning Multiple Layers of Features from Tiny Images*, Alex Krizhevsky, 2009.

    The code is as follows:

    ```
    def load_dataset(batch_size):
        train_dataloader = torch.utils.data.DataLoader(
            datasets.CIFAR10('dataset', transform=transform_
    train_dataset, train=True, download=True),
            batch_size=batch_size,  shuffle=True)
    ```

```
    return train_dataloader, test_dataloader
train_dataloader, test_dataloader = load_dataset(batch_
size)
```

This should give us the following output:

```
Downloading https://www.cs.toronto.edu/~kriz/cifar-10-python.tar.gz to dataset/cifar-10-python.tar.gz

████████████████████████  170500096/? [03:10<00:00, 889623.81it/s]

Extracting dataset/cifar-10-python.tar.gz to dataset
```

Figure 5.6 – RandWireNN data loading

We will now move on to designing the neural network model. For this, we will need to design the randomly wired graph.

Defining the randomly wired graph

In this section, we will define a graph generator in order to generate a random graph that will be later used as a neural network. Let's get started:

As shown in the following code, we must define the random graph generator class:

```
class RndGraph(object):
    def __init__(self, num_nodes, graph_probability, nearest_
neighbour_k=4, num_edges_attach=5):
    def make_graph_obj(self):
        graph_obj = nx.random_graphs.connected_watts_strogatz_
graph(self.num_nodes, self.nearest_neighbour_k,
self.graph_probability)
        return graph_obj
```

In this exercise, we'll be using a well-known random graph model – the **Watts Strogatz (WS)** model. This is one of the three models that was experimented on in the original research paper about RandWireNNs. In this model, there are two parameters:

- The number of neighbors for each node (which should be strictly even), K

- A rewiring probability, P

First, all the N nodes of the graph are organized in a ring fashion and each node is connected to $K/2$ nodes to its left and $K/2$ to its right. Then, we traverse each node clockwise $K/2$ times. At the mth traversal ($0<m<K/2$), the edge between the current node and its mth neighbor to the right is *rewired* with a probability, P.

Here, rewiring means that the edge is replaced by another edge between the current node and another node different from itself, as well as the *m*th neighbor. In the preceding code, the make_graph_obj method of our random graph generator class instantiates the WS graph model using the networkx library.

In the preceding code, the make_graph_obj method of our random graph generator class instantiates the WS graph model using the networkx library.

Furthermore, we add a get_graph_config method to return the list of nodes and edges in the graph. This will come in handy while we're transforming the abstract graph into a neural network. We will also define some graph saving and loading methods for caching the generated graph both for reproducibility and efficiency reasons:

```
def get_graph_config(self, graph_obj):
    return node_list, incoming_edges
def save_graph(self, graph_obj, path_to_write):
    nx.write_yaml(graph_obj, "./cached_graph_obj/" + path_
to_write)
def load_graph(self, path_to_read):
    return nx.read_yaml("./cached_graph_obj/" + path_to_
read)
```

Next, we will work on creating the actual neural network model.

Defining RandWireNN model modules

Now that we have the random graph generator, we need to transform it into a neural network. But before that, we will design some neural modules to facilitate that transformation. Let's get started:

1. Starting from the lowest level of the neural network, first, we will define a separable 2D convolutional layer, as follows:

```
class SepConv2d(nn.Module):
    def __init__(self, input_ch, output_ch, kernel_
length=3, dilation_size=1, padding_size=1, stride_
length=1, bias_flag=True):
        super(SepConv2d, self).__init__()
        self.conv_layer = nn.Conv2d(input_ch, input_ch,
kernel_length, stride_length, padding_size, dilation_
size, bias=bias_flag, groups=input_ch)
```

```
        self.pointwise_layer = nn.Conv2d(input_
ch, output_ch, kernel_size=1, stride=1, padding=0,
dilation=1, groups=1, bias=bias_flag)
    def forward(self, x):
        return self.pointwise_layer(self.conv_layer(x))
```

The separable convolutional layer is a cascade of a regular 3x3 2D convolutional layer followed by a pointwise 1x1 2D convolutional layer.

Having defined the separable 2D convolutional layer, we can now define the ReLU-Conv-BN triplet unit:

```
class UnitLayer(nn.Module):
    def __init__(self, input_ch, output_ch, stride_
length=1):
        self.unit_layer = nn.Sequential(
            nn.ReLU(),
            SepConv2d(input_ch, output_ch, stride_
length=stride_length),nn.BatchNorm2d(output_ch),nn.
Dropout(self.dropout)
        )
    def forward(self, x):
        return self.unit_layer(x)
```

As we mentioned earlier, the triplet unit is a cascade of a ReLU layer, followed by a separable 2D convolutional layer, followed by a batch normalization layer. We must also add a dropout layer for regularization.

With the triplet unit in place, we can now define a node in the graph with all of the aggregation, transformation, and distribution functionalities we need, as discussed at the beginning of this exercise:

```
class GraphNode(nn.Module):
    def __init__(self, input_degree, input_ch, output_ch,
stride_length=1):
        self.unit_layer = UnitLayer(input_ch, output_ch,
stride_length=stride_length)
    def forward(self, *ip):
```

```
        if len(self.input_degree) > 1:
            op = (ip[0] * torch.sigmoid(self.params[0]))
            for idx in range(1, len(ip)):
                op += (ip[idx] * torch.sigmoid(self.
params[idx]))
            return self.unit_layer(op)
        else:
            return self.unit_layer(ip[0])
```

In the `forward` method, we can see that if the number of incoming edges to the node is more than 1, then a weighted average is calculated and these weights are learnable parameters of this node. The triplet unit is applied to the weighted average and the transformed (ReLU-Conv-BN-ed) output is returned.

2. We can now consolidate all of our graph and graph node definitions in order to define a randomly wired graph class, as shown here:

```
class RandWireGraph(nn.Module):
    def __init__(self, num_nodes, graph_prob, input_ch,
output_ch, train_mode, graph_name):
        # get graph nodes and in edges
        rnd_graph_node = RndGraph(self.num_nodes, self.
graph_prob)
        if self.train_mode is True:
            rnd_graph = rnd_graph_node.make_graph_obj()
            self.node_list, self.incoming_edge_list =
rnd_graph_node.get_graph_config(rnd_graph)
        else:
        # define source Node
        self.list_of_modules =
nn.ModuleList([GraphNode(self.incoming_edge_list[0],
self.input_ch, self.output_ch,
stride_length=2)])
        # define the sink Node
        self.list_of_modules.extend([GraphNode(self.incoming_
edge_list[n], self.output_ch, self.output_ch)
                                    for n in self.node_
list if n > 0])
```

In the __init__ method of this class, first, an abstract random graph is generated. Its list of nodes and edges are derived. Using the GraphNode class, each abstract node of this abstract random graph is encapsulated as a neuron of the desired neural network. Finally, a source or input node and a sink or an output node are added to the network to make the neural network ready for the image classification task.

The forward method is also unconventional, as shown here:

```
    def forward(self, x):
        # source vertex
        op = self.list_of_modules[0].forward(x)
        mem_dict[0] = op
        # the rest of the vertices
        for n in range(1, len(self.node_list) - 1):
            if len(self.incoming_edge_list[n]) > 1:
                op = self.list_of_modules[n].
forward(*[mem_dict[incoming_vtx]

for incoming_vtx in self.incoming_edge_list[n]])
            mem_dict[n] = op
        for incoming_vtx in range(1, len(self.incoming_
edge_list[self.num_nodes + 1])):
            op += mem_dict[self.incoming_edge_list[self.
num_nodes + 1][incoming_vtx]]
        return op / len(self.incoming_edge_list[self.num_
nodes + 1])
```

First, a forward pass is run for the source neuron, and then a series of forward passes are run for the subsequent neurons based on the list_of_nodes for the graph. The individual forward passes are executed using list_of_modules. Finally, the forward pass through the sink neuron gives us the output of this graph.

Next, we will use these defined modules and the randomly wired graph class to build the actual RandWireNN model class.

Transforming a random graph into a neural network

In the previous step, we defined one randomly wired graph. However, as we mentioned at the beginning of this exercise, a randomly wired neural network consists of several staged randomly wired graphs. The rationale behind that is to have a different (increasing) number of channels/features as we progress from the input neuron to the output neuron in an image classification task. This would be impossible with just one randomly wired graph because the number of channels is constant through one such graph, by design. Let's get started:

1. In this step, we define the ultimate randomly wired neural network. This will have three randomly wired graphs cascaded next to each other. Each graph will have double the number of channels compared to the previous graph to help us align with the general practice of increasing the number of channels (while downsampling spatially) in an image classification task:

```python
class RandWireNNModel(nn.Module):
    def __init__(self, num_nodes, graph_prob, input_ch,
output_ch, train_mode):
        self.conv_layer_1 = nn.Sequential(
            nn.Conv2d(in_channels=3, out_channels=self.
output_ch, kernel_size=3, padding=1),
            nn.BatchNorm2d(self.output_ch) )
        self.conv_layer_2 = …
        self.conv_layer_3 = …
        self.conv_layer_4 = …
        self.classifier_layer = nn.Sequential(
            nn.Conv2d(in_channels=self.input_ch*8, out_
channels=1280, kernel_size=1), nn.BatchNorm2d(1280))
        self.output_layer = nn.Sequential(nn.
Dropout(self.dropout), nn.Linear(1280, self.class_num))
```

The __init__ method starts with a regular 3x3 convolutional layer, followed by three staged randomly wired graphs with channels that double in terms of numbers. This is followed by a fully connected layer that flattens the convolutional output from the last neuron of the last randomly wired graph into a vector that's 1280 in size.

2. Finally, another fully connected layer produces a 10-sized vector containing the probabilities for the 10 classes, as follows:

```python
def forward(self, x):
    x = self.conv_layer_1(x)
```

```
x = self.conv_layer_2(x)
x = self.conv_layer_3(x)
x = self.conv_layer_4(x)
x = self.classifier_layer(x)
# global average pooling
_, _, h, w = x.size()
x = F.avg_pool2d(x, kernel_size=[h, w])
x = torch.squeeze(x)
x = self.output_layer(x)
return x
```

The `forward` method is quite self-explanatory, besides the global average pooling that is applied right after the first fully connected layer. This helps reduce dimensionality and the number of parameters in the network.

At this stage, we have successfully defined the RandWireNN model, loaded the datasets, and defined the model training routine. Now, we are all set to run the model training loop.

Training the RandWireNN model

In this section, we will set the model's hyperparameters and train the RandWireNN model. Let's get started:

1. We have defined all the building blocks for our exercise. Now, it is time to execute it. First, let's declare the necessary hyperparameters:

```
num_epochs = 5
graph_probability = 0.7
node_channel_count = 64
num_nodes = 16
lrate = 0.1
batch_size = 64
train_mode = True
```

2. Having declared the hyperparameters, we instantiate the RandWireNN model, along with the optimizer and loss function:

```
rand_wire_model = RandWireNNModel(num_nodes, graph_
probability, node_channel_count, node_channel_count,
train_mode).to(device)
```

```
optim_module = optim.SGD(rand_wire_model.parameters(),
lr=lrate, weight_decay=1e-4, momentum=0.8)
loss_func = nn.CrossEntropyLoss().to(device)
```

3. Finally, we begin training the model. We're training the model for 5 epochs here for demonstration purposes, but you are encouraged to train for longer to see the boost in performance:

```
for ep in range(1, num_epochs + 1):
    epochs.append(ep)
    training_loss, training_accuracy = train(rand_wire_
model, train_dataloader, optim_module, loss_func, ep,
lrate)
    test_accuracy = accuracy(rand_wire_model, test_
dataloader)
    test_accuracies.append(test_accuracy)
    training_losses.append(training_loss)
    training_accuracies.append(training_accuracy)
    if best_test_accuracy < test_accuracy:
        torch.save(model_state, './model_checkpoint/' +
model_filename + 'ckpt.t7')
    print("model train time: ", time.time() - start_time)
```

This should result in the following output:

```
epoch 1, loss: 1.8047572374343872, accuracy: 32.8125
epoch 1, loss: 1.8053011894226074, accuracy: 39.0625
epoch 1, loss: 1.5705406665802002, accuracy: 40.625
epoch 1, loss: 1.7380733489990234, accuracy: 29.6875
epoch 1, loss: 1.7764639854431152, accuracy: 32.8125
epoch 1, loss: 1.425702691078186, accuracy: 37.5
epoch 1, loss: 1.3414183855056763, accuracy: 51.5625
test acc: 43.24%, best test acc: 0.00%
model train time:  3522.6173169612885
epoch 2, loss: 1.5954769849777222, accuracy: 45.3125
epoch 2, loss: 1.3833452463150024, accuracy: 53.125
epoch 2, loss: 1.370549201965332, accuracy: 43.75
epoch 2, loss: 1.3685939311981201, accuracy: 54.6875
epoch 2, loss: 1.4633197784423828, accuracy: 48.4375
epoch 2, loss: 1.2918241024017334, accuracy: 50.0
epoch 2, loss: 1.317800521850586, accuracy: 50.0
test acc: 51.04%, best test acc: 43.24%
model train time:  6938.013380050659
epoch 3, loss: 1.0907424688339233, accuracy: 59.375
                        ⋮

epoch 5, loss: 1.2000718116760254, accuracy: 62.5
test acc: 67.45%, best test acc: 67.73%
```

Figure 5.7 – RandWireNN training logs

It is evident from these logs that the model is progressively learning as the epochs progress. The performance on the validation set seems to be consistently increasing, which indicates model generalizability.

With that, we have created a model with no particular architecture in mind that can reasonably perform the task of image classification on the CIFAR-10 dataset.

Evaluating and visualizing the RandWireNN model

Finally, we will look at this model's test set performance before briefly exploring the model architecture visually. Let's get started:

1. Once the model has been trained, we can evaluate it on the test set:

```
rand_wire_nn_model.load_state_dict(model_
checkpoint['model'])
for test_data, test_label in test_dataloader:
    success += pred.eq(test_label.data).sum()
    print(f"test accuracy: {float(success) * 100. /
len(test_dataloader.dataset)} %")
```

This should result in the following output:

```
best model accuracy: 67.73%, last epoch: 4
```

Figure 5.8 – RandWireNN evaluation results

The best performing model was found at the fourth epoch, with over 67% accuracy. Although the model is not perfect yet, we can train it for more epochs to achieve better performance. Also, a random model for this task would perform at an accuracy of 10% (because of 10 equally likely classes), so an accuracy of 67.73% is still promising, especially given the fact that we are using a randomly generated neural network architecture.

2. To conclude this exercise, let's look at the model architecture that was learned. The original image is too large to be displayed here. You can find the full image in .svg format at https://github.com/PacktPublishing/Mastering-PyTorch/blob/master/Chapter05/randwirenn.svg and in .png format at https://github.com/PacktPublishing/Mastering-PyTorch/blob/master/Chapter05/randwirenn%5Brepresentational_purpose_only%5D.png. In the following figure, we have vertically stacked three parts - the input section, a mid section and the output section, of the original neural network:

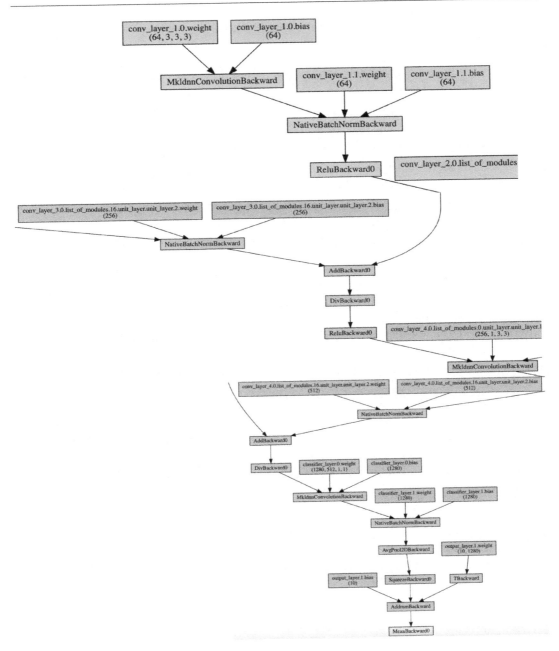

Figure 5.9 – RandWireNN architecture

From this graph, we can observe the following key points:

- At the top, we can see the beginning of this neural network, which consists of a 64-channel 3x3 2D convolutional layer, followed by a 64-channel 1x1 pointwise 2D convolutional layer.

- In the middle section, we can see the transition between the third- and fourth-stage random graphs, where we can see the sink neuron, `conv_layer_3`, of the stage 3 random graph followed by the source neuron `conv_layer_4`, of the stage 4 random graph.

- Lastly, the lowermost section of the graph shows the final output layers – the sink neuron (a 512-channel separable 2D convolutional layer) of the stage 4 random graph, followed by a fully connected flattening layer, resulting in a 1,280-size feature vector, followed by a fully connected softmax layer that produces the 10 class probabilities.

Hence, we have built, trained, tested, and visualized a neural network model for image classification without specifying any particular model architecture. We did specify some overarching constraints over the structure, such as the penultimate feature vector length (`1280`), the number of channels in the separable 2D convolutional layers (`64`), the number of stages in the RandWireNN model (`4`), the definition of each neuron (ReLU-Conv-BN triplet), and so on.

However, we didn't specify what the structure of this neural network architecture should look like. We used a random graph generator to do this for us, which opens up an almost infinite number of possibilities in terms of finding optimal neural network architectures.

Neural architecture search is an ongoing and promising area of research in the field of deep learning. Largely, this fits in well with the field of training custom machine learning models for specific tasks, referred to as AutoML.

AutoML stands for **automated machine learning** as it does away with the necessity of having to manually load datasets, predefine a particular neural network model architecture to solve a given task, and manually deploy models into production systems. In *Chapter 12, PyTorch and AutoML*, we will discuss AutoML in detail and learn how to build such systems with PyTorch.

Summary

In this chapter, we looked at two distinct hybrid types of neural networks. First, we looked at the transformer model – the attention-only-based models with no recurrent connections that have outperformed all recurrent models on multiple sequential tasks. We ran through an exercise where we built, trained, and evaluated a transformer model on a language modeling task with the WikiText-2 dataset using PyTorch. During this exercise, we explored the transformer architecture in detail, both through explained architectural diagrams as well as relevant PyTorch code.

We concluded the first section by briefly discussing the successors of transformers – models such as BERT, GPT, and so on. We demonstrated how PyTorch helps in getting started with loading pre-trained versions of most of these advanced models in less than five lines of code.

In the second and final section of this chapter, we took up from where we left off in *Chapter 3, Deep CNN Architectures*, where we discussed the idea of optimizing for model architectures rather than optimizing for just the model parameters while fixing the architecture. We explored one of the approaches to do that – using randomly wired neural networks (RandWireNNs) – where we generated random graphs, assigned meanings to the nodes and edges of these graphs, and interconnected these graphs to form a neural network.

We built, trained, and evaluated a RandWireNN model for the task of image classification on the CIFAR-10 dataset. We also visually investigated the resultant model architecture and zoomed into certain parts of it to understand what network structure had been generated for the task.

In the next chapter, we will switch gears and move away from model architectures and look at some interesting PyTorch applications. We will learn how to generate music and text through generative deep learning models using PyTorch.

Section 3: Generative Models and Deep Reinforcement Learning

In this section, we will dive deep into generative neural network models, including deep generative adversarial networks. We will also cover deep reinforcement learning using PyTorch. Upon completing this section, you will be able to train your own deep learning models so that they can generate music, text, images, and more. You will also know how to train players (agents) for a video game.

This section comprises the following chapters:

- *Chapter 6, Music and Text Generation with PyTorch*
- *Chapter 7, Neural Style Transfer*
- *Chapter 8, Deep Convolutional GANs*
- *Chapter 9, Deep Reinforcement Learning*

6
Music and Text Generation with PyTorch

PyTorch is a fantastic tool for both researching deep learning models and developing deep learning-based applications. In the previous chapters, we looked at model architectures across various domains and model types. We used PyTorch to build these architectures from scratch and used pre-trained models from the PyTorch model zoo. We will switch gears from this chapter onward and dive deep into generative models.

In the previous chapters, most of our examples and exercises revolved around developing models for classification, which is a supervised learning task. However, deep learning models have also proven extremely effective when it comes to unsupervised learning tasks. Deep generative models are one such example. These models are trained using lots of unlabeled data. Once trained, the model can generate similar meaningful data. It does so by learning the underlying structure and patterns in the input data.

In this chapter, we will develop text and music generators. For developing the text generator, we will utilize the transformer-based language model we trained in *Chapter 5, Hybrid Advanced Models*. We will extend the transformer model using PyTorch so that it works as a text generator. Furthermore, we will demonstrate how to use advanced pre-trained transformer models in PyTorch in order to set up a text generator in a few lines of code. Finally, we will build a music generator model that's been trained on an MIDI dataset from scratch using PyTorch.

By the end of this chapter, you should be able to create your own text and music generation models in PyTorch. You will also be able to apply different sampling or generation strategies to generate data from such models. This chapter covers the following topics:

- Building a transformer-based text generator with PyTorch

- Using a pre-trained GPT 2 model as a text generator

- Generating MIDI music with LSTMs using PyTorch

Technical requirements

We will be using Jupyter notebooks for all our exercises. The following is a list of Python libraries that you need to install for this chapter using `pip`; for example, run `pip install torch==1.4.0` on the command line:

```
jupyter==1.0.0
torch==1.4.0
tqdm==4.43.0
matplotlib==3.1.2
torchtext==0.5.0
transformers==3.0.2
scikit-image==0.14.2
```

All the code files that are relevant to this chapter are available at `https://github.com/PacktPublishing/Mastering-PyTorch/tree/master/Chapter06`.

Building a transformer-based text generator with PyTorch

We built a transformer-based language model using PyTorch in the previous chapter. Because a language model models the probability of a certain word following a given sequence of words, we are more than half-way through in building our own text generator. In this section, we will learn how to extend this language model as a deep generative model that can generate arbitrary yet meaningful sentences, given an initial textual cue in the form of a sequence of words.

Training the transformer-based language model

In the previous chapter, we trained a language model for 5 epochs. In this section, we will follow those exact same steps but will train the model for longer; that is, 50 epochs. The goal here is to obtain a better performing language model that can then generate realistic sentences. Please note that model training can take several hours. Hence, it is recommended to train it in the background; for example, overnight. In order to follow the steps for training the language model, please follow the complete code at `https://github.com/PacktPublishing/Mastering-PyTorch/blob/master/Chapter06/text_generation.ipynb`.

Upon training for 50 epochs, we get the following output:

```
epoch 1, 100/1018 batches, training loss 8.63, training perplexity 5614.45
epoch 1, 200/1018 batches, training loss 7.23, training perplexity 1380.31
epoch 1, 300/1018 batches, training loss 6.79, training perplexity 892.50
epoch 1, 400/1018 batches, training loss 6.55, training perplexity 701.84
epoch 1, 500/1018 batches, training loss 6.45, training perplexity 634.57
epoch 1, 600/1018 batches, training loss 6.32, training perplexity 553.86
epoch 1, 700/1018 batches, training loss 6.24, training perplexity 513.65
epoch 1, 800/1018 batches, training loss 6.13, training perplexity 459.07
epoch 1, 900/1018 batches, training loss 6.11, training perplexity 450.48
epoch 1, 1000/1018 batches, training loss 6.07, training perplexity 433.88

epoch 1, validation loss 5.82, validation perplexity 337.70

epoch 2, 100/1018 batches, training loss 5.98, training perplexity 395.15
epoch 2, 200/1018 batches, training loss 5.90, training perplexity 363.99

                                 :
                                 :
                                 :

epoch 50, 100/1018 batches, training loss 4.45, training perplexity 85.55
epoch 50, 200/1018 batches, training loss 4.38, training perplexity 79.68
epoch 50, 300/1018 batches, training loss 4.39, training perplexity 80.61
epoch 50, 400/1018 batches, training loss 4.39, training perplexity 80.27
epoch 50, 500/1018 batches, training loss 4.39, training perplexity 80.31
epoch 50, 600/1018 batches, training loss 4.38, training perplexity 80.17
epoch 50, 700/1018 batches, training loss 4.41, training perplexity 82.47
epoch 50, 800/1018 batches, training loss 4.26, training perplexity 71.00
epoch 50, 900/1018 batches, training loss 4.33, training perplexity 76.24
epoch 50, 1000/1018 batches, training loss 4.36, training perplexity 78.51

epoch 50, validation loss 4.98, validation perplexity 145.72
```

Figure 6.1 – Language model training logs

Now that we have successfully trained the transformer model for 50 epochs, we can move on to the actual exercise, where we will extend this trained language model as a text generation model.

Saving and loading the language model

Here, we will simply save the best performing model checkpoint once the training is complete. We can then separately load this pre-trained model:

1. Once the model has been trained, it is ideal to save it locally so that you avoid having to retrain it from scratch. You can save it as follows:

```
mdl_pth = './transformer.pth'
torch.save(best_model_so_far.state_dict(), mdl_pth)
```

2. We can now load the saved model so that we can extend this language model as a text generation model:

```
# load the best trained model
transformer_cached = Transformer(num_tokens, embedding_
size, num_heads, num_hidden_params, num_layers, dropout).
to(device)
transformer_cached.load_state_dict(torch.load(mdl_pth))
```

In this section, we re-instantiated a transformer model object and then loaded the pre-trained model weights into this new model object. Next, we will use this model to generate text.

Using the language model to generate text

Now that the model has been saved and loaded, we can extend the trained language model to generate text:

1. First, we must define the target number of words we want to generate and provide an initial sequence of words as a cue to the model:

```
ln = 10
sntc = 'It will _'
sntc_split = sntc.split()
```

2. Finally, we can generate the words one by one in a loop. At each iteration, we can
    append the predicted word in that iteration to the input sequence. This extended
    sequence becomes the input to the model in the next iteration and so on. The
    random seed is added to ensure consistency. By changing the seed, we can generate
    different texts, as shown in the following code block:

```
torch.manual_seed(799)
with torch.no_grad():
    for i in range(ln):
        sntc = ' '.join(sntc_split)
        txt_ds = TEXT.numericalize([sntc_split])
        num_b = txt_ds.size(0)
        txt_ds = txt_ds.narrow(0, 0, num_b)
        txt_ds = txt_ds.view(1, -1).t().contiguous().
to(device)
        ev_X, _ = return_batch(txt_ds, i+1)
        op = transformer_cached(ev_X)
        op_flat = op.view(-1, num_tokens)
        res = TEXT.vocab.itos[op_flat.argmax(1)[0]]
        sntc_split.insert(-1, res)
print(sntc[:-2])
```

This should output the following:

It will be used to the first season , and the

Figure 6.2 – Transformer generated text

As we can see, using PyTorch, we can train a language model (a transformer-based model,
in this case) and then use it to generate text with a few additional lines of code. The
generated text seems to make sense. The result of such text generators is limited by the
amount of data the underlying language model is trained on, as well as how powerful the
language model is. In this section, we have essentially built a text generator from scratch.

In the next section, we will load the pre-trained language model and use it as a text
generator. We will be using an advanced successor of the transformer model – the
generative pre-trained transformer (GPT-2). We will demonstrate how to build an
out-of-the-box advanced text generator using PyTorch in less than 10 lines of code. We
will also look at some strategies involved in generating text from a language model.

Using a pre-trained GPT-2 model as a text generator

Using the `transformers` library together with PyTorch, we can load most of the latest advanced transformer models for performing various tasks such as language modeling, text classification, machine translation, and so on. We demonstrated how to do so in *Chapter 5, Hybrid Advanced Models*.

In this section, we will load the pre-trained GPT-2-based language model. We will then extend this model so that we can use it as a text generator. Then, we will explore the various strategies we can follow to generate text from a pre-trained language model and use PyTorch to demonstrate those strategies.

Out-of-the-box text generation with GPT-2

In the form of an exercise, we will load a pre-trained GPT-2 language model using the transformers library and extend this language model as a text generation model to generate arbitrary yet meaningful texts. We will only show the important parts of the code for demonstration purposes. In order to access the full code, go to https://github.com/PacktPublishing/Mastering-PyTorch/blob/master/Chapter06/text_generation_out_of_the_box.ipynb. Follow these steps:

1. First, we need to import the necessary libraries:

   ```
   from transformers import GPT2LMHeadModel, GPT2Tokenizer
   import torch
   ```

   We will import the GPT-2 multi-head language model and corresponding tokenizer to generate the vocabulary.

2. Next, we will instantiate `GPT2Tokenizer` and the language model. Setting a random seed will ensure repeatable results. We can change the seed to generate different texts each time. Finally, we will provide an initial set of words as a cue to the model, as follows:

   ```
   torch.manual_seed(799)
   tkz = GPT2Tokenizer.from_pretrained("gpt2")
   mdl = GPT2LMHeadModel.from_pretrained('gpt2')
   ln = 10
   cue = "It will"
   ```

```
gen = tkz.encode(cue)
ctx = torch.tensor([gen])
```

3. Finally, we will iteratively predict the next word for a given input sequence of words using the language model. At each iteration, the predicted word is appended to the input sequence of words for the next iteration:

```
prv=None
for i in range(ln):
    op, prv = mdl(ctx, past=prv)
    tkn = torch.argmax(op[..., -1, :])
    gen += [tkn.tolist()]
    ctx = tkn.unsqueeze(0)
seq = tkz.decode(gen)
print(seq)
```

The output should be as follows:

`It will be interesting to see how the new system works`

Figure 6.3 – GPT-2 generated text

This way of generating text is also called **greedy search**. In the next section, we will look at greedy search in more detail and some other text generation strategies as well.

Text generation strategies using PyTorch

When we use a trained text generation model to generate text, we typically make predictions word by word. We then consolidate the resulting sequence of predicted words as predicted text. When we are in a loop iterating over word predictions, we need to specify a method of finding/predicting the next word given the previous k predictions. These methods are also known as text generation strategies, and we will discuss some well-known strategies in this section.

Greedy search

The name *greedy* is justified by the fact that the model selects the word with the maximum probability at the current iteration, regardless of how many time steps further ahead they are. With this strategy, the model could potentially miss a highly probable word hiding (further ahead in time) behind a low probability word, merely because the model did not pursue the low probability word. The following diagram demonstrates the greedy search strategy by illustrating a hypothetical scenario of what might be happening under the hood in *step 3* of the previous exercise. At each time step, the text generation model outputs possible words, along with their probabilities:

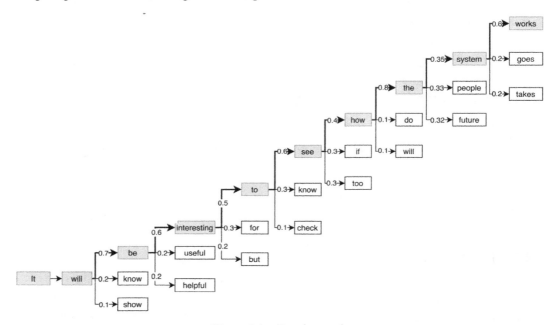

Figure 6.4 – Greedy search

As we can see, at each step, the word with the highest probability is picked up by the model under the greedy search strategy of text generation. Note the penultimate step, where the model predicts the words **system**, **people**, and **future** with roughly equal probabilities. With greedy search, **system** is selected as the next word due to it having a slightly higher probability than the rest. However, you could argue that **people** or **future** could have led to a better or more meaningful generated text.

This is the core limitation of the greedy search approach. Besides, greedy search also results in repetitive results due to a lack of randomness. If someone wants to use such a text generator artistically, greedy search is not the best approach, merely due to its monotonicity.

In the previous section, we manually wrote the text generation loop. Thanks to the transformers library, we can write the text generation step in three lines of code:

```
ip_ids = tkz.encode(cue, return_tensors='pt')
op_greedy = mdl.generate(ip_ids, max_length=ln)
seq = tkz.decode(op_greedy[0], skip_special_tokens=True)
print(seq)
```

This should output the following:

It will be interesting to see how the new system

Figure 6.5 – GPT-2 generated text (concise)

Notice that the generated sentence shown in Figure 6.5 has one word less than the sentence that was generated in *Figure 6.3*. This difference is because in the latter code, the max_length argument includes the cue words. So, if we have one cue word, nine new words would be predicted. If we have two cue words, eight new words would be predicted (as is the case here), and so on.

Beam search

Greedy search is not the only way of generating texts. **Beam search** is a development of the greedy search method wherein we maintain a list of potential candidate sequences based on the overall predicted sequence probability, rather than just the next word probability. The number of candidate sequences to be pursued is the number of beams along the tree of word predictions.

The following diagram demonstrates how beam search with a beam size of three would be used to produce three candidate sequences (ordered as per the overall sequence probability) of five words each:

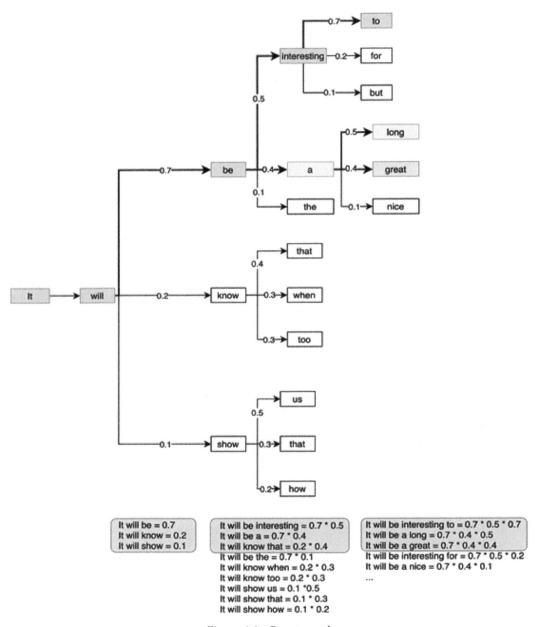

Figure 6.6 – Beam search

At each iteration in this beam search example, the three most likely candidate sequences are maintained. As we proceed further in the sequence, the possible number of candidate sequences increases exponentially. However, we are only interested in the top three sequences. This way, we do not miss potentially better sequences as we might with greedy search.

In PyTorch, we can use beam search out of the box in one line of code. The following code demonstrates beam search-based text generation with three beams generating the three most likely sentences, each containing five words:

```
op_beam = mdl.generate(
    ip_ids,
    max_length=5,
    num_beams=3,
    num_return_sequences=3,
)
for op_beam_cur in op_beam:
    print(tkz.decode(op_beam_cur, skip_special_tokens=True))
```

This gives us the following output:

```
It will be interesting to
It will be a long
It will be a great
```

Figure 6.7 – Beam search results

The problem of repetitiveness or monotonicity still remains with the beam search. Different runs would result in the same set of results as it deterministically looks for the sequence with the maximum overall probabilities. In the next section, we will look at some of the ways we can make the generated text more unpredictable or creative.

Top-k and top-p sampling

Instead of always picking the next word with the highest probability, we can randomly sample the next word out of the possible set of next words based on their relative probabilities. For example, in *Figure 6.6*, the words **be**, **know**, and **show** have probabilities of **0.7**, **0.2**, and **0.1**, respectively. Instead of always picking **be** against **know** and **show**, we can randomly sample any one of these three words based on their probabilities. If we repeat this exercise 10 times to generate 10 separate texts, **be** will be chosen roughly seven times and **know** and **show** will be chosen two and one times, respectively. This gives us far too many different possible combinations of words that beam or greedy search would never generate.

Two of the most popular ways of generating texts using sampling techniques are known as **top-k** and **top-p** sampling. Under top-k sampling, we predefine a parameter, *k*, which is the number of candidate words that should be considered while sampling the next word. All the other words are discarded, and the probabilities are normalized among the top *k* words. In our previous example, if *k* is 2, then the word **show** will be discarded and the words **be** and **know** will have their probabilities (**0.7** and **0.2**, respectively) normalized to **0.78** and **0.22**, respectively.

The following code demonstrates the top-k text generation method:

```
for i in range(3):
    torch.manual_seed(i)
    op = mdl.generate(
        ip_ids,
        do_sample=True,
        max_length=5,
        top_k=2
    )
    seq = tkz.decode(op[0], skip_special_tokens=True)
    print(seq)
```

This should generate the following output:

```
It will also be a
It will be a long
It will also be interesting
```

Figure 6.8 – Top-k search results

To sample from all possible words, instead of just the top-k words, we shall set the `top-k` argument to 0 in our code. As shown in the preceding screenshot, different runs produce different results as opposed to greedy search, which would result in the exact same result on each run, as shown in the following screenshot:

```
for i in range(3):
    torch.manual_seed(i)
    op_greedy = mdl.generate(ip_ids, max_length=5)
    seq = tkz.decode(op_greedy[0], skip_special_tokens=True)
    print(seq)
```

```
It will be interesting to
It will be interesting to
It will be interesting to
```

Figure 6.9 – Repetitive greedy search results

Under the top-p sampling strategy, instead of defining the top *k* words to look at, we can define a cumulative probability threshold (*p*) and then retain words whose probabilities add up to *p*. In our example, if *p* is between **0.7** and **0.9**, then we discard **know** and **show**, if *p* is between **0.9** and **1.0**, then we discard **show**, and if *p* is **1.0**, then we keep all three words; that is, **be**, **know**, and **show**.

The top-k strategy can sometimes be unfair in scenarios where the probability distribution is flat. This is because it clips off words that are almost as probable as the ones that have been retained. In those cases, the top-p strategy would retain a larger pool of words to sample from and would retain a smaller pool of words in cases where the probability distribution is rather sharp.

The following code demonstrates the top-p sampling method:

```
for i in range(3):
    torch.manual_seed(i)
    op = mdl.generate(
        ip_ids,
        do_sample=True,
        max_length=5,
        top_p=0.75,
        top_k=0
    )
    seq = tkz.decode(op[0], skip_special_tokens=True)
    print(seq)
```

This should output the following:

```
It will require work in
It will be an interesting
It will likely be important
```

Figure 6.10 – Top-p search results

We can set both top-k and top-p strategies together. In this example, we have set `top-k` to `0` to essentially disable the top-k strategy, and `p` is set to `0.75`. Once again, this results in different sentences across runs and can lead us to more creatively generated texts as opposed to greedy or beam search. There are many more text generation strategies available, and a lot of research is happening in this area. We encourage you to follow up on this further.

A great starting point is playing around with the available text generation strategies in the `transformers` library. You can read more about it by going to this illustrative blog post from the makers of this library: `https://huggingface.co/blog/how-to-generate`.

This concludes our exploration of using PyTorch to generate text. In the next section, we will perform a similar exercise but this time for music instead of text. The idea is to train an unsupervised model on a music dataset and use the trained model to generate melodies similar to those in the training dataset.

Generating MIDI music with LSTMs using PyTorch

Moving on from text, in this section, we will use PyTorch to create a machine learning model that can compose classical-like music. We used transformers for generating text in the previous section. Here, we will use an LSTM model to process sequential music data. We will train the model on Mozart's classical music compositions.

Each musical piece will essentially be broken down into a sequence of piano notes. We will be reading music data in the form of **Musical Instruments Digital Interface** (**MIDI**) files, which is a well-known and commonly used format for conveniently reading and writing musical data across devices and environments.

After converting the MIDI files into sequences of piano notes (which we call the piano roll), we will use them to train a next-piano-note detection system. In this system, we will build an LSTM-based classifier that will predict the next piano note for the given preceding sequence of piano notes, of which there are 88 in total (as per the standard 88 piano keys).

We will now demonstrate the entire process of building the AI music composer in the form of an exercise. Our focus will be on the PyTorch code that's used for data loading, model training, and generating music samples. Please note that the model training process may take several hours and therefore it is recommended to run the training process in the background; for example, overnight. The code presented here has been curtailed in the interest of keeping the text short.

Details of handling the MIDI music files are beyond the scope of this book, although you are encouraged to explore the full code, which is available at `https://github.com/PacktPublishing/Mastering-PyTorch/blob/master/Chapter06/music_generation.ipynb`.

Loading the MIDI music data

First, we will demonstrate how to load the music data that is available in MIDI format. We will briefly mention the code for handling MIDI data, and then illustrate how to make PyTorch dataloaders out of it. Let's get started:

1. As always, we will begin by importing the important libraries. Some of the new ones we'll be using in this exercise are as follows:

    ```
    import skimage.io as io
    from struct import pack, unpack
    from io import StringIO, BytesIO
    ```

    skimage is used to visualize the sequences of the music samples that are generated by the model. struct and io are used for handling the process of converting MIDI music data into piano rolls.

2. Next, we will write the helper classes and functions for loading MIDI files and converting them into sequences of piano notes (matrices) that can be fed to the LSTM model. First, we define some MIDI constants in order to configure various music controls such as pitch, channels, start of sequence, end of sequence, and so on:

    ```
    NOTE_MIDI_OFF = 0x80
    NOTE_MIDI_ON = 0x90
    CHNL_PRESS = 0xD0
    MIDI_PITCH_BND = 0xE0
    ...
    ```

3. Then, we will define a series of classes that will handle MIDI data input and output streams, the MIDI data parser, and so on, as follows:

    ```
    class MOStrm:
    # MIDI Output Stream
    ...
    class MIFl:
    # MIDI Input File Reader
    ...
    class MOFl(MOStrm):
    # MIDI Output File Writer
    ...
    ```

```
class RIStrFl:
# Raw Input Stream File Reader
...
class ROStrFl:
# Raw Output Stream File Writer
...
class MFlPrsr:
# MIDI File Parser
...
class EvtDspch:
# Event Dispatcher
...
class MidiDataRead(MOStrm):
# MIDI Data Reader
...
```

4. Having handled all the MIDI data I/O-related code, we are all set to instantiate our own PyTorch dataset class. Before we do that, we must define two crucial functions – one for converting the read MIDI file into a piano roll and one for padding the piano roll with empty notes. This will normalize the lengths of the musical pieces across the dataset:

```
def md_fl_to_pio_rl(md_fl):
    md_d = MidiDataRead(md_fl, dtm=0.3)
    pio_rl = md_d.pio_rl.transpose()
    pio_rl[pio_rl > 0] = 1
    return pio_rl
def pd_pio_rl(pio_rl, mx_l=132333, pd_v=0):
    orig_rol_len = pio_rl.shape[1]
    pdd_rol = np.zeros((88, mx_l))
    pdd_rol[:] = pd_v
    pdd_rol[:, - orig_rol_len:] = pio_rl
    return pdd_rol
```

5. Now, we can define our PyTorch dataset class, as follows:

```
class NtGenDataset(data.Dataset):
    def __init__(self, md_pth, mx_seq_ln=1491):
        ...
    def mx_len_upd(self):
        ...
    def __len__(self):
        return len(self.md_fnames_ful)
    def __getitem__(self, index):
        md_fname_ful = self.md_fnames_ful[index]
        pio_rl = md_fl_to_pio_rl(md_fname_ful)
        seq_len = pio_rl.shape[1] - 1
        ip_seq = pio_rl[:, :-1]
        gt_seq = pio_rl[:, 1:]
        ...
        return (torch.FloatTensor(ip_seq_pad),
                torch.LongTensor(gt_seq_pad), torch.
LongTensor([seq_len]))
```

6. Besides the dataset class, we must add another helper function to post-process the
    music sequences in a batch of training data into three separate lists. These will be
    input sequences, output sequences, and lengths of sequences, ordered by the lengths
    of the sequences in descending order:

```
def pos_proc_seq(btch):
    ip_seqs, op_seqs, lens = btch
    ...
    ord_tr_data_tups = sorted(tr_data_tups,
                                        key=lambda c:
int(c[2]),
                                        reverse=True)
    ip_seq_splt_btch, op_seq_splt_btch, btch_splt_lens =
zip(*ord_tr_data_tups)
    ...
    return tps_ip_seq_btch, ord_op_seq_btch, list(ord_
btch_lens_l)
```

7. For this exercise, we will be using a set of Mozart's compositions. You can download the dataset from here: `http://www.piano-midi.de/mozart.htm`. The downloaded folder consists of 21 MIDI files, which we will split into 18 training and three validation set files. The downloaded data is stored under `./mozart/train` and `./mozart/valid`. Once downloaded, we can read the data and instantiate our own training and validation dataset loaders:

```
training_dataset = NtGenDataset('./mozart/train', mx_seq_
ln=None)
```
```
training_datasetloader = data.DataLoader(training_
dataset, batch_size=5,shuffle=True, drop_last=True)
```
```
validation_dataset = NtGenDataset('./mozart/valid/', mx_
seq_ln=None)
```
```
validation_datasetloader = data.DataLoader(validation_
dataset, batch_size=3, shuffle=False, drop_last=False)
```
```
X_validation = next(iter(validation_datasetloader))
```
```
X_validation[0].shape
```

This should give us the following output:

torch.Size([3, 1587, 88])

Figure 6.11 – Sample music data dimensions

As we can see, the first validation batch consists of three sequences of length 1,587 (notes), where each sequence is encoded into an 88-size vector, with 88 being the total number of piano keys. For those of you who are trained musicians, here is a music sheet equivalent of the first few notes of one of the validation set music files:

Figure 6.12 – Music sheet of a Mozart composition

Alternatively, we can visualize the sequence of notes as a matrix with 88 rows, one per piano key. The following is a visual matrix representation of the preceding melody (the first 300 notes out of 1,587):

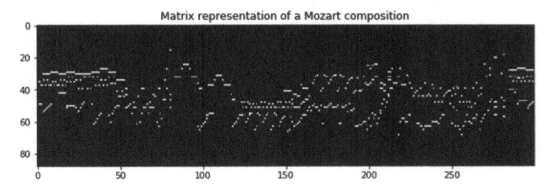

Figure 6.13 – Matrix representation of a Mozart composition

Dataset citation

The MIDI, audio (MP3, OGG), and video files of Bernd Krueger are licensed under the CC BY-SA Germany License.

Name: Bernd Krueger

Source: `http://www.piano-midi.de`

The distribution or public playback of these files is only allowed under identical license conditions.

The scores are open source.

We will now define the LSTM model and training routine.

Defining the LSTM model and training routine

So far, we have managed to successfully load a MIDI dataset and use it to create our own training and validation data loaders. In this section, we will define the LSTM model architecture, as well as the training and evaluation routines that shall be run during the model training loop. Let's get started:

1. First, we must define the model architecture. As we mentioned earlier, we will use an LSTM model that consists of an encoder layer that encodes the 88-dimensional representation of the input data at each time step of the sequence into a 512-dimensional hidden layer representation. The encoder is followed by two LSTM layers, followed by a fully connected layer that finally softmaxes into the 88 classes.

As per the different types of **recurrent neural networks** (**RNNs**) we discussed in *Chapter 4, Deep Recurrent Model Architectures*, this is a many-to-one sequence classification task, where the input is the entire sequence from time step *0* to time step *t* and the output is one of the 88 classes at time step *t+1*, as follows:

```python
class MusicLSTM(nn.Module):
    def __init__(self, ip_sz, hd_sz, n_cls, lyrs=2):
        ...
        self.nts_enc = nn.Linear(in_features=ip_sz, out_
features=hd_sz)
        self.bn_layer = nn.BatchNorm1d(hd_sz)
        self.lstm_layer = nn.LSTM(hd_sz, hd_sz, lyrs)
        self.fc_layer = nn.Linear(hd_sz, n_cls)

    def forward(self, ip_seqs, ip_seqs_len, hd=None):
        ...
        pkd = torch.nn.utils.rnn.pack_padded_
sequence(nts_enc_ful, ip_seqs_len)
        op, hd = self.lstm_layer(pkd, hd)
        ...
        lgts = self.fc_layer(op_nrm_drp.permute(2,0,1))
        ...
        zero_one_lgts = torch.stack((lgts, rev_lgts),
dim=3).contiguous()
        flt_lgts = zero_one_lgts.view(-1, 2)
        return flt_lgts, hd
```

2. Once the model architecture has been defined, we can specify the model training routine. We will use the Adam optimizer with gradient clipping to avoid overfitting. Another measure that's already in place to counter overfitting is the use of a dropout layer, as specified in the previous step:

```python
def lstm_model_training(lstm_model, lr, ep=10, val_loss_
best=float("inf")):
    ...
    for curr_ep in range(ep):
        ...
        for batch in training_datasetloader:
            ...
```

```
            lgts, _ = lstm_model(ip_seq_b_v, seq_l)
            loss = loss_func(lgts, op_seq_b_v)
            ...
        if vl_ep_cur < val_loss_best:
            torch.save(lstm_model.state_dict(), 'best_
model.pth')
            val_loss_best = vl_ep_cur
    return val_loss_best, lstm_model
```

3. Similarly, we will define the model evaluation routine, where a forward pass is run on the model with its parameters remaining unchanged:

```
def evaluate_model(lstm_model):
    ...
    for batch in validation_datasetloader:
        ...
        lgts, _ = lstm_model(ip_seq_b_v, seq_l)
        loss = loss_func(lgts, op_seq_b_v)
        vl_loss_full += loss.item()
        seq_len += sum(seq_l)
    return vl_loss_full/(seq_len*88)
```

Now, let's train and test the music generation model.

Training and testing the music generation model

In this final section, we will actually train the LSTM model. We will then use the trained music generation model to generate a music sample that we can listen to and analyze. Let's get started:

1. We are all set to instantiate our model and start training it. We have used categorical cross-entropy as the loss function for this classification task. We are training the model with a learning rate of 0.01 for 10 epochs:

```
loss_func = nn.CrossEntropyLoss().cpu()
lstm_model = MusicLSTM(ip_sz=88, hd_sz=512, n_cls=88).
cpu()
val_loss_best, lstm_model = lstm_model_training(lstm_
model, lr=0.01, ep=10)
```

This should output the following:

```
ep 0 , train loss = 1.2445591886838276
ep 0 , val loss = 1.3352128363692468e-06

ep 1 , train loss = 2.1156165103117623
ep 1 , val loss = 1.6539533744088603e-06

ep 2 , train loss = 1.6429476936658223
ep 2 , val loss = 6.44313576921296e-07

ep 3 , train loss = 1.3036367297172546
ep 3 , val loss = 7.910344729101428e-07

ep 4 , train loss = 0.6105860968430837
ep 4 , val loss = 1.2166870756004527e-06

ep 5 , train loss = 0.582861324151357
ep 5 , val loss = 5.687958283017817e-07

ep 6 , train loss = 0.28131235639254254
ep 6 , val loss = 4.83049781240143e-07

ep 7 , train loss = 0.1561812162399292
ep 7 , val loss = 5.472248898085979e-07

ep 8 , train loss = 0.14845856527487436
ep 8 , val loss = 4.1753687837465244e-07

ep 9 , train loss = 0.1285532539089521
ep 9 , val loss = 3.899009367655375e-07
```

Figure 6. 14 – Music LSTM training logs

2. Here comes the fun part. Once we have a next-musical-note-predictor, we can use it as a music generator. All we need to do is simply initiate the prediction process by providing an initial note as a cue. The model can then recursively make predictions for the next note at each time step, wherein the predictions at time step *t* are appended to the input sequence at time *t+1*.

Here, we will write a music generation function that takes in the trained model object, the intended length of music to be generated, a starting note to the sequence, and temperature. Temperature is a standard mathematical operation over the softmax function at the classification layer. It is used to manipulate the distribution of softmax probabilities, either by broadening or shrinking the softmaxed probabilities distribution. The code is as follows:

```
def generate_music(lstm_model, ln=100, tmp=1, seq_
st=None):

    ...
```

```
for i in range(ln):
    op, hd = lstm_model(seq_ip_cur, [1], hd)
    probs = nn.functional.softmax(op.div(tmp), dim=1)
    ...
gen_seq = torch.cat(op_seq, dim=0).cpu().numpy()
return gen_seq
```

Finally, we can use this function to create a brand-new music composition:

```
seq = generate_music(lstm_model, ln=100, tmp=1, seq_
st=None)
```

```
midiwrite('generated_music.mid', seq, dtm=0.2)
```

This should create the musical piece and save it as a MIDI file in the current directory. We can open the file and play it to hear what the model has produced. Nonetheless, we can also view the visual matrix representation of the produced music:

```
io.imshow(seq)
```

This should give us the following output:

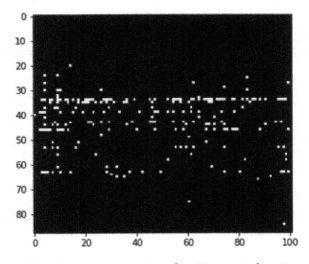

Figure 6.15 – Matrix representation of an AI generated music sample

Furthermore, here is what the generated music would look like as a music sheet:

Figure 6.16 – Music sheet of an AI generated music sample

Here, we can see that the generated melody seems to be not quite as melodious as Mozart's original compositions. Nonetheless, you can see consistencies in some key combinations that the model has learned. Moreover, the generated music quality can be enhanced by training the model on more data, as well as training it for more epochs.

This concludes our exercise on using machine learning to generate music. In this section, we have demonstrated how to use existing musical data to train a note predictor model from scratch and use the trained model to generate music. In fact, you can extend the idea of using generative models to generate samples of any kind of data. PyTorch is an extremely effective tool when it comes to such use cases, especially due to its straightforward APIs for data loading, model building/training/testing, and using trained models as data generators. You are encouraged to try out more such tasks on different use cases and data types.

Summary

In this chapter, we explored generative models using PyTorch. Beginning with text generation, we utilized the transformer-based language model we built in the previous chapter to develop a text generator. We demonstrated how PyTorch can be used to convert a model that's been trained without supervision (a language model, in this case) into a data generator. After that, we exploited the pre-trained advanced transformer models that are available under the transformers library and used them as text generators. We discussed various text generation strategies, such as greedy search, beam search, and top-k and top-p sampling.

Next, we built an AI music composer from scratch. Using Mozart's piano compositions, we trained an LSTM model to predict the next piano note given by the preceding sequence of piano notes. After that, we used the classifier we trained without supervision as a data generator to create music. The results of both the text and the music generators are promising and show how powerful PyTorch can be as a resource for developing artistic AI generative models.

In the same artistic vein, in the next chapter, we shall learn how machine learning can be used to transfer the style of one image to another. With PyTorch at our disposal, we will use CNNs to learn artistic styles from various images and impose those styles on different images – a task better known as neural style transfer.

7
Neural Style Transfer

In the previous chapter, we started exploring generative models using PyTorch. We built machine learning models that can generate text and music by training the models without supervision on text and music data, respectively. We will continue exploring generative modeling in this chapter by applying a similar methodology to image data.

We will mix different aspects of two different images, **A** and **B**, to generate a resultant image, **C**, that contains the content of image **A** and the style of image **B**. This task is also popularly known as **neural style transfer** because, in a way, we are transferring the style of image **B** to image **A** in order to achieve image **C**, as illustrated in the following figure:

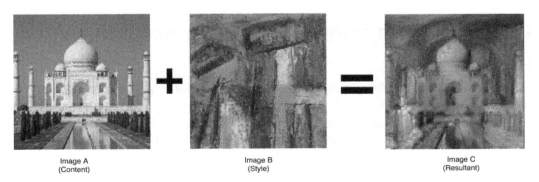

Figure 7.1 – Neural style transfer example

First, we will briefly discuss how to approach this problem and understand the idea behind achieving style transfer. Using PyTorch, we will then implement our own neural style transfer system and apply it to a pair of images. Through this implementation exercise, we will also try to understand the effects of different parameters in the style transfer mechanism.

By the end of this chapter, you will understand the concepts behind neural style transfer and be able to build and test your own neural style transfer model using PyTorch.

This chapter covers the following topics:

- Understanding how to transfer style between images
- Implementing neural style transfer using PyTorch

Technical requirements

We will be using Jupyter notebooks for all of our exercises.

Here's the list of Python libraries that must be installed for this chapter using `pip`. For example, here, you must run `pip install torch==1.4.0` on the command line and so on:

```
jupyter==1.0.0
torch==1.4.0
torchvision==0.5.0
matplotlib==3.1.2
Pillow==8.0.1
```

All the code files that are relevant to this chapter are available at `https://github.com/PacktPublishing/Mastering-PyTorch/tree/master/Chapter07`.

Understanding how to transfer style between images

In *Chapter 3, Deep CNN Architectures*, we discussed **convolutional neural networks (CNNs)** in detail. CNNs are largely the most successful class of models when working with image data. We have seen how CNN-based architectures are the best-performing architectures of neural networks on tasks such as image classification, object detection, and so on. One of the core reasons behind this success is the ability of convolutional layers to learn spatial representations.

For example, in a dog versus cat classifier, the CNN model is essentially able to capture the content of an image in its higher-level features, which helps it detect dog-specific features against cat-specific features. We will leverage this ability of an image classifier CNN to grasp the content of an image.

We know that VGG is a powerful image classification model, as discussed in *Chapter 3, Deep CNN Architectures*. We are going to use the convolutional part of the VGG model (excluding the linear layers) to extract content-related features from an image.

We know that each convolutional layer produces, say, N feature maps of dimensions $X*Y$ each. For example, let's say we have a single channel (grayscale) input image of size $(3,3)$ and a convolutional layer where the number of output channels (N) is 3, the kernel size is $(2,2)$ with a stride of $(1,1)$, and there's no padding. This convolutional layer will produce 3 (N) feature maps each of size 2x2, hence $X=2$ and $Y=2$ in this case.

We can represent these N feature maps produced by the convolutional layer as a 2D matrix of size $N*M$, where $M=X*Y$. By defining the output of each convolutional layer as a 2D matrix, we can define a loss function that's attached to each convolutional layer. This loss function, called the **content loss**, is the squared loss between the expected and predicted outputs of the convolutional layers, as demonstrated in the following diagram, with $N=3$, $X=2$, and $Y=2$:

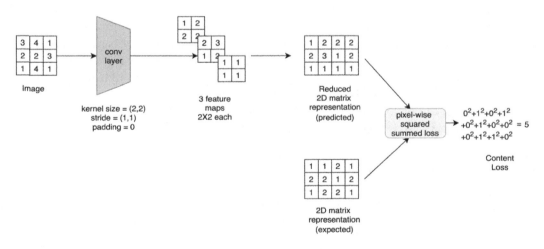

Figure 7.2 – Content loss schematic

As we can see, the input image (image C, as per our notation in *Figure 7.1*) in this example is transformed into **three feature maps** by the **convolutional (conv) layer**. These three feature maps, of size 2x2 each, are formatted into a 3x4 matrix. This matrix is compared with the expected output, which is obtained by passing image A (the content image) through the same flow. The pixel-wise squared summed loss is then calculated, which we call the **content loss**.

Now, for extracting style from an image, we will use gram matrices derived from the inner product between the rows of the reduced 2D matrix representations, as demonstrated in the following diagram:

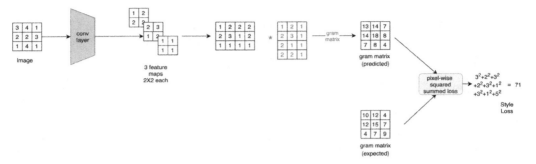

Figure 7.3 – Style loss schematic

> **Gram matrices**
>
> You can read more about gram matrices here: `https://mathworld.wolfram.com/GramMatrix.html`.

The **gram matrix** computation is the only extra step here compared to the content loss calculations. Also, as we can see, the output of the pixel-wise squared summed loss is quite a large number compared to the content loss. Hence, this number is normalized by dividing it by $N*X*Y$; that is, the number of feature maps (N) times the length (X) times the breadth (Y) of a feature map. This also helps standardize the **style loss** metric across different convolutional layers, which have a different N, X, and Y. Details of the implementation can be found in the original paper that introduced neural style transfer: `https://arxiv.org/pdf/1508.06576.pdf`.

Now that we understand the concept of content and style loss, let's take a look at how neural style transfer works, as follows:

1. For the given VGG (or any other CNN) network, we define which convolutional layers in the network should have a content loss attached to them. Repeat this exercise for style loss.

2. Once we have those lists, we pass the content image through the network and compute the expected convolutional outputs (2D matrices) at the convolutional layers where the content loss is to be calculated.

3. Next, we pass the style image through the network and compute the expected gram matrices at the convolutional layers. This is where the style loss is to be calculated, as demonstrated in the following diagram.

In the following diagram, for example, the content loss is to be calculated at the second and third convolutional layers, while the style loss is to be calculated at the second, third, and fifth convolutional layers:

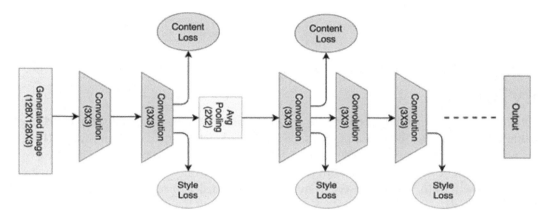

Figure 7.4 – Style transfer architecture schematic

Now that we have the content and style targets at the decided convolutional layers, we are all set to generate an image that contains the content of the content image and the style of the style image.

For initialization, we can either use a random noise matrix as our starting point for the generated image, or directly use the content image to start with. We pass this image through the network and compute the style and content losses at the pre-selected convolutional layers. We add style losses to get the total style loss and content losses to get the total content loss. Finally, we obtain a total loss by summing these two components in a weighted fashion.

If we give more weight to the style component, the generated image will have more style reflected on it and vice versa. Using gradient descent, we backpropagate the loss all the way back to the input in order to update our generated image. After a few epochs, the generated image should evolve in a way that it produces the content and style representations that minimize the respective losses, thereby producing a style transferred image.

In the preceding diagram, the pooling layer is average pooling-based instead of the traditional max pooling. Average pooling is deliberately used for style transfer to ensure smooth gradient flow. We want the generated images not to have sharp changes between pixels. Also, it is worth noticing that the network in the preceding diagram ends at the layer where the last style or content loss is calculated. Hence, in this case, because there is no loss associated with the sixth convolutional layer of the original network, it is meaningless to talk about layers beyond the fifth convolutional layer in the context of style transfer.

In the next section, we will implement our own neural style transfer system using PyTorch. With the help of a pre-trained VGG model, we will use the concepts we've discussed in this section to generate artistically styled images. We will also explore the impact of tuning the various model parameters on the content and texture/style of generated images.

Implementing neural style transfer using PyTorch

Having discussed the internals of a neural style transfer system, we are all set to build one using PyTorch. In the form of an exercise, we will load a style and a content image. Then, we will load the pre-trained VGG model. After defining which layers to compute the style and content loss on, we will trim the model so that it only retains the relevant layers. Finally, we will train the neural style transfer model in order to refine the generated image epoch by epoch.

Loading the content and style images

In this exercise, we will only show the important parts of the code for demonstration purposes. To access the full code, go to `https://github.com/PacktPublishing/Mastering-PyTorch/blob/master/Chapter07/neural_style_transfer.ipynb`. Follow these steps:

1. Firstly, we need to import the necessary libraries by running the following lines of code:

```
from PIL import Image
import matplotlib.pyplot as pltimport torch
import torch.nn as nn
import torch.optim as optim
import torchvisiondvc = torch.device("cuda" if torch.cuda.is_available() else "cpu")
```

We import image I/O-related libraries to load the content and style images and display the generated image. We also import standard Torch dependencies for the style transfer model's training, along with the `torchvision` library to load the pre-trained VGG model and other computer vision-related utilities.

2. Next, we need a style and content image. We will use `https://unsplash.com/` to download an image of each kind. The downloaded images are included in the code repository for this book. In the following code, we are writing a function that will load the images as tensors:

```
def image_to_tensor(image_filepath, image_
dimension=128):
    img = Image.open(image_filepath).convert('RGB')
    # display image
    ...
    torch_transformation =      torchvision.transforms.
Compose([
        torchvision.transforms.Resize(img_size),
        torchvision.transforms.ToTensor()
                            ])
    img = torch_transformation(img).unsqueeze(0)
    return img.to(dvc, torch.float)
style_image = image_to_tensor("./images/style.jpg")
content_image =image_to_tensor("./images/content.jpg")
```

This should give us the following output:

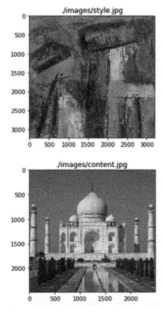

Figure 7.5 – Style and content images

So, the content image is a real-life photograph of the *Taj Mahal*, whereas the style image is an art painting. Using style transfer, we hope to generate an artistic *Taj Mahal* painting. However, before we do that, we need to load and trim the VGG19 model.

Loading and trimming the pre-trained VGG19 model

In this part of the exercise, we will use a pre-trained VGG model and retain its convolutional layers. We will make some minor changes to the model to make it usable for neural style transfer. Let's get started:

1. We already have the content and style images. Here, we will load the pre-trained VGG19 model and use its convolutional layers to generate the content and style targets to yield the content and style losses, respectively:

```
vgg19_model = torchvision.models.vgg19(pretrained=True).
to(dvc)
print(vgg19_model)
```

The output should be as follows:

```
VGG(
  (features): Sequential(
    (0): Conv2d(3, 64, kernel_size=(3, 3), stride=(1, 1), padding=(1, 1))
    (1): ReLU(inplace=True)
    (2): Conv2d(64, 64, kernel_size=(3, 3), stride=(1, 1), padding=(1, 1))
    (3): ReLU(inplace=True)
    (4): MaxPool2d(kernel_size=2, stride=2, padding=0, dilation=1, ceil_mode=False)
    (5): Conv2d(64, 128, kernel_size=(3, 3), stride=(1, 1), padding=(1, 1))
    (6): ReLU(inplace=True)
    (7): Conv2d(128, 128, kernel_size=(3, 3), stride=(1, 1), padding=(1, 1))
    (8): ReLU(inplace=True)
    (9): MaxPool2d(kernel_size=2, stride=2, padding=0, dilation=1, ceil_mode=False)
    (10): Conv2d(128, 256, kernel_size=(3, 3), stride=(1, 1), padding=(1, 1))
    (11): ReLU(inplace=True)
    (12): Conv2d(256, 256, kernel_size=(3, 3), stride=(1, 1), padding=(1, 1))
    (13): ReLU(inplace=True)
    (14): Conv2d(256, 256, kernel_size=(3, 3), stride=(1, 1), padding=(1, 1))
    (15): ReLU(inplace=True)
    (16): Conv2d(256, 256, kernel_size=(3, 3), stride=(1, 1), padding=(1, 1))
    (17): ReLU(inplace=True)
    (18): MaxPool2d(kernel_size=2, stride=2, padding=0, dilation=1, ceil_mode=False)
    (19): Conv2d(256, 512, kernel_size=(3, 3), stride=(1, 1), padding=(1, 1))
    (20): ReLU(inplace=True)
    (21): Conv2d(512, 512, kernel_size=(3, 3), stride=(1, 1), padding=(1, 1))
    (22): ReLU(inplace=True)
    (23): Conv2d(512, 512, kernel_size=(3, 3), stride=(1, 1), padding=(1, 1))
    (24): ReLU(inplace=True)
    (25): Conv2d(512, 512, kernel_size=(3, 3), stride=(1, 1), padding=(1, 1))
    (26): ReLU(inplace=True)
    (27): MaxPool2d(kernel_size=2, stride=2, padding=0, dilation=1, ceil_mode=False)
    (28): Conv2d(512, 512, kernel_size=(3, 3), stride=(1, 1), padding=(1, 1))
    (29): ReLU(inplace=True)
    (30): Conv2d(512, 512, kernel_size=(3, 3), stride=(1, 1), padding=(1, 1))
    (31): ReLU(inplace=True)
    (32): Conv2d(512, 512, kernel_size=(3, 3), stride=(1, 1), padding=(1, 1))
    (33): ReLU(inplace=True)
    (34): Conv2d(512, 512, kernel_size=(3, 3), stride=(1, 1), padding=(1, 1))
    (35): ReLU(inplace=True)
    (36): MaxPool2d(kernel_size=2, stride=2, padding=0, dilation=1, ceil_mode=False)
  )
  (avgpool): AdaptiveAvgPool2d(output_size=(7, 7))
  (classifier): Sequential(
    (0): Linear(in_features=25088, out_features=4096, bias=True)
    (1): ReLU(inplace=True)
    (2): Dropout(p=0.5, inplace=False)
    (3): Linear(in_features=4096, out_features=4096, bias=True)
    (4): ReLU(inplace=True)
    (5): Dropout(p=0.5, inplace=False)
    (6): Linear(in_features=4096, out_features=1000, bias=True)
  )
)
```

Figure 7.6 – VGG19 model

2. We do not need the linear layers; that is, we only need the convolutional part of the model. In the preceding code, this can be achieved by only retaining the `features` attribute of the model object, as follows:

```
vgg19_model = vgg19_model.features
```

> **Note**
>
> In this exercise, we are not going to tune the parameters of the VGG model. All we are going to tune is the pixels of the generated image, right at the input end of the model. Hence, we will ensure that the parameters of the loaded VGG model are fixed.

3. We must freeze the parameters of the VGG model with the following code:

```
for param in vgg19_model.parameters():
    param.requires_grad_(False)
```

4. Now that we've loaded the relevant section of the VGG model, we need to change the `maxpool` layers into average pooling layers, as discussed in the previous section. While doing so, we will take note of where the convolutional layers are located in the model:

```
conv_indices = []for i in range(len(vgg19_model)):
    if vgg19_model[i]._get_name() == 'MaxPool2d':
        vgg19_model[i] = nn.AvgPool2d(kernel_size=vgg19_model[i].kernel_size,
stride=vgg19_model[i].stride, padding=vgg19_model[i].padding)
    if vgg19_model[i]._get_name() == 'Conv2d':
        conv_indices.append(i)

conv_indices = dict(enumerate(conv_indices, 1))
print(vgg19_model)
```

The output should be as follows:

```
Sequential(
  (0): Conv2d(3, 64, kernel_size=(3, 3), stride=(1, 1), padding=(1, 1))
  (1): ReLU(inplace=True)
  (2): Conv2d(64, 64, kernel_size=(3, 3), stride=(1, 1), padding=(1, 1))
  (3): ReLU(inplace=True)
  (4): AvgPool2d(kernel_size=2, stride=2, padding=0)
  (5): Conv2d(64, 128, kernel_size=(3, 3), stride=(1, 1), padding=(1, 1))
  (6): ReLU(inplace=True)
  (7): Conv2d(128, 128, kernel_size=(3, 3), stride=(1, 1), padding=(1, 1))
  (8): ReLU(inplace=True)
  (9): AvgPool2d(kernel_size=2, stride=2, padding=0)
  (10): Conv2d(128, 256, kernel_size=(3, 3), stride=(1, 1), padding=(1, 1))
  (11): ReLU(inplace=True)
  (12): Conv2d(256, 256, kernel_size=(3, 3), stride=(1, 1), padding=(1, 1))
  (13): ReLU(inplace=True)
  (14): Conv2d(256, 256, kernel_size=(3, 3), stride=(1, 1), padding=(1, 1))
  (15): ReLU(inplace=True)
  (16): Conv2d(256, 256, kernel_size=(3, 3), stride=(1, 1), padding=(1, 1))
  (17): ReLU(inplace=True)
  (18): AvgPool2d(kernel_size=2, stride=2, padding=0)
  (19): Conv2d(256, 512, kernel_size=(3, 3), stride=(1, 1), padding=(1, 1))
  (20): ReLU(inplace=True)
  (21): Conv2d(512, 512, kernel_size=(3, 3), stride=(1, 1), padding=(1, 1))
  (22): ReLU(inplace=True)
  (23): Conv2d(512, 512, kernel_size=(3, 3), stride=(1, 1), padding=(1, 1))
  (24): ReLU(inplace=True)
  (25): Conv2d(512, 512, kernel_size=(3, 3), stride=(1, 1), padding=(1, 1))
  (26): ReLU(inplace=True)
  (27): AvgPool2d(kernel_size=2, stride=2, padding=0)
  (28): Conv2d(512, 512, kernel_size=(3, 3), stride=(1, 1), padding=(1, 1))
  (29): ReLU(inplace=True)
  (30): Conv2d(512, 512, kernel_size=(3, 3), stride=(1, 1), padding=(1, 1))
  (31): ReLU(inplace=True)
  (32): Conv2d(512, 512, kernel_size=(3, 3), stride=(1, 1), padding=(1, 1))
  (33): ReLU(inplace=True)
  (34): Conv2d(512, 512, kernel_size=(3, 3), stride=(1, 1), padding=(1, 1))
  (35): ReLU(inplace=True)
  (36): AvgPool2d(kernel_size=2, stride=2, padding=0)
)
```

Figure 7.7 – Modified VGG19 model

As we can see, the linear layers have been removed and the max pooling layers have been replaced by average pooling layers, as indicated by the red boxes in the preceding figure.

In the preceding steps, we loaded a pre-trained VGG model and modified it in order to use it as a neural style transfer model. Next, we will transform this modified VGG model into a neural style transfer model.

Building the neural style transfer model

At this point, we can define which convolutional layers we want the content and style losses to be calculated on. In the original paper, style loss was calculated on the first five convolutional layers, while content loss was calculated on the fourth convolutional layer only. We will follow the same convention, although you are encouraged to try out different combinations and observe their effects on the generated image. Follow these steps:

1. First, we list the layers we need to have the style and content loss on:

    ```
    layers = {1: 's', 2: 's', 3: 's', 4: 'sc', 5: 's'}
    ```

    Here, we have defined the first to fifth convolutional layers, which are attached to the style loss, and the fourth convolutional layer, which is attached to the content loss.

2. Now, let's remove the unnecessary parts of the VGG model. We shall only retain it until the fifth convolutional layer, as shown here:

    ```
    vgg_layers = nn.ModuleList(vgg19_model)
    last_layer_idx = conv_indices[max(layers.keys())]
    vgg_layers_trimmed = vgg_layers[:last_layer_idx+1]
    neural_style_transfer_model = nn.Sequential(*vgg_layers_
    trimmed)
    print(neural_style_transfer_model)
    ```

    This should give us the following output:

```
Sequential(
  (0): Conv2d(3, 64, kernel_size=(3, 3), stride=(1, 1), padding=(1, 1))
  (1): ReLU()
  (2): Conv2d(64, 64, kernel_size=(3, 3), stride=(1, 1), padding=(1, 1))
  (3): ReLU()
  (4): AvgPool2d(kernel_size=2, stride=2, padding=0)
  (5): Conv2d(64, 128, kernel_size=(3, 3), stride=(1, 1), padding=(1, 1))
  (6): ReLU()
  (7): Conv2d(128, 128, kernel_size=(3, 3), stride=(1, 1), padding=(1, 1))
  (8): ReLU()
  (9): AvgPool2d(kernel_size=2, stride=2, padding=0)
  (10): Conv2d(128, 256, kernel_size=(3, 3), stride=(1, 1), padding=(1, 1))
)
```

Figure 7.8 – Neural style transfer model object

As we can see, we have transformed the VGG model with 16 convolutional layers into a neural style transfer model with five convolutional layers.

Training the style transfer model

In this section, we'll start working on the image that will be generated. We can initialize this image in many ways, such as by using a random noise image or using the content image as the initial image. Currently, we are going to start with random noise. Later, we will also see how using the content image as the starting point impacts the results. Follow these steps:

1. The following code demonstrates the process of initializing a `torch` tensor with random numbers:

```
# initialize as the content image
# ip_image = content_image.clone()
# initialize as random noise:
ip_image = torch.randn(content_image.data.size(),
device=dvc)
plt.figure()
plt.imshow(ip_image.squeeze(0).cpu().detach().numpy().
transpose(1,2,0).clip(0,1));
```

This should give us the following output:

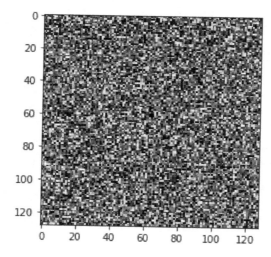

Figure 7.9 – Random noise image

2. Finally, we can start the model training loop. First, we will define the number of epochs to train for, the relative weightage to provide for the style and content losses, and instantiate the Adam optimizer for gradient descent-based optimization with a learning rate of 0.1:

```
num_epochs=180
wt_style=1e6
wt_content=1
style_losses = []
content_losses = []
opt = optim.Adam([ip_image.requires_grad_()], lr=0.1)
```

3. Upon starting the training loop, we initialize the style and content losses to zero at the beginning of the epoch, and then clip the pixel values of the input image between 0 and 1 for numerical stability:

```
for curr_epoch in range(1, num_epochs+1):
    ip_image.data.clamp_(0, 1)
    opt.zero_grad()
    epoch_style_loss = 0
    epoch_content_loss = 0
```

4. At this stage, we have reached a crucial step in the training iteration. Here, we must calculate the style and content losses for each of the pre-defined style and content convolutional layers. The individual style losses and content losses for each of the respective layers are added together to get the total style and content loss for the current epoch:

```
for k in layers.keys():
    if 'c' in layers[k]:
        target = neural_style_transfer_model[:conv_
indices[k]+1](content_image).detach()
        ip = neural_style_transfer_model[:conv_
indices[k]+1](ip_image)
        epoch_content_loss += torch.nn.functional.
mse_loss(ip, target)
    if 's' in layers[k]:
        target = gram_matrix(neural_style_transfer_
model[:conv_indices[k]+1](style_image)).detach()
```

```
        ip = gram_matrix(neural_style_transfer_
model[:conv_indices[k]+1](ip_image))
```

```
        epoch_style_loss += torch.nn.functional.mse_
loss(ip, target)
```

As shown in the preceding code, for both the style and content losses, first, we compute the style and content targets (ground truths) using the style and content image. We use .detach() for the targets to indicate that these are not trainable but just fixed target values. Next, we compute the predicted style and content outputs based on the generated image as input, at each of the style and content layers. Finally, we compute the style and content losses.

5. For the style loss, we also need to compute the gram matrix using a pre-defined gram matrix function, as shown in the following code:

```
def gram_matrix(ip):
    num_batch, num_channels, height, width = ip.size()
    feats = ip.view(num_batch * num_channels, width *
height)
    gram_mat = torch.mm(feats, feats.t())
    return gram_mat.div(num_batch * num_channels *
width * height)
```

As we mentioned earlier, we can compute an inner dot product using the torch.mm function. This computes the gram matrix and normalizes the matrix by dividing it by the number of feature maps times the width times the height of each feature map.

6. Moving on in our training loop, now that we've computed the total style and content losses, we need to compute the final total loss as a weighted sum of these two, using the weights we defined earlier:

```
    epoch_style_loss *= wt_style
    epoch_content_loss *= wt_content
    total_loss = epoch_style_loss + epoch_content_loss
    total_loss.backward()
```

Finally, at every *k* epochs, we can see the progression of our training by looking at the losses as well as looking at the generated image. The following figure shows the evolution of the generated style transferred image for the previous code for a total of 180 epochs recorded at every 20 epochs:

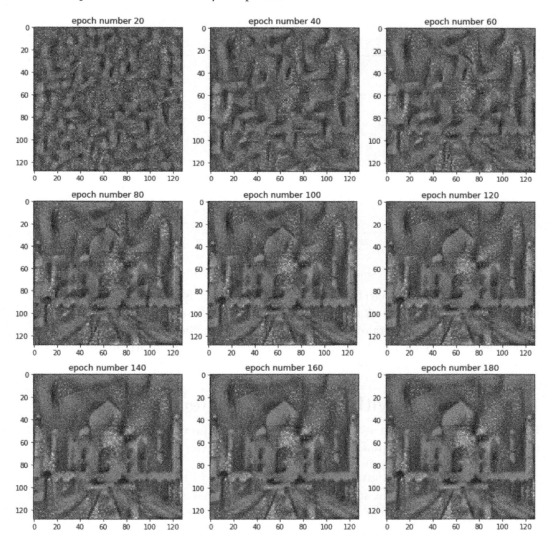

Figure 7.10 – Neural style transfer epoch-wise generated image

It is quite clear that the model begins by applying the style from the style image to the random noise. As training proceeds, the content loss starts playing its role, thereby imparting content to the styled image. By epoch **180**, we can see the generated image, which looks like a good approximation of an artistic painting of the *Taj Mahal*. The following graph shows the decreasing style and content losses as the epochs progress from **0** to **180**:

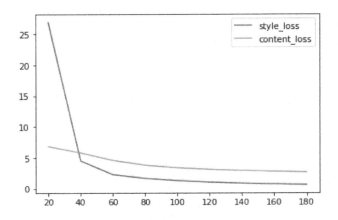

Figure 7.11 – Style and content loss curves

Noticeably, the style loss sharply goes down initially, which is also evident in *Figure 7.10* in that the initial epochs mark the imposition of style on the image more than the content. At the advanced stages of training, both losses decline together gradually, resulting in a style transferred image, which is a decent compromise between the artwork of the style image and the realism of a photograph that's been taken with a camera.

Experimenting with the style transfer system

Having successfully trained a style transfer system in the previous section, we will now look at how the system responds to different hyperparameter settings. Follow these steps:

1. In the preceding section, we set the content weight to 1 and the style weight to 1e6. Let's increase the style weight 10x further – that is, to 1e7 – and observe how it affects the style transfer process. Upon training with the new weights for 600 epochs, we get the following progression of style transfer:

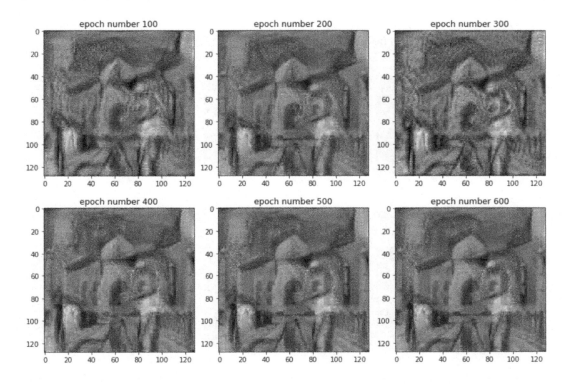

Figure 7.12 – Style transfer epochs with higher style weights

Here, we can see that initially, it required many more epochs than in the previous scenario to reach a reasonable result. More importantly, the higher style weight does seem to have an effect on the generated image. When we look at the images in the preceding figure compared to the ones in *Figure 7.10*, we find that the former have a stronger resemblance to the style image shown in *Figure 7.5*.

2. Likewise, reducing the style weight from `1e6` to `1e5` produces a more content-focused result, as can be seen in the following screenshot:

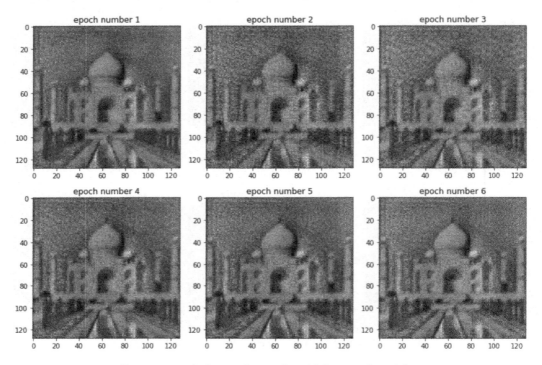

Figure 7.13 – Style transfer epochs with lower style weights

Compared to the scenario with a higher style weight, having a lower style weight means it takes far fewer epochs to get a reasonable-looking result. The amount of style in the generated image is much smaller and is mostly filled with the content image data. We only trained this scenario for 6 epochs as the results saturate after that point.

3. A final change could be to initialize the generated image with the content image instead of the random noise, while using the original style and content weights of `1e6` and `1`, respectively. The following figure shows the epoch-wise progression in this scenario:

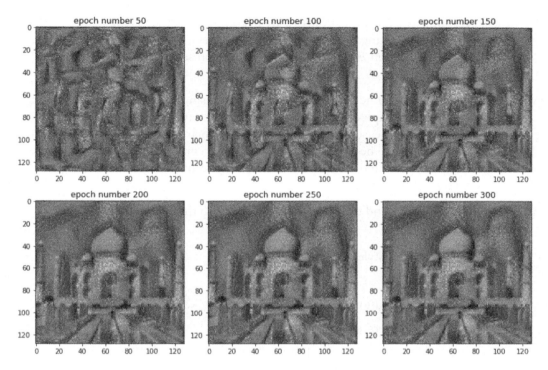

Figure 7.14 – Style transfer epochs with content image initialization

By comparing the preceding figure to *Figure 7.10*, we can see that having the content image as a starting point gives us a different path of progression to getting a reasonable style transferred image. It seems that both the content and style components are being imposed on the generated image more simultaneously than in *Figure 7.10*, where the style got imposed first, followed by the content. The following graph confirms this hypothesis:

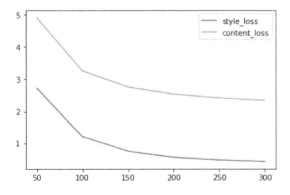

Figure 7.15 – Style and content loss curves with content image initialization

As we can see, both style and content losses are decreasing together as the epochs progress, eventually saturating toward the end. Nonetheless, the end results in both *Figures 7.10* and *7.14* or even *Figures 7.12* and *7.13* all represent reasonable artistic impressions of the *Taj Mahal*.

We have successfully built a neural style transfer model using PyTorch, wherein using a content image – a photograph of the beautiful *Taj Mahal* – and a style image – a canvas painting – we generated a reasonable approximation of an artistic painting of the *Taj Mahal*. This application can be extended to various other combinations. Swapping the content and style images could also produce interesting results and give more insight into the inner workings of the model.

You are encouraged to extend the exercise we discussed in this chapter by doing the following:

- Changing the list of style and content layers

- Using larger image sizes

- Trying more combinations of style and content loss weights

- Using other optimizers, such as SGD and LBFGS

- Training for longer epochs with different learning rates, in order to observe the differences in the generated images across all these approaches

Summary

In this chapter, we applied the concept of generative machine learning to images by generating an image that contains the content of one image and the style of another – a task known as neural style transfer. First, we understood the idea behind the style transfer algorithm, especially the use of the gram matrix in order to extract styles from an image.

Next, we used PyTorch to build our own neural style transfer model. We used parts of a pre-trained VGG19 model to extract content and style information through some of its convolutional layers. We replaced the max pooling layers of the VGG19 model with average pooling layers for a smooth gradient flow. We then input a random initial image to the style transfer model and with the help of a style and a content loss, we fine-tuned the image pixels using gradient descent.

This input image evolves over epochs and gives us the final generated image, which contains the content of the content image and style of the style image. Finally, we conducted style experiments by changing the relative style loss weight and the initial input image to observe the effects on the evolution of the generated image along epochs.

This concludes our discussions on neural style transfer using PyTorch. Note that in style transfer, we aren't generating data that looks like the data the model is being trained on (VGG19, in this case). In fact, we are generating data that is supposed to find the best compromise between two worlds – content and style. In the next chapter, we will expand on this paradigm, where we'll have a generator that generates *fake* data and there is a discriminator that tells apart *fake* versus *real* data. Such models are popularly known as **generative adversarial networks (GANs)**. We will be exploring deep convolutional GANs in the next chapter.

8
Deep Convolutional GANs

Generative neural networks have become a popular and active area of research and development. A huge amount of credit for this trend goes to a class of models that we are going to discuss in this chapter. These models are called **generative adversarial networks (GANs)** and were introduced in 2014. Ever since the introduction of the basic GAN model, various types of GANs have been, and are being, invented for different applications.

Essentially, a GAN is composed of two neural networks – a **generator** and a **discriminator**. Let's look at an example of the GAN that is used to generate images. For such a GAN, the task of the generator would be to generate realistic-looking fake images, and the task of the discriminator would be to tell the real images apart from the fake images.

In a joint optimization procedure, the generator would ultimately learn to generate such good fake images that the discriminator will essentially be unable to tell them apart from real images. Once such a model is trained, the generator part of it can then be used as a reliable data generator. Besides being used as a generative model for unsupervised learning, GANs have also proven useful in semi-supervised learning.

In the image example, for instance, the features learned by the discriminator model could be used to improve the performance of classification models trained on the image data. Besides semi-supervised learning, GANs have also proven to be useful in reinforcement learning, which is a topic that we will discuss in *Chapter 9, Deep Reinforcement Learning*.

A particular type of GAN that we will focus on in this chapter is the **deep convolutional GAN (DCGAN)**. A DCGAN is essentially an unsupervised **convolution neural network (CNN)** model. Both the generator and the discriminator in a DCGAN are purely *CNNs with no fully connected layers*. DCGANs have performed well in generating realistic images, and they can be a good starting point for learning how to build, train, and run GANs from scratch.

In this chapter, we will first understand the various components within a GAN – the generator and the discriminator models and the joint optimization schedule. We will then focus on building a DCGAN model using PyTorch. Next, we will use an image dataset to train and test the performance of the DCGAN model. We will conclude this chapter by revisiting the concept of style transfer on images and exploring the Pix2Pix GAN model, which can efficiently perform a style transfer on any given pair of images.

We will also learn how the various components of a Pix2Pix GAN model relate to that of a DCGAN model. After finishing this chapter, we will truly understand how GANs work and will be able to build any type of GAN model using PyTorch. This chapter is broken down into the following topics:

- Defining the generator and discriminator networks
- Training a DCGAN using PyTorch
- Using GANs for style transfer

Technical requirements

We will be using Jupyter notebooks for all of our exercises. The following is a list of Python libraries that should be installed for this chapter using `pip`. For example, run `pip install torch==1.4.0` on the command line:

```
jupyter==1.0.0
torch==1.4.0
torchvision==0.5.0
```

All code files relevant to this chapter are available here: `https://github.com/PacktPublishing/Mastering-PyTorch/tree/master/Chapter08`.

Defining the generator and discriminator networks

As mentioned earlier, GANs are composed of two components – the generator and the discriminator. Both of these are essentially neural networks. Generators and discriminators with different neural architectures produce different types of GANs. For example, DCGANs purely have CNNs as the generator and discriminator. You can find a list of different types of GANs along with their PyTorch implementations at `https://github.com/eriklindernoren/PyTorch-GAN`.

For any GAN that is used to generate some kind of real data, the generator usually takes random noise as input and produces an output with the same dimensions as the real data. We call this generated output **fake data**. The discriminator, on the other hand, works as a **binary classifier**. It takes in the generated fake data and the real data (one at a time) as input and predicts whether the input data is real or fake. *Figure 8.1* shows a diagram of the overall GAN model schematic:

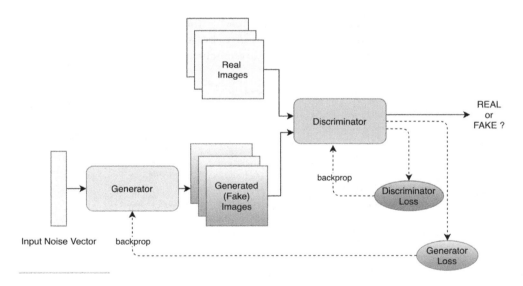

Figure 8.1 – A GAN schematic

The discriminator network is optimized like any binary classifier, that is, using the binary cross-entropy function. Therefore, the discriminator model's motivation is to correctly classify real images as real and fake images as fake. The generator network has quite the opposite motivation. The generator loss is mathematically expressed as $-log(D(G(x)))$, where x is random noise inputted into the generator model, G; $G(x)$ is the generated fake image by the generator model; and $D(G(x))$ is the output probability of the discriminator model, D, that is, the probability of the image being real.

Therefore, the generator loss is minimized when the discriminator thinks that the generated fake image is real. Essentially, the generator is trying to fool the discriminator in this joint optimization problem.

In execution, these two loss functions are backpropagated alternatively. That is, at every iteration of training, first, the discriminator is frozen, and the parameters of the generator networks are optimized by backpropagating the gradients from the generator loss.

Then, the tuned generator is frozen while the discriminator is optimized by backpropagating the gradients from the discriminator loss. This is what we call joint optimization. It has also been referred to as being equivalent to a two-player Minimax game in the original GAN paper, which you can find at `https://arxiv.org/pdf/1406.2661.pdf`.

Understanding the DCGAN generator and discriminator

For the particular case of DCGANs, let's consider what the generator and discriminator model architectures look like. As already mentioned, both are purely convolutional models. *Figure 8.2* shows the generator model architecture for a DCGAN:

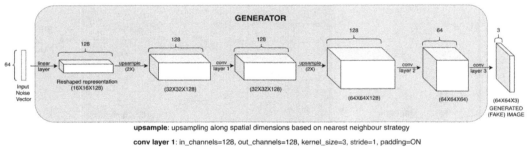

Figure 8.2 – The DCGAN generator model architecture

First, the random noise input vector of size **64** is reshaped and projected into **128** feature maps of size **16x16** each. This projection is achieved using a linear layer. From there on, a series of upsampling and convolutional layers follow. The first upsampling layer simply transforms the **16x16** feature maps into **32x32** feature maps using the nearest neighbor upsampling strategy.

This is followed by a 2D convolutional layer with a **3x3** kernel size and **128** output feature maps. The **128 32x32** feature maps outputted by this convolutional layer are further upsampled to **64x64**-sized feature maps, which is followed by two **2D** convolutional layers resulting in the generated (fake) RGB image of size **64x64**.

> **Note**
>
> We have omitted the batch normalization and leaky ReLU layers to avoid clutter in the preceding architectural representation. The PyTorch code in the next section will have these details mentioned and explained.

Now that we know what the generator model looks like, let's examine what the discriminator model looks like. *Figure 8.3* shows the discriminator model architecture:

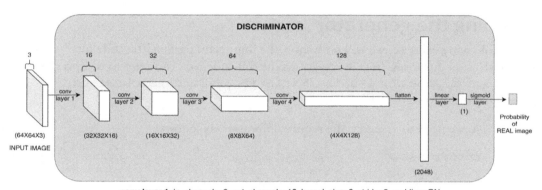

conv layer 1: in_channels=3, out_channels=16, kernel_size=3, stride=2, padding=ON
conv layer 2: in_channels=16, out_channels=32, kernel_size=3, stride=2, padding=ON
conv layer 3: in_channels=32, out_channels=64, kernel_size=3, stride=2, padding=ON
conv layer 4: in_channels=64, out_channels=128, kernel_size=3, stride=2, padding=ON

Figure 8.3 – The DCGAN discriminator model architecture

As you can see, a stride of **2** at every convolutional layer in this architecture helps to reduce the spatial dimension, while the depth (that is, the number of feature maps) keeps growing. This is a classic CNN-based binary classification architecture being used here to classify between real images and generated fake images.

Having understood the architectures of the generator and the discriminator network, we can now build the entire DCGAN model based on the schematic in *Figure 8.1* and train the DCGAN model on an image dataset.

In the next section, we will use PyTorch for this task. We will discuss, in detail, the DCGAN model instantiation, loading the image dataset, jointly training the DCGAN generator and discriminator, and generating sample fake images from the trained DCGAN generator.

Training a DCGAN using PyTorch

We have discussed the architectures of the generator and discriminator models within the DCGAN model in the previous section. In this section, we will build, train, and test a DCGAN model using PyTorch in the form of an exercise. We will use an image dataset to train the model and test how well the generator of the trained DCGAN model performs when producing fake images.

Defining the generator

In the following exercise, we will only show the important parts of the code for demonstration purposes. In order to access the full code, you can refer to https://github.com/PacktPublishing/Mastering-PyTorch/blob/master/Chapter08/dcgan.ipynb:

1. First, we need to import the required libraries, as follows:

```
import os
import numpy as np
import torch
import torch.nn as nn
import torch.nn.functional as F
from torch.utils.data import DataLoader
from torch.autograd import Variable
import torchvision.transforms as transforms
from torchvision.utils import save_image
from torchvision import datasets
```

In this exercise, we only need torch and torchvision to build the DCGAN model. By using torchvision, we will be able to directly use the available image datasets.

2. After importing the libraries, we specify some model hyperparameters, as shown in the following code:

```
num_eps=10
bsize=32
lrate=0.001
lat_dimension=64
image_sz=64
chnls=1
logging_intv=200
```

We will be training the model for 10 epochs with a batch size of 32 and a learning rate of 0.001. The expected image size is *64x64x3*. lat_dimension is the length of the random noise vector, which essentially means that we will draw the random noise from a *64*-dimensional latent space as input to the generator model.

3. Now we define the generator model object. The following code is in direct accordance with the architecture shown in *Figure 8.2*:

```
class GANGenerator(nn.Module):
    def __init__(self):
        super(GANGenerator, self).__init__()
        self.inp_sz = image_sz // 4
        self.lin =   nn.Sequential(nn.Linear(lat_
dimension, 128 * self.inp_sz ** 2))
        self.bn1 = nn.BatchNorm2d(128)
        self.up1 = nn.Upsample(scale_factor=2)
        self.cn1 = nn.Conv2d(128, 128, 3, stride=1,
padding=1)
        self.bn2 = nn.BatchNorm2d(128, 0.8)
        self.rl1 = nn.LeakyReLU(0.2, inplace=True)
        self.up2 = nn.Upsample(scale_factor=2)
        self.cn2 = nn.Conv2d(128, 64, 3, stride=1,
padding=1)
        self.bn3 = nn.BatchNorm2d(64, 0.8)
        self.rl2 = nn.LeakyReLU(0.2, inplace=True)
        self.cn3 = nn.Conv2d(64, chnls, 3, stride=1,
padding=1)
        self.act = nn.Tanh()
```

4. After defining the _init_ method, we define the `forward` method, which is essentially just calling the layers in a sequential manner:

```
def forward(self, x):
    x = self.lin(x)
    x = x.view(x.shape[0], 128, self.inp_sz, self.inp_sz)
    x = self.bn1(x)
    x = self.up1(x)
    x = self.cn1(x)
    x = self.bn2(x)
    x = self.rl1(x)
    x = self.up2(x)
    x = self.cn2(x)
    x = self.bn3(x)
    x = self.rl2(x)
    x = self.cn3(x)
    out = self.act(x)
    return out
```

We have used the explicit layer-by-layer definition in this exercise as opposed to the nn.Sequential method; this is because it makes it easier to debug the model if something goes wrong.

We can also see the batch normalization and leaky ReLU layers in the code, which are not mentioned in *Figure 8.2*. Batch normalization is used after the linear or convolutional layers to both fasten the training process and reduce sensitivity to the initial network weights.

Additionally, a leaky ReLU is used as an activation function in a DCGAN instead of a regular ReLU because a ReLU might lose all the information for inputs with negative values. A leaky ReLU set with a 0.2 negative slope gives 20% weightage to incoming negative information, which might help us to avoid vanishing gradients during the training of a GAN model.

Next, we will take a look at the PyTorch code to define the discriminator network.

Defining the discriminator

Similar to the generator, we will now define the discriminator model as follows:

1. Once again, the following code is the PyTorch equivalent for the model architecture shown in *Figure 8.3*:

```
class GANDiscriminator(nn.Module):
    def __init__(self):
        super(GANDiscriminator, self).__init__()
        def disc_module(ip_chnls, op_chnls, bnorm=True):
            mod = [nn.Conv2d(ip_chnls, op_chnls, 3, 2,
1), nn.LeakyReLU(0.2, inplace=True),
                    nn.Dropout2d(0.25)] if bnorm:
                mod += [nn.BatchNorm2d(op_chnls, 0.8)]
            return mod
        self.disc_model = nn.Sequential(
            *disc_module(chnls, 16, bnorm=False),
            *disc_module(16, 32),
            *disc_module(32, 64),
            *disc_module(64, 128),
        )
        # width and height of the down-sized image
        ds_size = image_sz // 2 ** 4
        self.adverse_lyr = nn.Sequential(nn.Linear(128 *
ds_size ** 2, 1), nn.Sigmoid())
```

First, we have defined a general discriminator module, which is a cascade of a convolutional layer, an optional batch normalization layer, a leaky ReLU layer, and a dropout layer. In order to build the discriminator model, we repeat this module sequentially four times – each time with a different set of parameters for the convolutional layer.

The goal is to input a 64x64x3 RGB image and to increase the depth (that is, the number of channels) and decrease the height and width of the image as it is passed through the convolutional layers.

The final discriminator module's output is flattened and passed through the adversarial layer. Essentially, the adversarial layer fully connects the flattened representation to the final model output (that is, a single number). This model output is then passed through a sigmoid activation function to give us the probability of the image being real (or not fake).

2. The following is the `forward` method for the discriminator, which takes in a 64x64 RGB image as input and produces the probability of it being a real image:

```
def forward(self, x):
    x = self.disc_model(x)
    x = x.view(x.shape[0], -1)
    out = self.adverse_lyr(x)
    return out
```

3. Having defined the generator and discriminator models, we can now instantiate one of each. We can also define our adversarial loss function as the binary cross-entropy loss function in the following code:

```
# instantiate the discriminator and generator models
gen = GANGenerator()
disc = GANDiscriminator()
# define the loss metric
adv_loss_func = torch.nn.BCELoss()
```

The adversarial loss function will be used to define the generator and discriminator loss functions later in the training loop. Conceptually, we are using binary cross-entropy as the loss function because the targets are essentially binary – that is, either real images or fake images. And, binary cross-entropy loss is a well-suited loss function for binary classification tasks.

Loading the image dataset

For the task of training a DCGAN to generate realistic-looking fake images, we are going to use the well-known `MNIST` dataset. The `MNIST` dataset contains images of handwritten digits from 0 to 9. By using `torchvision.datasets`, we can directly download the `MNIST` dataset and create a `dataset` and a `dataloader` instance out of it:

```
# define the dataset and corresponding dataloader
dloader = torch.utils.data.DataLoader(
    datasets.MNIST(
```

```
        "./data/mnist/", download=True,
      transform=transforms.Compose(
          [transforms.Resize((image_sz, image_sz)),
            transforms.ToTensor(), transforms.Normalize([0.5],
  [0.5])]),), batch_size=bsize, shuffle=True,)
```

Here is an example of a real image from the MNIST dataset:

Figure 8.4 – A real image from the MNIST dataset

> **Dataset citation**
>
> [LeCun et al., 1998a] Y. LeCun, L. Bottou, Y. Bengio, and P. Haffner. "Gradient-based learning applied to document recognition." Proceedings of the IEEE, 86(11):2278-2324, November 1998.
>
> Yann LeCun (Courant Institute, NYU) and Corinna Cortes (Google Labs, New York) hold the copyright of the MNIST dataset, which is a derivative work from the original NIST datasets. The MNIST dataset is made available under the terms of the Creative Commons Attribution-Share Alike 3.0 license.

So far, we have defined the model architecture and the data pipeline. Now it is time for us to actually write the DCGAN model training routine, which we will do in the following section.

Training loops for DCGANs

We have already defined the model architecture and loaded the dataset. In this section, we will actually train the DCGAN model:

1. **Defining the optimization schedule**: Before starting the training loop, we will define the optimization schedule for both the generator and the discriminator. We will use the Adam optimizer for our model. In the original DCGAN paper (https://arxiv.org/pdf/1511.06434.pdf), the *beta1* and *beta2* parameters of the Adam optimizer are set to *0.5* and *0.999*, as opposed to the usual *0.9* and *0.999*.

We have retained the default values of *0.9* and *0.999* in our exercise. However, you are encouraged to use the exact same values mentioned in the paper for similar results:

```
# define the optimization schedule for both G and D
opt_gen = torch.optim.Adam(gen.parameters(), lr=lrate)
opt_disc = torch.optim.Adam(disc.parameters(), lr=lrate)
```

2. **Training the generator**: Finally, we can now run the training loop to train the DCGAN. As we will be jointly training the generator and the discriminator, the training routine will consist of both these steps – training the generator model and training the discriminator model – in an alternate fashion. We will begin with training the generator in the following code:

```
os.makedirs("./images_mnist", exist_ok=True)
for ep in range(num_eps):
    for idx, (images, _) in enumerate(dloader):
        # generate ground truths for real and fake images
        good_img = Variable(torch.FloatTensor(images.
shape[0], 1).fill_(1.0), requires_grad=False)
        bad_img = Variable(torch.FloatTensor(images.
shape[0], 1) .fill_(0.0), requires_grad=False)
        # get a real image
        actual_images = Variable(images.type(torch.
FloatTensor))
        # train the generator model
        opt_gen.zero_grad()
        # generate a batch of images based on random
noise as input
        noise = Variable(torch.FloatTensor(np.random.
normal(0, 1, (images.shape[0], lat_dimension))))
        gen_images = gen(noise)
        # generator model optimization - how well can it
fool the discriminator
        generator_loss = adv_loss_func(disc(gen_images),
good_img)
        generator_loss.backward()
        opt_gen.step()
```

In the preceding code, we first generate the ground truth labels for real and fake images. Real images are labeled as 1, and fake images are labeled as 0. These labels will serve as the target outputs for the discriminator model, which is a binary classifier.

Next, we load a batch of real images from the MINST dataset loader, and we also use the generator to generate a batch of fake images using random noise as input.

Finally, we define the generator loss as the adversarial loss between the following:

i) The probability of realness of the fake images (produced by the generator model) as predicted by the discriminator model.

ii) The ground truth value of 1.

Essentially, if the discriminator is fooled to perceive the fake generated image as a real image, then the generator has succeeded in its role, and the generator loss will be low. Once we have formulated the generator loss, we can use it to backpropagate gradients along the generator model in order to tune its parameters.

In the preceding optimization step of the generator model, we left the discriminator model parameters unchanged and simply used the discriminator model for a forward pass.

3. **Training the discriminator**: Next, we will do the opposite, that is, we will retain the parameters of the generator model and train the discriminator model:

```
        # train the discriminator model
        opt_disc.zero_grad()
        # calculate discriminator loss as average of
mistakes(losses) in confusing real images as fake and
vice versa
        actual_image_loss = adv_loss_func(disc(actual_
images), good_img)
        fake_image_loss = adv_loss_func(disc(gen_images.
detach()), bad_img)
        discriminator_loss = (actual_image_loss + fake_
image_loss) / 2
        # discriminator model optimization
        discriminator_loss.backward()
        opt_disc.step()
        batches_completed = ep * len(dloader) + idx
        if batches_completed % logging_intv == 0:
```

```
            print(f"epoch number {ep} | batch number
{idx} | generator loss = {generator_loss.item()} \
            | discriminator loss = {discriminator_loss.
item()}")
            save_image(gen_images.data[:25], f"images_
mnist/{batches_completed}.png", nrow=5, normalize=True)
```

Remember that we have a batch of both real and fake images. In order to train the discriminator model, we will need both. We define the discriminator loss simply to be the adversarial loss or the binary cross entropy loss as we do for any binary classifier.

We compute the discriminator loss for the batches of both real and fake images, keeping the target values at 1 for the batch of real images and at 0 for the batch of fake images. We then use the mean of these two losses as the final discriminator loss, and use it to backpropagate gradients to tune the discriminator model parameters.

After every few epochs and batches, we log the model's performance results, that is, the generator loss and the discriminator loss. For the preceding code, we should get an output similar to the following:

```
epoch number 0 | batch number 0    | generator loss = 0.683123 | discriminator loss = 0.693203
epoch number 0 | batch number 200  | generator loss = 5.871073 | discriminator loss = 0.032416
epoch number 0 | batch number 400  | generator loss = 2.876508 | discriminator loss = 0.288186
epoch number 0 | batch number 600  | generator loss = 3.705342 | discriminator loss = 0.049239
epoch number 0 | batch number 800  | generator loss = 2.727477 | discriminator loss = 0.542196
epoch number 0 | batch number 1000 | generator loss = 3.382538 | discriminator loss = 0.282721
epoch number 0 | batch number 1200 | generator loss = 1.695523 | discriminator loss = 0.304907
epoch number 0 | batch number 1400 | generator loss = 2.297853 | discriminator loss = 0.655593
epoch number 0 | batch number 1600 | generator loss = 1.397890 | discriminator loss = 0.599436


epoch number 10 | batch number 3680 | generator loss = 1.407570 | discriminator loss = 0.409708
epoch number 10 | batch number 3880 | generator loss = 0.667673 | discriminator loss = 0.808560
epoch number 10 | batch number 4080 | generator loss = 0.793113 | discriminator loss = 0.679659
epoch number 10 | batch number 4280 | generator loss = 0.902015 | discriminator loss = 0.709771
epoch number 10 | batch number 4480 | generator loss = 0.640646 | discriminator loss = 0.321178
epoch number 10 | batch number 4680 | generator loss = 1.235740 | discriminator loss = 0.465171
epoch number 10 | batch number 4880 | generator loss = 0.896295 | discriminator loss = 0.451197
epoch number 10 | batch number 5080 | generator loss = 0.690564 | discriminator loss = 0.285500
```

Figure 8.5 – DCGAN training logs

Notice how the losses are fluctuating a bit; that generally tends to happen during the training of GAN models due to the adversarial nature of the joint training mechanism. Besides outputting logs, we also save some network-generated images at regular intervals. *Figure 8.6* shows the progression of those generated images along the first few epochs:

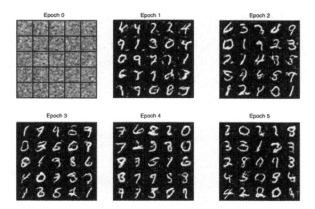

Figure 8.6 – DCGAN epoch-wise image generation

If we compare the results from the later epochs to the original MNIST images in *Figure 8.4*, it looks like the DCGAN has learned reasonably well how to generate realistic-looking fake images of handwritten digits.

That is it. We have learned how to use PyTorch to build a DCGAN model from scratch. The original DCGAN paper has a few nuanced details, such as the normal initialization of the layer parameters of the generator and discriminator models, using specific *beta1* and *beta2* values for the Adam optimizers, and more. We have omitted some of those details in the interest of focusing on the main parts of the GAN code. You are encouraged to incorporate those details and see how that changes the results.

Additionally, we have only used the MNIST database in our exercise. However, we can use any image dataset to train the DCGAN model. You are encouraged to try out this model on other image datasets. One popular image dataset that is used for DCGAN training is the celebrity faces dataset (http://mmlab.ie.cuhk.edu.hk/projects/CelebA.html).

A DCGAN trained with this model can then be used to generate the faces of celebrities who do not exist. *ThisPersonDoesntExist* (https://thispersondoesnotexist.com/) is one such project that generates the faces of humans that do not exist. Spooky? Yes. That is how powerful DCGANs and GANs, in general, are. Also, thanks to PyTorch, we can now build our own GANs in a few lines of code.

In the next and final section of this chapter, we will go beyond DCGANs and take a brief look at another type of GAN – the pix2pix model. The pix2pix model can be used to generalize the task of style transfer in images and, more generally, the task of image-to-image translation. We will discuss the architecture of the pix2pix model, its generator and discriminator, and use PyTorch to define the generator and discriminator models. We will also contrast Pix2Pix with a DCGAN in terms of their architecture and implementation.

Using GANs for style transfer

So far, we have only looked at DCGANs in detail. Although there exist hundreds of different types of GAN models already, and many more are in the making, some of the well-known GAN models include the following:

- GAN
- DCGAN
- Pix2Pix
- CycleGAN
- **SuperResolutionGAN (SRGAN)**
- Context encoders
- Text-2-Image
- **LeastSquaresGAN (LSGAN)**
- SoftmaxGAN
- WassersteinGAN

Each of these GAN variants differ by either the application they are catering to, their underlying model architecture, or due to some tweaks in their optimization strategy, such as modifying the loss function. For example, SRGANs are used to enhance the resolution of a low-resolution image. The CycleGAN uses two generators instead of one, and the generators consist of ResNet-like blocks. The LSGAN uses the mean square error as the discriminator loss function instead of the usual cross-entropy loss used in most GANs.

It is impossible to discuss all of these GAN variants in a single chapter or even a book. However, in this section, we will explore one more type of GAN model that relates to both the DCGAN model discussed in the previous section and the neural style transfer model discussed in *Chapter 7, Neural Style Transfer* .

This special type of GAN generalizes the task of style transfer between images and, furthermore, provides a general image-to-image translation framework. It is called **Pix2Pix**, and we will briefly explore its architecture and the PyTorch implementation of its generator and discriminator components.

Understanding the pix2pix architecture

In *Chapter 7, Neural Style Transfer*, you may recall that a fully trained neural style transfer model only works on a given pair of images. Pix2Pix is a more general model that can transfer style between any pair of images once trained successfully. In fact, the model goes beyond just style transfer and can be used for any image-to-image translation application, such as background masking, color palette completion, and more.

Essentially, Pix2Pix works like any GAN model. There is a generator and a discriminator involved. Instead of taking in random noise as input and generating an image, as shown in *Figure 8.1*, the generator in a `pix2pix` model takes in a real image as input and tries to generate a translated version of that image. If the task at hand is style transfer, then the generator will try to generate a style-transferred image.

Subsequently, the discriminator now looks at a pair of images instead of just a single image, as was the case in *Figure 8.1*. A real image and its equivalent translated image is fed as input to the discriminator. If the translated image is a genuine one, then the discriminator is supposed to output *1*, and if the translated image is generated by the generator, then the discriminator is supposed to output *0*. *Figure 8.7* shows the schematic for a `pix2pix` model:

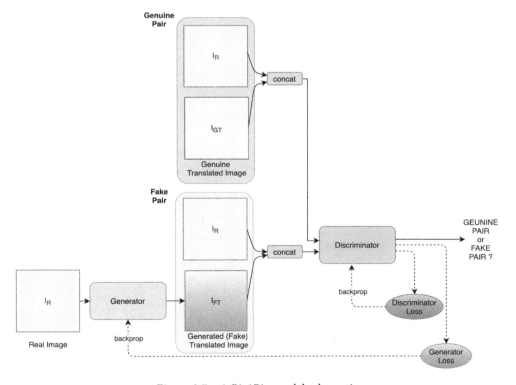

Figure 8.7 – A Pix2Pix model schematic

Figure 8.7 shows significant similarities to *Figure 8.1*, which implies that the underlying idea is the same as a regular GAN. The only difference is that the real or fake question to the discriminator is posed on a pair of images as opposed to a single image.

Exploring the Pix2Pix generator

The generator sub-model used in the `pix2pix` model is a well-known CNN used for image segmentation – the **UNet**. *Figure 8.8* shows the architecture of the UNet, which is used as a generator for the `pix2pix` model:

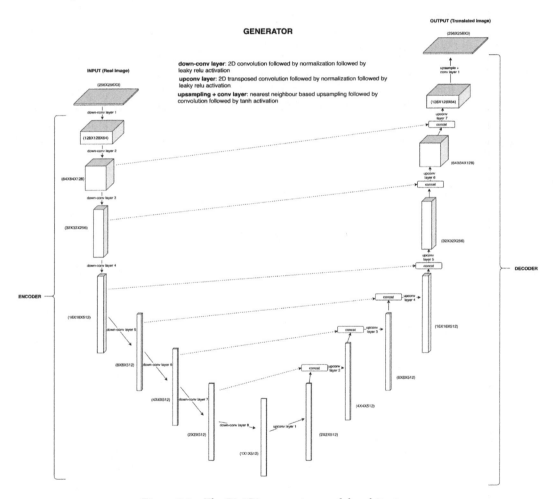

Figure 8.8 – The Pix2Pix generator model architecture

Firstly, the name, UNet, comes from the *U* shape of the network, as is made evident from the preceding diagram. There are two main components in this network, as follows:

- From the upper-left corner to the bottom lies the encoder part of the network, which encodes the **256x256** RGB input image into a **512**-sized feature vector.

- From the upper-right corner to the bottom lies the decoder part of the network, which generates an image from the embedding vector of size **512**.

A key property of UNet is the **skip connections**, that is, the concatenation of features from the encoder section to the decoder section, as shown by the dotted arrows in *Figure 8.8*. Using features from the encoder section helps the decoder to better localize the high-resolution information at each upsampling step. The concatenation always takes place along the depth dimension.

Essentially, the encoder section is a sequence of down-convolutional blocks, where each down-convolutional block is itself a sequence of a 2D convolutional layer, an instance normalization layer, and a leaky ReLU activation. Similarly, the decoder section consists of a sequence of up-convolutional blocks, where each block is a sequence of a 2D-transposed convolutional layer, an instance normalization layer, and a ReLU activation layer.

The final part of this UNet generator architecture is a nearest neighbor-based upsampling layer, followed by a 2D convolutional layer, and, finally, a `tanh` activation. Let's now look at the PyTorch code for the UNet generator:

1. Here is the equivalent PyTorch code for defining the UNet-based generator architecture:

```python
class UNetGenerator(nn.Module):
    def __init__(self, chnls_in=3, chnls_op=3):
        super(UNetGenerator, self).__init__()
        self.down_conv_layer_1 = DownConvBlock(chnls_in,
64, norm=False)
        self.down_conv_layer_2 = DownConvBlock(64, 128)
        self.down_conv_layer_3 = DownConvBlock(128, 256)
        self.down_conv_layer_4 = DownConvBlock(256, 512,
dropout=0.5)
        self.down_conv_layer_5 = DownConvBlock(512, 512,
dropout=0.5)
        self.down_conv_layer_6 = DownConvBlock(512, 512,
dropout=0.5)
        self.down_conv_layer_7 = DownConvBlock(512, 512,
dropout=0.5)
```

```
        self.down_conv_layer_8 = DownConvBlock(512, 512,
norm=False, dropout=0.5)
        self.up_conv_layer_1 = UpConvBlock(512, 512,
dropout=0.5)
        self.up_conv_layer_2 = UpConvBlock(1024, 512,
dropout=0.5)
        self.up_conv_layer_3 = UpConvBlock(1024, 512,
dropout=0.5)
        self.up_conv_layer_4 = UpConvBlock(1024, 512,
dropout=0.5)
        self.up_conv_layer_5 = UpConvBlock(1024, 256)
        self.up_conv_layer_6 = UpConvBlock(512, 128)
        self.up_conv_layer_7 = UpConvBlock(256, 64)
        self.upsample_layer = nn.Upsample(scale_factor=2)
        self.zero_pad = nn.ZeroPad2d((1, 0, 1, 0))
        self.conv_layer_1 = nn.Conv2d(128, chnls_op, 4,
padding=1)
        self.activation = nn.Tanh()
```

As you can see, there are 8 down-convolutional layers and 7 up-convolutional layers. The up-convolutional layers have two inputs, one from the previous up-convolutional layer output and another from the equivalent down-convolutional layer output, as shown by the dotted lines in *Figure 8.7*.

2. We have used the UpConvBlock and DownConvBlock classes to define the layers of the UNet model. The following is the definition of these blocks, starting with the UpConvBlock class:

```
class UpConvBlock(nn.Module):
    def __init__(self, ip_sz, op_sz, dropout=0.0):
        super(UpConvBlock, self).__init__()
        self.layers = [
            nn.ConvTranspose2d(ip_sz, op_sz, 4, 2, 1),
            nn.InstanceNorm2d(op_sz), nn.ReLU(),]
        if dropout:
            self.layers += [nn.Dropout(dropout)]
    def forward(self, x, enc_ip):
        x = nn.Sequential(*(self.layers))(x)
```

```
op = torch.cat((x, enc_ip), 1)
return op
```

The transpose convolutional layer in this up-convolutional block consists of a 4x4 kernel with a stride of 2 steps, which essentially doubles the spatial dimensions of its output compared to the input.

In this transpose convolution layer, the 4x4 kernel is passed through every other pixel (due to a stride of 2) in the input image. At each pixel, the pixel value is multiplied with each of the 16 values in the 4x4 kernel.

The overlapping values of the kernel multiplication results across the image are then summed up, resulting in an output twice the length and twice the breadth of the input image. Also, in the preceding `forward` method, the concatenation operation is performed after the forward pass is done via the up-convolutional block.

3. Next, here is the PyTorch code for defining the `DownConvBlock` class:

```
class DownConvBlock(nn.Module):
    def __init__(self, ip_sz, op_sz, norm=True,
dropout=0.0):
        super(DownConvBlock, self).__init__()
        self.layers = [nn.Conv2d(ip_sz, op_sz, 4, 2, 1)]
        if norm:
            self.layers.append(nn.InstanceNorm2d(op_sz))
        self.layers += [nn.LeakyReLU(0.2)]
        if dropout:
            self.layers += [nn.Dropout(dropout)]
    def forward(self, x):
        op = nn.Sequential(*(self.layers))(x)
        return op
```

The convolutional layer inside the down-convolutional block has a kernel of size 4x4, a stride of 2, and the padding is activated. Because the stride value is 2, the output of this layer is half the spatial dimensions of its input.

A leaky ReLU activation is also used for similar reasons as DCGANs – the ability to deal with negative inputs, which also helps with alleviating the vanishing gradients problem.

So far, we have seen the `__init__` method of our UNet-based generator. The `forward` method is pretty straightforward hereafter:

```python
def forward(self, x):
    enc1 = self.down_conv_layer_1(x)
    enc2 = self.down_conv_layer_2(enc1)
    enc3 = self.down_conv_layer_3(enc2)
    enc4 = self.down_conv_layer_4(enc3)
    enc5 = self.down_conv_layer_5(enc4)
    enc6 = self.down_conv_layer_6(enc5)
    enc7 = self.down_conv_layer_7(enc6)
    enc8 = self.down_conv_layer_8(enc7)
    dec1 = self.up_conv_layer_1(enc8, enc7)
    dec2 = self.up_conv_layer_2(dec1, enc6)
    dec3 = self.up_conv_layer_3(dec2, enc5)
    dec4 = self.up_conv_layer_4(dec3, enc4)
    dec5 = self.up_conv_layer_5(dec4, enc3)
    dec6 = self.up_conv_layer_6(dec5, enc2)
    dec7 = self.up_conv_layer_7(dec6, enc1)
    final = self.upsample_layer(dec7)
    final = self.zero_pad(final)
    final = self.conv_layer_1(final)
    return self.activation(final)
```

Having discussed the generator part of the `pix2pix` model, let's take a look at the discriminator model as well.

Exploring the Pix2Pix discriminator

The discriminator model, in this case, is also a binary classifier – just as it was for the DCGAN. The only difference is that this binary classifier takes in two images as inputs. The two inputs are concatenated along the depth dimension. *Figure 8.9* shows the discriminator model's high-level architecture:

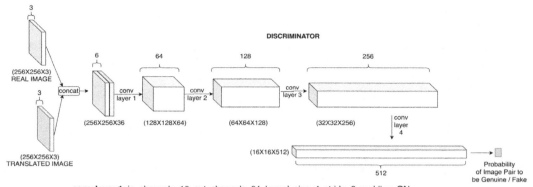

conv layer 1: in_channels=16, out_channels=64, kernel_size=4, stride=2, padding=ON
conv layer 2: in_channels=64, out_channels=128, kernel_size=4, stride=2, padding=ON
conv layer 3: in_channels=128, out_channels=256, kernel_size=4, stride=2, padding=ON
conv layer 4: in_channels=256, out_channels=512, kernel_size=4, stride=2, padding=ON

Figure 8.9 – The Pix2Pix discriminator model architecture

It is a CNN where the last 3 convolutional layers are followed by a normalization layer as well as a leaky ReLU activation. The PyTorch code to define this discriminator model will be as follows:

```
class Pix2PixDiscriminator(nn.Module):
    def __init__(self, chnls_in=3):
        super(Pix2PixDiscriminator, self).__init__()
        def disc_conv_block(chnls_in, chnls_op, norm=1):
            layers = [nn.Conv2d(chnls_in, chnls_op, 4,
stride=2, padding=1)]
            if normalization:
                layers.append(nn.InstanceNorm2d(chnls_op))
            layers.append(nn.LeakyReLU(0.2, inplace=True))
            return layers
        self.lyr1 = disc_conv_block(chnls_in * 2, 64, norm=0)
        self.lyr2 = disc_conv_block(64, 128)
        self.lyr3 = disc_conv_block(128, 256)
        self.lyr4 = disc_conv_block(256, 512)
```

As you can see, the 4 convolutional layers subsequently double the depth of the spatial representation at each step. Layers 2, 3, and 4 have added normalization layers after the convolutional layer, and a leaky ReLU activation with a negative slope of 20% is applied at the end of every convolutional block. Finally, here is the `forward` method of the discriminator model class in PyTorch:

```
def forward(self, real_image, translated_image):
    ip = torch.cat((real_image, translated_image), 1)
    op = self.lyr1(ip)
    op = self.lyr2(op)
    op = self.lyr3(op)
    op = self.lyr4(op)
    op = nn.ZeroPad2d((1, 0, 1, 0))(op)
    op = nn.Conv2d(512, 1, 4, padding=1)(op)
    return op
```

First, the input images are concatenated and passed through the four convolutional blocks and finally led into a single binary output that tells us the probability of the pair of images being genuine or fake (that is, generated by the generator model). In this way, the `pix2pix` model is trained at runtime so that the generator of the `pix2pix` model can take in any image as input and apply the image translation function that it has learned during training.

The `pix2pix` model will be considered successful if the generated fake-translated image is difficult to tell apart from a genuine translated version of the original image.

This concludes our exploration of the `pix2pix` model. In principle, the overall model schematic for Pix2Pix is quite similar to that of the DCGAN model. The discriminator network for both of these models is a CNN-based binary classifier. The generator network for the `pix2pix` model is a slightly more complex architecture inspired by the UNet image segmentation model.

Overall, we have been able to both successfully define the generator and discriminator models for DCGAN and Pix2Pix using PyTorch, and understand the inner workings of these two GAN variants.

After finishing this section, you should be able to get started with writing PyTorch code for the many other GAN variants out there. Building and training various GAN models using PyTorch can be a good learning experience and certainly a fun exercise. We encourage you to use the information from this chapter to work on your own GAN projects using PyTorch.

Summary

GANs have been an active area of research and development in recent years, ever since their inception in 2014. This chapter was an exploration of the concepts behind GANs, including the components of GANs, namely, the generator and the discriminator. We discussed the architectures of each of these components and the overall schematic of a GAN model.

Next, we did a deep dive into a particular type of GAN – the DCGAN. With the help of an exercise, we built a DCGAN model from scratch using PyTorch. We used the MNIST dataset to train the model. The generator of the trained DCGAN model successfully generated realistic-looking fake images of handwritten digits after 10 epochs of training.

In the last section of this chapter, we explored another type of GAN, which is used for the task of image-to-image translation – the `pix2pix` model. Instead of working on just a pair of images, the `pix2pix` GAN model is architectured to generalize any image-to-image translation task, including a style transfer for any given pair of images.

Additionally, we discussed how the `pix2pix` model schematic and the architecture of its generator and discriminator models differ from that of the DCGAN model. This concludes our ongoing discussion on generative models, which began in *Chapter 6, Music and Text Generation with PyTorch*, continued in *Chapter 7, Neural Style Transfer*, and now ends with GANs.

In the next chapter, we will change tracks and discuss one of the most exciting and upcoming areas of deep learning – deep reinforcement learning. This branch of deep learning is still maturing. We will explore what PyTorch already has to offer and how it is helping to further developments in this challenging field of deep learning.

9
Deep Reinforcement Learning

Machine learning is usually classified into three different paradigms: **supervised learning**, **unsupervised learning**, and **reinforcement learning** (**RL**). Supervised learning requires labeled data and has been the most popularly used machine learning paradigm so far. However, applications based on unsupervised learning, which does not require labels, have been steadily on the rise, especially in the form of generative models.

An RL, on the other hand, is a different branch of machine learning that is considered to be the closest we have reached in terms of emulating how humans learn. It is an area of active research and development and is in its early stages, with some promising results. A prominent example is the famous AlphaGo model, built by Google's DeepMind, that defeated the world's best Go player.

In supervised learning, we usually feed the model with atomic input-output data pairs and hope for the model to learn the output as a function of the input. In RL, we are not keen on learning such individual input to individual output functions. Instead, we are interested in learning a strategy (or policy) that enables us to take a sequence of steps (or actions), starting from the input (state), in order to obtain the final output or achieve the final goal.

Looking at a photo and deciding whether it's a cat or a dog is an atomic input-output learning task that can be solved through supervised learning. However, looking at a chess board and deciding the next move with the aim of winning the game requires strategy, and we need RL for complex tasks like these.

In the previous chapters, we came across examples of supervised learning such as building a classifier to classify handwritten digits using the MNIST dataset. We also explored unsupervised learning while building a text generation model using an unlabeled text corpus.

In this chapter, we will uncover some of the basic concepts of RL and **deep reinforcement learning (DRL)**. We will then focus on a specific and popular type of DRL model – the **deep Q-learning Network (DQN)** model. Using PyTorch, we will build a DRL application. We will train a DQN model to learn how to play the game of Pong against a computer opponent (bot).

By the end of this chapter, you will have all the necessary context to start working on your own DRL project in PyTorch. Additionally, you will have hands-on experience of building a DQN model for a real-life problem. The skills you'll have gained in this chapter will be useful for working on other such RL problems.

This chapter is broken down into the following topics:

- Reviewing reinforcement learning concepts
- Discussing Q-learning
- Understanding deep Q-learning
- Building a DQN model in PyTorch

Technical requirements

We will be using Jupyter notebooks for all of our exercises. The following is a list of Python libraries that must be installed for this chapter using `pip`. For example, run `pip install torch==1.4.0` on the command line:

```
jupyter==1.0.0
torch==1.4.0
atari-py==0.2.6
gym==0.17.2
```

All the code files that are relevant to this chapter are available at `https://github.com/PacktPublishing/Mastering-PyTorch/tree/master/Chapter09`.

Reviewing reinforcement learning concepts

In a way, RL can be defined as learning from mistakes. Instead of getting the feedback for every data instance, as is the case with supervised learning, the feedback is received after a sequence of actions. The following diagram shows the high-level schematic of an RL system:

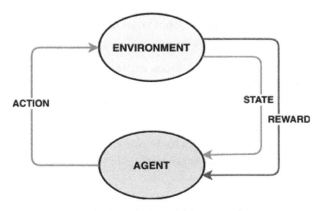

Figure 9.1 – Reinforcement learning schematic

In an RL setting, we usually have an **agent**, which does the learning. The agent learns to make decisions and take **actions** according to these decisions. The agent operates within a provided **environment**. This environment can be thought of as a confined world where the agent lives, takes actions, and learns from its actions. An action here is simply the implementation of the decision the agent makes based on what it has learned.

We mentioned earlier that unlike supervised learning, RL does not have an output for each and every input; that is, the agent does not necessarily receive a feedback for each and every action. Instead, the agent works in **states**. Suppose it starts at an initial state, S_0. It then takes an action, say a_0. This action transitions the state of the agent from S_0 to S_1, after which the agent takes another action, a_1, and the cycle goes on.

Occasionally, the agent receives **rewards** based on its state. The sequence of states and actions that the agent traverses is also known as a **trajectory**. Let's say the agent received a reward at state S_2. In that case, the trajectory that resulted in this reward would be S_0, a_0, S_1, a_1, S_2.

Note

The rewards could either be positive or negative.

Based on the rewards, the agent learns to adjust its behavior so that it takes actions in a way that maximizes the long-term rewards. This is the essence of RL. The agent learns a strategy regarding how to act optimally (that is, to maximize the reward) based on the given state and reward.

This learned strategy, which is basically actions expressed as a function of states and rewards, is called the **policy** of the agent. The ultimate goal of RL is to compute a policy that enables the agent to always receive the maximum reward from the given situation the agent is placed in.

Video games are one of the best examples to demonstrate RL. Let's use the video game Pong as an example, which is a virtual version of table tennis. The following is a snapshot of this game:

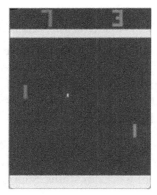

Figure 9.2 – Pong video game

Consider that the player to the right is the agent, which is represented by a short vertical line. Notice that there is a well-defined environment here. The environment consists of the playing area, which is denoted by the brown pixels. The environment also consists of a ball, which is denoted by a white pixel. As well as this, the environment consists of the boundaries of the playing area, denoted by the gray stripes and edges that the ball may bounce off. Finally, and most importantly, the environment includes an opponent, which looks like the agent but is placed on the left-hand side, opposite the agent.

Usually, in an RL setting, the agent at any given state has a finite set of possible actions, referred to as a discrete action space (as opposed to a continuous action space). In this example, the agent has two possible actions at all states – move up or move down, but with two exceptions. First, it can only move down when it is at the top-most position (state), and second, it can only move up when it is at the bottom-most position (state).

The concept of reward in this case can be directly mapped to what happens in an actual table tennis game. If you miss the ball, your opponent gains a point. Whoever scores 21 points first wins the game and receives a positive reward. Losing a game means negative rewards. Scoring a point or losing a point also results in smaller intermediate positive and negative rewards, respectively. A sequence of play starting from score 0-0 and leading to either of the players scoring 21 points is called an **episode**.

Training our agent for a Pong game using RL is equivalent to training someone to play table tennis from scratch. Training results in a policy that the agent follows while playing the game. In any given situation – which includes the position of the ball, the position of the opponent, the scoreboard, as well as the previous reward – a successfully trained agent moves up or down to maximize its chances of winning the game.

So far, we have discussed the basic concepts behind RL by providing an example. In doing so, we have repeatedly mentioned terms such as strategy, policy, and learning. But how does the agent actually learn the policy? The answer is through an RL model, which works based on a pre-defined algorithm. Next, we will explore the different kinds of RL algorithms.

Types of reinforcement learning algorithms

In this section, we will look at the types of RL algorithms, as per the literature. We will then explore some of the subtypes within these types. Broadly speaking, RL algorithms can be categorized as either of the following:

- **Model-based**
- **Model-free**

Let's look at these one by one.

Model-based

As the name suggests, in model-based algorithms, the agent knows about the model of the environment. The model here refers to the mathematical formulation of a function that can be used to estimate rewards and how the states transition within the environment. Because the agent has some idea about the environment, it helps reduce the sample space to choose the next action from. This helps with the efficiency of the learning process.

However, in reality, a modeled environment is not directly available most of the time. If we, nonetheless, want to use the model-based approach, we need to have the agent learn the environment model with its own experience. In such cases, the agent is highly likely to learn a biased representation of the model and perform poorly in the real environment. For this reason, model-based approaches are less frequently used for implementing RL systems. We will not be discussing models based on this approach in detail in this book, but here are some examples:

- **Model-Based DRL with Model-Free Fine-Tuning (MBMF)**.
- **Model-Based Value Estimation (MBVE)** for efficient Model-Free RL.
- **Imagination-Augmented Agents (I2A)** for DRL.
- **AlphaZero**, the famous AI bot that defeated Chess and Go champions.

Now, let's look at the other set of RL algorithms that work with a different philosophy.

Model-free

The model-free approach works without any model of the environment and is currently more popularly used for RL research and development. There are primarily two ways of training the agent in a model-free RL setting:

- **Policy optimization**
- **Q-learning**

Policy optimization

In this method, we formulate the policy in the form of a function of an action, given the current state, as demonstrated in the following equation:

$$Policy = F_\beta(a \mid S)$$

Here, β represents the internal parameters of this function, which is updated to optimize the policy function via gradient ascent. The objective function is defined using the policy function and the rewards. An approximation of the objective function may also be used in some cases for the optimization process. Furthermore, in some cases, an approximation of the policy function could be used instead of the actual policy function for the optimization process.

Usually, the optimizations that are performed under this approach are **on-policy**, which means that the parameters are updated based on the data gathered using the latest policy version. Some examples of policy optimization-based RL algorithms are as follows:

- **Policy gradient**: This is the most basic policy optimization method and is where we directly optimize the policy function using gradient ascent. The policy function outputs the probabilities of different actions to be taken next, at each time step.

- **Actor-critic**: Because of the on-policy nature of optimization under the policy gradient algorithm, every iteration of the algorithm needs the policy to be updated. This takes a lot of time. The actor-critic method introduces the use of a value function, as well as a policy function. The actor models the policy function and the critic models the value function.

    By using a critic, the policy update process becomes faster. We will discuss the value function in more detail in the next section. However, we will not go into the mathematical details of the actor-critic method in this book.

- **Trust region policy optimization** (**TRPO**): Like the policy gradient method, TRPO consists of an on-policy optimization approach. In the policy-gradient approach, we use the gradient for updating the policy function parameters, β. Since the gradient is a first-order derivative, it can be noisy for sharp curvatures in the function. This may lead us to making large policy changes that may destabilize the learning trajectory of the agent.

    To avoid that, TRPO proposes a trust region. It defines an upper limit on how much the policy may change in a given update step. This ensures the stability of the optimization process.

- **Proximal policy optimization** (**PPO**): Similar to TRPO, PPO aims to stabilize the optimization process. During gradient ascent, an update is performed per data sample in the policy gradient approach. PPO, however, uses a surrogate objective function, which facilitates updates over batches of data samples. This results in estimating gradients more conservatively, thereby improving the chances of the gradient ascent algorithm converging.

Policy optimization functions directly work on optimizing the policy and hence are extremely intuitive algorithms. However, due to the on-policy nature of most of these algorithms, data needs to be resampled at each step after the policy is updated. This can be a limiting factor in solving RL problems. Next, we will discuss the other kind of model-free algorithm that is more sample-efficient, known as Q-learning.

Q-learning

Contrary to policy optimization algorithms, **Q-learning** relies on a value function instead of a policy function. From here on, this chapter will focus on Q-learning. We will explore the fundamentals of Q-learning in detail in the next section.

Discussing Q-learning

The key difference between policy optimization and Q-learning is the fact that in the latter, we are not directly optimizing the policy. Instead, we optimize a value function. What is a **value function**? We have already learned that RL is all about an agent learning to gain the maximum overall rewards while traversing a trajectory of states and actions. A value function is a function of a given state the agent is currently at, and this function outputs the expected sum of rewards the agent will receive by the end of the current episode.

In Q-learning, we optimize a specific type of value function, known as the **action-value function**, which depends on both the current state and the action. At a given state, S, the action-value function determines the long-term rewards (rewards until the end of the episode) the agent will receive for taking action a. This function is usually expressed as $Q(S, a)$, and hence is also called the Q-function. The action-value is also referred to as the **Q-value**.

The Q-values for every (state, action) pair can be stored in a table where the two dimensions are state and action. For example, if there are four possible states, S_1, S_2, S_3, and S_4, and two possible actions, a_1 and a_2, then the eight Q-values will be stored in a 4x2 table. The goal of Q-learning, therefore, is to create this table of Q-values. Once the table is available, the agent can look up the Q-values for all possible actions from the given state and take the action with the maximum Q-value. However, the question is, where do we get the Q-values from? The answer lies in the **Bellman equation**, which is mathematically expressed as follows:

$$Q(S_t, a_t) = R + \gamma * Q(S_{t+1}, a_{t+1})$$

The Bellman equation is a recursive way of calculating Q-values. R in this equation is the reward received by taking action a_t at state S_t, while γ (gamma) is the **discount factor**, which is a scalar value between *0* and *1*. Basically, this equation states that the Q-value for the current state, S_t, and action, a_t, is equal to the reward, R, received by taking action a_t at state S_t, plus the Q-value resulting from the most optimal action, a_t+1, taken from the next state, S_t+1, multiplied by a discount factor. The discount factor defines how much weightage is to be given to the immediate reward versus the long-term future rewards.

Now that we have defined most of the underlying concepts of Q-learning, let's walk through an example to demonstrate how Q-learning exactly works. The following diagram shows an environment that consists of five possible states:

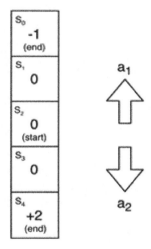

Figure 9.3 – Q-learning example environment

There are two different possible actions – moving up (**a₁**) or down (**a₂**). There are different rewards at different states ranging from **+2** at state **S₄** to **-1** at state **S₀**. Every episode in this environment starts from state **S₂** and ends at either **S₀** or **S₄**. Because there are five states and two possible actions, the Q-values can be stored in a 5x2 table. The following code snippet shows how rewards and Q-values can be written in Python:

```
rwrds = [-1, 0, 0, 0, 2]
Qvals = [[0.0, 0.0],
         [0.0, 0.0],
         [0.0, 0.0],
         [0.0, 0.0],
         [0.0, 0.0]]
```

We initialize all the Q-values to zero. Also, because there are two specific end states, we need to specify those in the form of a list, as shown here:

```
end_states = [1, 0, 0, 0, 1]
```

This basically indicates that states S_0 and S_4 are end states. There is one final piece we need to look at before we can run the complete Q-learning loop. At each step of Q-learning, the agent has two options with regards to taking the next action:

- Take the action that has the highest Q-value.

- Randomly choose the next action.

Why would the agent choose an action randomly?

Remember that in *Chapter 6, Music and Text Generation with PyTorch*, in the *Text generation* section, we discussed how greedy search or beam search results in repetitive results, and hence introducing randomness helps in producing better results. With a similar approach, if the agent always chooses the next action based on Q-values, then it might get stuck choosing an action repeatedly that gives an immediate high reward in the short term. Hence, taking actions randomly once in a while will help the agent get out of such sub-optimal conditions.

Now that we've established that the agent has two possible ways of taking an action at each step, we need to decide which way the agent goes. This is where the **epsilon-greedy-action** mechanism comes into play. The following diagram shows how it works:

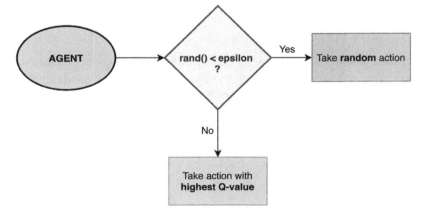

Figure 9.4 – Epsilon-greedy-action mechanism

Under this mechanism, at each episode, an epsilon value is pre-decided, which is a scalar value between 0 and 1. In a given episode, for taking each next action, the agent generates a random number between 0 to 1. If the generated number is less than the pre-defined epsilon value, the agent chooses the next action randomly from the available set of next actions. Otherwise, the Q-values for each of the next possible actions are retrieved from the Q-value table, and the action with the highest Q-value is chosen. The Python code for the epsilon-greedy-action mechanism is as follows:

```python
def eps_greedy_action_mechanism(eps, S):
    rnd = np.random.uniform()
    if rnd < eps:
        return np.random.randint(0, 2)
    else:
        return np.argmax(Qvals[S])
```

Typically, we start with an epsilon value of 1 at the first episode and then linearly decrease it as the episodes progress. The idea here is that we want the agent to explore different options initially. However, as the learning process progresses, the agent is less susceptible to getting stuck collecting short-term rewards and hence it can better exploit the Q-values table.

We are now in a position to write the Python code for the main Q-learning loop, which will look as follows:

```python
n_epsds = 100
eps = 1
gamma = 0.9
for e in range(n_epsds):
    S_initial = 2 # start with state S2
    S = S_initial
    while not end_states[S]:
        a = eps_greedy_action_mechanism(eps, S)
        R, S_next = take_action(S, a)
        if end_states[S_next]:
            Qvals[S][a] = R
        else:
            Qvals[S][a] = R + gamma * max(Qvals[S_next])
        S = S_next
    eps = eps - 1/n_epsds
```

First, we define that the agent shall be trained for `100` episodes. We begin with an epsilon value of `1` and we define the discounting factor (gamma) as `0.9`. Next, we run the Q-learning loop, which loops over the number of episodes. In each iteration of this loop, we run through an entire episode. Within the episode, we first initialize the state of the agent to `S2`.

Thereon, we run another internal loop, which only breaks if the agent reaches an end state. Within this internal loop, we decide on the next action for the agent using the epsilon-greedy-action mechanism. The agent then takes the action, which transitions the agent to a new state and may possibly yield a reward. The implementation for the `take_action` function is as follows:

```
def take_action(S, a):
  if a == 0: # move up
    S_next = S - 1
  else:
    S_next = S + 1
  return rwrds[S_next], S_next
```

Once we obtain the reward and the next state, we update the Q-value for the current state-action pair using the *Bellman* equation. The next state now becomes the current state and the process repeats. At the end of each episode, the epsilon value is reduced linearly. Once the entire Q-learning loop is over, we obtain a Q-values table. This table is essentially all that the agent needs to operate in this environment in order to gain the maximum long-term rewards.

Ideally, a well-trained agent for this example would always move downward to receive the maximum reward of *+2* at S_4, and would avoid going toward S_0, which contains a negative reward of *-1*.

This completes our discussion on Q-learning. The preceding code should help you get started with Q-learning in simple environments such as the one provided here. For more complex and realistic environments, such as video games, this approach will not work. Why?

We have noticed that the essence of Q-learning lies in creating the Q-values table. In our example, we only had 5 states and 2 actions, and therefore the table was of size 10, which is manageable. But in video games such as Pong, there are far too many possible states. This explodes the Q-values table's size, which makes our Q-learning algorithm extremely memory intensive and impractical to run.

Thankfully, there is a solution where we can still use the concept of Q-learning without our machines running out of memory. This solution combines the worlds of Q-learning and deep neural networks and provides the extremely popular RL algorithm known as **DQN**. In the next section, we will discuss the basics of DQN and some of its novel characteristics.

Understanding deep Q-learning

Instead of creating a Q-values table, **DQN** uses a **deep neural network** (**DNN**) that outputs a Q-value for a given state-action pair. DQN is used with complex environments such as video games, where there are far too many states for them to be managed in a Q-values table. The current image frame of the video game is used to represent the current state and is fed as input to the underlying DNN model, together with the current action.

The DNN outputs a scalar Q-value for each such input. In practice, instead of just passing the current image frame, N number of neighboring image frames in a given time window are passed as input to the model.

We are using a DNN to solve an RL problem. This has an inherent concern. While working with DNNs, we have always worked with **independent and identically distributed** (**iid**) data samples. However, in RL, every current output impacts the next input. For example, in the case of Q-learning, the Bellman equation itself suggests that the Q-value is dependent on another Q-value; that is, the Q-value of the next state-action pair impacts the Q-value of the current-state pair.

This implies that we are working with a constantly moving target and there is a high correlation between the target and the input. DQN addresses these issues with two novel features:

- Using two separate DNNs
- Experience replay buffer

Let's look at these in more detail.

Using two separate DNNs

Let's rewrite the Bellman equation for DQNs:

$$Q\left(S_t, a_t, \theta\right) = R + \gamma * Q\left(S_{t+1}, a_{t+1}, \theta\right)$$

This equation is mostly the same as for Q-learning except for the introduction of a new term, θ (theta). θ represents the weights of the DNN that the DQN model uses to get Q-values. But something is odd with this equation.

Notice that θ is placed on both the left hand-side and the right-hand side of the equation. This means that at every step, we are using the same neural network for getting the Q-values of the current state-action, pair as well as the next state-action pair. This means that we are chasing a non-stationary target because every step, θ, will be updated, which will change both the left-hand side as well as the right-hand side of the equation for the next step, causing instability in the learning process.

This can be more clearly seen by looking at the loss function, which the DNN will be trying to minimize using gradient descent. The loss function is as follows:

$$L = E[(R + \gamma * Q\,(S_{t+1}, a_{t+1}, \theta) - Q\,(S_t, a_t, \theta))^2]$$

Keeping R (reward) aside for a moment, having the exact same network producing Q-values for current and next state-action pairs will lead to volatility in the loss function as both terms will be constantly changing. To address this issue, DQN uses two separate networks – a main DNN and a target DNN. Both DNNs have the exact same architecture.

The main DNN is used for computing the Q-values of the current state-action pair, while the target DNN is used for computing the Q-values of the next (or target) state-action pair. However, although the weights of the main DNN are updated at every learning step, the weights of the target DNN are frozen. After every K gradient descent iterations, the weights of the main network are copied to the target network. This mechanism keeps the training procedure relatively stable. The weights-copying mechanism ensures accurate predictions from the target network.

Experience replay buffer

Because the DNN expects iid data as input, we simply cache the last X number of steps (frames of the video game) into a buffer memory and then randomly sample batches of data from the buffer. These batches are then fed as inputs to the DNN. Because the batches consist of randomly sampled data, the distribution looks similar to that of iid data samples. This helps stabilize the DNN training process.

> **Note**
> Without the buffer trick, the DNN would receive correlated data, which would result in poor optimization results.

These two tricks have proven significant in contributing to the success of DQNs. Now that we have a basic understanding of how DQN models work and their novel characteristics, let's move on to the final section of this chapter, where we will implement our own DQN model. Using PyTorch, we will build a CNN-based DQN model that will learn to play the Atari video game known as Pong and potentially learn to win the game against the computer opponent.

Building a DQN model in PyTorch

We discussed the theory behind DQNs in the previous section. In this section, we will take a hands-on approach. Using PyTorch, we will build a CNN-based DQN model that will train an agent to play the video game known as Pong. The goal of this exercise is to demonstrate how to develop DRL applications using PyTorch. Let's get straight into the exercise.

Initializing the main and target CNN models

In this exercise, we will only show the important parts of the code for demonstration purposes. In order to access the full code, visit `https://github.com/PacktPublishing/Mastering-PyTorch/blob/master/Chapter09/pong.ipynb`. Follow these steps:

1. First, we need to import the necessary libraries:

```
# general imports
import cv2
import math
import numpy as np
import random
# reinforcement learning related imports
import re
import atari_py as ap
from collections import deque
from gym import make, ObservationWrapper, Wrapper
from gym.spaces import Box
# pytorch imports
```

```
import torch
import torch.nn as nn
from torch import save
from torch.optim import Adam
```

In this exercise, besides the usual Python- and PyTorch-related imports, we are also using a Python library called gym. It is a Python library produced by OpenAI that provides a set of tools for building DRL applications. Essentially, importing gym does away with the need of writing all the scaffolding code for the internals of an RL system. It also consists of built-in environments, including one for the video game Pong, which we will use in this exercise.

2. After importing the libraries, we must define the CNN architecture for the DQN model. This CNN model essentially takes in the current state input and outputs the probability distribution over all possible actions. The action with the highest probability gets chosen as the next action by the agent. Instead of using a regression model to predict the Q-values for each state-action pair, we cleverly turn this into a classification problem.

The Q-value regression model will have to be run separately for all possible actions, and we will choose the action with the highest predicted Q-value. But using this classification model combines the task of calculating Q-values and predicting the best next action into one:

```
class ConvDQN(nn.Module):
    def __init__(self, ip_sz, tot_num_acts):
        super(ConvDQN, self).__init__()
        self._ip_sz = ip_sz
        self._tot_num_acts = tot_num_acts
        self.cnv1 = nn.Conv2d(ip_sz[0], 32, kernel_
size=8, stride=4)
        self.rl = nn.ReLU()
        self.cnv2 = nn.Conv2d(32, 64, kernel_size=4,
stride=2)
        self.cnv3 = nn.Conv2d(64, 64, kernel_size=3,
stride=1)
        self.fc1 = nn.Linear(self.feat_sz, 512)
        self.fc2 = nn.Linear(512, tot_num_acts)
```

As we can see, the model consists of three convolutional layers – cnv1, cnv2, and cnv3 – with ReLU activations in-between them, followed by two fully connected layers. Now, let's look at what a forward pass through this model entails:

```python
def forward(self, x):
    op = self.cnv1(x)
    op = self.rl(op)
    op = self.cnv2(op)
    op = self.rl(op)
    op = self.cnv3(op)
    op = self.rl(op).view(x.size()[0], -1)
    op = self.fc1(op)
    op = self.rl(op)
    op = self.fc2(op)
    return op
```

The forward method simply demonstrates a forward pass by the model, where the input is passed through the convolutional layers, flattened, and finally fed to the fully connected layers. Finally, let's look at the other model methods:

```python
@property
def feat_sz(self):
    x = torch.zeros(1, *self._ip_sz)
    x = self.cnv1(x)
    x = self.rl(x)
    x = self.cnv2(x)
    x = self.rl(x)
    x = self.cnv3(x)
    x = self.rl(x)
    return x.view(1, -1).size(1)
def perf_action(self, stt, eps, dvc):
    if random.random() > eps:
        stt=torch.from_numpy(np.float32(stt)).unsqueeze(0).to(dvc)
        q_val = self.forward(stt)
        act = q_val.max(1)[1].item()
    else:
        act = random.randrange(self._tot_num_acts)
    return act
```

In the preceding code snippet, the `feat_size` method is simply meant to calculate the size of the feature vector after flattening the last convolutional layer output. Finally, the `perf_action` method is the same as the `take_action` method we discussed previously in the *Discussing Q-learning* section.

3. In this step, we define a function that instantiates the main neural network and the target neural network:

```
def models_init(env, dvc):
    mdl = ConvDQN(env.observation_space.shape, env.
action_space.n).to(dvc)
    tgt_mdl = ConvDQN(env.observation_space.shape, env.
action_space.n).to(dvc)
    return mdl, tgt_mdl
```

These two models are instances of the same class and hence share the same architecture. However, they are two separate instances and hence will evolve differently with different sets of weights.

Defining the experience replay buffer

As we discussed in the *Understanding deep Q-learning* section, the experience replay buffer is a significant feature of DQNs. With the help of this buffer, we can store several thousand transitions (frames) of a game and then randomly sample those video frames to train the CNN model. The following is the code for defining the replay buffer:

```
class RepBfr:
    def __init__(self, cap_max):
        self._bfr = deque(maxlen=cap_max)
    def push(self, st, act, rwd, nxt_st, fin):
        self._bfr.append((st, act, rwd, nxt_st, fin))
    def smpl(self, bch_sz):
        idxs = np.random.choice(len(self._bfr), bch_sz, False)
        bch = zip(*[self._bfr[i] for i in idxs])
        st, act, rwd, nxt_st, fin = bch
        return (np.array(st), np.array(act), np.array(rwd,
dtype=np.float32),np.array(nxt_st), np.array(fin, dtype=np.
uint8))
    def __len__(self):
        return len(self._bfr)
```

Here, `cap_max` is the defined buffer size; that is, the number of video game state transitions that shall be stored in the buffer. The `smpl` method is used during the CNN training loop to sample the stored transitions and generate batches of training data.

Setting up the environment

So far, we have mostly focused on the neural network side of DQNs. In this section, we will focus on building one of the foundational aspects in an RL problem – the environment. Follow these steps:

1. First, we must define some video game environment initialization-related functions:

```
def gym_to_atari_format(gym_env):
    ...
def check_atari_env(env):
    ...
```

Using the `gym` library, we have access to a pre-built Pong video game environment. But here, we will augment the environment in a series of steps, which will include downsampling the video game image frames, pushing image frames to the experience replay buffer, converting images into PyTorch tensors, and so on.

2. The following are the defined classes that implement each of the environment control steps:

```
class CCtrl(Wrapper):
    ...
class FrmDwSmpl(ObservationWrapper):
    ...
class MaxNSkpEnv(Wrapper):
    ...
class FrRstEnv(Wrapper):
    ...
class FrmBfr(ObservationWrapper):
    ...
class Img2Trch(ObservationWrapper):
    ...
class NormFlts(ObservationWrapper):
    ...
```

These classes will now be used for initializing and augmenting the video game environment.

3. Once the environment-related classes have been defined, we must define a final method that takes in the raw Pong video game environment as input and augments the environment, as follows:

```python
def wrap_env(env_ip):
    env = make(env_ip)
    is_atari = check_atari_env(env_ip)
    env = CCtrl(env, is_atari)
    env = MaxNSkpEnv(env, is_atari)
    try:
        env_acts = env.unwrapped.get_action_meanings()
        if "FIRE" in env_acts:
            env = FrRstEnv(env)
    except AttributeError:
        pass
    env = FrmDwSmpl(env)
    env = Img2Trch(env)
    env = FrmBfr(env, 4)
    env = NormFlts(env)
    return env
```

Some of the code in this step have been omitted as our focus is on the PyTorch aspect of this exercise. Please refer to this book's GitHub repository for the full code.

Defining the CNN optimization function

In this section, we will define the loss function for training our DRL model, as well as define what needs to be done at the end of each model training iteration. Follow these steps:

1. We initialized our main and target CNN models in *step 2* of the *Initializing the main and target CNN models* section. Now that we have defined the model architecture, we shall define the loss function, which the model will be trained to minimize:

```python
def calc_temp_diff_loss(mdl, tgt_mdl, bch, gm, dvc):
    st, act, rwd, nxt_st, fin = bch

    st = torch.from_numpy(np.float32(st)).to(dvc)
```

```
    nxt_st =           torch.from_numpy(np.float32(nxt_st)).
to(dvc)

    act = torch.from_numpy(act).to(dvc)

    rwd = torch.from_numpy(rwd).to(dvc)

    fin = torch.from_numpy(fin).to(dvc)
    q_vals = mdl(st)

    nxt_q_vals = tgt_mdl(nxt_st)
    q_val = q_vals.gather(1, act.unsqueeze(-1)).squeeze(-
1)

    nxt_q_val = nxt_q_vals.max(1)[0]

    exp_q_val = rwd + gm * nxt_q_val * (1 - fin)
    loss = (q_val -exp_q_val.data.to(dvc)).pow(2).
mean()

    loss.backward()
```

The loss function defined here is derived from our earlier discussions of the loss function equation. This loss is known as the **time/temporal difference loss** and is one of the foundational concepts of DQNs.

2. Now that the neural network architecture and loss function are in place, we shall define the model updation function, which is called at every iteration of neural network training:

```
def upd_grph(mdl, tgt_mdl, opt, rpl_bfr, dvc, log):
    if len(rpl_bfr) > INIT_LEARN:
        if not log.idx % TGT_UPD_FRQ:
            tgt_mdl.load_state_dict(mdl.state_dict())
        opt.zero_grad()
        bch = rpl_bfr.smpl(B_S)
        calc_temp_diff_loss(mdl, tgt_mdl, bch, G, dvc)
        opt.step()
```

This function samples a batch of data from the experience replay buffer, computes the time difference loss on this batch of data, and also copies the weights of the main neural network to the target neural network once every TGT_UPD_FRQ iterations. TGT_UPD_FRQ will be assigned a value later.

Managing and running episodes

Now, let's learn how to define the epsilon value:

1. First, we will define a function that will update the epsilon value after each episode:

```
def upd_eps(epd):
    last_eps = EPS_FINL
    first_eps = EPS_STRT
    eps_decay = EPS_DECAY
    eps = last_eps + (first_eps - last_eps) * math.exp(-1
* ((epd + 1) / eps_decay))
    return eps
```

This function is the same as the epsilon update step in our Q-learning loop, as discussed in the *Discussing Q-learning* section. The goal of this function is to linearly reduce the epsilon value per episode.

2. The next function is to define what happens at the end of an episode. If the overall reward that's scored in the current episode is the best we've achieved so far, we save the CNN model weights and print the reward value:

```
def fin_epsd(mdl, env, log, epd_rwd, epd, eps):
    bst_so_far = log.upd_rwds(epd_rwd)
    if bst_so_far:
        print(f"checkpointing current model weights.
highest running_average_reward of\
  {round(log.bst_avg, 3)} achieved!")
        save(mdl.state_dict(), f"{env}.dat")
    print(f"episode_num {epd}, curr_reward: {epd_rwd},
best_reward: {log.bst_rwd},\running_avg_reward:
{round(log.avg, 3)}, curr_epsilon: {round(eps, 4)}")
```

At the end of each episode, we also log the episode number, the reward at the end of the current episode, a running average of reward values across the past few episodes, and finally, the current epsilon value.

3. We have finally reached one of the most crucial function definitions of this exercise. Here, we must specify the DQN loop. This is where we define the steps that shall be executed in an episode:

```
def run_epsd(env, mdl, tgt_mdl, opt, rpl_bfr, dvc, log,
epd):
    epd_rwd = 0.0
    st = env.reset()
    while True:
        eps = upd_eps(log.idx)
        act = mdl.perf_action(st, eps, dvc)
        env.render()
        nxt_st, rwd, fin, _ = env.step(act)
        rpl_bfr.push(st, act, rwd, nxt_st, fin)
        st = nxt_st
        epd_rwd += rwd
        log.upd_idx()
        upd_grph(mdl, tgt_mdl, opt, rpl_bfr, dvc, log)
        if fin:
            fin_epsd(mdl, ENV, log, epd_rwd, epd, eps)
            break
```

The rewards and states are reset at the beginning of the episode. Then, we run an endless loop that only breaks if the agent reaches one of the end states. Within this loop, in each iteration, the following steps are executed:

i) First, the epsilon value is modified as per the *linear depreciation scheme.*

ii) The next action is predicted by the main CNN model. This action is executed, resulting in the next state and a reward. This state transition is recorded in the experience replay buffer.

iii) The next state now becomes the current state and we calculate the time difference loss, which is used to update the main CNN model while keeping the target CNN model frozen.

iv) If the new current state is an end state, then we break the loop (that is, end the episode) and log the results for this episode.

4. We have mentioned logging results throughout the training process. In order to store the various metrics around rewards and model performance, we must define a training metadata class, which will consist of various metrics as attributes:

```python
class TrMetadata:
    def __init__(self):
        self._avg = 0.0
        self._bst_rwd = -float("inf")
        self._bst_avg = -float("inf")
        self._rwds = []
        self._avg_rng = 100
        self._idx = 0
```

We will use these metrics to visualize model performance later in this exercise, once we've trained the model.

5. We store the model metric attributes in the previous step as private members and publicly expose their corresponding getter functions instead:

```python
    @property
    def bst_rwd(self):
        ...

    @property
    def bst_avg(self):
        ...

    @property
    def avg(self):
        ...

    @property
    def idx(self):
        ...

    ...
```

The `idx` attribute is critical for deciding when to copy the weights from the main CNN to the target CNN, while the `avg` attribute is useful for computing the running average of rewards that have been received in the past few episodes.

Training the DQN model to learn Pong

Now, we have all the necessary ingredients to start training the DQN model. Let's get started:

1. The following is a training wrapper function that will do everything we need it to do:

```
def train(env, mdl, tgt_mdl, opt, rpl_bfr, dvc):
    log = TrMetadata()
    for epd in range(N_EPDS):
        run_epsd(env, mdl, tgt_mdl, opt, rpl_bfr, dvc,
log, epd)
```

Essentially, we initialize a logger and just run the DQN training system for a predefined number of episodes.

2. Before we actually run the training loop, we need to define the hyperparameter values, which are as follows:

i) The batch size for each iteration of gradient descent to tune the CNN model

ii) The environment, which in this case is the Pong video game

iii) The epsilon value for the first episode

iv) The epsilon value for the last episode

v) The rate of depreciation for the epsilon value

vi) Gamma; that is, the discounting factor

vii) The initial number of iterations that are reserved just for pushing data to the replay buffer

viii) The learning rate

ix) The size or capacity of the experience replay buffer

x) The total number of episodes to train the agent for

xi) The number of iterations after which we copy the weights from the main CNN to the target CNN

We can instantiate all of these hyperparameters in the following piece of code:

```
B_S = 64
ENV = "Pong-v4"
EPS_STRT = 1.0
EPS_FINL = 0.005
EPS_DECAY = 100000
G = 0.99
INIT_LEARN = 10000
LR = 1e-4
MEM_CAP = 20000
N_EPDS = 2000
TGT_UPD_FRQ = 1000
```

These values are experimental, and I encourage you to try changing them and observe the impact they have on the results.

3. This is the last step of the exercise and is where we actually execute the DQN training routine, as follows:

    i) First, we instantiate the game environment.

    ii) Then, we define the device that the training will happen on – either CPU or GPU, based on availability.

    iii) Next, we instantiate the main and target CNN models. We also define *Adam* as the optimizer for the CNN models.

    iv) We then instantiate an experience replay buffer.

    v) Finally, we begin training the main CNN model. Once the training routine finishes, we close the instantiated environment.

The code for this is as follows:

```
env = wrap_env(ENV)
dvc = torch.device("cuda") if torch.cuda.is_available()
else torch.device("cpu")
mdl, tgt_mdl = models_init(env, dvc)
opt = Adam(mdl.parameters(), lr=LR)
rpl_bfr = RepBfr(MEM_CAP)
train(env, mdl, tgt_mdl, opt, rpl_bfr, dvc)
env.close()
```

This should give us the following output:

```
episode_num 0, curr_reward: -20.0, best_reward: -20.0, running_avg_reward: -20.0, curr_epsilon: 0.9971
checkpointing current model weights. highest running_average_reward of -19.5 achieved!
episode_num 1, curr_reward: -19.0, best_reward: -19.0, running_avg_reward: -19.5, curr_epsilon: 0.9937
episode_num 2, curr_reward: -21.0, best_reward: -19.0, running_avg_reward: -20.0, curr_epsilon: 0.991
episode_num 3, curr_reward: -21.0, best_reward: -19.0, running_avg_reward: -20.25, curr_epsilon: 0.9881
episode_num 4, curr_reward: -19.0, best_reward: -19.0, running_avg_reward: -20.0, curr_epsilon: 0.9846
episode_num 5, curr_reward: -20.0, best_reward: -19.0, running_avg_reward: -20.0, curr_epsilon: 0.9811

episode_num 500, curr_reward: -13.0, best_reward: -11.0, running_avg_reward: -16.52, curr_epsilon: 0.1053
episode_num 501, curr_reward: -20.0, best_reward: -11.0, running_avg_reward: -16.52, curr_epsilon: 0.1049
episode_num 502, curr_reward: -19.0, best_reward: -11.0, running_avg_reward: -16.59, curr_epsilon: 0.1041
episode_num 503, curr_reward: -12.0, best_reward: -11.0, running_avg_reward: -16.53, curr_epsilon: 0.1034
checkpointing current model weights. highest running_average_reward of -16.51 achieved!
episode_num 504, curr_reward: -13.0, best_reward: -11.0, running_avg_reward: -16.51, curr_epsilon: 0.1026
checkpointing current model weights. highest running_average_reward of -16.5 achieved!
episode_num 505, curr_reward: -18.0, best_reward: -11.0, running_avg_reward: -16.5, curr_epsilon: 0.1019
checkpointing current model weights. highest running_average_reward of -16.46 achieved!

episode_num 1000, curr_reward: -4.0, best_reward: 13.0, running_avg_reward: -6.64, curr_epsilon: 0.0059
checkpointing current model weights. highest running_average_reward of -6.61 achieved!
episode_num 1001, curr_reward: -9.0, best_reward: 13.0, running_avg_reward: -6.61, curr_epsilon: 0.0059

episode_num 1002, curr_reward: -15.0, best_reward: 13.0, running_avg_reward: -6.72, curr_epsilon: 0.0059
episode_num 1003, curr_reward: -3.0, best_reward: 13.0, running_avg_reward: -6.66, curr_epsilon: 0.0059
episode_num 1004, curr_reward: -7.0, best_reward: 13.0, running_avg_reward: -6.72, curr_epsilon: 0.0059
episode_num 1005, curr_reward: -12.0, best_reward: 13.0, running_avg_reward: -6.69, curr_epsilon: 0.0059

episode_num 1500, curr_reward: 11.0, best_reward: 17.0, running_avg_reward: -0.22, curr_epsilon: 0.005
checkpointing current model weights. highest running_average_reward of -0.05 achieved!
episode_num 1501, curr_reward: 7.0, best_reward: 17.0, running_avg_reward: -0.05, curr_epsilon: 0.005
checkpointing current model weights. highest running_average_reward of 0.01 achieved!
episode_num 1502, curr_reward: -1.0, best_reward: 17.0, running_avg_reward: 0.01, curr_epsilon: 0.005

checkpointing current model weights. highest running_average_reward of 0.11 achieved!
episode_num 1503, curr_reward: 3.0, best_reward: 17.0, running_avg_reward: 0.11, curr_epsilon: 0.005
checkpointing current model weights. highest running_average_reward of 0.2 achieved!
episode_num 1504, curr_reward: 2.0, best_reward: 17.0, running_avg_reward: 0.2, curr_epsilon: 0.005
episode_num 1505, curr_reward: -8.0, best_reward: 17.0, running_avg_reward: 0.19, curr_epsilon: 0.005

episode_num 1000, curr_reward: -4.0, best_reward: 13.0, running_avg_reward: -6.64, curr_epsilon: 0.0059
checkpointing current model weights. highest running_average_reward of -6.61 achieved!
episode_num 1001, curr_reward: -9.0, best_reward: 13.0, running_avg_reward: -6.61, curr_epsilon: 0.0059

episode_num 1002, curr_reward: -15.0, best_reward: 13.0, running_avg_reward: -6.72, curr_epsilon: 0.0059
episode_num 1003, curr_reward: -3.0, best_reward: 13.0, running_avg_reward: -6.66, curr_epsilon: 0.0059
episode_num 1004, curr_reward: -7.0, best_reward: 13.0, running_avg_reward: -6.72, curr_epsilon: 0.0059
episode_num 1005, curr_reward: -12.0, best_reward: 13.0, running_avg_reward: -6.69, curr_epsilon: 0.0059
```

Figure 9.5 – DQN training logs

Furthermore, the following graph shows the progression of the current rewards, best rewards, and average rewards, as well as the epsilon values against the progression of the episodes:

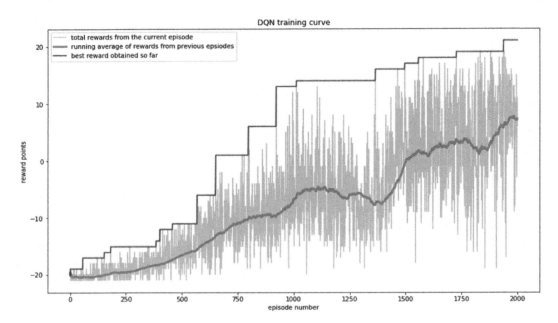

Figure 9.6 – DQN training curves

The following graph shows how the epsilon value decreases over episodes during the training process:

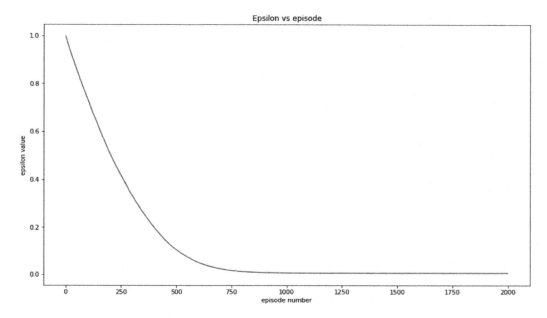

Figure 9.7 – Epsilon variation over episodes

Notice that in *Figure 9.6*, the running average value of rewards in an episode (red curve) starts at **-20**, which is the scenario where the agent scores **0** points in a game and the opponent scores all **20** points. As the episodes progress, the average rewards keep increasing and by episode number **1500**, it crosses the zero mark. This means that after **1500** episodes of training, the agent has leveled up against the opponent.

From here onward, the average rewards are positive, which indicates that the agent is winning against the opponent on average. We have only trained until **2000** episodes, which already results in the agent winning by a margin of over **7** average points against the opponent. I encourage you to train it for longer and see if the agent can absolutely crush the opponent by always scoring all the points and winning by a margin of **20** points.

This concludes our deep dive into the implementation of a DQN model. DQN has been vastly successful and popular in the field of RL and is definitely a great starting point for those interested in exploring the field further. PyTorch, together with the gym library, is a great resource that enables us to work in various RL environments and work with different kinds of DRL models.

In this chapter, we have only focused on DQNs, but the lessons we've learned can be transferred to working with other variants of Q-learning models and other DRL algorithms.

Summary

RL is one of the fundamental branches of machine learning and is currently one of the hottest, if not the hottest, areas of research and development. RL-based AI breakthroughs such as AlphaGo from Google's DeepMind have further increased enthusiasm and interest in the field. This chapter provided an overview of RL and DRL and walked us through a hands-on exercise of building a DQN model using PyTorch.

First, we briefly review the basic concepts of RL. We then explored the different kinds of RL algorithms that have been developed over the years. We took a closer look at one such RL algorithm – the Q-learning algorithm. We then discussed the theory behind Q-learning, including the Bellman equation and the epsilon-greedy-action mechanism. We also explained how Q-learning differs from other RL algorithms, such as policy optimization methods.

Next, we explored a specific type of Q-learning model – the deep Q-learning model. We discussed the key concepts behind DQNs and uncovered some of its novel features, such as the experience replay buffer mechanism and separating main and target neural networks. Finally, we ran an exercise where we built a DQN system using the PyTorch and gym libraries, with CNNs as the underlying neural networks. In this exercise, we built an AI agent that successfully learned to play the video game Pong. Toward the end of training, the agent managed to win against the computer Pong player.

This concludes our discussion on DRL using PyTorch. RL is a vast field and one chapter is not enough to cover everything. I encourage you to use the high-level discussions from this chapter to explore the details around those discussions. From the next chapter onward, we will focus on the practical aspects of working with PyTorch, such as model deployment, parallelized training, automated machine learning, and so on. In the next chapter, we will start by discussing how to effectively use PyTorch to put trained models into production systems.

Section 4:
PyTorch in
Production Systems

In this section, we will explore how to use PyTorch as a powerful tool for running light to extremely heavy deep learning applications. We'll then explore the journey of building a model and putting it into a live production system while grasping some optimization tricks along the way. We'll also dig deeper into the topics of neural architecture search, as well as explainability in AI. The final chapter of this book covers the various additional tools that can be used to accelerate model prototyping and productionizing in PyTorch.

Upon completing this section, you will have an understanding of using PyTorch in production systems at industrial scale. You will be further equipped with the latest PyTorch tools such as Captum and fast.ai and skills such as distributed training and AutoML that are crucial for building advanced deep learning systems.

This section comprises the following chapters:

- *Chapter 10, Operationalizing PyTorch Models into Production*
- *Chapter 11, Distributed Training*
- *Chapter 12, PyTorch and AutoML*
- *Chapter 13, PyTorch and Explainable AI*
- *Chapter 14, Rapid Prototyping with PyTorch*

10
Operationalizing PyTorch Models into Production

So far in this book, we have covered how to train and test different kinds of machine learning models using PyTorch. We started by reviewing the basic elements of PyTorch that enable us to work on deep learning tasks efficiently. Then, we explored a wide range of deep learning model architectures and applications that can be written using PyTorch.

In this chapter, we will be focusing on taking these models into production. But what does that mean? Basically, we will be discussing the different ways of taking a trained and tested model (object) into a separate environment where it can be used to make predictions or inferences on incoming data. This is what is referred to as the **productionization** of a model, as the model is being deployed into a production system.

We will begin by discussing some common approaches you can take to serve PyTorch models in production environments, starting from defining a simple model inference function and going all the way to using model microservices. We will then take a look at TorchServe, which is a scalable PyTorch model-serving framework that has been recently (at the time of writing) and jointly developed by AWS and Facebook.

We will then dive into the world of exporting PyTorch models using **TorchScript**, which, through **serialization**, makes our models independent of the Python ecosystem so that they can be, for instance, loaded in a **C++** code base. We will also look beyond the Torch framework and the Python ecosystem as we explore **ONNX** – an open source universal format for machine learning models – which will help us export PyTorch trained models to non-PyTorch and non-Pythonic environments.

Finally, we will briefly discuss how to use PyTorch for model serving with some of the well-known cloud platforms such as **Amazon Web Services (AWS)**, **Google Cloud**, and **Microsoft Azure**.

Throughout this chapter, we will use the handwritten digits image classification **convolutional neural network (CNN)** model that we trained in *Chapter 1, Overview of Deep Learning Using PyTorch*, as our reference. We will demonstrate how that trained model can be deployed and exported using the different approaches discussed in this chapter.

This chapter is broken down into the following sections:

- Model serving in PyTorch
- Serving a PyTorch model using TorchServe
- Exporting universal PyTorch models using TorchScript and ONNX
- Serving PyTorch model in the cloud

Technical requirements

We will be using Jupyter notebooks and Python scripts for our exercises. Shown next is a list of Python libraries that shall be installed for this chapter using `pip`. To install them, run `pip install torch==1.4.0` and so on at the command line:

```
jupyter==1.0.0
torch==1.4.0
torchvision==0.5.0
matplotlib==3.1.2
Pillow==6.2.2
torch-model-archiver==0.2.0
torchserve==0.2.0
Flask==1.1.1
onnx==1.7.0
onnx-tf==1.5.0
tensorflow==1.15.0
```

All code files relevant to this chapter are available at the following URL: `https://github.com/PacktPublishing/Mastering-PyTorch/tree/master/Chapter10`.

Model serving in PyTorch

In this section, we will begin with building a simple PyTorch inference pipeline that can make predictions given some input data and the location of a previously trained and saved PyTorch model. We will proceed thereafter to place this inference pipeline on a model server that can listen to incoming data requests and return predictions. Finally, we will advance from developing a model server to creating a model microservice using Docker.

Creating a PyTorch model inference pipeline

We will be working on the handwritten digits image classification CNN model that we built in *Chapter 1, Overview of Deep Learning Using PyTorch*, on the MNIST dataset. Using this trained model, we will build an inference pipeline that shall be able to predict a digit between 0 to 9 for a given handwritten-digit input image.

For the process of building and training the model, please refer to the *Training a neural network using PyTorch* section of *Chapter 1, Overview of Deep Learning Using PyTorch*. For the full code of this exercise, you can refer to `https://github.com/PacktPublishing/Mastering-PyTorch/blob/master/Chapter10/mnist_pytorch.ipynb`.

Saving and loading a trained model

In this section, we will demonstrate how to efficiently load a saved pre-trained PyTorch model, which will later be used for serving requests.

So, using the notebook code from *Chapter 1, Overview of Deep Learning Using PyTorch*, we have trained a model and evaluated it against test data samples. But what next? In real life, we would like to close this notebook and, later on, still be able to use this model that we worked hard on training to make inferences on handwritten-digit images. This is where the concept of serving a model comes in.

From here, we will get into a position where we can use the preceding trained model in a separate Jupyter notebook without having to do any (re)training. The crucial next step is to save the model object into a file that can later be restored/de-serialized. PyTorch provides two main ways of doing this:

- The less recommended way is to save the entire model object as follows:

```
torch.save(model, PATH_TO_MODEL)
```

And then, the saved model can be later read as follows:

```
model = torch.load(PATH_TO_MODEL)
```

Although this approach looks the most straightforward, this can be problematic in some cases. This is because we are not only saving the model parameters, but also the model classes and directory structure used in our source code. If our class signatures or directory structures change later, loading the model will fail in potentially unfixable ways.

- The second and more recommended way is to only save the model parameters as follows:

```
torch.save(model.state_dict(), PATH_TO_MODEL)
```

Later, when we need to restore the model, first we instantiate an empty model object and then load the model parameters into that model object as follows:

```
model = ConvNet()
model.load_state_dict(torch.load(PATH_TO_MODEL))
```

We will use the more recommended way to save the model as shown in the following code:

```
PATH_TO_MODEL = "./convnet.pth"
torch.save(model.state_dict(), PATH_TO_MODEL)
```

The convnet.pth file is essentially a pickle file containing model parameters.

At this point, we can safely close the notebook we were working on and open another one, which is available at: https://github.com/PacktPublishing/Mastering-PyTorch/blob/master/Chapter10/run_inference.ipynb:

1. As a first step, we will once again need to import libraries:

```
import torch
```

2. Next, we need to instantiate an empty CNN model once again. Ideally, the model definition done in *step 1* would be written in a Python script (say, cnn_model.py), and then we would simply need to write this:

```
from cnn_model import ConvNet
model = ConvNet()
```

However, since we are operating in Jupyter notebooks in this exercise, we shall rewrite the model definition and then instantiate it as follows:

```
class ConvNet(nn.Module):
    def __init__(self):
        ...
    def forward(self, x):
        ...
model = ConvNet()
```

3. We can now restore the saved model parameters into this instantiated model object as follows:

```
PATH_TO_MODEL = "./convnet.pth"
model.load_state_dict(torch.load(PATH_TO_MODEL, map_
location="cpu"))
```

You shall see the following output:

<All keys matched successfully>

Figure 10.1 – Model parameter loading

This essentially means that the parameter loading is successful. That is, the model that we have instantiated has the same structure as the model whose parameters were saved and are now being restored. We specify that we are loading the model on a CPU device as opposed to GPU (CUDA).

4. Finally, we want to specify that we do not wish to update or change the parameter values of the loaded model, and we will do so with the following line of code:

```
model.eval()
```

This should give the following output:

```
ConvNet(
  (cn1): Conv2d(1, 16, kernel_size=(3, 3), stride=(1, 1))
  (cn2): Conv2d(16, 32, kernel_size=(3, 3), stride=(1, 1))
  (dp1): Dropout2d(p=0.1, inplace=False)
  (dp2): Dropout2d(p=0.25, inplace=False)
  (fc1): Linear(in_features=4608, out_features=64, bias=True)
  (fc2): Linear(in_features=64, out_features=10, bias=True)
)
```

Figure 10.2 – Loaded model in evaluation mode

This again verifies that we are indeed working with the same model (architecture) that we trained.

Building the inference pipeline

Having successfully loaded a pre-trained model in a new environment (notebook) in the previous section, we shall now build our model inference pipeline and use it to run model predictions:

1. At this point, we have the previously trained model object fully restored to us. We shall now load an image that we can run the model prediction on using the following code:

```
image = Image.open("./digit_image.jpg")
```

The image file should be available in the exercise folder and is as follows:

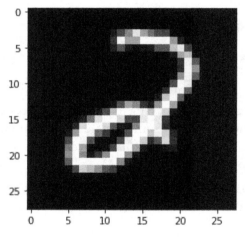

Figure 10.3 – Model inference input image

It is not necessary to use this particular image in the exercise. You may use any image you want, to check how the model reacts to it.

2. In any inference pipeline, there are three main components at the core of it: (a) the data preprocessing component, (b) the model inference (forward pass in the case of neural networks), and (c) the post-processing step.

We will begin with the first part by defining a function that takes in an image and transforms it into the tensor that shall be fed to the model as input as follows:

```
def image_to_tensor(image):
    gray_image = transforms.functional.to_
grayscale(image)
    resized_image = transforms.functional.resize(gray_
image, (28, 28))
    input_image_tensor = transforms.functional.to_
tensor(resized_image)
    input_image_tensor_norm = transforms.functional.
normalize(input_image_tensor, (0.1302,), (0.3069,))
    return input_image_tensor_norm
```

This can be seen as a series of steps as follows:

i) First, the RGB image is converted to a grayscale image.

ii) The image is then resized to a 28x28 pixels image because this is the image size the model is trained with.

iii) Then, the image array is converted to a PyTorch tensor.

iv) And finally, the pixel values in the tensor are normalized with the same mean and standard deviation values as those used during model training time.

Having defined this function, we call it to convert our loaded image into a tensor:

```
input_tensor = image_to_tensor(image)
```

3. Next, we define the **model inference functionality**. This is where the model takes in a tensor as input and outputs the predictions. In this case, the prediction will be any digit between 0 to 9 and the input tensor will be the tensorized form of the input image:

```
def run_model(input_tensor):
    model_input = input_tensor.unsqueeze(0)
    with torch.no_grad():
        model_output = model(model_input)[0]
    model_prediction = model_output.detach().numpy().
argmax()
    return model_prediction
```

`model_output` contains the raw predictions of the model, which contains a list of predictions for each image. Because we have only one image in the input, this list of predictions will just have one entry at index 0. The raw prediction at index 0 is essentially a tensor with 10 probability values for digits 0,1,2...9, in that order. This tensor is converted to a numpy array, and finally, we choose the digit that has the highest probability.

4. We can now use this function to generate our model prediction. The following code uses the `run_model` model inference function from *step 3* to generate the model prediction for the given input data, `input_tensor`:

```
output = run_model(input_tensor)
print(output)
print(type(output))
```

This should output the following:

```
output = run_model(input_tensor)
print(output)
print(type(output))

2
<class 'numpy.int64'>
```

Figure 10.4 – Model inference output

As we can see from the preceding screenshot, the model outputs a numpy integer. And based on the image shown in *Figure 10.3*, the model output seems rather correct.

5. Besides just outputting the model prediction, we can also write a debug function to dig deeper into metrics such as raw prediction probabilities, as shown in the following code snippet:

```
def debug_model(input_tensor):
    model_input = input_tensor.unsqueeze(0)
    with torch.no_grad():
        model_output = model(model_input)[0]
    model_prediction = model_output.detach().numpy()
    return np.exp(model_prediction)
```

This function is exactly the same as the `run_model` function except that it returns the raw list of probabilities for each digit. The model originally returns the logarithm of softmax outputs because of the `log_softmax` layer being used as the final layer in the model (refer to *step 2* of this exercise).

Hence, we need to exponentiate those numbers to return the softmax outputs, which are equivalent to model prediction probabilities. Using this debug function, we can look at how the model is performing in more detail, such as whether the probability distribution is flat or has clear peaks:

```
print(debug_model(input_tensor))
```

This should output the following:

```
[8.69212745e-05 5.61913612e-06 9.97763395e-01 1.33050999e-04
 5.43686365e-05 1.59305739e-06 1.17863165e-04 5.08185963e-07
 1.83202932e-03 4.63086781e-06]
```

Figure 10.5 – Model inference debug output

We can see that the third probability in the list is the highest by far, which corresponds to digit 2.

6. Finally, we shall post-process the model prediction so that it can be used by other applications. In our case, we are just going to transform the digit predicted by the model from the integer type to the string type.

    The post-processing step can be more complex in other scenarios, such as speech recognition, where we might want to process the output waveform by smoothening, removing outliers, and so on:

```
def post_process(output):
    return str(output)
```

Because string is a serializable format, this enables the model predictions to be communicated easily across servers and applications. We can check whether our final post-processed data is as expected:

```
final_output = post_process(output)
print(final_output)
print(type(final_output))
```

This should provide you with the following output:

```
final_output = post_process(output)
print(final_output)
print(type(final_output))
```
```
2
<class 'str'>
```

Figure 10.6 – Post-processed model prediction

As expected, the output is now of the type string.

This concludes our exercise of loading a saved model architecture, restoring its trained weights, and using the loaded model to generate predictions for sample input data (an image). We loaded a sample image, pre-processed it to transform it into a PyTorch tensor, passed it to the model as input to obtain the model prediction, and post-processed the prediction to generate the final output.

This is a step forward in the direction of serving trained models with a clearly defined input and output interface. In this exercise, the input was an externally provided image file and the output was a generated string containing a digit between 0 to 9. Such a system can be embedded by copying and pasting the provided code into any application that requires the functionality of digitizing hand-written digits.

In the next section, we will go a level deeper into model serving, where we aim to build a system that can be interacted with by any application to use the digitizing functionality without copying and pasting any code.

Building a basic model server

We have so far built a model inference pipeline that has all the code necessary to independently perform predictions from a pre-trained model. Here, we will work on building our first model server, which is essentially a machine that hosts the model inference pipeline, actively listens to any incoming input data via an interface, and outputs model predictions on any input data through the interface.

Writing a basic app using Flask

To develop our server, we will use a popular Python library – Flask. **Flask** will enable us to build our model server in a few lines of code. You can read about the library in detail here: https://flask.palletsprojects.com/en/1.1.x/. A good example of how this library works is shown with the following code:

```python
from flask import Flask
app = Flask(__name__)
@app.route('/')
def hello_world():
    return 'Hello, World!'
if __name__ == '__main__':
    app.run(host='localhost', port=8890)
```

Say we saved this Python script as example.py and ran it from the terminal:

```
python example.py
```

It would show the following output in the terminal:

```
* Serving Flask app "example" (lazy loading)
* Environment: production
  WARNING: This is a development server. Do not use it in a production deployment.
  Use a production WSGI server instead.
* Debug mode: off
* Running on http://localhost:8890/ (Press CTRL+C to quit)
```

Figure 10.7 – Flask example app launch

Basically, it will launch a Flask server that will serve an app called **example**. Let's open a browser and go to the following URL:

```
http://localhost:8890/
```

It will result in the following output in the browser:

Hello, World!

Figure 10.8 – Flask example app testing

Essentially, the Flask server is listening to port number `8890` on the IP address `0.0.0.0` (`localhost`) at the endpoint `/`. As soon as we input `localhost:8890/` in a browser search bar and press *Enter*, a request is received by this server. The server then runs the `hello_world` function, which in turn returns the string `Hello, World!` as per the function definition provided in `example.py`.

Using Flask to build our model server

Using the principles of running a Flask server demonstrated in the preceding section, we will now use the model inference pipeline built in the previous section to create our first model server. At the end of the exercise, we will launch the server that will be listening to incoming requests (image data input).

We will furthermore write another Python script that will make a request to this server by sending the sample image shown in *Figure 10.3*. The Flask server shall run the model inference on this image and output the post-processed predictions.

The full code for this exercise is available on GitHub: go to `https://github.com/ PacktPublishing/Mastering-PyTorch/blob/master/Chapter10/server. py` for the Flask server code and `https://github.com/PacktPublishing/ Mastering-PyTorch/blob/master/Chapter10/make_request.py` for the request maker (client) code.

Setting up model inference for Flask serving

In this section, we will load a pre-trained model and write the model inference pipeline code:

1. First, we will build the Flask server. And for that, we once again start by importing the necessary libraries:

    ```
    from flask import Flask, request
    import torch
    ```

    Both `flask` and `torch` are vital necessities for this task, besides other basic libraries such as `numpy` and `json`.

2. Next, we will need to define the model class (architecture):

    ```
    class ConvNet(nn.Module):
        def __init__(self):
        def forward(self, x):
    ```

Ideally, this piece of code will already exist in a separate Python script, say, `model.py`, and all we need to do then is `from model import ConvNet`.

3. Now that we have the empty model class defined, we can instantiate a model object and load the pre-trained model parameters into this model object as follows:

```
model = ConvNet()
PATH_TO_MODEL = "./convnet.pth"
model.load_state_dict(torch.load(PATH_TO_MODEL, map_
location="cpu"))
model.eval()
```

We set the restored model to evaluation mode to indicate no tuning of model parameters.

4. We will reuse the exact `run_model` function defined in *step 3* of the *Building the inference pipeline* section:

```
def run_model(input_tensor):
    ...
    return model_prediction
```

As a reminder, this function takes in the tensorized input image and outputs the model prediction, which is any digit between 0 to 9.

5. Next, we will reuse the exact `post_process` function defined in *step 6* of the *Building the inference pipeline* section:

```
def post_process(output):
    return str(output)
```

This will essentially convert the integer output from the `run_model` function to a string.

Building a Flask app to serve model

Having established the inference pipeline in the previous section, we will now build our own Flask app and use it to serve the loaded model:

1. We will instantiate our Flask app as shown in the following line of code:

```
app = Flask(__name__)
```

This creates a Flask app with the same name as the Python script, which in our case is `server(.py)`.

2. This is the critical step, where we will be defining an endpoint functionality of the Flask server. We will expose a /test endpoint and define what happens when a POST request is made to that endpoint on the server as follows:

```
@app.route("/test", methods=["POST"])
def test():
    data = request.files['data'].read()
    md = json.load(request.files['metadata'])
    input_array = np.frombuffer(data, dtype=np.float32)
    input_image_tensor = torch.from_numpy(input_array).
view(md["dims"])
    output = run_model(input_image_tensor)
    final_output = post_process(output)
    return final_output
```

Let's go through the steps one by one:

a) First, we add a decorator to the function – test – defined underneath. This decorator tells the Flask app to run this function whenever someone makes a POST request to the /test endpoint.

b) Next, we get to defining what exactly happens inside the test function. First, we read the data and metadata from the POST request. Because the data is in serialized form, we need to convert it into a numerical format – we convert it to a numpy array. And from a numpy array, we swiftly cast it as a PyTorch tensor.

c) Next, we use the image dimensions provided in the metadata to reshape the tensor.

d) Finally, we run a forward pass of the model loaded earlier with this tensor. This gives us the model prediction, which is then post-processed and returned by our test function.

3. We have all the necessary ingredients to launch our Flask app. We will add these last two lines to our server.py Python script:

```
if __name__ == '__main__':
    app.run(host='0.0.0.0', port=8890)
```

This indicates that the Flask server will be hosted at IP address 0.0.0.0 (also known as localhost) and port number 8890. We may now save the Python script and in a new terminal window simply execute the following:

```
python server.py
```

This will run the entire script written in the previous steps and you shall see the following output:

```
* Serving Flask app "server" (lazy loading)
* Environment: production
  WARNING: This is a development server. Do not use it in a production deployment.
  Use a production WSGI server instead.
* Debug mode: off
* Running on http://0.0.0.0:8890/ (Press CTRL+C to quit)
```

Figure 10.9 – Flask server launch

This looks similar to the example demonstrated in *Figure 10.7*. The only difference is the app name.

Using a Flask server to run predictions

We have successfully launched our model server, which is actively listening to requests. Let's now work on making a request:

1. We will write a separate Python script in the next few steps to do this job. We begin with importing libraries:

    ```python
    import requests
    from PIL import Image
    from torchvision import transforms
    ```

    The `requests` library will help us make the actual POST request to the Flask server. `Image` helps us to read a sample input image file, and `transforms` will help us to preprocess the input image array.

2. Next, we read an image file:

    ```python
    image = Image.open("./digit_image.jpg")
    ```

    The image read here is an RGB image and may have any dimensions (not necessarily 28x28 as expected by the model as input).

3. We now define a preprocessing function that converts the read image into a format that is readable by the model:

    ```python
    def image_to_tensor(image):
        gray_image = transforms.functional.to_
    grayscale(image)
        resized_image = transforms.functional.resize(gray_
    image, (28, 28))
    ```

```
    input_image_tensor = transforms.functional.to_
tensor(resized_image)
    input_image_tensor_norm = transforms.functional.
normalize(input_image_tensor, (0.1302,), (0.3069,))
    return input_image_tensor_norm
```

First the RGB image is converted to a grayscale image. Then, the image is resized to 28x28 pixels. Next, the image is casted from an array into a PyTorch tensor. Lastly, the 28x28 pixel values are normalized based on the mean and standard deviation values obtained during the training of our model in the previous exercise.

Having defined the function, we can execute it:

```
image_tensor = image_to_tensor(image)
```

image_tensor is what we need to send as input data to the Flask server.

4. Let's now get into packaging our data together to send it over. We want to send both the pixel values of the image as well as the shape of the image (28x28) so that the Flask server at the receiving end knows how to reconstruct the stream of pixel values as an image:

```
dimensions = io.StringIO(json.dumps({'dims': list(image_
tensor.shape)}))
data = io.BytesIO(bytearray(image_tensor.numpy()))
```

We stringify the shape of our tensor and convert the image array into bytes to make it all serializable.

5. This is the most critical step in this request making script. This is where we actually make the POST request:

```
r = requests.post('http://localhost:8890/test',
                    files={'metadata': dimensions,
                           'data' : data})
```

Using the requests library, we make the POST request at the URL localhost:8890/test. This is where the Flask server is listening for requests. We send both the actual image data (as bytes) and the metadata (as string) in the form of a dictionary

6. The r variable in the preceding code will receive the response of the request from the Flask server. This response should contain the post-processed model prediction. We will now read that output:

```
response = json.loads(r.content)
```

The response variable will essentially contain what the Flask server outputs, which is a digit between 0 and 9 as a string.

7. We can print the response just to be sure:

```
print("Predicted digit :", response)
```

At this point, we can save this Python script as make_request.py and execute the following command in the terminal:

```
python make_request.py
```

This should output the following:

Predicted digit : 2

Figure 10.10 – Flask server response

Based on the input image (see *Figure 10.3*), the response seems rather correct. This concludes our current exercise.

Thus, we have successfully built a standalone model server that can render predictions for handwritten digit images. The same set of steps can easily be extended to any other machine learning model, and so this opens up endless possibilities with regards to creating machine learning applications using PyTorch and Flask.

So far, we have moved from simply writing inference functions to creating model servers that can be hosted remotely and render predictions over the network. In our next and final model serving venture, we will go a level further. You might have noticed that in order to follow the steps in the previous two exercises, there were inherent dependencies to be considered. We are required to install certain libraries, save and load the models at particular locations, read image data, and so on. All of these manual steps slow down the development of a model server.

Up next, we will work on creating a model microservice that can be spun up with one command and replicated across several machines, say, for scalability reasons.

Creating a model microservice

Imagine you know nothing about training machine learning models but want to use an already-trained model without having to get your hands dirty with any PyTorch code. This is where a paradigm such as the machine learning model microservice comes into play.

A machine learning model microservice can be thought of as a black box to which you send input data and it sends back predictions to you. Moreover, it is easy to spin up this black box on a given machine with just a few lines of code. The best part is that it scales effortlessly. You can scale a microservice vertically by using a bigger machine (more memory, more processing power) as well as horizontally, by replicating the microservice across multiple machines. You may read in detail about microservices here: `https://opensource.com/resources/what-are-microservices`.

How do we go about deploying a machine learning model as a microservice? Thanks to the work done using Flask and PyTorch in the previous exercise, we are already a few steps ahead. We have already built a standalone model server using Flask.

In this section, we will take that idea forward and build a standalone model-serving environment using **Docker**. Docker helps containerize software, which essentially means that it helps virtualize the entire **operating system (OS)**, including software libraries, configuration files, and even data files.

> **Note**
>
> Docker is a huge topic of discussion in itself. However, because the book is focused on PyTorch, we will only cover the basic concepts and usage of Docker for our limited purposes. If you are interested in reading about Docker further, their own documentation is a great place to start: `https://docs.docker.com/get-started/overview/`.

In our case, we have so far used the following libraries in building our model server:

- Python
- PyTorch
- Pillow (for image I/O)
- Flask

And, we have used the following data file:

- Pre-trained model checkpoint file (`convnet.pth`)

We have had to manually arrange for these dependencies by installing the libraries and placing the file in the current working directory. What if we have to redo all of this in a new machine? We would have to manually install the libraries and copy and paste the file once again. This way of working is neither efficient nor failproof, as we might end up installing different library versions across different machines, for example.

To solve this problem, we would like to create an OS-level blueprint that can be consistently repeated across machines. This is where Docker comes in handy. Docker lets us create that blueprint in the form of a Docker image. This image can then be built on any empty machine with no assumptions regarding pre-installed Python libraries or an already-available model.

Let's actually create such a blueprint using Docker for our digits classification model. In the form of an exercise, we will go from a Flask-based standalone model server to a Docker-based model microservice. Before delving into the exercise, you will need to install Docker. And based on your OS and machine configurations, you can find the Docker installation instructions here: `https://docs.docker.com/engine/install/`:

1. First, we need to list the Python library requirements for our Flask model server. The requirements (with their versions) are as follows:

```
torch==1.5.0
torchvision==0.5.0
Pillow==6.2.2
Flask==1.1.1
```

As a general practice, we will save this list as a text file – `requirements.txt`. This file is also available at `https://github.com/PacktPublishing/Mastering-PyTorch/blob/master/Chapter10/requirements.tx`. This list will come in handy for installing the libraries consistently in any given environment.

2. Next, we get straight to the blueprint, which, in Docker terms, will be `Dockerfile`. A `Dockerfile` is a script that is essentially a list of instructions. The machine where this `Dockerfile` is run needs to execute the listed instructions in the file. This results in a Docker image, and the process is called *building an image*.

An **image** here is a system snapshot that can be effectuated on any machine, provided that the machine has the minimum necessary hardware resources (for example, installing PyTorch 1.5.0 alone requires 750 MB of memory space).

Let's look at our `Dockerfile` and try to understand what it does step by step. The full code for the `Dockerfile` is available at `https://github.com/PacktPublishing/Mastering-PyTorch/blob/master/Chapter10/Dockerfile`.

a) The FROM keyword instructs Docker to fetch a standard Linux OS with `python 3.8` baked in:

```
FROM python:3.8-slim
```

This ensures that we will have Python installed.

b) Next, install `wget`, which is a Unix command useful for downloading resources from the internet via the command line:

```
RUN apt-get -q update && apt-get -q install -y wget
```

The `&&` symbol indicates the sequential execution of commands written before and after the symbol.

c) Here, we are copying two files from our local development environment into this virtual environment:

```
COPY ./server.py ./
COPY ./requirements.txt ./
```

We copy the requirements file as discussed in *step 1* as well as the Flask model server code that we worked on in the previous exercise.

d) Next, we download the pre-trained PyTorch model checkpoint file:

```
RUN wget -q https://github.com/PacktPublishing/Mastering-
PyTorch/blob/master/Chapter10/convnet.pth
```

This is the same model checkpoint file that we had saved in the *Saving and loading a trained model* section of this chapter.

e) Here, we are installing all the relevant libraries listed under `requirements.txt`:

```
RUN pip install -r requirements.txt
```

This `txt` file is the one we wrote under *step 1*.

e) Next, we give `root` access to the Docker client:

```
USER root
```

This step is important in this exercise as it ensures that the client has the credentials to perform all necessary operations on our behalf, such as saving model inference logs on the disk.

> **Note**
> In general, though, it is advised not to give root privileges to the client as per the principle of least privilege in data security (https://snyk.io/blog/10-docker-image-security-best-practices/).

f) Finally, we specify that after performing all the previous steps, Docker should execute the `python server.py` command:

```
ENTRYPOINT ["python", "server.py"]
```

This will ensure the launch of a Flask model server in the virtual machine.

3. Let's now run this Dockerfile. In other words, let's build a Docker image using the Dockerfile from *step 2*. In the current working directory, on the command line, simply run this:

```
docker build -t digit_recognizer .
```

We are allocating a tag with the name `digit_recognizer` to our Docker image. This should output the following:

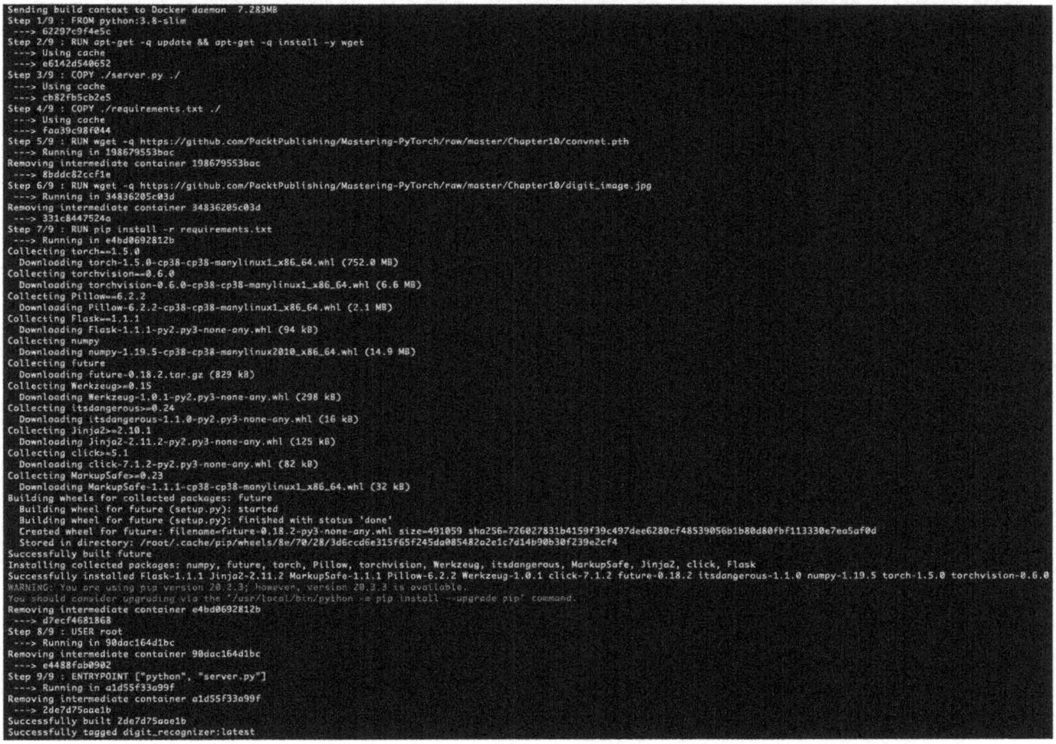

Figure 10.11 – Building a Docker image

Figure 10.11 shows the sequential execution of the steps mentioned in *step 2*. Running this step might take a while, depending on your internet connection, as it downloads the entire PyTorch library among others to build the image.

4. At this stage, we already have a Docker image with the name `digit_recognizer`. We are all set to deploy this image on any machine. In order to deploy the image on your own machine for now, just run the following command:

```
docker run -p 8890:8890 digit_recognizer
```

With this command, we are essentially starting a virtual machine inside our machine using the `digit_recognizer` Docker image. Because our original Flask model server was designed to listen to port `8890`, we have forwarded our actual machine's port `8890` to the virtual machine's port `8890` using the `-p` argument. Running this command should output this:

```
* Serving Flask app "server" (lazy loading)
* Environment: production
  WARNING: This is a development server. Do not use it in a production deployment.
  Use a production WSGI server instead.
* Debug mode: off
* Running on http://0.0.0.0:8890/ (Press CTRL+C to quit)
```

Figure 10.12 – Running a Docker instance

The preceding screenshot is remarkably similar to *Figure 10.9* from the previous exercise, which is no surprise because the Docker instance is running the same Flask model server that we were manually running in our previous exercise.

5. We can now test whether our Dockerized Flask model server (model microservice) works as expected by using it to make model predictions. We will once again use the `make_request.py` file used in the previous exercise to send a prediction request to our model. From the current local working directory, simply execute this:

```
python make_request.py
```

This should output the following:

Predicted digit : 2

Figure 10.13 – Microservice model prediction

The microservice seems to be doing the job, and thus we have successfully built and tested our own machine learning model microservice using Python, PyTorch, Flask, and Docker.

6. Upon successful completion of the preceding steps, you can close the launched Docker instance from *step 4* by pressing *Ctrl+C* as indicated in *Figure 10.12*. And once the running Docker instance is stopped, you can delete the instance by running the following command:

```
docker rm $(docker ps -a -q | head -1)
```

This command basically removes the most recent inactive Docker instance, which in our case is the Docker instance that we just stopped.

7. Finally, you can also delete the Docker image that we had built under *step 3*, by running the following command:

```
docker rmi $(docker images -q "digit_recognizer")
```

This will basically remove the image that has been tagged with the digit_recognizer tag.

This concludes our section for serving models written in PyTorch. We started off by designing a local model inference system. We took this inference system and wrapped a Flask-based model server around it to create a standalone model serving system.

Finally, we used the Flask-based model server inside a Docker container to essentially create a model serving microservice. Using both the theory as well as the exercises discussed in this section, you should be able to get started with hosting/serving your trained models across different use cases, system configurations, and environments.

In the next section, we will stay with the model-serving theme but will discuss a particular tool that has been developed precisely to serve PyTorch models: **TorchServe**. We will also do a quick exercise to demonstrate how to use this tool.

Serving a PyTorch model using TorchServe

TorchServe, released in April 2020, is a dedicated PyTorch model-serving framework. Using the functionalities offered by TorchServe, we can serve multiple models at the same time with low prediction latency and without having to write much custom code. Furthermore, TorchServe offers features such as model versioning, metrics monitoring, and data preprocessing and post-processing.

This clearly makes TorchServe a more advanced model-serving alternative than the model microservice we developed in the previous section. However, making custom model microservices still proves to be a powerful solution for complicated machine learning pipelines (which is more common than we might think).

In this section, we will continue working with our handwritten digits classification model and demonstrate how to serve it using TorchServe. After reading this section, you should be able to get started with TorchServe and go further in utilizing its full set of features.

Installing TorchServe

Before starting with the exercise, we will need to install Java 11 SDK as a requirement. For Linux OS, run the following:

```
sudo apt-get install openjdk-11-jdk
```

And for macOS, we need to run the following command on the command line:

```
brew tap AdoptOpenJDK/openjdk
brew cask install adoptopenjdk11
```

And thereafter, we need to install `torchserve` by running this:

```
pip install torchserve torch-model-archiver
```

For detailed installation instructions, refer to `https://github.com/pytorch/serve/blob/master/README.md#install-torchserve`.

Notice that we also install a library called `torch-model-archiver`. This archiver aims at creating one model file that will contain both the model parameters as well as the model architecture definition in an independent serialized format as a `.mar` file. You can read about the archiver in detail here: `https://pytorch.org/serve/model-archiver.html`.

Launching and using a TorchServe server

Now that we have installed all that we need, we can start putting together our existing code from the previous exercises to serve our model using TorchServe. We will hereon go through a number of steps in the form of an exercise:

1. First, we will place the existing model architecture code in a model file saved as `convnet.py`:

```
============================convnet.
py============================
import torch
import torch.nn as nn
import torch.nn.functional as F
class ConvNet(nn.Module):
    def __init__(self):
        ...
```

```
def forward(self, x):
    …
```

We will need this model file as one of the inputs to `torch-model-archiver` to produce a unified `.mar` file. You can find the full model file here: `https://github.com/PacktPublishing/Mastering-PyTorch/blob/master/Chapter10/convnet.pth`.

Remember we had discussed the three parts of any model inference pipeline: data pre-processing, model prediction, and post-processing. TorchServe provides *handlers*, which handle the pre-processing and post-processing parts of popular kinds of machine learning tasks: `image_classifier`, `image_segmenter`, `object_detector`, and `text_classifier`.

This list might grow in the future as TorchServe is actively being developed at the time of writing this book.

2. For our task, we will create a custom image handler that is inherited from the default `Image_classifier` handler. We choose to create a custom handler because as opposed to the usual image classification models that deal with color (RGB) images, our model deals with grayscale images of a specific size (28x28 pixels). The following is the code for our custom handler, which you can also find at `https://github.com/PacktPublishing/Mastering-PyTorch/blob/master/10_operationalizing_pytorch_models_into_production/convnet_handler.py`:

```
==========================convnet_handler.
py========================
from torchvision import transforms
from ts.torch_handler.image_classifier import
ImageClassifier
class ConvNetClassifier(ImageClassifier):
    image_processing = transforms.Compose([
        transforms.Grayscale(), transforms.Resize((28,
28)),
        transforms.ToTensor(),  transforms.
Normalize((0.1302,), (0.3069,))])
    def postprocess(self, output):
        return output.argmax(1).tolist()
```

First, we imported the `image_classifer` default handler, which will provide most of the basic image classification inference pipeline handling capabilities. Next, we inherit the `ImageClassifer` handler class to define our custom `ConvNetClassifier` handler class.

There are two blocks of custom code:

i) The data pre-processing step, where we apply a sequence of transformations to the data exactly as we did in *step 3* of the *Building the inference pipeline* section.

ii) The postprocessing step, defined under the `postprocess` method, where we extract the predicted class label from the list of prediction probabilities of all classes

3. We already produced a `convnet.pth` file in *the Saving and loading a trained model section* of this chapter while creating the model inference pipeline. Using `convnet.py`, `convnet_handler.py`, and `convnet.pth`, we can finally create the `.mar` file using `torch-model-archiver` by running the following command:

```
torch-model-archiver --model-name convnet --version 1.0
--model-file ./convnet.py --serialized-file ./convnet.pth
--handler  ./convnet_handler.py
```

This command should result in a `convnet.mar` file written to the current working directory. We have specified a `model_name` argument, which names the `.mar` file. We have specified a `version` argument, which will be helpful in model versioning while working with multiple variations of a model at the same time.

We have located where our `convnet.py` (for model architecture), `convnet.pth` (for model weights) and `convnet_handler.py` (for pre- and post-processing) files are, using the `model_file`, `serialzed_file`, and `handler` arguments, respectively.

4. Next, we need to create a new directory in the current working directory and move the `convnet.mar` file created in *step 3* to that directory, by running the following on the command line:

```
mkdir model_store
mv convnet.mar model_store/
```

We have to do so to follow the design requirements of the TorchServe framework.

5. Finally, we may launch our model server using TorchServe. On the command line, simply run the following:

```
torchserve --start --ncs --model-store model_store
--models convnet.mar
```

This will silently start the model inference server and you will see some logs on the screen, including the following:

```
Number of GPUs: 0
Number of CPUs: 8
Max heap size: 4096 M
Python executable: /Users/ashish.jha/opt/anaconda3/bin/python
Config file: N/A
Inference address: http://127.0.0.1:8080
Management address: http://127.0.0.1:8081
Metrics address: http://127.0.0.1:8082
```

Figure 10.14 – TorchServe launch output

As you can see, TorchServe investigates the available devices on the machine among other details. It allocates three separate URLs for *inference*, *management*, and *metrics*. To check whether the launched server is indeed serving our model, we can ping the management server with the following command:

```
curl http://localhost:8081/models
```

This should output the following:

```
{
  "models": [
    {
      "modelName": "convnet",
      "modelUrl": "convnet.mar"
    }
  ]
}
```

Figure 10.15 – TorchServe-served models

This verifies that the TorchServe server is indeed hosting the model.

6. Finally, we can test our TorchServe model server by making an inference request. This time, we won't need to write a Python script, because the handler will already take care of processing any input image file. So, we can directly make a request using the digit_image.jpg sample image file by running this:

```
curl http://127.0.0.1:8080/predictions/convnet -T ./
digit_image.jpg
```

This should output 2 in the terminal, which is indeed the correct prediction as evident from *Figure 10.3*.

7. Finally, once we are done with using the model server, it can be stopped by running the following on the command line:

```
torchserve --stop
```

This concludes our exercise on how to use TorchServe to spin up our own PyTorch model server and use it to make predictions. There is a lot more to unpack here, such as model monitoring (metrics), logging, versioning, benchmarking, and so on. `https://pytorch.org/serve/` is a great place to pursue these advanced topics in detail.

After finishing this section, you should be able to use TorchServe to serve your own models. I encourage you to write custom handlers for your own use cases, explore the various TorchServe configuration settings (read more here: `https://pytorch.org/serve/configuration.html`), and try out other advanced features of TorchServe (read more here: `https://pytorch.org/serve/server.html#advanced-features`).

> **Note**
> TorchServe is in an experimental phase at the time of writing this book, with a lot of promise. My advice would be to keep an eye on the rapid updates in this territory of PyTorch.

In the next section, we will take a look at exporting PyTorch models so that they can be used in different environments, programming languages, and deep learning libraries.

Exporting universal PyTorch models using TorchScript and ONNX

We have discussed serving PyTorch models extensively in the previous sections of this chapter, which is perhaps the most critical aspect of operationalizing PyTorch models in production systems. In this section, we will look at another important aspect – exporting PyTorch models. We have already learned how to save PyTorch models and load them back from disk in the classic Python scripting environment. But we need more ways of exporting PyTorch models. Why?

Well, for starters, the Python interpreter allows only one thread to run at a time using the **global interpreter lock (GIL)**. This keeps us from parallelizing operations. Secondly, Python might not be supported in every system or device that we might want to run our models on. To address these problems, PyTorch offers support for exporting its models in an efficient format and in a platform- or language-agnostic manner such that a model can be run in environments different from the one it was trained in.

We will first explore TorchScript, which enables us to export serialized and optimized PyTorch models into an intermediate representation that can then be run in a Python-independent program (say, a C++ program).

Next, we will look at ONNX and how it lets us save PyTorch models into a universal format that can then be loaded into other deep learning frameworks and different programming languages.

Understanding the utility of TorchScript

There are two key reasons why TorchScript is a vital tool when it comes to putting PyTorch models into production:

- PyTorch works on an eager execution basis, as discussed in *Chapter 1, Overview of Deep Learning Using PyTorch*, of this book. This has its advantages, such as easier debugging. However, executing steps/operations one by one by writing and reading intermediate results to and from memory may lead to high inference latency as well as limiting us from overall operational optimizations. To tackle this problem, PyTorch provides its own **just-in-time** (**JIT**) compiler, which is based on the PyTorch-centered parts of Python.

  The JIT compiler compiles PyTorch models instead of interpreting, which is equivalent to creating one composite graph for the entire model by looking at all of its operations at once. The JIT-compiled code is TorchScript code, which is basically a statically typed subset of Python. This compilation leads to several performance improvements and optimizations, such as getting rid of the GIL and thereby enabling multithreading.

- PyTorch is essentially built to be used with the Python programming language. Remember, we have used Python in almost the entirety of this book too. However, when it comes to productionizing models, there are more performant (that is, quicker) languages than Python, such as C++. And also, we might want to deploy our trained models on systems or devices that do not work with Python.

This is where TorchScript kicks in. As soon as we compile our PyTorch code into TorchScript code, which is an intermediate representation of our PyTorch model, we can serialize this representation into a C++-friendly format using the TorchScript compiler. Thereafter, this serialized file can be read in a C++ model inference program using LibTorch – the PyTorch C++ API.

We have mentioned JIT compilation of PyTorch models several times in this section. Let's now look at two of the possible options of compiling our PyTorch models into TorchScript format.

Model tracing with TorchScript

One way of translating PyTorch code to TorchScript is tracing the PyTorch model. Tracing requires the PyTorch model object along with a dummy example input to the model. As the name suggests, the tracing mechanism traces the flow of this dummy input through the model (neural network), records the various operations, and renders a TorchScript **Intermediate Representation** (**IR**), which can be visualized both as a graph as well as TorchScript code.

We will now walk through the steps involved in tracing a PyTorch model using our handwritten digits classification model. The full code for this exercise is available at `https://github.com/PacktPublishing/Mastering-PyTorch/blob/master/Chapter10/model_tracing.ipynb`.

The first five steps of this exercise are the same as the steps of the *Saving and loading a trained model* and *Building the inference pipeline* sections, where we built the model inference pipeline:

1. We will start with importing libraries by running the following code:

    ```
    import torch
    ...
    ```

2. Next, we will define and instantiate the `model` object:

    ```
    class ConvNet(nn.Module):
        def __init__(self):
            ...
        def forward(self, x):
            ...
    model = ConvNet()
    ```

3. Next, we will restore the model weights using the following lines of code:

    ```
    PATH_TO_MODEL = "./convnet.pth"
    model.load_state_dict(torch.load(PATH_TO_MODEL, map_
    location="cpu"))
    model.eval()
    ```

4. We then load a sample image:

```
image = Image.open("./digit_image.jpg")
```

5. Next, we define the data pre-processing function:

```
def image_to_tensor(image):
    gray_image = transforms.functional.to_
grayscale(image)
    resized_image = transforms.functional.resize(gray_
image, (28, 28))
    input_image_tensor = transforms.functional.to_
tensor(resized_image)
    input_image_tensor_norm = transforms.functional.
normalize(input_image_tensor, (0.1302,), (0.3069,))
    return input_image_tensor_norm
```

And we then apply the pre-processing function to the sample image:

```
input_tensor = image_to_tensor(image)
```

6. In addition to the code under *step 3*, we also execute the following lines of code:

```
for p in model.parameters():
    p.requires_grad_(False)
```

If we do not do this, the traced model will have all parameters requiring gradients and we will have to load the model within the `torch.no_grad()` context.

7. We already have the loaded PyTorch model object with pre-trained weights. We are ready to trace the model with a dummy input as shown next:

```
demo_input = torch.ones(1, 1, 28, 28)
traced_model = torch.jit.trace(model, demo_input)
```

The dummy input is an image with all pixel values set to 1.

8. We can now look at the traced model graph by running this:

```
print(traced_model.graph)
```

This should output the following:

```
graph(%self.1 : __torch__.torch.nn.modules.module.___torch_mangle_6.Module,
      %input.1 : Float(1, 1, 28, 28)):
  %113 : __torch__.torch.nn.modules.module.___torch_mangle_5.Module = prim::GetAttr[name="fc2"](%self.1)
  %110 : __torch__.torch.nn.modules.module.___torch_mangle_3.Module = prim::GetAttr[name="dp2"](%self.1)
  %109 : __torch__.torch.nn.modules.module.___torch_mangle_4.Module = prim::GetAttr[name="fc1"](%self.1)
  %106 : __torch__.torch.nn.modules.module.___torch_mangle_2.Module = prim::GetAttr[name="dp1"](%self.1)
  %105 : __torch__.torch.nn.modules.module.___torch_mangle_1.Module = prim::GetAttr[name="cn2"](%self.1)
  %102 : __torch__.torch.nn.modules.module.Module = prim::GetAttr[name="cn1"](%self.1)
  %120 : Tensor = prim::CallMethod[name="forward"](%102, %input.1)
  %input.3 : Float(1, 16, 26, 26) = aten::relu(%120) # /Users/ashish.jha/opt/anaconda3/lib/python3.7/site-packages/to
rch/nn/functional.py:914:0
  %121 : Tensor = prim::CallMethod[name="forward"](%105, %input.3)
  %input.5 : Float(1, 32, 24, 24) = aten::relu(%121) # /Users/ashish.jha/opt/anaconda3/lib/python3.7/site-packages/to
rch/nn/functional.py:914:0




  %input.9 : Float(1, 64) = aten::relu(%123) # /Users/ashish.jha/opt/anaconda3/lib/python3.7/site-packages/torch/nn/f
unctional.py:914:0
  %124 : Tensor = prim::CallMethod[name="forward"](%110, %input.9)
  %125 : Tensor = prim::CallMethod[name="forward"](%113, %124)
  %91 : int = prim::Constant[value=1]() # /Users/ashish.jha/opt/anaconda3/lib/python3.7/site-packages/torch/nn/functi
onal.py:1317:0
  %92 : None = prim::Constant()
  %93 : Float(1, 10) = aten::log_softmax(%125, %91, %92) # /Users/ashish.jha/opt/anaconda3/lib/python3.7/site-package
s/torch/nn/functional.py:1317:0
  return (%93)
```

Figure 10.16 – Traced model graph

Intuitively, the first few lines in the graph show the initialization of layers of this model, such as `cn1`, `cn2`, and so on. Toward the end, we see the last layer, that is, the softmax layer. Evidently, the graph is written in a lower-level language with statically typed variables and closely resembles the TorchScript language.

9. Besides the graph, we can also look at the exact TorchScript code behind the traced model by running this:

```
print(traced_model.code)
```

This should output the following lines of Python-like code that define the forward pass method for the model:

```
def forward(self,
    input: Tensor) -> Tensor:
  _0 = self.fc2
  _1 = self.dp2
  _2 = self.fc1
  _3 = self.dp1
  _4 = self.cn2
  input0 = torch.relu((self.cn1).forward(input, ))
  input1 = torch.relu((_4).forward(input0, ))
  input2 = torch.max_pool2d(input1, [2, 2], annotate(List[int], []), [0, 0], [1, 1], False)
  input3 = torch.flatten((_3).forward(input2, ), 1, -1)
  input4 = torch.relu((_2).forward(input3, ))
  _5 = (_0).forward((_1).forward(input4, ), )
  return torch.log_softmax(_5, 1, None)
```

Figure 10.17 – Traced model code

This precisely is the TorchScript equivalent for the code that we wrote using PyTorch in *step 2*.

10. Next, we will export or save the traced model:

```
torch.jit.save(traced_model, 'traced_convnet.pt')
```

11. Now we load the saved model:

```
loaded_traced_model = torch.jit.load('traced_convnet.pt')
```

Note that we didn't need to load the model architecture and parameters separately.

12. Finally, we can use this model for inference:

```
loaded_traced_model(input_tensor.unsqueeze(0))
```

The output is as follows:

```
tensor([[-9.3505e+00, -1.2089e+01, -2.2391e-03, -8.9248e+00, -9.8197e+00,
         -1.3350e+01, -9.0460e+00, -1.4492e+01, -6.3023e+00, -1.2283e+01]])
```

Figure 10.18 – Traced model inference

13. We can check these results by re-running model inference on the original model:

```
model(input_tensor.unsqueeze(0))
```

This should produce the same output as in *Figure 10.18*, which verifies that our traced model is working properly.

You can use the traced model instead of the original PyTorch model object to build more efficient Flask model servers and Dockerized model microservices, thanks to the GIL-free nature of TorchScript. While tracing is a viable option for JIT compiling PyTorch models, it has some drawbacks.

For instance, if the forward pass of the model consists of control flows such as `if` and `for` statements, then the tracing will only render one of the multiple possible paths in the flow. In order to accurately translate PyTorch code to TorchScript code for such scenarios, we will use the other compilation mechanism called scripting.

Model scripting with TorchScript

Please follow *steps 1 to 6* from the previous exercise and then follow up with the steps given in this exercise. The full code is available at `https://github.com/PacktPublishing/Mastering-PyTorch/blob/master/Chapter10/model_scripting.ipynb`:

1. For scripting, we need not provide any dummy input to the model, and the following line of code transforms PyTorch code to TorchScript code directly:

   ```
   scripted_model = torch.jit.script(model)
   ```

2. Let's look at the scripted model graph by running the following line of code:

   ```
   print(scripted_model.graph)
   ```

   This should output the scripted model graph in a similar fashion as the traced model graph, as shown in the following figure:

```
graph(%self : __torch__.ConvNet,
      %x.1 : Tensor):
  %51 : Function = prim::Constant[name="log_softmax"]()
  %49 : int = prim::Constant[value=3]()
  %33 : int = prim::Constant[value=-1]()
  %26 : Function = prim::Constant[name="_max_pool2d"]()
  %20 : int = prim::Constant[value=0]()
  %19 : None = prim::Constant()
  %7 : Function = prim::Constant[name="relu"]()
  %6 : bool = prim::Constant[value=0]()

           ┆
           ┆
           ┆

  %x.19 : Tensor = prim::CallFunction(%7, %x.17, %6) # <ipython-input-3-936a1c5cab85>:20:12
  %42 : __torch__.torch.nn.modules.dropout.___torch_mangle_1.Dropout2d = prim::GetAttr[name
="dp2"](%self)
  %x.21 : Tensor = prim::CallMethod[name="forward"](%42, %x.19) # <ipython-input-3-936a1c5cab
85>:21:12
  %45 : __torch__.torch.nn.modules.linear.___torch_mangle_2.Linear = prim::GetAttr[name="fc
2"](%self)
  %x.23 : Tensor = prim::CallMethod[name="forward"](%45, %x.21) # <ipython-input-3-936a1c5cab
85>:22:12
  %op.1 : Tensor = prim::CallFunction(%51, %x.23, %32, %49, %19) # <ipython-input-3-936a1c5ca
b85>:23:13
  return (%op.1)
```

Figure 10.19 – Scripted model graph

Once again, we can see similar, verbose, low-level script that lists the various edges of the graph per line. Notice that the graph here is not the same as in *Figure 10.16*, which indicates differences in code compilation strategy in using tracing rather than scripting.

3. We can also look at the equivalent TorchScript code by running this:

```
print(scripted_model.code)
```

This should output the following:

```
def forward(self,
    x: Tensor) -> Tensor:
  _0 = __torch__.torch.nn.functional.___torch_mangle_12.relu
  _1 = __torch__.torch.nn.functional._max_pool2d
  _2 = __torch__.torch.nn.functional.___torch_mangle_13.relu
  _3 = __torch__.torch.nn.functional.log_softmax
  x0 = (self.cn1).forward(x, )
  x1 = __torch__.torch.nn.functional.relu(x0, False, )
  x2 = (self.cn2).forward(x1, )
  x3 = _0(x2, False, )
  x4 = _1(x3, [2, 2], None, [0, 0], [1, 1], False, False, )
  x5 = (self.dp1).forward(x4, )
  x6 = torch.flatten(x5, 1, -1)
  x7 = (self.fc1).forward(x6, )
  x8 = _2(x7, False, )
  x9 = (self.dp2).forward(x8, )
  x10 = (self.fc2).forward(x9, )
  return _3(x10, 1, 3, None, )
```

Figure 10.20 – Scripted model code

In essence, the flow is similar to that in *Figure 10.17*; however, there are subtle differences in the code signature resulting from differences in compilation strategy.

4. Once again, the scripted model can be exported and loaded back in the following way:

```
torch.jit.save(scripted_model, 'scripted_convnet.pt')
loaded_scripted_model = torch.jit.load('scripted_convnet.
pt')
```

5. Finally, we use the scripted model for inference using this:

```
loaded_scripted_model(input_tensor.unsqueeze(0))
```

This should produce the exact same results as in *Figure 10.18*, which verifies that the scripted model is working as expected.

Similar to tracing, a scripted PyTorch model is GIL-free and hence can improve model serving performance when used with Flask or Docker. *Table 10.1* shows a quick comparison between the model tracing and scripting approaches:

Tracing	Scripting
• Dummy input is needed.	• No need for dummy input.
• Records a fixed sequence of mathematical operations by passing the dummy input to the model.	• Generates TorchScript code/graph by inspecting the `nn.Module` contents within the PyTorch code.
• Cannot handle multiple control flows (if-else) within the model forward pass.	• Useful in handling all types of control flows.
• Works even if the model has PyTorch functionalities that are not supported by TorchScript (`https://pytorch.org/docs/stable/jit_unsupported.html`).	• Scripting can work only if the PyTorch model does not contain any functionalities which are not supported by TorchScript.

Table 10.1 – Tracing versus scripting

We have so far demonstrated how PyTorch models can be translated and serialized as TorchScript models. In the next section, we will completely get rid of Python for a moment and demonstrate how to load the TorchScript serialized model using C++.

Running a PyTorch model in C++

Python can sometimes be limiting or unable to run machine learning models trained using PyTorch. In this section, we will use the serialized TorchScript model objects (using tracing and scripting) that we exported in the previous section to run model inferences inside C++ code.

> **Note**
>
> Basic working knowledge of C++ is assumed for this section. If you want to learn the basics of C++ coding, this could be a good starting point: `https://www.learncpp.com/`. This section specifically talks a lot about C++ code compilation. You can read more about how C++ code compilation works here: `https://www.toptal.com/c-plus-plus/c-plus-plus-understanding-compilation`.

For this exercise, follow the steps here, `https://cmake.org/install/`, to install CMake to be able to build the C++ code. Following that, we will create a folder named `cpp_convnet` in the current working directory and work from that directory:

1. Let's get straight into writing the C++ file that will run the model inference pipeline. The full C++ code is available here: `https://github.com/PacktPublishing/Mastering-PyTorch/blob/master/Chapter10/cpp_convnet/cpp_convnet.cpp`:

```cpp
#include <torch/script.h>
...
int main(int argc, char **argv) {
    Mat img = imread(argv[2], IMREAD_GRAYSCALE);
```

First the `.jpg` image file is read as a grayscale image using the OpenCV library. You will need to install the OpenCV library for C++ using the following links:

a) **Mac**: `https://docs.opencv.org/master/d0/db2/tutorial_macos_install.html`

b) **Linux**: `https://docs.opencv.org/3.4/d7/d9f/tutorial_linux_install.html`

c) **Win**: `https://docs.opencv.org/master/d3/d52/tutorial_windows_install.html`

2. The grayscale image is then resized to `28x28` pixels as that is the requirement for our CNN model:

```cpp
resize(img, img, Size(28, 28));
```

3. The image array is then converted to a PyTorch tensor:

```cpp
auto input_ = torch::from_blob(img.data, { img.rows, img.cols, img.channels() }, at::kByte);
```

For all `torch`-related operations as in this step, we use the `libtorch` library, which is the home for all `torch` C++-related APIs. If you have PyTorch installed, you need not install LibTorch separately.

4. Because OpenCV reads the grayscale in (28, 28, 1) dimension, we need to turn it around as (1, 28, 28) to suit the PyTorch requirements. The tensor is then reshaped to shape (1,1,28,28), where the first 1 is `batch_size` for inference and the second 1 is the number of channels, which is 1 for grayscale:

```
auto input = input_.permute({2,0,1}).unsqueeze_(0).
reshape({1, 1, img.rows, img.cols}).toType(c10::kFloat).
div(255);
```
```
input = (input - 0.1302) / 0.3069;
```

Because OpenCV read images have pixel values ranging from 0 to 255, we normalize these values to the range of 0 to 1. Thereafter, we standardize the image with mean 0.1302 and std 0.3069, as we did in a previous section (see *step 2* of the *Building the inference pipeline* section).

5. In this step, we load the JIT-ed TorchScript model object that we exported in the previous exercise:

```
auto module = torch::jit::load(argv[1]);
std::vector<torch::jit::IValue> inputs;
inputs.push_back(input);
```

Once again, we have used the LibTorch JIT API to load the JIT-ed model compiled using TorchScript in Python.

6. Finally, we come to the model prediction, where we use the loaded model object to make a forward pass with the supplied input data (an image, in this case):

```
auto output_ = module.forward(inputs).toTensor();
```

The `output_` variable contains a list of probabilities for each class. Let's extract the class label with the highest probability and print it:

```
auto output = output_.argmax(1);
cout << output << '\n';
```

Finally, we successfully exit the C++ routine:

```
    return 0;
}
```

7. While *steps 1-6* concern the various parts of our C++, we also need to write a `CMakeLists.txt` file in the same working directory. The full code for this file is available at `https://github.com/PacktPublishing/Mastering-PyTorch/blob/master/Chapter10/cpp_convnet/CMakeLists.txt`:

```
cmake_minimum_required(VERSION 3.0 FATAL_ERROR)
project(cpp_convnet)
find_package(Torch REQUIRED)
find_package(OpenCV REQUIRED)
add_executable(cpp_convnet cpp_convnet.cpp)
...
```

This file is basically the library installation and building script similar to `setup.py` in a Python project. In addition to this code, the `OpenCV_DIR` environment variable needs to be set to the path where the OpenCV build artifacts are created, shown in the following code block:

```
export OpenCV_DIR=/Users/ashish.jha/code/personal/
Mastering-PyTorch/tree/master/Chapter10/cpp_convnet/
build_opencv/
```

8. Next, we need to actually run the `CMakeLists` file to create build artifacts. We do so by creating a new directory in the current working directory and run the build process from there. In the command line, we simply need to run the following:

```
mkdir build
cd build
cmake -DCMAKE_PREFIX_PATH=/Users/ashish.jha/opt/
anaconda3/lib/python3.7/site-packages/torch/share/cmake/
..
cmake --build . --config Release
```

In the third line, you shall provide the path to LibTorch. To find your own, open Python and execute this:

```
import torch; torch.__path__
```

For me, it outputs this:

```
['/Users/ashish.jha/opt/anaconda3/lib/python3.7/site-
packages/torch']
```

Executing the third line shall output the following:

```
-- The C compiler identification is AppleClang 10.0.1.10010046
-- The CXX compiler identification is AppleClang 10.0.1.10010046
-- Check for working C compiler: /Library/Developer/CommandLineTools/usr/bin/cc
-- Check for working C compiler: /Library/Developer/CommandLineTools/usr/bin/cc -- works
-- Detecting C compiler ABI info
-- Detecting C compiler ABI info - done
-- Detecting C compile features
-- Detecting C compile features - done
-- Check for working CXX compiler: /Library/Developer/CommandLineTools/usr/bin/c++
-- Check for working CXX compiler: /Library/Developer/CommandLineTools/usr/bin/c++ -- works
-- Detecting CXX compiler ABI info
-- Detecting CXX compiler ABI info - done
-- Detecting CXX compile features
-- Detecting CXX compile features - done
-- Looking for pthread.h
-- Looking for pthread.h - found
-- Performing Test CMAKE_HAVE_LIBC_PTHREAD
-- Performing Test CMAKE_HAVE_LIBC_PTHREAD - Success
-- Found Threads: TRUE
-- Found Torch: /Users/ashish.jha/opt/anaconda3/lib/python3.7/site-packages/torch/lib/libtorch.dylib
-- Found OpenCV: /Users/ashish.jha/code/personal/Mastering-PyTorch/Chapter10/cpp_convnet/build_opencv (found version "4.5.0")
-- Configuring done
-- Generating done
-- Build files have been written to: /Users/ashish.jha/code/personal/Mastering-PyTorch/Chapter10/cpp_convnet/build
```

Figure 10.21 – The C++ CMake output

And the fourth line should result in this:

```
Scanning dependencies of target cpp_convnet
[ 50%] Building CXX object CMakeFiles/cpp_convnet.dir/cpp_convnet.cpp.o
[100%] Linking CXX executable cpp_convnet
[100%] Built target cpp_convnet
```

Figure 10.22 – C++ model building

9. Upon successful execution of the previous step, we will have produced a C++ compiled binary with the name cpp_convnet. It is now time to execute this binary program. In other words, we can now supply a sample image to our C++ model for inference. We may use the scripted model as input:

```
./cpp_convnet ../../scripted_convnet.pt ../../digit_
image.jpg
```

Alternatively, we may use the traced model as input:

```
./cpp_convnet ../../traced_convnet.pt ../../digit_image.
jpg
```

Either of these should result in the following output:

```
2
[ CPULongType{1} ]
```

Figure 10.23 – C++ model prediction

According to *Figure 10.3*, the C++ model seems to be working correctly. Because we have used a different image handling library in C++ (that is, OpenCV) as compared to in Python (PIL), the pixel values are slightly differently encoded, which will result in slightly different prediction probabilities, but the final model prediction in the two languages should not differ significantly if correct normalizations are applied.

This concludes our exploration of PyTorch model inference using C++. This exercise shall help you get started with transporting your favorite deep learning models written and trained using PyTorch into a C++ environment, which should make predictions more efficient as well as opening up the possibility of hosting models in Python-less environments (for example, certain embedded systems, drones, and so on).

In the next section, we will move away from TorchScript and discuss a universal neural network modeling format – ONNX – that has enabled model usage across deep learning frameworks, programming languages, and OSes. We will work on loading a PyTorch trained model for inference in TensorFlow.

Using ONNX to export PyTorch models

There are scenarios in production systems where most of the already-deployed machine learning models are written in a certain deep learning library, say, TensorFlow, with its own sophisticated model-serving infrastructure. However, if a certain model is written using PyTorch, we would like it to be runnable using TensorFlow to conform to the the serving strategy. This is one among various other use cases where a framework such as ONNX is useful.

ONNX is a universal format where the essential operations of a deep learning model such as matrix multiplications and activations, written differently in different deep learning libraries, are standardized. It enables us to interchangeably use different deep learning libraries, programming languages, and even operating environments to run the same deep learning model.

Here, we will demonstrate how to run a model, trained using PyTorch, in TensorFlow. We will first export the PyTorch model into ONNX format and then load the ONNX model inside TensorFlow code.

ONNX works with restricted versions of TensorFlow and hence we will work with `tensorflow==1.15.0`. We will also need to install the `onnx==1.7.0` and `onnx-tf==1.5.0` libraries for the exercise. The full code for this exercise is available at `https://github.com/PacktPublishing/Mastering-PyTorch/blob/master/Chapter10/onnx.ipynb`. Please follow *steps 1 to 11* from the *Model tracing with TorchScript* section, and then follow up with the steps given in this exercise:

1. Similar to model tracing, we again pass a dummy input through our loaded model:

    ```
    demo_input = torch.ones(1, 1, 28, 28)
    torch.onnx.export(model, demo_input, "convnet.onnx")
    ```

    This should save a model onnx file. Under the hood, the same mechanism is used for serializing the model as was used in model tracing.

2. Next, we load the saved onnx model and convert it into a TensorFlow model:

    ```
    import onnx
    from onnx_tf.backend import import prepare
    model_onnx = onnx.load("./convnet.onnx")
    tf_rep = prepare(model_onnx)
    tf_rep.export_graph("./convnet.pb")
    ```

3. Next, we load the serialized `tensorflow` model to parse the model graph. This will help us in verifying that we have loaded the model architecture correctly as well as in identifying the input and output nodes of the graph:

    ```
    with tf.gfile.GFile("./convnet.pb", "rb") as f:
        graph_definition = tf.GraphDef()
        graph_definition.ParseFromString(f.read())
    with tf.Graph().as_default() as model_graph:
        tf.import_graph_def(graph_definition, name="")
    for op in model_graph.get_operations():
        print(op.values())
    ```

This should output the following:

```
(<tf.Tensor 'Const:0' shape=(16,) dtype=float32>,)
(<tf.Tensor 'Const_1:0' shape=(16, 1, 3, 3) dtype=float32>,)
(<tf.Tensor 'Const_2:0' shape=(32,) dtype=float32>,)
(<tf.Tensor 'Const_3:0' shape=(32, 16, 3, 3) dtype=float32>,)
(<tf.Tensor 'Const_4:0' shape=(64,) dtype=float32>,)
(<tf.Tensor 'Const_5:0' shape=(64, 4608) dtype=float32>,)
(<tf.Tensor 'Const_6:0' shape=(10,) dtype=float32>,)
(<tf.Tensor 'Const_7:0' shape=(10, 64) dtype=float32>,)
(<tf.Tensor 'input.1:0' shape=(1, 1, 28, 28) dtype=float32>,)
(<tf.Tensor 'transpose/perm:0' shape=(4,) dtype=int32>,)
(<tf.Tensor 'transpose:0' shape=(3, 3, 1, 16) dtype=float32>,)

                        :
                        :
                        :

(<tf.Tensor 'mul_2/x:0' shape=() dtype=float32>,)
(<tf.Tensor 'mul_2:0' shape=(1, 10) dtype=float32>,)
(<tf.Tensor 'mul_3/x:0' shape=() dtype=float32>,)
(<tf.Tensor 'mul_3:0' shape=(10,) dtype=float32>,)
(<tf.Tensor 'add_3:0' shape=(1, 10) dtype=float32>,)
(<tf.Tensor '18:0' shape=(1, 10) dtype=float32>,)
```

Figure 10.24 – TensorFlow model graph

From the graph, we are able to identify the input and output nodes, as marked.

4. Finally, we can assign variables to the input and output nodes of the neural network model, instantiate a TensorFlow session, and run the graph to generate predictions for our sample image:

```
model_output = model_graph.get_tensor_by_name('18:0')
model_input = model_graph.get_tensor_by_name('input.1:0')
sess = tf.Session(graph=model_graph)
output = sess.run(model_output, feed_dict={model_input:
input_tensor.unsqueeze(0)})
print(output)
```

This should output the following:

```
[[-9.35050774e+00 -1.20893326e+01 -2.23922171e-03 -8.92477798e+00
  -9.81972313e+00 -1.33498535e+01 -9.04598618e+00 -1.44924192e+01
  -6.30233145e+00 -1.22827682e+01]]
```

Figure 10.25 – TensorFlow model prediction

As you can see, in comparison with *Figure 10.18*, the predictions are exactly the same for the TensorFlow and PyTorch versions of our model. This validates the successful functioning of the ONNX framework. I encourage you to dissect the TensorFlow model further and understand how ONNX helps regenerate the exact same model in a different deep learning library by utilizing the underlying mathematical operations in the model graph.

This concludes our discussion of the different ways of exporting PyTorch models. The techniques covered here will be useful in deploying PyTorch models in production systems as well as in working across various platforms. As new versions of deep learning libraries, programming languages, and even OSes keep coming, this is an area that will rapidly evolve accordingly.

Hence, it is highly advisable to keep an eye on the developments and make sure to use the latest and most efficient ways of exporting models as well as operationalizing them into production.

So far, we have been working on our local machines for serving and exporting our PyTorch models. In the next and final section of this chapter, we will briefly look at serving PyTorch models on some of the well-known cloud platforms, such as AWS, Google Cloud, and Microsoft Azure.

Serving PyTorch models in the cloud

Deep learning is computationally expensive and therefore demands powerful and sophisticated computational hardware. Not everyone might have access to a local machine that has enough CPUs and GPUs to train gigantic deep learning models in a reasonable time. Furthermore, we cannot guarantee 100 percent availability for a local machine that is serving a trained model for inference. For reasons such as these, cloud computing platforms are a vital alternative for both training and serving deep learning models.

In this section, we will discuss how to use PyTorch with some of the most popular cloud platforms – **AWS**, **Google Cloud**, and **Microsoft Azure**. We will explore the different ways of serving a trained PyTorch model in each of these platforms. The model-serving exercises we discussed in the earlier sections of this chapter were executed on a local machine. The goal of this section is to enable you to perform similar exercises using **virtual machines** (**VMs**) on the cloud.

Using PyTorch with AWS

AWS is the oldest and one of the most popular cloud computing platforms. It has deep integrations with PyTorch. We have already seen an example of it in the form of TorchServe, which is jointly developed by AWS and Facebook.

In this section, we will look at some of the common ways of serving PyTorch models using AWS. First, we will simply learn how to use an AWS instance as a replacement for our local machine (laptop) to serve PyTorch models. Then, we will briefly discuss Amazon SageMaker, which is a fully dedicated cloud machine learning platform. We will briefly discuss how TorchServe can be used together with SageMaker for model serving.

> **Note**
>
> This section assumes basic familiarity with AWS. Therefore, we will not be elaborating on topics such as what an AWS EC2 instance is, what AMIs are, how to create an instance, and so on. To review such topics, please go to `https://aws.amazon.com/getting-started/`. We will instead focus on the components of AWS that are related to PyTorch.

Serving a PyTorch model using an AWS instance

In this section, we will demonstrate how we can use PyTorch within a VM – an AWS instance, in this case. After reading this section, you will be able to execute the exercises discussed in the *Model serving in PyTorch* section inside an AWS instance.

First, you will need to create an AWS account if you haven't done so already. Creating an account requires an email address and a payment method (credit card). You can find details on account creation here: `https://aws.amazon.com/premiumsupport/knowledge-center/create-and-activate-aws-account/`.

Once you have an AWS account, you may log in to enter the AWS console (`https://aws.amazon.com/console/`). From here, we basically need to instantiate a VM (AWS instance) where we can start using PyTorch for training and serving models. Creating a VM requires two decisions:

- Choosing the hardware configuration of the VM, also known as the **AWS instance type**
- Choosing the **Amazon Machine Image** (**AMI**), which entails all the required software, such as the OS (Ubuntu or Windows), Python, PyTorch, and so on

You can read in more detail about the interaction between the preceding two components here: `https://docs.aws.amazon.com/AWSEC2/latest/UserGuide/ec2-instances-and-amis.html`. Typically, when we refer to an AWS instance, we are referring to an **Elastic Cloud Compute** instance, also known as an **EC2** instance.

Based on the computational requirements of the VM (RAM, CPUs, and GPUs), you can choose from a long list of EC2 instances provided by AWS, which can be found here: `https://aws.amazon.com/ec2/instance-types/`. Because PyTorch heavily leverages GPU compute power, it is recommended to use EC2 instances that include GPUs, though they are generally costlier than CPU-only instances.

Regarding AMIs, there are two possible approaches to choosing an AMI. You may go for a barebones AMI that only has an OS installed, such as Ubuntu (Linux). In this case, you can then manually install Python (using the documentation here: `https://docs.python-guide.org/starting/install3/linux/`) and subsequently install PyTorch (using the documentation here: `https://pytorch.org/get-started/locally/#linux-prerequisites`).

An alternative and more recommended way is to start with a pre-built AMI that has PyTorch installed already. AWS offers Deep Learning AMIs, which make the process of getting started with PyTorch on AWS much faster and easier. You can read this well-written blog for starting your own AWS EC2 instance with a Deep Learning AMI: `https://aws.amazon.com/blogs/machine-learning/get-started-with-deep-learning-using-the-aws-deep-learning-ami/`.

Once you have launched an instance successfully using either of the suggested approaches, you may simply connect to the instance using one of the various available methods: `https://docs.aws.amazon.com/AWSEC2/latest/UserGuide/AccessingInstances.html`.

SSH is one of the most common ways of connecting to an instance. Once you are inside the instance, it will have the same layout as working on a local machine. One of the first logical steps would then be to test whether PyTorch is working inside the machine.

To test, first open a Python interactive session by simply typing `python` on the command line. Then, execute the following line of code:

```
import torch
```

If it executes without error, it means that you have PyTorch installed on the system.

At this point, you can simply fetch all the code that we wrote in the preceding sections of this chapter on model serving. On the command line inside your home directory, simply clone this book's GitHub repository by running this:

```
git clone https://github.com/PacktPublishing/Mastering-PyTorch.git
```

Then, within the `Chapter10` subfolder, you will have all the code to serve the MNIST model that we worked on in the previous sections. You can basically re-run the exercises, this time on the AWS instance instead of your local computer.

Let's review the steps we need to take for working with PyTorch on AWS:

1. Create an AWS account.

2. Log in to the AWS console.

3. Click on the **Launch a virtual machine** button in the console.

4. Select an AMI. For example, select the Deep Learning AMI (Ubuntu).

5. Select an AWS instance type. For example, select **p.2x large**, as it contains a GPU.

6. Click **Launch**.

7. Click **Create a new key pair**. Give the key pair a name and download it locally.

8. Modify permissions of this key-pair file by running this on the command line:

    ```
    chmod 400 downloaded-key-pair-file.pem
    ```

9. On the console, click on **View Instances** to see the details of the launched instance and specifically note the public IP address of the instance.

10. Using SSH, connect to the instance by running this on the command line:

    ```
    ssh -i downloaded-key-pair-file.pem ubuntu@<Public IP
    address>
    ```

    The public IP address is the same as obtained in the previous step.

11. Once connected, start a `python` shell and run `import torch` in the shell to ensure that PyTorch is correctly installed on the instance.

12. Clone this book's GitHub repository by running the following on the instance's command line:

    ```
    git clone https://github.com/PacktPublishing/Mastering-
    PyTorch.git
    ```

13. Go to the `chapter10` folder within the repository and start working on the various model-serving exercises that are covered in the preceding sections of this chapter.

This brings us to the end of this section, where we have essentially learned how to start working with PyTorch on a remote AWS instance. You can read more about this topic on PyTorch's website: `https://pytorch.org/get-started/cloud-partners/#aws-quick-start`. Next, we will look at AWS's fully dedicated cloud machine learning platform –Amazon SageMaker.

Using TorchServe with Amazon SageMaker

We have already discussed TorchServe in detail in the preceding section. As we know, TorchServe is a PyTorch model-serving library developed by AWS and Facebook. Instead of manually defining a model inference pipeline, model-serving APIs, and microservices, you can use TorchServe, which provides all of these functionalities.

Amazon SageMaker, on the other hand, is a cloud machine learning platform that offers functionalities such as the training of massive deep learning models as well as deploying and hosting trained models on custom instances. When working with SageMaker, all we need to do is this:

- Specify the type and number of AWS instances we would like to spin up to serve the model.
- Provide the location of the stored pre-trained model object.

We do not need to manually connect to the instance and serve the model using TorchServe. SageMaker takes care of all that. To get started with using SageMaker and TorchServe to serve PyTorch models on an industrial scale and within a few clicks, refer to this tutorial: `https://aws.amazon.com/blogs/machine-learning/deploying-pytorch-models-for-inference-at-scale-using-torchserve/`. You can also explore use cases of Amazon SageMaker when working with PyTorch, here: `https://docs.aws.amazon.com/sagemaker/latest/dg/pytorch.html`.

Tools such as SageMaker are incredibly useful for scalability during both model training and serving. However, while using such one-click tools, we often tend to lose some flexibility and debuggability. Therefore, it is for you to decide what set of tools works best for your use case. This concludes our discussion on using AWS as a cloud platform for working with PyTorch. Next, we will look at another cloud platform – Google Cloud.

Serving PyTorch model on Google Cloud

Similar to AWS, you first need to create a Google account (*@gmail.com) if you do not have one already. Furthermore, to be able to log in to the Google Cloud console (`https://console.cloud.google.com`), you will need to add a payment method (credit card details).

> **Note**
>
> We will not be covering the basics of Google Cloud here. We will instead focus on using Google Cloud for serving PyTorch models within a VM. To review the basics of Google Cloud, please refer to `https://console.cloud.google.com/getting-started`.

Once inside the console, we need to follow the steps similar to AWS to launch a VM where we can serve our PyTorch model. You can always start with a barebones VM and manually install PyTorch. But we will be using Google's Deep Learning VM Image (`https://cloud.google.com/deep-learning-vm`), which has PyTorch pre-installed. Here are the steps for launching a Google Cloud VM and using it to serve PyTorch models:

1. Launch Deep Learning VM Image on Google Cloud by visiting the following link in the marketplace: `https://console.cloud.google.com/marketplace/product/click-to-deploy-images/deeplearning`.

2. Input the deployment name in the command window. This name suffixed with `-vm` acts as the name of the launched VM. The command prompt inside this VM will look like this:

```
<user>@<deployment-name>-vm:~/
```

Here, `user` is the client connecting to the VM and `deployment-name` is the name of the VM chosen in this step.

3. Select `PyTorch` as the `Framework` in the next command window. This tells the platform to pre-install PyTorch in the VM.

4. Select the zone for this machine. Preferably, choose the zone geographically closest to you. Also, different zones have slightly different hardware offerings (VM configurations) and hence you might want to choose a specific zone for a specific machine configuration.

5. Having specified the software requirement in *step 3*, we shall now specify the hardware requirements. In the GPU section of the command window, we need to specify the GPU type and subsequently the number of GPUs to be included in the VM.

   The list of GPU types available for Google Cloud can be found here: `https://cloud.google.com/compute/docs/gpus`. In the GPU section, also tick the checkbox that will automatically install the NVIDIA drivers that are necessary to utilize the GPUs for deep learning.

6. Similarly, under the CPU section, we need to provide the machine type. The list of machine types offered by Google Cloud can be found here: `https://cloud.google.com/compute/docs/machine-types`. Regarding *step 5* and *step 6*, please be aware that different zones provide different machine and GPU types as well as different combinations of GPU types and GPU numbers.

7. Finally, click on the **Deploy** button. This will launch the VM and lead you to a page that will have all the instructions needed to connect to the VM from your local computer.

8. At this point, you may connect to the VM and ensure that PyTorch is correctly installed by trying to import PyTorch from within a Python shell. Once verified, clone this book's GitHub repository. Go to the `Chapter10` folder and start working on the model-serving exercises within this VM.

You can read more about creating the PyTorch deep learning VM here: `https://cloud.google.com/ai-platform/deep-learning-vm/docs/pytorch_start_instance`. This concludes our discussion of using Google Cloud as a cloud platform to work with PyTorch model serving. As you may have noticed, the process is very similar to that of AWS. In the next and final section, we will briefly look at using Microsoft's cloud platform, Azure, to work with PyTorch.

Serving PyTorch models with Azure

Once again, similar to AWS and Google Cloud, Azure requires a Microsoft-recognized email ID for signing up, along with a valid payment method.

> **Note**
> We assume a basic understanding of the Microsoft Azure cloud platform for this section. In order to review the Azure basics, you may visit this link: `https://azure.microsoft.com/en-us/get-started/`.

Once you have access to the Azure portal (`https://portal.azure.com/`), there are broadly two recommended ways of getting started with using PyTorch on Azure:

- **Data Science Virtual Machine (DSVM)**
- **Azure Machine Learning**

We will now discuss these approaches briefly.

Working on Azure's Data Science Virtual Machine

Similar to Google Cloud's Deep Learning VM Image, Azure offers its own DSVM image (`https://azure.microsoft.com/en-us/services/virtual-machines/data-science-virtual-machines/`), which is a fully dedicated VM image for data science and machine learning, including deep learning.

These images are available for Windows as well as Linux/Ubuntu. Links to the machine images are provided in the *References* section at the end of this chapter.

The steps to create a DSVM instance using this image are quite similar to the steps discussed for Google Cloud. You can follow the steps to create a Linux or a Windows DSVM by following the appropriate links provided in the *References* section.

Once you have created the DSVM, you can launch a Python shell and try to import the PyTorch library to ensure that it is correctly installed. You may further test the functionalities available in this DSVM by following the steps provided in the this well-written articles for Linux as well as Windows, links to which are provided in the *References* section.

Finally, you may clone this book's GitHub repository within the DSVM instance and use the code within the `Chapter10` folder to work on the PyTorch model-serving exercises discussed in this chapter.

Discussing Azure Machine Learning Service

Similar to and predating Amazon's SageMaker, Azure provides an end-to-end cloud machine learning platform. The Azure Machine Learning Service (AMLS) comprises the following (to name just a few):

- Azure Machine Learning VMs
- Notebooks
- Virtual environments
- Datastores
- Tracking machine learning experiments
- Data labeling

A key difference between AMLS VMs and DSVMs is that the former are fully managed. For instance, they can be scaled up or down based on the model training or serving requirements. You can read more about the differences between the Azure Machine Learning VMs and DSVMs here: `https://docs.microsoft.com/en-gb/azure/machine-learning/data-science-virtual-machine/overview`.

Just like SageMaker, Azure Machine Learning is useful both for training large-scale models as well as deploying and serving those models. Azure website has a great tutorial for training PyTorch models on AMLS as well as for deploying PyTorch models on AMLS. Links to these tutorials can be found in the *References* section.

Azure Machine Learning aims at providing a one-click interface to the user for all machine learning tasks. Hence, it is important to keep in mind the flexibility trade-off. Although we have not covered all the details about Azure Machine Learning here, Azure's website is a good resource for reading further: `https://docs.microsoft.com/en-us/azure/machine-learning/overview-what-is-azure-ml`.

This brings us to the end of discussing what Azure has to offer as a cloud platform for working with PyTorch. You can read more about working with PyTorch on Azure here: `https://azure.microsoft.com/en-us/develop/pytorch/`.

And that also concludes our discussion of using PyTorch to serve models on the cloud. We have discussed AWS, Google Cloud, and Microsoft Azure in this section. Although there are more cloud platforms available out there, the nature of their offerings and the ways of using PyTorch within those platforms will be similar to what we have discussed. This section will help you in getting started with working on your PyTorch projects on a VM in the cloud.

Summary

In this chapter, we have explored the world of deploying trained PyTorch deep learning models in production systems. We began with building a local model inference pipeline to be able to make predictions using a pre-trained model with a few lines of Python code. We then utilized the model inference logic of this pipeline to build our own model server using Python's Flask library. We went further with the model server to build a self-contained model microservice using Docker that can be deployed and scaled with a one-line command.

Next, we explored TorchServe, which is a recently developed dedicated model-serving framework for PyTorch. We learned how to use this tool to serve PyTorch models with a few lines of code and discussed the advanced capabilities it offers, such as model versioning and metrics monitoring. Thereafter, we elaborated on how to export PyTorch models.

We first learned the two different ways of doing so using TorchScript: tracing and scripting. We also demonstrated how to use an exported model using TorchScript to make predictions inside C++ code. And then, we discussed another way of exporting models using ONNX. We demonstrated how we can export a trained PyTorch model into ONNX format and thereon to TensorFlow, to make predictions using TensorFlow code.

In the final section of this chapter, we explored the various cloud platforms where we can train and serve PyTorch models. In particular, we looked at the AWS, Google Cloud, and Microsoft Azure cloud platforms.

After finishing this chapter, you are all set to start building model inference pipelines of your own. The possibilities to develop a model-serving infrastructure are many and the optimal design choice will depend on the specific requirements of the model. Some models might require heavy performance optimizations to reduce inference latency. Some models might need to be deployed in a very sophisticated environment with limited software options. The topics covered in this chapter will surely help you in thinking reasonably through such different scenarios and preparing a solid model serving system.

In the next chapter, we will look at another practical aspect of working with models in PyTorch that helps immensely in saving time and resources while training and validating deep learning models – distributed training.

References

- Azure Linux/Ubuntu Image: `https://azuremarketplace.microsoft.com/en-us/marketplace/apps/microsoft-dsvm.ubuntu-1804?tab=Overview`

- Azure Windows Image: `https://azuremarketplace.microsoft.com/en-us/marketplace/apps/microsoft-dsvm.dsvm-win-2019?tab=Overview`

- Steps to create Linux DSVM: `https://docs.microsoft.com/en-gb/azure/machine-learning/data-science-virtual-machine/dsvm-ubuntu-intro`

- Steps to create Windows DSVM: `https://docs.microsoft.com/en-gb/azure/machine-learning/data-science-virtual-machine/provision-vm`

- Linux DSVM walkthrough: `https://docs.microsoft.com/en-gb/azure/machine-learning/data-science-virtual-machine/linux-dsvm-walkthrough`

- Windows DSVM walkthrough : `https://docs.microsoft.com/en-gb/azure/machine-learning/data-science-virtual-machine/vm-do-ten-things`

- Tutorial for training PyTorch model on AMLS: `https://docs.microsoft.com/en-us/azure/machine-learning/how-to-train-pytorch`

- Tutorial for deploying PyTorch model on AMLS: `https://docs.microsoft.com/en-us/azure/machine-learning/how-to-deploy-and-where?tabs=azcli`

11
Distributed Training

Before serving pre-trained machine learning models, which we discussed extensively in the previous chapter, we need to train our machine learning models. In *Chapter 3, Deep CNN Architectures*; *Chapter 4, Deep Recurrent Model Architectures*; and *Chapter 5, Hybrid Advanced Models*, we have seen the vast expanse of increasingly complex deep learning model architectures.

Such gigantic models often have millions and even billions of parameters. The recent (at the time of writing) **Generative Pre-Trained Transformer 3 (GPT3)** language model has 175 billion parameters. Using backpropagation to tune many parameters requires enormous amounts of memory and compute power. And even then, model training can take days to finish.

In this chapter, we will explore ways of speeding up the model training process by distributing the training task across machines and processes within machines. We will learn about the distributed training APIs offered by PyTorch – **torch.distributed, torch.multiprocessing**, and **torch.utils.data.distributed.DistributedSampler** – that will make distributed training look easy.

Using the handwritten digits classification example from *Chapter 1*, *Overview of Deep Learning Using PyTorch*, we will demonstrate the speedup in training on CPU by using PyTorch's distributed training tools. We will then discuss similar ways of speeding up on GPU.

By the end of this chapter, you will be able to fully utilize the hardware at your disposal for model training. For training extremely large models, the tools discussed in this chapter will prove vital, if not necessary.

In this chapter, we will cover the following topics:

- Distributed training with PyTorch
- Distributed training on GPUs with CUDA

Technical requirements

We will be using Python scripts for all our exercises. The following is a list of Python libraries that must be installed for this chapter using pip. For example, run `pip install torch==1.4.0` on the command line, like so to install `torch`:

```
jupyter==1.0.0
torch==1.4.0
torchvision==0.5.0
```

All the code files that are relevant to this chapter are available at `https://github.com/PacktPublishing/Mastering-PyTorch/tree/master/Chapter11`.

Distributed training with PyTorch

In the previous exercises in this book, we have implicitly assumed that model training happens in one machine and in a single Python process in that machine. In this section, we will revisit the exercise from *Chapter 1*, *Overview of Deep Learning Using PyTorch* – the handwritten digit classification model – and transform the model training routine from regular training into distributed training. While doing so, we will explore the tools PyTorch offers for distributing the training process, thereby making it both faster and more hardware-efficient.

First, let's look at how the `MNIST` model can be trained without using distributed training. We will then contrast this with a distributed training PyTorch pipeline.

Training the MNIST model in a regular fashion

The handwritten digits classification model that we built in *Chapter 1, Overview of Deep Learning Using Python*, was in the form of a Jupyter notebook. Here, we will put that notebook code together as a single Python script file. The full code can be found here: `https://github.com/PacktPublishing/Mastering-PyTorch/blob/master/Chapter11/convnet_undistributed.py`.

In the following steps, we will recap on the different parts of the model training code:

1. In the Python script, we must import the relevant libraries:

    ```
    import torch
    …
    import argparse
    ```

2. Next, we must define the CNN model architecture:

    ```
    class ConvNet(nn.Module):
        def __init__(self): …
        def forward(self, x): …
    ```

3. We must then define the model training routine. The full code has been deliberately written here so that we can compare it to the distributed training mode later:

    ```
    def train(args):
        torch.manual_seed(0)
        device = torch.device("cpu")
        train_dataloader=torch.utils.data.DataLoader(...)
        model = ConvNet()
        optimizer = optim.Adadelta(model.parameters(),
    lr=0.5)
        model.train()
    ```

    In the first half of the function, we define our PyTorch training `dataloader` using the PyTorch training dataset. We then instantiate our deep learning model, known as the `ConvNet`, and also define the optimization module. In the second half, we run the training loop, which runs for a defined number of epochs, as shown in the following code:

    ```
        for epoch in range(args.epochs):
            for b_i, (X, y) in enumerate(train_dataloader):
                X, y = X.to(device), y.to(device)
    ```

```
pred_prob = model(X)
loss = F.nll_loss(pred_prob, y) # nll is the
negative likelihood loss
optimizer.zero_grad()
loss.backward()
optimizer.step()
```

Inside the loop, we run through the entire training dataset in batches with a defined batch size (128, in this case). For each batch containing 128 training data points, we run a forward pass through the model to compute prediction probabilities. We then use the predictions alongside ground truth labels to compute a batch loss. We use this loss to compute gradients in order to tune the model parameters using backpropagation.

4. We now have all the components we need. We can put this all together in a `main()` function:

```
def main():
    parser = argparse.ArgumentParser()
    ...
    train(args)
```

Here, we are using an arguments parser, which helps us enter hyperparameters such as the number of epochs while running our Python training program from the command line. We are also timing the training routine so that we can compare it with the distributed training routine later.

5. The final thing we must do in our Python script is to make sure that the `main()` function runs when we execute this script from the command line:

```
if __name__ == '__main__':
    main()
```

6. Now, we can execute the Python script by running the following command on the command line:

```
python convnet_undistributed.py --epochs 1
```

We are running the training data for just a single epoch as the focus is not on model accuracy but on the model training time. This should output the following:

```
epoch: 0 [0/469 (0%)]      training loss: 2.308408
epoch: 0 [10/469 (2%)]     training loss: 1.772532
epoch: 0 [20/469 (4%)]     training loss: 0.953913
epoch: 0 [30/469 (6%)]     training loss: 0.694977
epoch: 0 [40/469 (9%)]     training loss: 0.481864
epoch: 0 [50/469 (11%)]    training loss: 0.394739
epoch: 0 [60/469 (13%)]    training loss: 0.415441




epoch: 0 [430/469 (92%)]      training loss: 0.137537
epoch: 0 [440/469 (94%)]      training loss: 0.088957
epoch: 0 [450/469 (96%)]      training loss: 0.040298
epoch: 0 [460/469 (98%)]      training loss: 0.136536
Finished training in 50.57237482070923 secs
```

Figure 11.1 – Output of regular model training logs

It took roughly 50 seconds to train for 1 epoch, which equates to 469 batches, each of which has 128 data points. The only exception is the last batch, which has 32 fewer data points than usual (as there are 60,000 data points in total).

At this point, it is important to know what kind of machine this model is being trained on so that we know the reference context. As an example, the following screenshot shows the system specifications for my computer, which is a MacBook:

```
Hardware Overview:

    Model Name: MacBook Pro
    Model Identifier: MacBookPro15,2
    Processor Name: Intel Core i5
    Processor Speed: 2.4 GHz
    Number of Processors: 1
    Total Number of Cores: 4
    L2 Cache (per Core): 256 KB
    L3 Cache: 6 MB
    Hyper-Threading Technology: Enabled
    Memory: 16 GB
```

Figure 11.2 – Hardware specifications

The preceding information can be obtained by running the following command on a mac Terminal:

```
/Volumes/Macintosh\ HD/usr/sbin/system_profiler
SPHardwareDataType
```

It is important point to note that my machine consists of 4 CPU cores and 16 GB RAM. This is useful information when you're trying to parallelize the training routine, which we will look at next.

Training the MNIST model in a distributed fashion

In this section, we will basically repeat the *six steps* we provided of the previous section, but we will make a few edits to the code to enable distributed training, which should be faster than the regular training we performed. The full code for this distributed training Python script can be found here: `https://github.com/PacktPublishing/Mastering-PyTorch/blob/master/Chapter11/convnet_distributed.py`.

Defining a distributed training routine

In this section, we will import the additional PyTorch libraries that are crucial for facilitating distributed training. We will then redefine the model training routine, this time ensuring that different machines and processes can work together when training a single model. Let's get started:

1. Once again, we will start by importing the necessary libraries. This time, we will have a few additional imports:

    ```
    import torch
    import torch.multiprocessing as mp
    import torch.distributed as dist
    import argparse
    ```

    While `torch.multiprocessing` helps spawn multiple Python processes within a machine (typically, we may spawn as many processes as there are CPU cores in the machine), `torch.distributed` enables communications between different machines as they work together to train the model. During execution, we need to explicitly launch our model training script from within each of these machines.

    One of the built-in PyTorch communication backends, such as **Gloo**, will then take care of the communication between these machines. Inside each machine, multiprocessing will take care of parallelizing the training task across several processes. I encourage you to read about multiprocessing and distribution in further detail at `https://pytorch.org/docs/stable/multiprocessing.html` and `https://pytorch.org/docs/stable/distributed.html`, respectively.

2. The model architecture definition step remains unchanged for obvious reasons:

    ```
    class ConvNet(nn.Module):
        def __init__(self): ...
        def forward(self, x): ...
    ```

3. At this point, it's time to define the `train()` function, which is where most of the magic happens. The following highlighted code helps facilitate distributed training:

```
def train(cpu_num, args):
    rank = args.machine_id * args.num_processes + cpu_num
    dist.init_process_group(backend='gloo',
    init_method='env://', world_size=args.world_size,
    rank=rank)
    torch.manual_seed(0)
    device = torch.device("cpu")
```

As we can see, there is additional code at the very beginning that consists of two statements. First, a `rank` is calculated. This is essentially the ordinal ID of a process within the entire distributed system; for example, if we are using two machines with four CPU cores each. For full hardware utilization, we might want to launch a total of eight processes, with four per machine.

In this scenario, we will need to somehow label these eight processes in order to remember which process is which. We can do so by assigning IDs *0* and *1* to the two machines and then IDs *0* to *3* to the four processes in each machine. Finally, the rank of the *k*th process of the *n*th machine is given by the following equation:

$$rank = n * 4 + k$$

The second additional line of code uses the `torch.distributed` module's `init_process_group`, which, for each launched process, specifies the following:

a) The backend that will be used for communication between machines (Gloo, in this case).

b) The total number of processes involved in distributed training (given by `args.world_size`), otherwise called `world_size`.

c) The rank of the process being launched.

d) The `init_process_group` method blocks each process from performing further actions until all the processes across machines have been initiated using this method.

Regarding the backend, PyTorch provides the following three built-in backends for distributed training: **Gloo**, **NCCL**, and **MPI**. In short, for distributed training on CPUs, use Gloo, while for GPUs, use NCCL. You can read about these communication backends in detail here: `https://pytorch.org/tutorials/intermediate/dist_tuto.html#communication-backends`. The code is as follows:

```
train_dataset = …
train_sampler = torch.utils.data.distributed.
DistributedSampler(
    train_dataset, num_replicas=args.world_size,
    rank=rank)
train_dataloader = torch.utils.data.DataLoader(
  dataset=train_dataset, batch_size=args.batch_size,
  shuffle=False, num_workers=0, sampler=train_sampler)
model = ConvNet()
optimizer = optim.Adadelta(model.parameters(),
lr=0.5)
model = nn.parallel.DistributedDataParallel(model)
model.train()
```

Compared to the undistributed training exercise, we have separated the MNIST dataset instantiation from the dataloader instantiation. And in-between these two steps, we have inserted a data sampler; that is, `torch.utils.data.distributed.DistributedSampler`.

The sampler's task is to divide the training dataset into `world_size` number of partitions so that all the processes in the distributed training session get to work on equal portions of data. Note that we have set shuffle to `False` in the dataloader instantiation because we are using the sampler for distributing data.

Another addition to our code is the `nn.parallel.DistributedDataParallel` function, which is applied to the model object. This is perhaps the most important part of this code as `DistributedDataParallel` is a critical component/API that facilitates the gradient descent algorithm in a distributed fashion. The following happens under the hood:

a) Each spawned process in the distributed universe gets its own model copy.

b) Each model per process maintains its own optimizer and undergoes a local optimization step that's in sync with the global iteration.

c) At each distributed training iteration, individual losses and hence gradients are calculated in each process. These gradients are then averaged across processes.

d) The averaged gradient is then universally backpropagated to each of the model copies, which tune their parameters.

e) Because of the universal backpropagation step, all the model's parameters are the same at each iteration, which means they are automatically synced.

`DistributedDataParallel` ensures that each Python process runs on an independent Python interpreter. This does away with the GIL limitation that could occur if multiple models were instantiated in multiple threads under the same interpreter. This boosts performance even more, especially for models that require intense Python-specific processing:

```
for epoch in range(args.epochs):
    for b_i, (X, y) in enumerate(train_dataloader):
        X, y = X.to(device), y.to(device)
        pred_prob = model(X)
        ...
    if b_i % 10 == 0 and cpu_num==0:
        print(...)
```

Finally, the training loop is almost the same as it was previously. The only difference is that we restrict the logging to only the process with rank 0. We have done this because the machine with rank 0 is used to set up all communications. Hence, we notionally use the process with rank 0 as our reference to track the model's training performance. If we did not restrict this, we would get as many log lines per model training iteration as there are processes.

Executing distributed training on multiple processes

We defined the model, as well as the distributed training routine, in the previous section. In this section, we will execute that routine on multiple hardware settings and observe the impact of distributed training on model training time. Let's get started:

1. Moving on from the `train()` function to the `main()` function, we can see a lot of additions in the code:

```
def main():
    parser = argparse.ArgumentParser()
    parser.add_argument('--num-machines', default=1,
type=int,)
```

```
        parser.add_argument('--num-processes', default=1,
    type=int)
        parser.add_argument('--machine-id', default=0,
    type=int)
        parser.add_argument('--epochs', default=1, type=int)
        parser.add_argument('--batch-size', default=128,
    type=int)
        args = parser.parse_args()
        args.world_size = args.num_processes * args.num_
    machines
        os.environ['MASTER_ADDR'] = '127.0.0.1'
        os.environ['MASTER_PORT'] = '8892'
        start = time.time()
        mp.spawn(train, nprocs=args.num_processes,
    args=(args,))
        print(f"Finished training in {time.time()-start}
    secs")
```

First, we can observe the following additional arguments:

a) num_machines: As its name suggests, this specifies the number of machines.

b) num_processes: The number of processes to be spawned in each machine.

c) machine_id: The ordinal ID of the current machine. Remember, this Python script will need to be launched separately in each of the machines.

d) batch_size: The number of data points in a batch. Why do we suddenly need this?

As we mentioned earlier, there are two reasons why we need this. First, all the processes will have their own gradients, which will be averaged to get the overall gradient per iteration. Hence, we need to explicitly specify how many data points are processed by each process in one model training iteration. Secondly, the full training dataset is divided into world_size number of individual datasets.

Therefore, at each iteration, the full batch of data needs to be divided into world_size number of sub-batches of data per process. And because the batch_size is now coupled to world_size, we provide it as an input argument for easier training interface. So, for example, if the world_size is doubled, the batch_size needs to be halved in order to enable uniform distribution of data points across all machines and processes.

After providing the preceding additional arguments, we calculate `world_size` as a derived argument. Then, we specify two important environment variables:

a) `MASTER_ADDR`: The IP address of the machine that runs the process with rank 0.

b) `MASTER_PORT`: An available port on the machine that runs the process with rank 0.

As we mentioned in *step 3* of the previous section - *Defining a distributed training routine*, the machine with rank 0 sets up all the backend communications, and hence it is important for the entire system to be able to locate the hosting machine at all times. That is why we provide its IP address and port.

In this example, the training process will be run on a single local machine and hence a localhost address suffices. However, when running multi-machine training across servers located remotely, we need to provide the exact IP address of the rank 0 server with a free port.

The final change we've made is the use of multiprocessing to spawn `num_processes` number of processes in a machine, instead of simply running a single training process. The distributional arguments are passed to each of the spawned processes so that the processes and machines coordinate among themselves during the model training run.

2. The final piece of our distributed training code is the same as it was previously:

```
if __name__ == '__main__':
    main()
```

3. We are now in a position to launch the distributed training script. We will begin with an undistributed-like run using the distributed-like script. We can do so by simply setting the number of machines, as well as the number of processes, to 1:

```
python convnet_distributed.py --num-machines 1
--num-processes 1 --machine-id 0 --batch-size 128
```

> **Note**
>
> The Gloo backend only works with Linux and macOS at the time of writing. Unfortunately, this means that this code will not run on Windows operating systems.

Note that since only a single process is being used for training, `batch_size` remains unchanged in comparison to the previous exercise. You shall see the following output:

```
epoch: 0 [0/469 (0%)]      training loss: 2.310592
epoch: 0 [10/469 (2%)]     training loss: 1.276357
epoch: 0 [20/469 (4%)]     training loss: 0.693506
epoch: 0 [30/469 (6%)]     training loss: 0.666963
epoch: 0 [40/469 (9%)]     training loss: 0.318174
epoch: 0 [50/469 (11%)]    training loss: 0.567527
                    ⋮
epoch: 0 [430/469 (92%)]       training loss: 0.084474
epoch: 0 [440/469 (94%)]       training loss: 0.140898
epoch: 0 [450/469 (96%)]       training loss: 0.154369
epoch: 0 [460/469 (98%)]       training loss: 0.110312
Finished training in 44.398102045059204 secs
```

Figure 11.3 – Distributed training with a single process

If we compare this result to the one shown in *Figure 11.1*, the training time is slightly shorter, although it follows a similar pattern. The training loss' evolution is also quite similar.

4. We will now run a truly distributed training session with 2 processes instead of 1. Due to this, we will halve the batch size from 128 to 64:

```
python convnet_distributed.py --num-machines 1
--num-processes 2 --machine-id 0 --batch-size 64
```

You shall see the following output:

```
epoch: 0 [0/469 (0%)]      training loss: 2.309348
epoch: 0 [10/469 (2%)]     training loss: 1.524053
epoch: 0 [20/469 (4%)]     training loss: 0.993402
epoch: 0 [30/469 (6%)]     training loss: 0.777355
epoch: 0 [40/469 (9%)]     training loss: 0.407441
epoch: 0 [50/469 (11%)]    training loss: 0.655984
                    ⋮
epoch: 0 [420/469 (90%)]       training loss: 0.179646
epoch: 0 [430/469 (92%)]       training loss: 0.059710
epoch: 0 [440/469 (94%)]       training loss: 0.052976
epoch: 0 [450/469 (96%)]       training loss: 0.039953
epoch: 0 [460/469 (98%)]       training loss: 0.181595
Finished training in 30.58652114868164 secs
```

Figure 11.4 – Distributed training with two processes

As we can see, there is a quite a reduction in training time – from **44** seconds to **30** seconds. Once again, the training loss' evolution seems to be unaffected, which shows how distributed training can speed up training without there being any loss in model accuracy.

5. Now, let's go even further and use 4 processes instead of 2. Due to this, we will reduce the batch size from 64 to 32:

```
python convnet_distributed.py --num-machines 1
--num-processes 4 --machine-id 0 --batch-size 32
```

You shall see the following output:

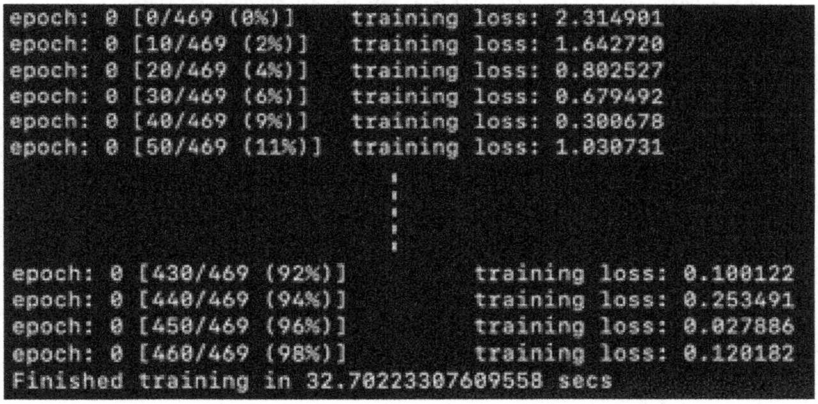

```
epoch: 0 [0/469 (0%)]      training loss: 2.314901
epoch: 0 [10/469 (2%)]     training loss: 1.642720
epoch: 0 [20/469 (4%)]     training loss: 0.802527
epoch: 0 [30/469 (6%)]     training loss: 0.679492
epoch: 0 [40/469 (9%)]     training loss: 0.300678
epoch: 0 [50/469 (11%)]    training loss: 1.030731
                        :
                        :
                        :
epoch: 0 [430/469 (92%)]       training loss: 0.100122
epoch: 0 [440/469 (94%)]       training loss: 0.253491
epoch: 0 [450/469 (96%)]       training loss: 0.027886
epoch: 0 [460/469 (98%)]       training loss: 0.120182
Finished training in 32.70223307609558 secs
```

Figure 11.5 – Distributed training with four processes

Contrary to our expectations, the training time doesn't reduce further and in fact increases slightly. This is where we need to go back to *Figure 11.2* – here, the machine has four CPU cores and all the cores are occupied by one process each.

Since this session is being run on a local machine, there are other processes running as well (such as Google Chrome), which may fight for resources with one or more of our distributed training processes.

In practice, training models in a distributed fashion is done on remote machines, whose only job is to perform model training. On such machines, it is advisable to use as many processes (or even more) as there are CPU cores.

You can still launch more processes than there are cores, but that will not yield significant training time improvements (if any) as multiple processes will be fighting for one resource (a CPU core). You can read more about cores and processes here: https://www.guru99.com/cpu-core-multicore-thread.html.

6. As a final note, because we have only used one machine in this exercise, we only needed to launch one Python script to start training. If, however, you are training on multiple machines, then besides applying the changes to MASTER_ADDR and MASTER_PORT, as advised in *step 4*, you need to launch one Python script in each machine. For example, if there are two machines, then on the first machine, run the following command:

```
python convnet_distributed.py --num-machines 2
--num-processes 2 --machine-id 0 --batch-size 32
```

Then, on the second machine, run the following command:

```
python convnet_distributed.py --num-machines 2
--num-processes 2 --machine-id 1 --batch-size 32
```

This concludes our hands-on discussion of training deep learning models on CPUs using PyTorch in a distributed fashion. With a few lines of added code, a general PyTorch model training script can be turned into a distributed training environment. The exercise we performed in this section was for a simple convolutional network. However, because we did not even touch the model architecture code, this exercise can easily be extended for more complex learning models, where the gains will be more visible and needed.

In the next and final section, we will briefly discuss how to apply similar code changes in order to facilitate distributed training on GPUs.

Distributed training on GPUs with CUDA

Throughout the various exercises in this book, you may have noticed a common line of PyTorch code:

```
device = torch.device('cuda' if torch.cuda.is_available() else
'cpu')
```

This code simply looks for the available compute device and prefers cuda (which uses the GPU) over cpu. This preference is because of the computational speedups that GPUs can provide on regular neural network operations, such as matrix multiplications and additions through parallelization.

In this section, we will learn how to speed this up further with the help of distributed training on GPUs. We will build upon the work done in the previous exercise. Note that most of the code looks the same. In the following steps, we will highlight the changes. Executing the script has been left to you as an exercise.

The full code is available here: `https://github.com/PacktPublishing/Mastering-PyTorch/blob/master/Chapter11/convnet_distributed_cuda.py`. Let's get started:

1. While the imports and model architecture definition code are exactly the same as they were previously, there are a few changes we need to make in the `train()` function:

```python
def train(gpu_num, args):
    rank = args.machine_id * args.num_processes + cpu_num
    dist.init_process_group(
    backend='nccl', init_method='env://',
    world_size=args.world_size, rank=rank)
        torch.manual_seed(0)
        model = ConvNet()
    torch.cuda.set_device(gpu_num)
    model.cuda(gpu_num)
    criterion = nn.NLLLoss().cuda(gpu_num) # nll is the
    negative likelihood loss
```

As we discussed in *step 3* of the previous section- *Defining a distributed training routine*, NCCL is the preferred choice of communication backend when working with GPUs. Both the model and the loss function need to be placed on the GPU device to ensure that the parallelized matrix operations offered by the GPUs are utilized and training is accordingly sped up:

```python
    train_dataset = ...
    train_sampler = ...
    train_dataloader = torch.utils.data.DataLoader(
        dataset=train_dataset, batch_size=args.batch_size,
        shuffle=False, num_workers=0, pin_memory=True,
        sampler=train_sampler)
    optimizer = optim.Adadelta(model.parameters(),
    lr=0.5)
    model = nn.parallel.DistributedDataParallel(model,
        device_ids=[gpu_num])
    model.train()
```

The `DistributedDataParallel` API takes in an additional parameter, called `device_ids`, which takes in the rank of the GPU process it is called from. There is also an additional parameter, `pin_memory`, under the dataloader, which is set to `True`. This essentially helps in faster data transfer from the host (the CPU, in this case, which is where the dataset is loaded) to the various devices (GPUs) during model training.

This parameter enables the dataloader to *pin* data into CPU memory – in other words, allocate the data samples to fixed page-locked CPU memory slots. The data from these slots is then copied to the respective GPUs during training. You can read more about the pinning strategy here: `https://developer. nvidia.com/blog/how-optimize-data-transfers-cuda-cc/`. The `pin_memory=True` mechanism works together with the `non_blocking=True` argument, as shown in the following code:

```
for epoch in range(args.epochs):
        for b_i, (X, y) in enumerate(train_dataloader):
        X, y = X.cuda(non_blocking=True), y.cuda(non_
blocking=True)
            pred_prob = model(X)
        ...
```

By invoking the `pin_memory` and `non_blocking` parameter, we enable overlap between the following:

a) CPU to GPU data (ground truth) transfer

b) GPU model training compute (or GPU kernel execution)

This basically makes the overall GPU training process more efficient (faster).

2. Besides the changes in the `train()` function, we must change a few lines in the `main()` function as well:

```
def main():
    parser.add_argument('--num-gpu-processes', default=1,
type=int)
    args.world_size = args.num_gpu_processes * args.num_
machines
    mp.spawn(train, nprocs=args.num_gpu_processes,
args=(args,))
```

Instead of num_process, we now have num_gpu_processes. The rest of the code changes accordingly. The rest of the GPU code is the same as it was previously. Now, we are all set to the run distributed training on GPUs by executing the following command:

```
python convnet_distributed_cuda.py --num-machines 1
--num-gpu-processes 2 --machine-id 0 --batch-size 64
```

This brings us to the end of briefly discussing distributed model training on GPUs using PyTorch. As we mentioned in the previous section, the code changes that have been suggested for the preceding example can be extended to other deep learning models. Using distributed training on GPUs is actually how most of the latest state-of-the-art deep learning models are trained. This should get you started with training your own amazing models using GPUs.

Summary

In this chapter, we covered an important practical aspect of machine learning; that is, how to optimize the model training process. We explored the extent and power of distributed training using PyTorch. First, we discussed distributed training on CPUs. We re-trained the model we trained in *Chapter 1*, *Overview of Deep Learning Using PyTorch*, using the principles of distributed training.

While working on this exercise, we learned about some of the useful PyTorch APIs that make distributed training work once we've made a few code changes. Finally, we ran the new training script and observed a significant speedup by distributing the training across multiple processes.

In the second half of this chapter, we briefly discussed distributed training on GPUs using PyTorch. We highlighted the basic code changes needed for model training to work on multiple GPUs in a distributed fashion, while leaving out the actual execution for you as an exercise.

In the next chapter, we will move on to another important and promising aspect of applied machine learning that we already touched upon in both *Chapter 3*, *Deep CNN Architectures*, and *Chapter 5*, *Hybrid Advanced Models*: we will learn how to effectively use PyTorch for **automated machine learning** (**AutoML**). By doing this, we will be able to use AutoML to train machine learning models automatically; that is, without having to decide on and define the model architecture.

12

PyTorch and AutoML

Automated machine learning (**AutoML**) provides methods to find the optimal neural architecture and the best hyperparameter settings for a given neural network. We have already covered neural architecture search in detail while discussing the `RandWireNN` model in *Chapter 5, Hybrid Advanced Models*.

In this chapter, we will look more broadly at the AutoML tool for PyTorch—**Auto-PyTorch**—which performs both neural architecture search and hyperparameter search. We will also look at another AutoML tool called **Optuna** that performs hyperparameter search for a PyTorch model.

At the end of this chapter, non-experts will be able to design machine learning models with little domain experience, and experts will drastically speed up their model selection process.

This chapter is broken down into the following topics:

- Finding the best neural architectures with AutoML
- Using Optuna for hyperparameter search

Technical requirements

We will be using Jupyter Notebooks for all of our exercises. Here is a list of the Python libraries that will be installed for this chapter, using `pip` (for example, by running `pip install torch==1.7.0` on the command line):

```
jupyter==1.0.0
torch==1.7.0
torchvision==0.8.1
torchviz==0.0.1
autoPyTorch==0.0.2
configspace==0.4.12
git+https://github.com/shukon/HpBandSter.git
optuna==2.2.0
```

> **Note**
>
> Auto-PyTorch is fully supported in Linux and macOS at the time of writing. However, Windows users might encounter issues while installing the library. It is therefore recommended to use macOS or Linux for working on Auto-PyTorch.

All code files relevant to this chapter are available at the following GitHub page: `https://github.com/PacktPublishing/Mastering-PyTorch/tree/master/Chapter12`.

Finding the best neural architectures with AutoML

One way to think of machine learning algorithms is that they automate the process of learning relationships between given inputs and outputs. In traditional software engineering, we would have to explicitly write/code these relationships in the form of functions that take in input and return output. In the machine learning world, machine learning models find such functions for us. Although we automate to a certain extent, there is still a lot to be done. Besides mining and cleaning data, here are a few routine tasks to be performed in order to get those functions:

- Choosing a machine learning model (or a model family and then a model)
- Deciding the model architecture (especially in the case of deep learning)
- Choosing hyperparameters

- Adjusting hyperparameters based on validation set performance
- Trying different models (or model families)

These are the kinds of tasks that justify the requirement of a human machine learning expert. Most of these steps are manual and either take a lot of time or need a lot of expertise to discount the required time, and we have far fewer machine learning experts than needed to create and deploy machine learning models that are increasingly popular, valuable, and useful across both industries and academia.

This is where AutoML comes to the rescue. AutoML has become a discipline within the field of machine learning that aims to automate the previously listed steps and beyond.

In this section, we will take a look at Auto-PyTorch—an AutoML tool created to work with PyTorch. In the form of an exercise, we will find an optimal neural network along with the hyperparameters to perform handwritten digit classification—a task that we worked on in *Chapter 1, Overview of Deep Learning Using PyTorch*.

The difference from the first chapter will be that this time, we do not decide the architecture or the hyperparameters, and instead let Auto-PyTorch figure that out for us. We will first load the dataset, then define an Auto-PyTorch model search instance, and finally run the model searching routine, which will provide us with a best-performing model.

Tool citation

Auto-PyTorch (`https://github.com/automl/Auto-PyTorch`)
Auto-PyTorch Tabular: Multi-Fidelity MetaLearning for Efficient and Robust AutoDL, Lucas Zimmer, Marius Lindauer, and *Frank Hutter* `https://arxiv.org/abs/2006.13799`

Using Auto-PyTorch for optimal MNIST model search

We will execute the model search in the form of a Jupyter Notebook. In the text, we only show the important parts of the code. The full code can be found here:

```
https://github.com/PacktPublishing/Mastering-PyTorch/blob/
master/Chapter12/automl-pytorch.ipynb
```

Loading the MNIST dataset

We will now discuss the code for loading the dataset step by step, as follows:

1. First, we import the relevant libraries, like this:

```
import torch
from autoPyTorch import AutoNetClassification
```

The last line is crucial, as we import the relevant Auto-PyTorch module here. This will help us set up and execute a model search session.

2. Next, we load the training and test datasets using Torch **application programming interfaces (APIs)**, as follows:

```
train_ds = datasets.MNIST(...)
test_ds = datasets.MNIST(...)
```

3. We then convert these dataset tensors into training and testing input (X) and output (y) arrays, like this:

```
X_train, X_test, y_train, y_test = train_ds.data.numpy().
reshape(-1, 28*28), test_ds.data.numpy().reshape(-1,
28*28) ,train_ds.targets.numpy(), test_ds.targets.numpy()
```

Note that we are reshaping the images into flattened vectors of size 784. In the next section, we will be defining an Auto-PyTorch model searcher that expects a flattened feature vector as input, and hence we do the reshaping.

Auto-PyTorch currently (at the time of writing) only provides support for featurized and image data in the form of `AutoNetClassification` and `AutoNetImageClassification` respectively. While we are using featurized data in this exercise, we leave it as an exercise for the reader to use image data instead, using the tutorial here: `https://github.com/automl/Auto-PyTorch/blob/master/examples/basics/Auto-PyTorch%20Tutorial.ipynb`.

Running a neural architecture search with Auto-PyTorch

Having loaded the dataset in the preceding section, we will now use Auto-PyTorch to define a model search instance and use it to perform the tasks of neural architecture search and hyperparameter search. We'll proceed as follows:

1. This is the most important step of the exercise, where we define an `autoPyTorch` model search instance, like this:

```
autoPyTorch = AutoNetClassification("tiny_cs",  # config
preset

                log_level='info', max_runtime=2000, min_
budget=100, max_budget=1500)
```

The configs here are derived from the examples provided in the Auto-PyTorch repository at `https://github.com/automl/Auto-PyTorch`. But generally, `tiny_cs` is used for faster searches with fewer hardware requirements.

The budget argument is all about setting constraints on resource consumption by the Auto-PyTorch process. As a default, the unit of a budget is time—that is, how much **central processing unit/graphics processing unit (CPU/GPU)** time we are comfortable spending on the model search.

2. After instantiating an Auto-PyTorch model search instance, we execute the search by trying to fit the instance on the training dataset, as follows:

```
autoPyTorch.fit(X_train, y_train, validation_split=0.1)
```

Internally, Auto-PyTorch will run several `trials` of different model architectures and hyperparameter settings based on methods mentioned in the original paper, which can be found at `https://arxiv.org/abs/2006.13799`.

The different `trials` will be benchmarked against the 10% validation dataset, and the best-performing `trial` will be returned as output. The command in the preceding code snippet should output the following:

```
{'optimized_hyperparameter_config': {'CreateDataLoader:batch_size': 125,
 'Imputation:strategy': 'median',
 'InitializationSelector:initialization_method': 'default',
 'InitializationSelector:initializer:initialize_bias': 'No',
 'LearningrateSchedulerSelector:lr_scheduler': 'cosine_annealing',
 'LossModuleSelector:loss_module': 'cross_entropy_weighted',
 'NetworkSelector:network': 'shapedresnet',
 'NormalizationStrategySelector:normalization_strategy': 'standardize',
 'OptimizerSelector:optimizer': 'sgd',
 'PreprocessorSelector:preprocessor': 'truncated_svd',
 'ResamplingStrategySelector:over_sampling_method': 'none',
 'ResamplingStrategySelector:target_size_strategy': 'none',
 'ResamplingStrategySelector:under_sampling_method': 'none',
 'TrainNode:batch_loss_computation_technique': 'standard',
 'LearningrateSchedulerSelector:cosine_annealing:T_max': 10,
 'LearningrateSchedulerSelector:cosine_annealing:eta_min': 2,
 'NetworkSelector:shapedresnet:activation': 'relu',
 'NetworkSelector:shapedresnet:blocks_per_group': 4,
 'NetworkSelector:shapedresnet:max_units': 13,
 'NetworkSelector:shapedresnet:num_groups': 2,
 'NetworkSelector:shapedresnet:resnet_shape': 'brick',
 'NetworkSelector:shapedresnet:use_dropout': 0,
 'NetworkSelector:shapedresnet:use_shake_drop': 0,
 'NetworkSelector:shapedresnet:use_shake_shake': 0,
 'OptimizerSelector:sgd:learning_rate': 0.06829146967649465,
 'OptimizerSelector:sgd:momentum': 0.9343847098348538,
 'OptimizerSelector:sgd:weight_decay': 0.0002425066735211845,
 'PreprocessorSelector:truncated_svd:target_dim': 100},
'budget': 40.0,
'loss': -96.45,
'info': {'loss': 0.12337125303244502,
 'model_parameters': 176110.0,
 'train_accuracy': 96.28550185873605,
 'lr_scheduler_converged': 0.0,
 'lr': 0.06829146967649465,
 'val_accuracy': 96.45}}
```

Figure 12.1 – Auto-PyTorch model accuracy

Figure 12.1 basically shows the hyperparameter setting that Auto-PyTorch finds optimal for the given task—for example, the learning rate is `0.068`, momentum is `0.934`, and so on. The preceding screenshot also shows the training and validation set accuracy for the chosen optimal model configuration.

3. Having converged to an optimal trained model, we can now make predictions on our test set using that model, as follows:

```
y_pred = autoPyTorch.predict(X_test)
print("Accuracy score", np.mean(y_pred.reshape(-1) == y_
test))
```

It should output something like this:

Accuracy score 0.964

Figure 12.2 – Auto-PyTorch model accuracy

As we can see, we have obtained a model with a decent test-set performance of 96.4%. For context, a random choice on this task would lead to a performance rate of 10%. We have obtained this good performance without defining either the model architecture or the hyperparameters. Upon setting a higher budget, a more extensive search could lead to an even better performance.

Also, the performance will vary based on the hardware (machine) on which the search is being performed. Hardware with more compute power and memory can run more searches in the same time budget, and hence can lead to a better performance.

Visualizing the optimal AutoML model

In this section, we will look at the best-performing model that we have obtained by running the model search routine in the previous section. We'll proceed as follows:

1. Having already looked at the hyperparameters in the preceding section, let's look at the optimal model architecture that Auto-PyTorch has devised for us, as follows:

```
pytorch_model = autoPyTorch.get_pytorch_model()
print(pytorch_model)
```

It should output something like this:

```
pytorch_model = autoPyTorch.get_pytorch_model()
print(pytorch_model)

Sequential(
  (0): Linear(in_features=100, out_features=100, bias=True)
  (1): Sequential(
    (0): ResBlock(
      (layers): Sequential(
        (0): BatchNorm1d(100, eps=1e-05, momentum=0.1, affine=True, track_running_stats=True)
        (1): ReLU()
        (2): Linear(in_features=100, out_features=100, bias=True)
        (3): BatchNorm1d(100, eps=1e-05, momentum=0.1, affine=True, track_running_stats=True)
        (4): ReLU()
        (5): Linear(in_features=100, out_features=100, bias=True)
      )
    )
    (1): ResBlock(
      (layers): Sequential(
        (0): BatchNorm1d(100, eps=1e-05, momentum=0.1, affine=True, track_running_stats=True)
        (1): ReLU()
        (2): Linear(in_features=100, out_features=100, bias=True)
        (3): BatchNorm1d(100, eps=1e-05, momentum=0.1, affine=True, track_running_stats=True)
        (4): ReLU()
        (5): Linear(in_features=100, out_features=100, bias=True)
      )
    )
    (2): ResBlock(
      (layers): Sequential(
        (0): BatchNorm1d(100, eps=1e-05, momentum=0.1, affine=True, track_running_stats=True)
        (1): ReLU()
        (2): Linear(in_features=100, out_features=100, bias=True)
        (3): BatchNorm1d(100, eps=1e-05, momentum=0.1, affine=True, track_running_stats=True)
        (4): ReLU()
        (5): Linear(in_features=100, out_features=100, bias=True)
      )
    )
    (3): ResBlock(

                              .
                              .
                              .
                              .

    )
    (3): ResBlock(
      (layers): Sequential(
        (0): BatchNorm1d(100, eps=1e-05, momentum=0.1, affine=True, track_running_stats=True)
        (1): ReLU()
        (2): Linear(in_features=100, out_features=100, bias=True)
        (3): BatchNorm1d(100, eps=1e-05, momentum=0.1, affine=True, track_running_stats=True)
        (4): ReLU()
        (5): Linear(in_features=100, out_features=100, bias=True)
      )
    )
  )
  (3): BatchNorm1d(100, eps=1e-05, momentum=0.1, affine=True, track_running_stats=True)
  (4): ReLU()
  (5): Linear(in_features=100, out_features=10, bias=True)
)
```

Figure 12.3 – Auto-PyTorch model architecture

The model consists of some structured residual blocks containing fully connected layers, batch normalization layers, and ReLU activations. At the end, we see a final fully connected layer with 10 outputs—one for each digit from 0 to 9.

2. We can also visualize the actual model graph using `torchviz`, as shown in the next code snippet:

```
x = torch.randn(1, pytorch_model[0].in_features)
y = pytorch_model(x)
arch = make_dot(y.mean(), params=dict(pytorch_model.
```

```
named_parameters()))
arch.format="pdf"
arch.filename = "convnet_arch"
arch.render(view=False)
```

This should save a `convnet_arch.pdf` file in the current working directory, which should look like this upon opening:

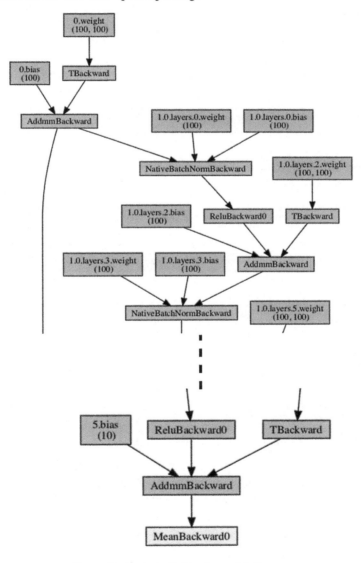

Figure 12.4 – Auto-PyTorch model diagram

3. To peek into how the model converged to this solution, we can look at the search space that was used during the model-finding process with the following code:

```
autoPyTorch.get_hyperparameter_search_space()
```

This should output the following:

```
Configuration space object:
  Hyperparameters:
    CreateDataLoader:batch_size, Type: Constant, Value: 125
    Imputation:strategy, Type: Categorical, Choices: {median}, Default: median
    InitializationSelector:initialization_method, Type: Categorical, Choices: {default}, Default: default
    InitializationSelector:initializer:initialize_bias, Type: Constant, Value: No
    LearningrateSchedulerSelector:cosine_annealing:T_max, Type: Constant, Value: 10
    LearningrateSchedulerSelector:cosine_annealing:eta_min, Type: Constant, Value: 2
    LearningrateSchedulerSelector:lr_scheduler, Type: Categorical, Choices: {cosine_annealing}, Default: cosine_annea
ling
    LossModuleSelector:loss_module, Type: Categorical, Choices: {cross_entropy_weighted}, Default: cross_entropy_weig
hted
    NetworkSelector:network, Type: Categorical, Choices: {shapedresnet}, Default: shapedresnet
    NetworkSelector:shapedresnet:activation, Type: Constant, Value: relu
    NetworkSelector:shapedresnet:blocks_per_group, Type: UniformInteger, Range: [1, 4], Default: 2
    NetworkSelector:shapedresnet:max_units, Type: UniformInteger, Range: [10, 1024], Default: 101, on log-scale
    NetworkSelector:shapedresnet:num_groups, Type: UniformInteger, Range: [1, 9], Default: 5
    NetworkSelector:shapedresnet:resnet_shape, Type: Constant, Value: brick
    NetworkSelector:shapedresnet:use_dropout, Type: Constant, Value: 0
    NetworkSelector:shapedresnet:use_shake_drop, Type: Constant, Value: 0
    NetworkSelector:shapedresnet:use_shake_shake, Type: Constant, Value: 0
    NormalizationStrategySelector:normalization_strategy, Type: Categorical, Choices: {standardize}, Default: standar
dize
    OptimizerSelector:optimizer, Type: Categorical, Choices: {sgd}, Default: sgd
    OptimizerSelector:sgd:learning_rate, Type: UniformFloat, Range: [0.0001, 0.1], Default: 0.0031622777, on log-scal
e
    OptimizerSelector:sgd:momentum, Type: UniformFloat, Range: [0.1, 0.999], Default: 0.5495
    OptimizerSelector:sgd:weight_decay, Type: UniformFloat, Range: [1e-05, 0.1], Default: 0.050005
    PreprocessorSelector:preprocessor, Type: Categorical, Choices: {truncated_svd}, Default: truncated_svd
    PreprocessorSelector:truncated_svd:target_dim, Type: Constant, Value: 100
    ResamplingStrategySelector:over_sampling_method, Type: Categorical, Choices: {none}, Default: none
    ResamplingStrategySelector:target_size_strategy, Type: Categorical, Choices: {none}, Default: none
    ResamplingStrategySelector:under_sampling_method, Type: Categorical, Choices: {none}, Default: none
    TrainNode:batch_loss_computation_technique, Type: Categorical, Choices: {standard}, Default: standard
  Conditions:
    LearningrateSchedulerSelector:cosine_annealing:T_max | LearningrateSchedulerSelector:lr_scheduler == 'cosine_anne
aling'
    LearningrateSchedulerSelector:cosine_annealing:eta_min | LearningrateSchedulerSelector:lr_scheduler == 'cosine_an
nealing'
    NetworkSelector:shapedresnet:activation | NetworkSelector:network == 'shapedresnet'
    NetworkSelector:shapedresnet:blocks_per_group | NetworkSelector:network == 'shapedresnet'
    NetworkSelector:shapedresnet:max_units | NetworkSelector:network == 'shapedresnet'
    NetworkSelector:shapedresnet:num_groups | NetworkSelector:network == 'shapedresnet'
    NetworkSelector:shapedresnet:resnet_shape | NetworkSelector:network == 'shapedresnet'
    NetworkSelector:shapedresnet:use_dropout | NetworkSelector:network == 'shapedresnet'
    NetworkSelector:shapedresnet:use_shake_drop | NetworkSelector:network == 'shapedresnet'
    NetworkSelector:shapedresnet:use_shake_shake | NetworkSelector:network == 'shapedresnet'
    OptimizerSelector:sgd:learning_rate | OptimizerSelector:optimizer == 'sgd'
    OptimizerSelector:sgd:momentum | OptimizerSelector:optimizer == 'sgd'
    OptimizerSelector:sgd:weight_decay | OptimizerSelector:optimizer == 'sgd'
    PreprocessorSelector:truncated_svd:target_dim | PreprocessorSelector:preprocessor == 'truncated_svd'
```

Figure 12.5 – Auto-PyTorch model search space

It essentially lists the various ingredients required to build the model, with an allocated range per ingredient. For instance, the learning rate is allocated a range of **0.0001** to **0.1** and this space is sampled in a log scale—this is not linear but logarithmic sampling.

In *Figure 12.1*, we have already seen the exact hyperparameter values that Auto-PyTorch samples from these ranges as optimal values for the given task. We can also alter these hyperparameter ranges manually, or even add more hyperparameters, using the `HyperparameterSearchSpaceUpdates` sub-module under the Auto-PyTorch module. You can find further details in the Auto-PyTorch GitHub documentation at `https://github.com/automl/Auto-PyTorch#configuration`.

This concludes our exploration of Auto-PyTorch—an AutoML tool for PyTorch. We successfully built an MNIST digit classification model using Auto-PyTorch, without specifying either the model architecture or the hyperparameters. This exercise will help you to get started with using this and other AutoML tools to build PyTorch models in an automated fashion. Some other similar tools are listed here:

- Hyperopt: `https://github.com/hyperopt/hyperopt`
- Tune: `https://docs.ray.io/en/latest/tune/index.html`
- Hypersearch: `https://github.com/kevinzakka/hypersearch`
- Skorch: `https://github.com/skorch-dev/skorch`
- BoTorch: `https://botorch.org/`
- Optuna: `https://optuna.org/`

While we cannot cover all of these tools in this chapter, in the next section we will discuss Optuna, which is a tool focused exclusively on finding an optimal set of hyperparameters and one that works well with PyTorch.

Using Optuna for hyperparameter search

Optuna is one of the hyperparameter search tools that supports PyTorch. You can read in detail about the search strategies used by the tool, such as **TPE (Tree-Structured Parzen Estimation)** and **CMA-ES (Covariance Matrix Adaptation Evolution Strategy)** in the *Optuna* paper, at `https://arxiv.org/pdf/1907.10902.pdf`. Besides the advanced hyperparameter search methodologies, the tool provides a sleek API, which we will explore in a moment.

> **Tool citation**
>
> *Optuna: A Next-Generation Hyperparameter Optimization Framework.*
>
> *Takuya Akiba, Shotaro Sano, Toshihiko Yanase, Takeru Ohta*, and *Masanori Koyama* (2019, in KDD).

In this section, we will once again build and train the `MNIST` model, this time using Optuna to figure out the optimal hyperparameter setting. We will discuss important parts of the code step by step, in the form of an exercise. The full code can be found here:

```
https://github.com/PacktPublishing/Mastering-PyTorch/blob/
master/Chapter12/optuna_pytorch.ipynb
```

Defining the model architecture and loading dataset

First, we will define an Optuna-compliant model object. By Optuna-compliant, we mean adding APIs within the model definition code that are provided by Optuna to enable the parameterization of the model hyperparameters. To do this, we'll proceed as follows:

1. First, we import the necessary libraries, as follows:

    ```
    import torch
    import optuna
    ```

    The `optuna` library will manage the hyperparameter search for us throughout the exercise.

2. Next, we define the model architecture. Because we want to be flexible with some of the hyperparameters—such as the number of layers and the number of units in each layer—we need to include some logic in the model definition code. So, first, we have declared that we need anywhere in between 1 to 4 convolutional layers and 1 to 2 fully connected layers thereafter, as illustrated in the following code snippet:

    ```
    class ConvNet(nn.Module):
        def __init__(self, trial):
            super(ConvNet, self).__init__()
            num_conv_layers =  trial.suggest_int("num_conv_
    layers", 1, 4)
            num_fc_layers = trial.suggest_int("num_fc_
    layers", 1, 2)
    ```

3. We then successively append the convolutional layers, one by one. Each convolutional layer is instantly followed by a ReLU activation layer, and for each convolutional layer, we declare the depth of that layer to be between 16 and 64.

The stride and padding are fixed to 3 and True respectively, and the whole convolutional block is then followed by a MaxPool layer, then a Dropout layer, with dropout probability ranging anywhere between 0.1 to 0.4 (another hyperparameter), as illustrated in the following code snippet:

```
self.layers = []
input_depth = 1 # grayscale image
for i in range(num_conv_layers):
        output_depth = trial.suggest_int(f"conv_
depth_{i}", 16, 64)
        self.layers.append(nn.Conv2d(input_depth,
output_depth, 3, 1))
        self.layers.append(nn.ReLU())
        input_depth = output_depth
    self.layers.append(nn.MaxPool2d(2))
        p = trial.suggest_float(f"conv_dropout_{i}", 0.1,
0.4)
    self.layers.append(nn.Dropout(p))
    self.layers.append(nn.Flatten())
```

4. Next, we add a flattening layer so that fully connected layers can follow. We have to define a _get_flatten_shape function to derive the shape of the flattening layer output. We then successively add fully connected layers, where the number of units is declared to be between 16 and 64. A Dropout layer follows each fully connected layer, again with the probability range of 0.1 to 0.4.

Finally, we append a fixed fully connected layer that outputs 10 numbers (one for each class/digit), followed by a LogSoftmax layer. Having defined all the layers, we then instantiate our model object, as follows:

```
input_feat = self._get_flatten_shape()
for i in range(num_fc_layers):
        output_feat = trial.suggest_int(f"fc_output_
feat_{i}", 16, 64)
        self.layers.append(nn.Linear(input_feat,
output_feat))
```

```
            self.layers.append(nn.ReLU())
            p = trial.suggest_float(f"fc_dropout_{i}",
0.1, 0.4)
            self.layers.append(nn.Dropout(p))
            input_feat = output_feat
        self.layers.append(nn.Linear(input_feat, 10))
        self.layers.append(nn.LogSoftmax(dim=1))
        self.model = nn.Sequential(*self.layers)
    def _get_flatten_shape(self):
        conv_model = nn.Sequential(*self.layers)
        op_feat = conv_model(torch.rand(1, 1, 28, 28))
        n_size = op_feat.data.view(1, -1).size(1)
        return n_size
```

This model initialization function is conditioned on the `trial` object, which is facilitated by Optuna and which will decide the hyperparameter setting for our model. Finally, the `forward` method is quite straightforward, as can be seen in the following code snippet:

```
    def forward(self, x):
        return self.model(x)
```

Thus, we have defined our model object and we can now move on to loading the dataset.

5. The code for dataset loading is the same as in *Chapter 1, Overview of Deep Learning Using PyTorch* and is shown again in the following snippet:

```
train_dataloader = torch.utils.data.DataLoader(...)
test_dataloader = ...
```

In this section, we have successfully defined our parameterized model object as well as loaded the dataset. We will now define the model training and testing routines, along with the optimization schedule.

Defining the model training routine and optimization schedule

Model training itself involves hyperparameters such as optimizer, learning rate, and so on. In this part of the exercise, we will define the model training procedure while utilizing Optuna's parameterization capabilities. We'll proceed as follows:

1. First, we define the training routine. Once again, the code is the same as the training routine code we had for this model in the exercise found in *Chapter 1, Overview of Deep Learning Using PyTorch*, and is shown again here:

```
def train(model, device, train_dataloader, optim, epoch):
    for b_i, (X, y) in enumerate(train_dataloader):
        …
```

2. The model testing routine needs to be slightly augmented. To operate as per Optuna API requirements, the test routine needs to return a model performance metric—accuracy, in this case—so that Optuna can compare different hyperparameter settings based on this metric, as illustrated in the following code snippet:

```
def test(model, device, test_dataloader):
    with torch.no_grad():
        for X, y in test_dataloader:
            …
    accuracy = 100. * success/ len(test_dataloader.
dataset)
    return accuracy
```

3. Previously, we would instantiate the model and the optimization function with the learning rate, and start the training loop outside of any function. But to follow the Optuna API requirements, we do all that under an `objective` function, which takes in the same `trial` object that was fed as an argument to the `__init__` method of our model object.

   The `trial` object is needed here too because there are hyperparameters associated with deciding the learning rate value and choosing an optimizer, as illustrated in the following code snippet:

```
def objective(trial):
    model = ConvNet(trial)
    opt_name = trial.suggest_categorical("optimizer",
["Adam", "Adadelta", "RMSprop", "SGD"])
```

```
    lr = trial.suggest_float("lr", 1e-1, 5e-1, log=True)
    optimizer = getattr(optim,opt_name)(model.
parameters(), lr=lr)
    for epoch in range(1, 3):
        train(model, device, train_dataloader, optimizer,
epoch)
        accuracy = test(model, device,test_dataloader)
        trial.report(accuracy, epoch)
        if trial.should_prune():
            raise optuna.exceptions.TrialPruned()
    return accuracy
```

For each epoch, we record the accuracy returned by the model testing routine. Additionally, at each epoch, we check if we will prune—that is, if we will skip—the current epoch. This is another feature offered by Optuna to speed up the hyperparameter search process so that we don't waste time on poor hyperparameter settings.

Running Optuna's hyperparameter search

In this final part of the exercise, we will instantiate what is called an **Optuna study** and, using the model definition and the training routine, we will execute Optuna's hyperparameter search process for the given model and the given dataset. We'll proceed as follows:

1. Having prepared all the necessary components in the preceding sections, we are ready to start the hyperparameter search process—something that is called a `study` in Optuna terminology. A `trial` is one hyperparameter-search iteration in a `study`. The code can be seen in the following snippet:

    ```
    study = optuna.create_study(study_name="mastering_
    pytorch", direction="maximize")
    study.optimize(objective, n_trials=10, timeout=2000)
    ```

    The `direction` argument helps Optuna compare different hyperparameter settings. Because our metric is accuracy, we will need to `maximize` the metric. We allow a maximum of `2000` seconds for the `study` or a maximum of `10` different searches—whichever finishes first. The preceding command should output the following:

```
[I 2020-10-24 18:39:34,357] A new study created in memory with name: mastering_pytorch

epoch: 1 [0/60000 (0%)]  training loss: 2.314928
epoch: 1 [16000/60000 (27%)]    training loss: 2.339143
epoch: 1 [32000/60000 (53%)]    training loss: 2.554311
epoch: 1 [48000/60000 (80%)]    training loss: 2.392770

Test dataset: Overall Loss: 2.4598, Overall Accuracy: 974/10000 (10%)

epoch: 2 [0/60000 (0%)]  training loss: 2.352818
epoch: 2 [16000/60000 (27%)]    training loss: 2.425988
epoch: 2 [32000/60000 (53%)]    training loss: 2.432955
epoch: 2 [48000/60000 (80%)]    training loss: 2.497166
```

```
[I 2020-10-24 18:44:51,667] Trial 0 finished with value: 9.82 and parameters: {'num_conv_layers': 4, 'num_fc_layers':
2, 'conv_depth_0': 20, 'conv_depth_1': 18, 'conv_depth_2': 38, 'conv_depth_3': 27, 'conv_dropout_3': 0.18560304003563
005, 'fc_output_feat_0': 54, 'fc_dropout_0': 0.18233257074201586, 'fc_output_feat_1': 55, 'fc_dropout_1': 0.104182596
77735323, 'optimizer': 'RMSprop', 'lr': 0.49822431360836333}. Best is trial 0 with value: 9.82.
```

```
[I 2020-10-24 18:46:24,551] Trial 1 finished with value: 95.68 and parameters: {'num_conv_layers': 1, 'num_fc_layer
s': 2, 'conv_depth_0': 39, 'conv_dropout_0': 0.3950204757059781, 'fc_output_feat_0': 54, 'fc_dropout_0': 0.3760852329
345368, 'fc_output_feat_1': 40, 'fc_dropout_1': 0.29727560678671294, 'optimizer': 'Adadelta', 'lr': 0.254984294053231
25}. Best is trial 1 with value: 95.68.
```

```
[I 2020-10-24 18:51:37,575] Trial 2 finished with value: 98.77 and parameters: {'num_conv_layers': 3, 'num_fc_layer
s': 2, 'conv_depth_0': 27, 'conv_depth_2': 28, 'conv_dropout_2': 0.3274565117338556, 'fc_output_f
eat_0': 57, 'fc_dropout_0': 0.1234849615378503, 'fc_output_feat_1': 54, 'fc_dropout_1': 0.36784682560478876, 'optimi
zer': 'Adadelta', 'lr': 0.4290610978292583}. Best is trial 2 with value: 98.77.
```

```
[I 2020-10-24 18:55:41,400] Trial 3 finished with value: 98.28 and parameters: {'num_conv_layers': 2, 'num_fc_layer
s': 1, 'conv_depth_0': 38, 'conv_depth_1': 40, 'conv_dropout_1': 0.3592746030824463, 'fc_output_feat_0': 20, 'fc_drop
out_0': 0.22476024022504099, 'optimizer': 'Adadelta', 'lr': 0.3167228174356792}. Best is trial 2 with value: 98.77.
```

```
[I 2020-10-24 18:59:54,755] Trial 4 finished with value: 10.28 and parameters: {'num_conv_layers': 2, 'num_fc_layer
s': 2, 'conv_depth_0': 26, 'conv_depth_1': 50, 'conv_dropout_1': 0.30220610162727457, 'fc_output_feat_0': 42, 'fc_dro
pout_0': 0.1561741472895425, 'fc_output_feat_1': 33, 'fc_dropout_1': 0.31642189637209367, 'optimizer': 'RMSprop', 'l
r': 0.45189990541514835}. Best is trial 2 with value: 98.77.
```

```
[I 2020-10-24 19:02:39,390] Trial 5 finished with value: 98.12 and parameters: {'num_conv_layers': 2, 'num_fc_layer
s': 1, 'conv_depth_0': 31, 'conv_depth_1': 22, 'conv_dropout_1': 0.361294491672082, 'fc_output_feat_0': 25, 'fc_drop
out_0': 0.2839369529837842, 'optimizer': 'SGD', 'lr': 0.11490140528643872}. Best is trial 2 with value: 98.77.
```

```
[I 2020-10-24 19:06:33,825] Trial 6 finished with value: 98.29 and parameters: {'num_conv_layers': 2, 'num_fc_layer
s': 2, 'conv_depth_0': 24, 'conv_depth_1': 55, 'conv_dropout_1': 0.34239043023224586, 'fc_output_feat_0': 35, 'fc_dro
pout_0': 0.17065510224232447, 'fc_output_feat_1': 46, 'fc_dropout_1': 0.19804499857448277, 'optimizer': 'Adadelta',
'lr': 0.4213881172164293}. Best is trial 2 with value: 98.77.
```

```
[I 2020-10-24 19:09:33,855] Trial 7 pruned.
```

```
[I 2020-10-24 19:10:33,804] Trial 8 pruned.
```

```
[I 2020-10-24 19:15:36,906] Trial 9 pruned.
```

Figure 12.6 – Optuna logs

As we can see, the third `trial` is the most optimal trial, producing a test set accuracy of 98.77%, and the last three `trials` are pruned. In the logs, we also see the hyperparameters for each non-pruned `trial`. For the most optimal `trial`, for example, there are three convolutional layers with 27, 28, and 46 feature maps respectively, and then there are two fully connected layers with 57 and 54 units/ neurons respectively, and so on.

2. Each `trial` is given a completed or a pruned status. We can demarcate those with the following code:

```
pruned_trials = [t for t in study.trials if t.state ==
optuna.trial.TrialState.PRUNED]
complete_trials = [t for t in study.trials if t.state ==
optuna.trial.TrialState.COMPLETE]
```

3. And finally, we can specifically look at all the hyperparameters of the most successful `trial` with the following code:

```
print("results: ")
trial = study.best_trial
for key, value in trial.params.items():
    print("{}: {}".format(key, value))
```

You will see the following output:

```
results:
num_trials_conducted:   10
num_trials_pruned:   3
num_trials_completed:   7
results from best trial:
accuracy:   98.77
hyperparameters:
num_conv_layers: 3
num_fc_layers: 2
conv_depth_0: 27
conv_depth_1: 28
conv_depth_2: 46
conv_dropout_2: 0.3274565117338556
fc_output_feat_0: 57
fc_dropout_0: 0.12348496153785013
fc_output_feat_1: 54
fc_dropout_1: 0.36784682560478876
optimizer: Adadelta
lr: 0.4290610978292583
```

Figure 12.7 – Optuna optimal hyperparameters

As we can see, the output shows us the total number of `trials` and the number of successful `trials` performed. It further shows us the model hyperparameters for the most successful `trial`, such as the number of layers, the number of neurons in layers, learning rate, optimization schedule, and so on.

This brings us to the end of the exercise. We have managed to use Optuna to define a range of hyperparameter values for different kinds of hyperparameters for a handwritten digit classification model. Using Optuna's hyperparameter search algorithm, we ran 10 different `trials` and managed to obtain the highest accuracy of 98.77% in one of those `trials`. The model (architecture and hyperparameters) from the most successful `trial` can be used for training with larger datasets, thereby serving in a production system.

Using the lessons from this section, you can use Optuna to find the optimal hyperparameters for any neural network model written in PyTorch. Optuna can also be used in a distributed fashion if the model is extremely large and/or there are way too many hyperparameters to tune. You can read more about distributed tuning here: `https://optuna.readthedocs.io/en/stable/tutorial/004_distributed.html#distributed`.

Lastly, Optuna supports not only PyTorch but other popular machine learning libraries too, such as `TensorFlow`, `Sklearn`, `MXNet`, and so on.

Summary

In this chapter, we discussed AutoML, which aims to provide methods for model selection and hyperparameter optimization. AutoML is useful for beginners who have little expertise on making decisions such as how many layers to put in a model, which optimizer to use, and so on. AutoML is also useful for experts to both speed up the model training process and discover superior model architectures for a given task that would be nearly impossible to figure manually.

We looked at two different AutoML tools that can be used with PyTorch. First, we discussed Auto-PyTorch, which does the task of both finding an optimal neural architecture and finding the perfect hyperparameter setting. We used the MNIST handwritten digit classification task from *Chapter 1*, *Overview of Deep Learning Using PyTorch*, to find the best model for this task, using Auto-PyTorch. We obtained a best accuracy of 96.4%.

Next, we explored Optuna which is another AutoML tool that automates hyperparameter search. We used this tool for the same task. A difference from Auto-PyTorch is that we needed to manually define the architecture on a high level (types of layers); however, lower-level details (number of layers and units) were hyperparameterized. Optuna gave us a best-performing model, with 98.77% accuracy.

Both of the exercises prove that we can find, train, and deploy performant PyTorch models without having to define the model architecture or the hyperparameter values. This opens up a lot of possibilities, and I encourage you to try AutoML in one of your machine learning projects by letting AutoML find the model for you instead of defining it manually. This can, for instance, save you several days' worth of time typically spent on experimentation over different model architectures.

In the next chapter, we will study another increasingly important and crucial aspect of machine learning, especially deep learning. We will closely look at how to interpret output produced by PyTorch models—a field popularly known as model interpretability or explainability.

13
PyTorch and Explainable AI

Throughout this book, we have built several deep learning models that can perform different kinds of tasks for us. For example, a handwritten digit classifier, an image-caption generator, a sentiment classifier, and more. Although we have mastered how to train and evaluate these models using PyTorch, we do not know what precisely is happening inside these models while they make predictions. Model interpretability or explainability is that field of machine learning where we aim to answer the question, why did the model make that prediction? More elaborately, what did the model see in the input data to make that particular prediction?

In this chapter, we will use the handwritten digit classification model from *Chapter 1, Overview of Deep Learning Using PyTorch*, to understand its inner workings and thereby explain why the model makes a certain prediction for a given input. We will first dissect the model using only PyTorch code. Then, we will use a specialized model interpretability toolkit, called **Captum**, to further investigate what is happening inside the model. Captum is a dedicated third-party library for PyTorch that provides model interpretability tools for deep learning models, including image- and text-based models.

This chapter should provide you with the skills that are necessary to uncover the internals of a deep learning model. Looking inside a model this way can help you to reason about the model's predictive behavior. At the end of this chapter, you will be able to use the hands-on experience to start interpreting your own deep learning models using PyTorch (and Captum).

This chapter is broken down into the following topics:

- Model interpretability in PyTorch
- Using Captum to interpret models

Technical requirements

We will be using Jupyter notebooks for all of our exercises. The following is a list of Python libraries that should be installed for this chapter using `pip`. For example, run `pip install torch==1.4.0` on the command line:

```
jupyter==1.0.0
torch==1.4.0
torchvision==0.5.0
matplotlib==3.1.2
captum==0.2.0
```

All code files relevant to this chapter are available at `https://github.com/PacktPublishing/Mastering-PyTorch/tree/master/Chapter13`.

Model interpretability in PyTorch

In this section, we will dissect a trained handwritten digits classification model using PyTorch in the form of an exercise. More precisely, we will be looking at the details of the convolutional layers of the trained handwritten digits classification model to understand what visual features the model is learning from the handwritten digit images. We will look at the convolutional filters/kernels along with the feature maps produced by those filters.

Such details will help us to understand how the model is processing input images and, therefore, making predictions. The full code for the exercise can be found at `https://github.com/PacktPublishing/Mastering-PyTorch/blob/master/Chapter13/pytorch_interpretability.ipynb`.

Training the handwritten digits classifier – a recap

We will quickly revisit the steps involved in training the handwritten digits classification model, as follows:

1. First, we import the relevant libraries, and then set the random seeds to be able to reproduce the results of this exercise:

```
import torch
np.random.seed(123)
torch.manual_seed(123)
```

2. Next, we will define the model architecture:

```
class ConvNet(nn.Module):
    def __init__(self):
    def forward(self, x):
```

3. Next, we will define the model training and testing routine:

```
def train(model, device, train_dataloader,
optim,  epoch):
def test(model, device, test_dataloader):
```

4. We then define the training and testing dataset loaders:

```
train_dataloader = torch.utils.data.DataLoader(...)
test_dataloader = torch.utils.data.DataLoader(...)
```

5. Next, we instantiate our model and define the optimization schedule:

```
device = torch.device("cpu")
model = ConvNet()
optimizer = optim.Adadelta(model.parameters(), lr=0.5)
```

6. Finally, we start the model training loop where we train our model for 20 epochs:

```
for epoch in range(1, 20):
    train(model, device, train_dataloader, optimizer,
epoch)
    test(model, device, test_dataloader)
```

This should output the following:

```
epoch: 1 [0/60000 (0%)]  training loss: 2.324445
epoch: 1 [320/60000 (1%)]        training loss: 1.727462
epoch: 1 [640/60000 (1%)]        training loss: 1.428922
epoch: 1 [960/60000 (2%)]        training loss: 0.717944
epoch: 1 [1280/60000 (2%)]       training loss: 0.572199

                              ┇

epoch: 19 [58880/60000 (98%)]    training loss: 0.016509
epoch: 19 [59200/60000 (99%)]    training loss: 0.118218
epoch: 19 [59520/60000 (99%)]    training loss: 0.000097
epoch: 19 [59840/60000 (100%)]   training loss: 0.000271

Test dataset: Overall Loss: 0.0387, Overall Accuracy: 9910/10000 (99%)
```

Figure 13.1 – Model training logs

7. Finally, we can test the trained model on a sample test image. The sample test image is loaded as follows:

```
test_samples = enumerate(test_dataloader)
b_i, (sample_data, sample_targets) = next(test_samples)
plt.imshow(sample_data[0][0], cmap='gray',
interpolation='none')
plt.show()
```

This should output the following:

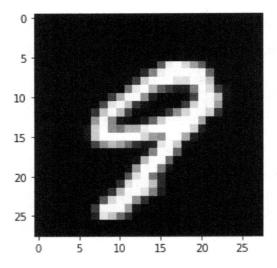

Figure 13.2 – An example of a handwritten image

8. Then, we use this sample test image to make a model prediction, as follows:

```
print(f"Model prediction is : {model(sample_data).data.
max(1)[1][0]}")
print(f"Ground truth is : {sample_targets[0]}")
```

This should output the following:

```
Model prediction is : 9
Ground truth is : 9
```

Figure 13.3 – Model prediction

Therefore, we have trained a handwritten digits classification model and used it to make inference on a sample image. We will now look at the internals of the trained model. We will also investigate what convolutional filters have been learned by this model.

Visualizing the convolutional filters of the model

In this section, we will go through the convolutional layers of the trained model and look at the filters that the model has learned during training. This will tell us how the convolutional layers are operating on the input image, what kinds of features are being extracted, and more:

1. First, we need to obtain a list of all the layers in the model, as follows:

```
model_children_list = list(model.children())
convolutional_layers = []
model_parameters = []
model_children_list
```

This should output the following:

```
[Conv2d(1, 16, kernel_size=(3, 3), stride=(1, 1)),
 Conv2d(16, 32, kernel_size=(3, 3), stride=(1, 1)),
 Dropout2d(p=0.1, inplace=False),
 Dropout2d(p=0.25, inplace=False),
 Linear(in_features=4608, out_features=64, bias=True),
 Linear(in_features=64, out_features=10, bias=True)]
```

Figure 13.4 – Model layers

As you can see, there are 2 convolutional layers that both have 3x3-sized filters. The first convolutional layer uses **16** such filters, whereas the second convolutional layer uses **32**. We are focusing on visualizing convolutional layers in this exercise because they are visually more intuitive. However, you can similarly explore the other layers, such as linear layers, by visualizing their learned weights.

2. Next, we select only the convolutional layers from the model and store them in a separate list:

```
for i in range(len(model_children_list)):
    if type(model_children_list[i]) == nn.Conv2d:
        model_parameters.append(model_children_
list[i].w        eight)
        convolutional_layers.append(model_children_
list[i])
```

In this process, we also make sure to store the parameters or weights learned in each convolutional layer.

3. We are now ready to visualize the learned filters of the convolutional layers. We begin with the first layer, which has 16 filters of size 3x3 each. The following code visualizes those filters for us:

```
plt.figure(figsize=(5, 4))
for i, flt in enumerate(model_parameters[0]):
    plt.subplot(4, 4, i+1)
    plt.imshow(flt[0, :, :].detach(), cmap='gray')
    plt.axis('off')
plt.show()
```

This should output the following:

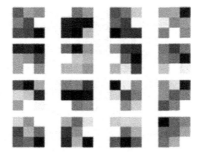

Figure 13.5 – The first convolutional layer's filters

Firstly, we can see that all the learned filters are slightly different from each other, which is a good sign. These filters usually have contrasting values inside them so that they can extract some types of gradients when convolved around an image. During model inference, each of these 16 filters operates independently on the input grayscale image and produces 16 different feature maps, which we will visualize in the next section.

4. Similarly, we can visualize the 32 filters learned in the second convolutional layer using the same code, as in the preceding step, but with the following change:

```
plt.figure(figsize=(5, 8))
for i, flt in enumerate(model_parameters[1]):
plt.show()
```

This should output the following:

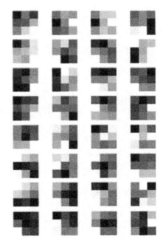

Figure 13.6 – The second convolutional layer's filters

Once again, we have 32 different filters/kernels that have contrasting values aimed at extracting gradients from the image. These filters are already applied to the output of the first convolutional layer, and hence produce even higher levels of output feature maps. The usual goal of CNN models with multiple convolutional layers is to keep producing more and more complex, or higher-level, features that can represent complex visual elements such as a nose on a face, traffic lights on the road, and more.

Next, we will take a look at what comes out of these convolutional layers as these filters operate/convolve on their given inputs.

Visualizing the feature maps of the model

In this section, we will run a sample handwritten image through the convolutional layers and visualize the outputs of these layers:

1. First, we need to gather the results of every convolutional layer output in the form of a list, which is achieved using the following code:

```
per_layer_results = [convolutional_layers[0](sample_
data)]
for i in range(1, len(convolutional_layers)):
    per_layer_results.append(convolutional_layers[i](per_
layer_results[-1]))
```

   Notice that we call the forward pass for each convolutional layer separately while ensuring that the *n*th convolutional layer receives as input the output of the (*n-1*)th convolutional layer.

2. We can now visualize the feature maps produced by the two convolutional layers. We will begin with the first layer by running the following code:

```
plt.figure(figsize=(5, 4))
layer_visualisation = per_layer_results[0][0, :, :, :]
layer_visualisation = layer_visualisation.data
print(layer_visualisation.size())
for i, flt in enumerate(layer_visualisation):
    plt.subplot(4, 4, i + 1)
    plt.imshow(flt, cmap='gray')
    plt.axis("off")
plt.show()
```

   This should output the following:

```
torch.Size([16, 26, 26])
```

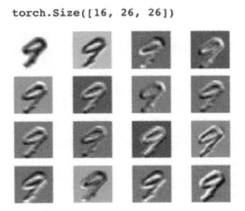

Figure 13.7 – The first convolutional layer's feature maps

The numbers, **(16, 26, 26)**, represent the output dimensions of the first convolution layer. Essentially, the sample image size is (28, 28), the filter size is (3,3), and there is no padding. Therefore, the resulting feature map size will be (26, 26). Because there are 16 such feature maps produced by the 16 filters (please refer to *Figure 13.5*), the overall output dimension is (16, 26, 26).

As you can see, each filter produces a feature map from the input image. Additionally, each feature map represents a different visual feature in the image. For example, the top-left feature map essentially inverts the pixel values in the image (please refer to *Figure 13.2*), whereas the bottom-right feature map represents some form of edge detection.

These 16 feature maps are then passed on to the second convolutional layer, where yet another 32 filters convolve separately on these 16 feature maps to produce 32 new feature maps. We will look at these next.

3. We can use the same code as the preceding one with minor changes (as highlighted in the following code) to visualize the 32 feature maps produced by the next convolutional layer:

```
plt.figure(figsize=(5, 8))
layer_visualisation = per_layer_results[1][0, :, :, :]
    plt.subplot(8, 4, i + 1)
plt.show()
```

This should output the following:

```
torch.Size([32, 24, 24])
```

Figure 13.8 – The second convolutional layer's feature maps

Compared to the earlier 16 feature maps, these 32 feature maps are evidently more complex. They seem to be doing more than just edge detection, and this is because they are already operating on the outputs of the first convolutional layer instead of the raw input image.

In this model, the 2 convolutional layers are followed by 2 linear layers with (4,608x64) and (64x10) number of parameters, respectively. Although the linear layer weights are also useful to visualize, the sheer number of parameters (4,608x64) is, visually, a lot to get your head around. Therefore, in this section, we will restrict our visual analysis to convolutional weights only.

And thankfully, we have more sophisticated ways of interpreting model prediction without having to look at such a large number of parameters. In the next section, we will explore Captum, which is a machine learning model interpretability toolkit that works with PyTorch and helps us to explain model decisions within a few lines of code.

Using Captum to interpret models

Captum (`https://captum.ai/`) is an open source model interpretability library built by Facebook on top of PyTorch, and it is currently (at the time of writing) under active development. In this section, we will use the handwritten digits classification model that we had trained in the preceding section. We will also use some of the model interpretability tools offered by Captum to explain the predictions made by this model. The full code for the following exercise can be found here: `https://github.com/PacktPublishing/Mastering-PyTorch/blob/master/Chapter13/captum_interpretability.ipynb`.

Setting up Captum

The model training code is similar to the code shown under the *Training the handwritten digits classifier – a recap* section. In the following steps, we will use the trained model and a sample image to understand what happens inside the model while making a prediction for the given image:

1. There are few extra imports related to Captum that we need to perform in order to use Captum's built-in model interpretability functions:

```
from captum.attr import IntegratedGradients
from captum.attr import Saliency
from captum.attr import DeepLift
from captum.attr import visualization as viz
```

2. In order to do a model forward pass with the input image, we reshape the input image to match the model input size:

```
captum_input = sample_data[0].unsqueeze(0)
captum_input.requires_grad = True
```

As per Captum's requirements, the input tensor (image) needs to be involved in gradient computation. Therefore, we set the `requires_grad` flag for input to `True`.

3. Next, we prepare the sample image to be processed by the model interpretability methods using the following code:

```
orig_image = np.tile(np.transpose((sample_data[0].cpu().
detach().numpy() / 2) + 0.5, (1, 2, 0)), (1,1,3))
```

```
_ = viz.visualize_image_attr(None, orig_image,
cmap='gray', method="original_image", title="Original
Image")
```

This should output the following:

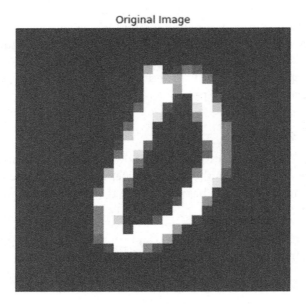

Figure 13.9 – The original image

We have tiled the grayscale image across the depth dimension so that it can be consumed by the Captum methods, which expect a 3-channel image.

Next, we will actually apply some of Captum's interpretability methods to the forward pass of the prepared grayscale image through the pretrained handwritten digits classification model.

Exploring Captum's interpretability tools

In this section, we will be looking at some of the model interpretability methods offered by Captum.

One of the most fundamental methods of interpreting model results is by looking at saliency, which represents the gradients of the output (class 0, in this example) with respect to the input (that is, the input image pixels). The larger the gradients with respect to a particular input, the more important that input is. You can read more about how these gradients are exactly calculated in the original saliency paper at https://arxiv.org/pdf/1312.6034.pdf. Captum provides an implementation of the saliency method:

1. In the following code, we use Captum's `Saliency` module to compute the gradients:

```
saliency = Saliency(model)
gradients = saliency.attribute(captum_input,
target=sample_targets[0].item())
gradients = np.reshape(gradients.squeeze().cpu().
detach().numpy(), (28, 28, 1))
_ = viz.visualize_image_attr(gradients, orig_image,
method="blended_heat_map", sign="absolute_value",
show_colorbar=True, title="Overlayed Gradients")
```

This should output the following:

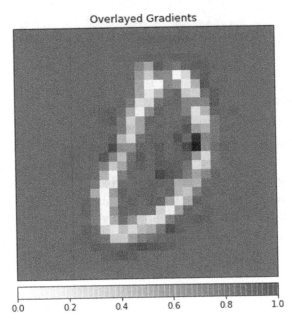

Figure 13.10 – Overlayed gradients

In the preceding code, we reshaped the obtained gradients to size (28,28,1) in order to overlay them on the original image, as shown in the preceding diagram. Captum's viz module takes care of the visualizations for us. We can further visualize only the gradients, without the original image, using the following code:

```
plt.imshow(np.tile(gradients/(np.max(gradients)),
(1,1,3)));
```

We will get the following output:

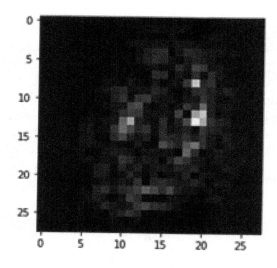

Figure 13.11 – Gradients

As you can see, the gradients awre spread across those pixel regions in the image that are likely to contain the digit 0.

2. Next, using a similar code fashion, we will look at another interpretability method – integrated gradients. With this method, we will look for **feature attribution** or **feature importance**. That is, we'll look for what pixels are important to use when making predictions. Under the integrated gradients technique, apart from the input image, we also need to specify a baseline image, which is usually set to an image with all of the pixel values set to zero.

An integral of gradients is then calculated with respect to the input image along the path from the baseline image to the input image. Details of the implementation of integrated gradients technique can be found in the original paper at https://arxiv.org/abs/1703.01365. The following code uses Captum's IntegratedGradients module to derive the importance of each input image pixel:

```
integ_grads = IntegratedGradients(model)

attributed_ig, delta=integ_grads.attribute(captum_input,
target=sample_targets[0], baselines=captum_input * 0,
return_convergence_delta=True)


attributed_ig = np.reshape(attributed_ig.squeeze().cpu().
detach().numpy(), (28, 28, 1))

_ = viz.visualize_image_attr(attributed_ig, orig_image,
method="blended_heat_map",sign="all",show_colorbar=True,
title="Overlayed Integrated Gradients")
```

This should output the following:

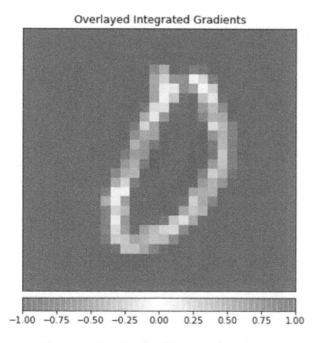

Figure 13.12 – Overlayed integrated gradients

As expected, the gradients are high in the pixel regions that contain the digit 0.

3. Finally, we will look at yet another gradient-based attribution technique, called
    deeplift. Deeplift also requires a baseline image besides the input image. Once
    again for the baseline, we use an image with all the pixel values set to zero. Deeplift
    computes the change in non-linear activation outputs with respect to the change in
    input from the baseline image to the input image (*Figure 13.9*). The following code
    uses the `DeepLift` module provided by Captum to compute the gradients and
    displays these gradients overlayed on the original input image:

```
deep_lift = DeepLift(model)

attributed_dl = deep_lift.attribute(captum_input,
target=sample_targets[0], baselines=captum_input * 0,
return_convergence_delta=False)

attributed_dl = np.reshape(attributed_dl.squeeze(0).
cpu().detach().numpy(), (28, 28, 1))

_ = viz.visualize_image_attr(attributed_dl, orig_image,
method="blended_heat_map",sign="all",show_colorbar=True,
title="Overlayed DeepLift")
```

You should see the following output:

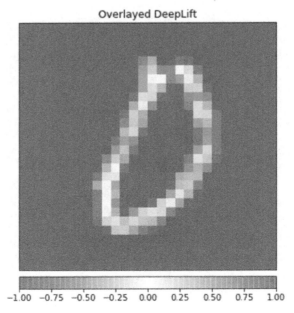

Figure 13.13 – Overlayed deeplift

Once again, the gradient values are extreme around the pixels that contain the digit 0.

This brings us to the end of this exercise and this section. There are more model interpretability techniques provided by Captum, such as *LayerConductance*, *GradCAM*, and *SHAP*. You can read more about these techniques at `https://captum.ai/docs/algorithms`. Model interpretability is an active area of research, and hence libraries such as Captum are likely to evolve rapidly. More such libraries are likely to be developed in the near future, which will enable us to make model interpretability a standard component of the machine learning life cycle.

Summary

In this chapter, we have briefly explored how to explain or interpret the decisions made by deep learning models using PyTorch. Using the handwritten digits classification model as an example, we first uncovered the internal workings of a CNN model's convolutional layers. We demonstrated how to visualize the convolutional filters and feature maps produced by convolutional layers.

We then used a dedicated third-party model interpretability library built on PyTorch, called Captum. We used out-of-the-box implementations provided by Captum for feature attribution techniques, such as saliency, integrated gradients, and deeplift. Using these techniques, we demonstrated how the model is using an input to make predictions and which parts of the input are more important for a model to make predictions.

In the next, and final, chapter of this book, we will learn how to rapidly train and test machine learning models on PyTorch – a skill that is useful for quickly iterating over various machine learning ideas. We will also discuss a few deep learning libraries and frameworks that enable rapid prototyping with PyTorch.

14
Rapid Prototyping with PyTorch

In the preceding chapters, we have seen multiple facets of PyTorch as a Python library. We have seen its use for training vision and text models. We have learned about its extensive **application programming interfaces (APIs)** for loading and processing datasets. We have explored the model inference support provided by PyTorch. We have also noticed the interoperability of PyTorch across programming languages (such as C++) as well as with other deep learning libraries (such as TensorFlow).

To accommodate all of these features, PyTorch provides a rich and extensive family of APIs, which makes it one of the best deep learning libraries of all time. However, the vast expanse of those features also makes PyTorch a heavy library, and this can sometimes intimidate users about performing streamlined or simple model training and testing tasks.

This chapter is focused on introducing some of the libraries that are built on top of PyTorch and that are aimed at providing intuitive and easy-to-use APIs for building quick model training and testing pipelines with a few lines of code. We will first discuss **fast.ai**, which is one of the most popular high-level deep learning libraries.

We will demonstrate how fast.ai helps speed up the deep learning research process as well as make deep learning accessible to all levels of expertise. Finally, we will look at **PyTorch Lightning**, which provides the ability to use the exact same code for training on any hardware configuration, be it multiple **central processing units (CPUs)**, **graphics processing units (GPUs)**, or even **tensor processing units (TPUs)**.

There are other such libraries too—such as `PyTorch Ignite`, `Poutyne`, and more—that aim to achieve similar goals, but we won't be covering them here. This chapter should familiarize you with these higher-level deep learning libraries that can be extremely useful to rapidly prototype your deep learning models.

By the end of this chapter, you will be able to use fast.ai and PyTorch Lightning in your own deep learning projects and hopefully see a significant reduction in the amount of time spent on model training and testing.

This chapter is broken down into the following topics:

- Using fast.ai to set up model training in a few minutes
- Training models on any hardware using PyTorch Lightning

Technical requirements

We will be using Jupyter Notebooks for all of our exercises. Here is a list of the Python libraries that will be installed for this chapter, using `pip` (for example, by running `pip install torch==1.4.0` on the command line:

```
jupyter==1.0.0
torch==1.4.0
torchvision==0.5.0
matplotlib==3.1.2
pytorch-lightning==1.0.5
fast.ai==2.1.8
```

All code files relevant to this chapter are available at the following GitHub page: `https://github.com/PacktPublishing/Mastering-PyTorch/tree/master/Chapter14`.

Using fast.ai to set up model training in a few minutes

In this section, we will use the fast.ai library (`https://docs.fast.ai/`) to train and evaluate a handwritten digit classification model in fewer than 10 lines of code, in the form of an exercise. We will also use fast.ai's `interpretability` module to understand where the trained model is still failing to perform well. The full code for the exercise can be found at the following GitHub page: `https://github.com/PacktPublishing/Mastering-PyTorch/blob/master/Chapter14/fast.ai.ipynb`.

Setting up fast.ai and loading data

In this section, we will first import the fast.ai library, load the `MNIST` dataset, and finally preprocess the dataset for model training. We'll proceed as follows:

1. First, we will import fast.ai in the recommended way, as shown here:

```
import os
from fast.ai.vision.all import *
```

Although `import *` is not the recommended way of importing libraries in Python, the fast.ai documentation suggests this format because of the **read-eval-print loop (REPL)** environment that fast.ai is designed to be used in. You can read more about that reasoning here: `https://www.fast.ai/2020/02/13/fast.ai-A-Layered-API-for-Deep-Learning/`.

Basically, this line of code imports some of the key modules from the fast.ai library that are usually necessary and mostly sufficient for a user to perform model training and evaluation. A list of implicitly imported modules can be found here: `https://fast.ai1.fast.ai/imports.html`.

2. Next, by using fast.ai's ready-to-use data modules, we will load the `MNIST` dataset, which is among the provided list of datasets under the fast.ai library, as follows:

```
path = untar_data(URLs.MNIST)
print(path)
```

An exhaustive list of available datasets under fast.ai can be seen at `https://docs.fast.ai/data.external`. The preceding code should output as follows:

/Users/ashish.jha/.fastai/data/mnist_png

Figure 14.1 – fast.ai dataset path

This is where the dataset will be stored, just so we know for future purposes.

3. We can now look at a sample image path under the stored dataset, so as to understand how the dataset is laid out, as follows:

```
files = get_image_files(path/"training")
print(len(files))
print(files[0])
```

This should output as follows:

60000
/Users/ashish.jha/.fastai/data/mnist_png/training/9/36655.png

Figure 14.2 – Fast.ai dataset sample

There are a total of 60,000 images in the training dataset. As we can see, inside the `training` folder, there is a 9 subfolder that refers to the digit 9, and inside that subfolder are images of the digit 9.

4. Using the information gathered in the preceding step, we can generate labels for the `MNIST` dataset. We first declare a function that takes an image path and uses its parent folder's name to derive the digit (class) that the image belongs to. Using this function and the `MNIST` dataset path, we instantiate a `DataLoader`, as shown in the following piece of code:

```
def label_func(f): return f.parent.name
dls = ImageDataLoaders.from_path_func(path, fnames=files,
label_func=label_func, num_workers=0)
dls.show_batch()
```

It should output something like this:

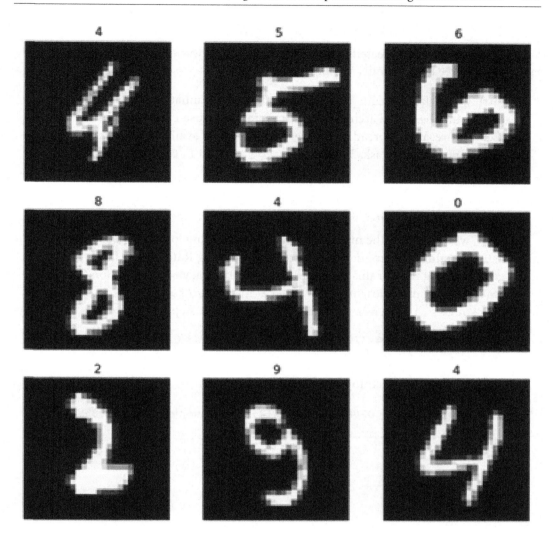

Figure 14.3 – fast.ai batch display

As we can see, the dataloader is correctly set up, and we are now ready to move on to model training, which we will do in the next section.

Training a MNIST model using fast.ai

Using the `DataLoader` created in the preceding section, we will now train a model with fast.ai using three lines of code, as follows:

1. First, we use fast.ai's `cnn_learner` module to instantiate our model. Instead of defining the model architecture from scratch, we use `resnet18` as the base architecture. You can read about the extensive list of available base architectures for computer vision tasks here: `https://fast.ai1.fast.ai/vision.models.html`.

    Also, feel free to review the model architecture details provided in *Chapter 3, Deep CNN Architectures*.

2. Next, we also define the metric that the model training logs should contain. Before actually training the model, we use fast.ai's **Learning Rate Finder** to suggest a good learning rate for this model architecture and dataset combination. You can read more about the learning rate finder at `https://fast.ai1.fast.ai/callbacks.lr_finder.html`. The code for this step is shown here:

    ```
    learn = cnn_learner(dls, arch=resnet18, metrics=accuracy)
    learn.lr_find()
    ```

    It should output something like this:

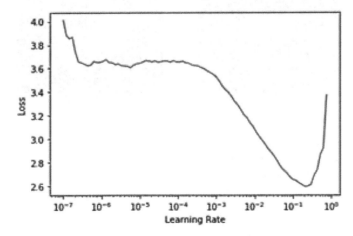

Figure 14.4 – Learning rate finder output

The learning rate finder essentially does model training with varying learning rates per iteration, starting from a low value and ending with a high value. It then plots the loss for each of those iterations against the corresponding learning rate value. As we can see in this plot, a learning rate of 0.0209 is where the loss is minimal. Hence, we will choose this as our base learning rate value for model training.

3. We are now ready to train our model. We could use `learn.fit` to train the model from scratch, but to aim for a better performance we will fine-tune a pre-trained `resnet18` model using the `learn.fine_tune` method, as shown in the following line of code:

```
learn.fine_tune(epochs=2, base_lr=0.0209, freeze_
epochs=1)
```

Here, `freeze_epochs` refers to the number of epochs the model is trained on initially with a frozen network where only the last layer is unfrozen. `epochs` refers to the number of epochs the model is trained on thereafter, by unfreezing the entire `resnet18` network. The code should output something like this:

epoch	train_loss	valid_loss	accuracy	time
0	0.281835	0.199095	0.946417	08:30

epoch	train_loss	valid_loss	accuracy	time
0	0.122436	0.080322	0.982583	10:24
1	0.033702	0.027708	0.991833	08:32

Figure 14.5 – Fast.ai training logs

As we can see, there is a first epoch of training with the frozen network, and then there are two subsequent epochs of training with the unfrozen network. We also see the accuracy metric in the logs, which we declared as our metric in *step 2*. The training logs look reasonable, and it looks like the model is indeed learning the task. In the next and final part of this exercise, we will look at the performance of this model on some samples and try to understand where it fails.

Evaluating and interpreting the model using fast.ai

We will first look at how the trained model performs on some of the sample images, and finally explore the top mistakes made by the model in order to understand the scope for improvement. We'll proceed as follows:

1. With the trained model, we can use the `show_results` method to look at some of the model's predictions, as shown in the following line of code:

    ```
    learn.show_results()
    ```

    It should output something like this:

    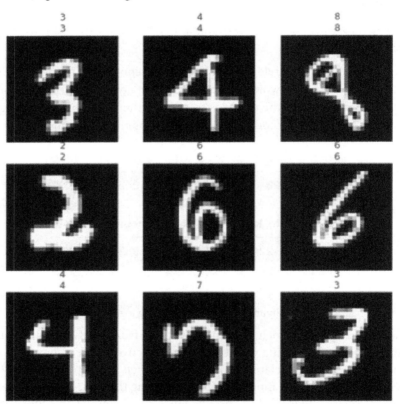

    Figure 14.6 – Fast.ai sample predictions

    In the preceding screenshot, we can see that the model has got all nine images right. Because the accuracy of the trained model is already at 99%, we will need 100 images to look at a wrong prediction. We will instead look exclusively at the mistakes made by the model in the next step.

2. In *Chapter 13, PyTorch and Explainable AI*, we learned about **model interpretability**. One of the ways of trying to understand how a trained model is working is to look at where it is failing the most. Using fast.ai's `Interpretation` module, we can do that in two lines of code, as shown here:

```
interp = Interpretation.from_learner(learn)
interp.plot_top_losses(9, figsize=(15,10))
```

This should output the following:

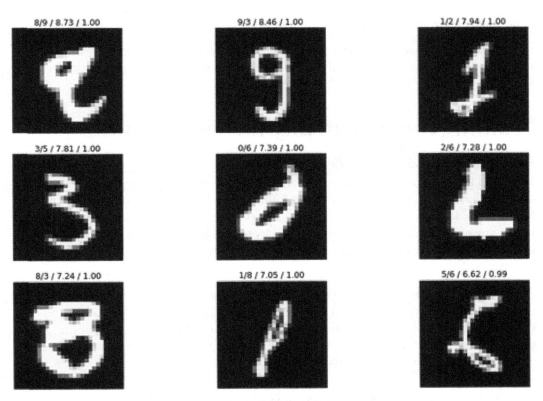

Figure 14.7 – fast.ai top model mistakes

In *Figure 14.7*, we can see that each image is titled with the prediction, ground truth, cross-entropy loss, and the prediction probability. Most of these cases are hard/wrong even for humans, and hence it is acceptable for the model to make mistakes. But for cases such as the one on the bottom right, the model is just plain wrong. This type of analysis can then be followed up by further dissecting the model, for such curious cases as we did in the previous chapter.

This concludes the exercise and our discussion on fast.ai. fast.ai has a lot to offer for machine learning engineers and researchers—both beginner and advanced users. This exercise was aimed at demonstrating fast.ai's speediness and ease of use. Lessons from this section can be used for working on other machine learning tasks with fast.ai. Under the hood, fast.ai uses PyTorch's functionalities, and therefore it is always possible to switch between these two frameworks.

In the next section, we will explore another such library that sits on top of PyTorch and facilitates users to train models with relatively few lines of code, rendering the code hardware-agnostic.

Training models on any hardware using PyTorch Lightning

PyTorch Lightning (`https://github.com/PyTorchLightning/pytorch-lightning`) is yet another library that is built on top of PyTorch to abstract out the boilerplate code needed for model training and evaluation. A special feature of this library is that any model training code written using PyTorch Lightning can be run without changes on any hardware configuration such as multiple CPUs, multiple GPUs, or even multiple TPUs.

In the following exercise, we will train and evaluate a handwritten digit classification model using PyTorch Lightning on CPUs. You can use the same code for training on GPUs or TPUs. The full code for the following exercise can be found here: `https://github.com/PacktPublishing/Mastering-PyTorch/blob/master/Chapter14/pytorch_lightning.ipynb`.

Defining the model components in PyTorch Lightning

In this part of the exercise, we will demonstrate how to initialize the `model` class in PyTorch Lightning. This library works on the philosophy of *self-contained model systems*— that is, the model class contains not only the model architecture definition but also the optimizer definition and dataset loaders, as well as the training, validation, and test set performance computation functions, all in one place.

We'll proceed as follows:

1. First, we need to import the relevant modules, as follows:

```
import torch
import torch.nn as nn
from torch.nn import functional as F
from torch.utils.data import DataLoader
from torchvision.datasets import MNIST
from torchvision import transforms
import pytorch_lightning as pl
```

As we can see, PyTorch Lightning still uses a lot of native PyTorch modules for the model class definition. We have additionally imported the MNIST dataset straight from the torchvision.datasets module to train the handwritten digit classifier on.

2. Next, we define the PyTorch Lightning model class, which contains everything that is needed to train and evaluate our model. Let's first look at the model architecture-related methods of the class, as follows:

```
class ConvNet(pl.LightningModule):
    def __init__(self):
        super(ConvNet, self).__init__()
        self.cn1 = nn.Conv2d(1, 16, 3, 1)
        ...
        self.fc2 = nn.Linear(64, 10)
    def forward(self, x):
        x = self.cn1(x)
        ...
        op = F.log_softmax(x, dim=1)
        return op
```

These two methods—__init__ and forward—work in the same manner as they did with the native PyTorch code.

3. Next, let's look at the other methods of the model class, as follows:

```python
    def training_step(self, batch, batch_num):
        ...
    def validation_step(self, batch, batch_num):
        ...
    def validation_epoch_end(self, outputs):
        ...
    def test_step(self, batch, batch_num):
        ...
    def test_epoch_end(self, outputs):
        ...
    def configure_optimizers(self):
        return torch.optim.Adadelta(self.parameters(),
lr=0.5)
    def train_dataloader(self):
        ...
    def val_dataloader(self):
        ...
    def test_dataloader(self):
        ...
```

While methods such as `training_step`, `validation_step`, and `test_step` are meant to evaluate per-iteration performances on the training, validation, and test sets, the `*_epoch_end` methods compute the per-epoch performances. There are `*_dataloader` methods for the training, validation, and test sets. And finally, there is the `configure_optimizer` method, which defines the optimizer to be used for training the model.

Training and evaluating the model using PyTorch Lightning

Having set up the model class, we will now train the model in this part of the exercise. Then, we will evaluate the performance of the trained model on the test set.

We'll proceed as follows:

1. **Instantiating the model object**: Here, we will first instantiate the model object using the model class defined in *step 3* of the previous section - *Defining the model components in PyTorch Lightning*. We will then use the `Trainer` module from PyTorch Lightning to define a `trainer` object.

    Note that we are relying on CPUs only for model training. However, you can easily switch to GPUs or TPUs. The beauty of PyTorch Lightning lies in the fact that you can add an argument such as `gpus=8` or `tpus=2` in the `trainer` definition code depending on your hardware settings, and the entire code will still run without any further modifications.

    We begin the model training process with the following lines of code:

    ```
    model = ConvNet()
    trainer = pl.Trainer(progress_bar_refresh_rate=20, max_
    epochs=10)
    trainer.fit(model)
    ```

    It should output something like this:

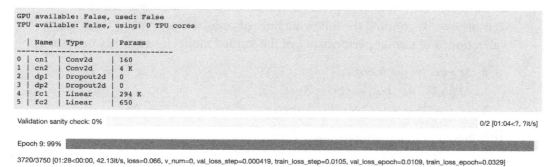

Figure 14.8 – PyTorch Lightning training logs

First, the `trainer` object assesses the available hardware, and then it also logs the entire model architecture that is to be trained, along with the number of parameters per layer in the architecture. Thereafter, it begins the model training epoch by epoch. It trains until `10` epochs as specified using the `max_epochs` argument while defining the `trainer` object. We can also see that the training and validation losses are being logged at every epoch.

2. **Testing the model**: Having trained the model for 10 epochs, we can now test it. Using the .test method, we request the trainer object, that was defined in *step 1* of this section, to run inference on the test set, as follows:

```
trainer.test()
```

It should output something like this:

```
Testing: 96% ████████████████████████████████████████----------------------------------------   300/313 [00:03<00:00, 92.65it/s]
-------------------------------------------------------------------------------------------
DATALOADER:0 TEST RESULTS
{'test_loss': tensor(4.2241e-05),
 'test_loss_epoch': tensor(0.0361),
 'train_loss': tensor(0.0105),
 'train_loss_epoch': tensor(0.0304),
 'train_loss_step': tensor(0.0105),
 'val_loss': tensor(0.0004),
 'val_loss_epoch': tensor(0.0109)}
-------------------------------------------------------------------------------------------
```

Figure 14.9 – PyTorch Lightning testing logs

We can see that the model outputs the train, validation, and test losses using the trained model.

3. **Exploring the trained model**: Finally, PyTorch Lightning also provides a neat interface with TensorBoard (https://www.tensorflow.org/tensorboard), which is a great visualization toolkit made originally for TensorFlow. By running the following lines of code, we can explore the training, validation, and test set performance of the trained model interactively in a web app:

```
# Start TensorBoard.
%reload_ext tensorboard
%tensorboard --logdir lightning_logs/
```

This should output the following:

```
Reusing TensorBoard on port 6007 (pid 21690), started 22:03:23 ago. (Use '!kill 21690' to kill it.)
```

Figure 14.10 – PyTorch Lightning TensorBoard logs

As suggested in the output prompt, if we go to http://localhost:6007/ on a web browser, it will open a TensorBoard session that should look something like this:

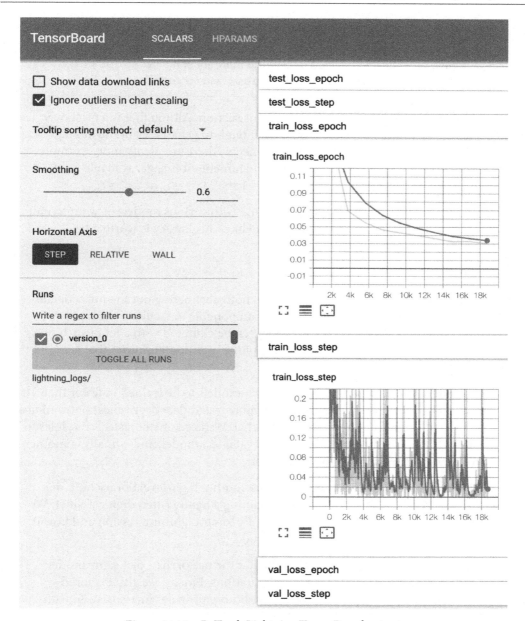

Figure 14.11 – PyTorch Lightning TensorBoard output

Within this interactive visualization toolkit, we can look at the epoch-wise model training progress in terms of loss, accuracy, and various other metrics. This is another neat feature of PyTorch Lightning that enables us to have a rich model evaluation and debugging experience with just a few lines of code.

> **Note**
>
> Regular PyTorch code also provides an interface with TensorBoard, although the code is lengthier. You can read more about it here: `https://pytorch.org/docs/stable/tensorboard.html`.

This brings us to the end of this exercise and this section. Although it is a brief overview of the PyTorch Lightning library, it should be enough to get an idea of the library, how it works, and how it can work for your projects. There are plenty more examples and tutorials available at PyTorch Lightning's documentation page, available at `https://pytorch-lightning.readthedocs.io/en/stable/`.

If you are in the process of rapidly experimenting with various models or want to reduce the scaffolding code in your model training pipeline, this library is worth a try.

Summary

In this final chapter of the book, we focused on both abstracting out the noisy details involved in model training code and the core components to facilitate the rapid prototyping of models. As PyTorch code can often be cluttered with a lot of such noisy detailed code components, we looked at some of the high-level libraries that are built on top of PyTorch.

First, we explored fast.ai, which enables PyTorch models to be trained in fewer than 10 lines of code. In the form of an exercise, we demonstrated the effectiveness of training a handwritten digit classification model using fast.ai. We used one of fast.ai's modules to load the dataset, another module to train and evaluate a model, and—finally—another module to interpret the trained model behavior.

Next, we looked at PyTorch Lightning, which is another high-level library built on top of PyTorch. We did a similar exercise of training a handwritten digit classifier. We demonstrated the code layout used in a typical PyTorch Lightning session and how it reduces clutter compared to regular PyTorch code.

We highlighted how PyTorch Lightning facilitates the use of the exact same model training code across different hardware configurations. Finally, we also explored the model evaluation interface that PyTorch Lightning provides in association with TensorBoard.

While we discussed these two libraries, more of these are available, such as PyTorch `Ignite` and `Poutyne`. As PyTorch keeps evolving and expanding, such high-level libraries are going to be more and more prevalent among PyTorch users. Hence, similar to many other aspects of PyTorch that we have discussed in the preceding chapters—such as interpretability in *Chapter 13, PyTorch and Explainable AI*, and automated machine learning in *Chapter 12, PyTorch and AutoML*—this area is another one to keep an eye on.

We have reached the end of this book! I hope the various topics covered here will help you in using PyTorch effectively and efficiently for deep learning. Besides writing various deep learning architectures and interesting applications in PyTorch, we have explored some useful practical concepts such as model deployment, distribution, and prototyping. This book can therefore also act as a guide whenever you are in doubt regarding any particular aspect of working with PyTorch.

Now, it is your turn to apply the PyTorch skills you have mastered in this book to your deep learning projects. Thank you for reading this book, and keep learning!

Other Books You May Enjoy

If you enjoyed this book, you may be interested in these other books by Packt:

PyTorch 1.x Reinforcement Learning

Yuxi (Hayden) Liu

ISBN: 978-1-83855-196-4

- Use Q-learning and the state–action–reward–state–action (SARSA) algorithm to solve various Gridworld problems
- Develop a multi-armed bandit algorithm to optimize display advertising
- Scale up learning and control processes using Deep Q-Networks
- Simulate Markov Decision Processes, OpenAI Gym environments, and other common control problems
- Select and build RL models, evaluate their performance, and optimize and deploy them

Hands-On Natural Language Processing with PyTorch 1.x

Thomas Dop

ISBN: 978-1-78980-274-0

- Use NLP techniques for understanding, processing, and generating text
- Understand PyTorch, its applications and how it can be used to build deep linguistic models
- Explore the wide variety of deep learning architectures for NLP
- Develop the skills you need to process and represent both structured and unstructured NLP data
- Become well-versed with state-of-the-art technologies and exciting new developments in the NLP domain
- Create chatbots using attention-based neural networks

Leave a review - let other readers know what you think

Please share your thoughts on this book with others by leaving a review on the site that you bought it from. If you purchased the book from Amazon, please leave us an honest review on this book's Amazon page. This is vital so that other potential readers can see and use your unbiased opinion to make purchasing decisions, we can understand what our customers think about our products, and our authors can see your feedback on the title that they have worked with Packt to create. It will only take a few minutes of your time, but is valuable to other potential customers, our authors, and Packt. Thank you!

Index

S

Made in the USA
Monee, IL
04 September 2021